SHANTIES FROM THE SEVEN SEAS

Shanties from the Seven Seas

SHIPBOARD WORK-SONGS
AND SONGS USED AS WORK-SONGS
FROM THE GREAT DAYS OF SAIL

collected by

STAN HUGILL

Mystic Seaport Museum
Mystic, Connecticut
1994

First published in 1961
Reprinted 1966 (with corrections), 1979 and 1984
Second (abridged) edition 1984
Reprinted 1987
by Routledge & Kegan Paul Ltd.
11 New Fetter Lane, London EC4P 4EE

First published in the United States by
Routledge & Kegan Paul, Inc.
29 West 35th Street, New York, NY 10001

This new U.S. edition published by
Mystic Seaport Museum, Inc.
75 Greenmanville Avenue, Mystic, CT 06355

Library of Congress Cataloging in Publication Data
I. Hugill, Stan, 1906-1992.
Shanties from the seven seas.
1. Sea songs.   2. Work songs.
I. Hugill, Stan.
M1977. S2SH8   1994   84-757301
ISBN 0-913372-70-6

Thanks
to my two sons
Philip and Martin
for having kept
the tradition alive

CONTENTS

~~~~~~

ILLUSTRATIONS

FOREWORD

HE singing of sea shanties as working songs at sea is a
lost art. It died with the last of the British Cape Horners. The Finns and the Germans didn't use such songs—
not in the last of their ships, at any rate. Nobody sang
much in the Aaland Islands square-riggers. Nobody knew the songs,
nor the use of them. Work was a hard slog on deck or aloft there all
the time, aided by brace-winches and halyard winches and such
things.

In the last of the Limejuice Cape Horners Stan Hugill was shanteyman—the last shanteyman anywhere, I'd think. I'm not reckoning
the odd mouthers who moon with microphones. If you need a micro-
phone, real shantey-singing is not your line. Stan was a good shanteyman. I never was shipmates with him, but I heard of him. My brother
Frank was prisoner of war with him in the Marlag-und-Milag Nord.
Stan's cheerful shanteys were a help even there, just as they were in
the big four-masted barque *Garthpool*. Such shanteys were part of the
old sea life. They were *real*, and so were the men who led them and
worked to them. There just is no place for them now.

I'm glad that Stan Hugill has got this collection together. Nobody
could do the job better: very soon, nobody could do it at all.

ALAN VILLIERS

Oxford, 1960

ix

PREFACE

~~~~~~

*T*HE bulk of the shanties in this book I carried around for years, safely stowed away in the saltwater recesses of my figurehead, and they would never have been unloaded if it had not been for the interest shown and pressure applied by Dr. Kurt Hahn, headmaster of Gordonstoun, the famous public school near Elgin in the north of Scotland.

Being brought up in a seafaring environment I was made familiar with shanties and sea-songs even when very small. Pictures of merchant and naval sailing ships lining the walls of our living-room once caused my mother to remark, 'A good gust of wind in here would make us take off!'

Not only did my sailor father, in a fine bass-baritone voice, accompanying himself with a button-type accordion, frequently render sea-songs and shanties, but my mother, a sailor's daughter, would sing them too when working about the house or rocking the babies to sleep—my younger brother always needed *The Lowlands Low* to make him doze off. (Strangely enough, the first melody to fascinate my own small son was the melancholy *Stormalong*, or rather the 'Ay! ay! ay!' part of its refrain.)

On my obviously choosing seafaring as a career I soon picked up from older shipmates, men who had spent their lives under sail, many variants, of both words and music, of those songs I had learnt at my father's knee. I had the opportunity also to ship in some British and foreign sailing vessels before the demise of sail, on the decks of which ships I at times enacted the role of shantyman. In coastal sailing ships of Britain, New Zealand, and Australia, too, I had the opportunity to acquire 'new' shanties. Then I spent some time in the Windward Islands of the West Indies and was lucky enough to rope in many shanties which are to be seen in print in this book for the first time. I was fortunate, too, in having for my tutors men from the two main sections of seafarers from which the bulk of the shanties stemmed— Irish Merchant Johns from Liverpool, New York, and Ireland herself, and West Indian coloured seamen.

All my own material was collected in the main during my first twenty years at sea.

After the Second World War I became an Instructor and later Bosun of the Outward Bound Sea School at Aberdovey. During my first year here Wilfred Pickles visited us for a *Have a Go* programme and I was asked to lead the lads in the singing of shanties as part of the programme. This led to the weekly *Shanty Night*, which has run for many years as one of the evening entertainments for the lads. I also introduced the singing of shanties at work—when hauling our heavy cutters up on the slipway for their periodical overhaul, lifting the lifeboat, heaving the anchor at the little brass capstan aboard our sail-training-ship *Warspite*, and sometimes when setting her heavy mainsail. In fact we used them for any lifting or pulling jobs whether connected with the sea or not.

In 1951 the two four-masted barques *Pamir* and *Passat* were saved from the knacker's yard by a certain Hamburg shipowner, Herr Schlievman, and a scheme was devised to send them to sea again with a mixed crowd of German, British, and Continental youths. However, the international angle failed, and in the end Germans predominated, with about twenty-four British lads, most of whom had been accepted as Alfred Holt midshipmen and were ex-Outward-Bounders. Many of the German lads and all of the British lads were sent to Gordonstoun to learn the elements of sail-seamanship under a certain German instructor, Captain Schwabauer, once of the Flensberg Naval Academy. Dr. Kurt Hahn sent for me to be a sort of liaison instructor between the Germans and British, as I had shipped in both British and German sailing ships, and also he wanted to revive the singing of shanties aboard of these two vessels. A 'Hahnism' was: 'The international common denominator—seasickness and a song.'

After being at Gordonstoun for a while I went over to Hamburg by plane and thence to Kiel and the castle of Nehemten, where the lads were furthering their seamanship before sailing in *Pamir* and *Passat*. Here, too, we had evenings singing shanties in the hope that they would be resuscitated aboard the ships. Captain Schmidt of the Flying P Line, a well-known marine historian—the German Basil Lubbock—was an enthusiastic visitor. But, mainly on account of the added mechanical devices, the shantying, although occasionally attempted, did not have the glorious come-back we had all hoped for.

Hahn was so pleased with this attempted shanty revival that he told me it was essential that I should get down on paper all the shanties I knew, but I tarried for a year or two until, thanks to an injury to my left foot and being dry-docked for three months, I decided to make a start. This book is the result.

During the next year or two I made a host of pen friends—a letter of enquiry about shanty material in the monthly nautical magazine *Sea Breezes* brought me in a flood of letters relating to the subject. Old sailors, master mariners, landsmen, foreigners—of all types and ages—wrote to me, and I must say I received a great amount of fresh material in this way. When foreign lads who had attended our school returned to their homelands, they searched diligently for new material and also helped me with the translations. Eventually I contacted the Folk Song Department of the B.B.C., where I recorded several of the rarer shanties for their Permanent Records Library. I also became known at Cecil Sharp House, the headquarters of the English Folk Dance and Song Society, where I was asked to give talks on the subject of shantying and shanties and where I met many well-known collectors of sea-songs and shanties, with whom I exchanged notes on the subject. Prior to his death, Richard Runciman Terry had intended to write a historical and critical study of shanties, and this induced me to add to my collection a historical account of shanties and shantying as detailed as extensive research could make it.

Twenty odd years ago shanties were very popular, thanks to Terry and other collectors, but they were presented on records and by the B.B.C. in far too grandiose a fashion, and in the years between many of the old tunes have been altered beyond all recognition by prominent musical editors for radio and community singing, destroying all their nautical character and salty atmosphere. On H.M.V. records twenty years or so ago John Goss and his Cathedral Quartet produced a fine collection of shanties (mainly from Terry's *Shanty Book*) with part-singing and a fine instrumental background. At the time this method of preserving them was considered correct, but in recent years, thanks to 'folk-songers', there has been a tendency to revive the shanties in a manner closer to what is believed to have been Sailor John's way of singing them. In book form the only collector to have attempted this is the American writer W. M. Doerflinger in his excellent book *Shantymen and Shantyboys* (1951). All Doerflinger's shanties were taken down from sailor-singers by tape-recorder.

In record-form Mr. Stanley Slade of Bristol (who died recently) has on H.M.V. given quite a good example of how the songs should be sung, and the Workers' Music Association has recently issued an excellent recording of sixteen sea-songs (forebitters) and shanties sung in fine imitation of the true style, and in particular the Liverpool sailorman's style. These two records have little musical accompaniment, mainly a concertina, accordion, or fiddle, and the solos of the shanties are unaccompanied and so *sound* much more like the real thing. The forebitters are, too, sung realistically in the drawn-out nasal fashion of the time.

Recently skiffle and calypso groups have brought before the public many of these old work songs of the 'Sailor of the Sail', and, although they have altered them and speeded them up somewhat, it is a pleasure to me to find that young people have helped to resuscitate these fine old 'hooraw choruses'.

Previous shanty collections have been grouped in two ways: (1)

under capstan, halyard, and pump headings; and (2) starting with a capstan song and finishing with *Leave Her, Johnny, Leave Her*, with a variety of other shanties coming in between, as they would on a voyage. I have chosen what might be called the 'family tree' method, placing songs of a similar type together, e.g. the Stormalong family, the Hilo family, and the roll and blow families. In some cases I have classed them under 'girls' names', 'men's names', 'ships' names', or 'place names'. Those that do not fit into any category I have put in Part V. My reason for moulding the book in this fashion is that I find it too dogmatic to state that this shanty is a capstan or that a halyard song. 'Different ships, different long splices,' sailors used to say, and this adage applies particularly to shanties.

With the exception of those words and lines indicated in the text as having been camouflaged, all the words of the shanties given in this collection were actually sung. Although I have numbered all the verses in the halyard songs, in actual fact those verses in shanties which have no 'theme' were sung in any order in which they came to the mind of the shantyman.

Alternative ways of singing the words are given in brackets, and in the hauling songs the 'pulls' are in italics. In order to help would-be shantymen to sing these songs correctly I have drawn this symbol, MVW, to indicate at which note sailormen would give vent to anything from a quavering 'hitch' to an unearthly yelp.

An unusual feature of shantying, which makes it so different from most kinds of singing, is the fact that these songs had no audiences—except of course in the early passenger and emigrant ships, where obviously the spiciest would be tabu—and were never sung by women, although Captain Robinson in *The Bellman* tells a yarn of how a certain bevy of actresses bound to the New World helped in the mastheading of sails aboard the ship *Denmark* of the National Steamship Co. in the seventies!

In these days of racial equality many readers may object to the constant appearance of the word 'nigger' in the shanties. But many of the shanties in which this word is found were products of the Negro himself, and *he* sang 'nigger' in those far-off days. Coloured shantymen and 'chequerboard crews' were in the main singers of such work-songs. I myself object to the use of the word in normal conversation, but I deplore the extremists who have gone so far as to alter such a phrase as 'niggerhead' (a part of a ship's equipment) to 'negrohead' in modern seamanship books. I think this is carrying things a little too far!

And now I must make mention of the many sailing-ship Johns and shantymen, most, if not all, now dead, from whom I learnt the bulk of my shanties. I will call these my

Deck Sources

Paddy Griffiths. Master Mariner, deserted the Royal Navy, where he had served in brigs, and so on; sailed in the Colonies Trade—*Birkdale, Bidston Hill*, etc.—and had shipped in many coastwise schooners. Was once shanghaied aboard a whaler.

Paddy Delaney. Sailed in the Blackball Line when a young man.

Jack Connolly. Irish A.B., served in the Saltpetre Trade and Australian Trade; a fine example of a 'square-rig' seaman; never swore—'Holy Sailor!' and 'By the Great Hook Block!' being his only epithets.

Spike Sennit. Colonies and West Coast of South America Trades.

Mike O'Rourke. Had shipped in many Yankee Blood Boats and Bluenose (Nova Scotian) ships.

Paddy McArty. Ex *Falls of Garry* and other vessels of the 'Fall' Line.

Big MacDonald. Shipped in several Colonial Packets and finished up in New Zealand schooners.

W. G. Chenoworth. Bosun of the *Mount Stewart* for eight years. Ex Dundee whalers. Also shipped in many vessels of the 'Garth' Line. Had been on Polar expeditions and held the White Ribbon of Antarctica.

Harding the Barbarian. A coloured seaman from the Island of Barbadoes; had sailed in many Yankee, British, and Bluenose sailing vessels as well as in West Indian barques; a fine shantyman and first-rate seaman.

'Harry Lauder.' Coloured shantyman from the Island of St. Lucia.

'Tobago' Smith. A coloured seaman who had sailed in many British 'Tanker' squareriggers.

'Old' Louis. Coloured cook from Mauritius, shantyman, ex 'Dale' and 'Milne' Lines of sailing ships.

H. Groetzmann. German sailing-ship man and Whaler of Punta Arenas.

Jean Loro. French seaman, served many years in the 'Borde' Cape-Horners.

Ezra Cobb. A Bluenose seaman of the old school.

Oswald Ziemer; G. Biemer; and H. Hesschen. German seamen from the Flying P Line, all Friesian Islanders.

Captain P. A. Kihlberg. Swedish Master Mariner; ex Scotch barque *Fasces*.

Also the following Seamen of the Sail:

Arthur Spencer, W. J. Reeds, W. Dowling, T. Southwood, 'Scottie', F. Shaw, Ira Croker, J. Birch, Bill Morris, Bill Fuller, J. Reed, 'Chips' Anderson, H. J. Hugill, Taff Davies, Big Skan, Sullivan, 'Archie', T. W. Jones, Paddy Cunningham, A. Macmillan, and Bosun Chamberlain.

And then there are the many people who have helped me in more recent years to gather together data for this work. In particular my thanks are due to the following:

Fred G. Carver (Coseley, Staffs), Jack Knapman (Bristol), Capt. E. R. W. Allen (S.S. *Cornwall*, Cory Co.), Mansel Thomas (Head of Welsh Music, B.B.C., Cardiff), Prof. J. Glyn-Davies (Llanfairfechan, Caerns), Wm. A. Bryce (Sutton Coldfield), T. E. Elwell (Caretaker, Manx Nautical Museum, Castletown, I.O.M.), Sir Maurice Bowra (Wadham College, Oxford University), Mrs. Irma Hoffmeister (Hamburg), Kenneth Lodewick (University Eugene, Oregon), Seamus Ennis (*As I Roved Out* Team, B.B.C., London), Dan McDonald (Croftfoot, Glasgow), Miss Dorothy Laird (Hampstead, London), W. J. Hughes (M.T. *Hoegh Eagle*), Peter Kennedy (English Folk Dance and Song Society, London), Patrick Shuldam-Shaw (Folk Song, B.B.C., London), Gwion Davies (Llanfairfechan, Caerns), D. Maloney (Porchester, Hants), John Strueman (Town Clerk Depute, Campbeltown, Argyll), Fritz Kalb (Gothenburg), Henrik Reimers (Oslo), Mrs. Parton (Aberdovey), G. Morris (Aberdovey), Admiral Bernard Rogge (ex-German Navy), Capt. Dolo (Cape Horn Master's Association, France), B. O. Streiffert (Gothenburg), Earl Checkley (Ottawa, Canada), Berta Ruck (Aberdovey), H. M. Tunstall-Behrens (Cornwall), G. Legman (Cagnes, France), Rainer M. v. Barsewisch (Hamburg), Ingo Scharf, J. Francis, B.A. (Aberdovey), Dr. D. J. Davies, M.A. (Towyn), Mrs. B. Williams, B.A. (Bala), Bert Kingdon (British Overseas Service, B.B.C.) and Mr. Shortland (British Vice-Consul, Oslo).

Desk Sources

Besides these shipmates, personal friends, and pen-friends, I must also remember the 'desk sources' from whom I obtained so many variants. My deepest thanks are due for the kind permission to use copyright material granted me by the following:

Kegan Paul, Trench & Co., London (shanties from Laura A. Smith's *Music of the Waters*, 1888),

English Folk Dance and Song Society, London (shanties collected by Miners and Thomas, Miss Gilchrist, H. E. Piggot, etc.),

George Philip & Son, Ltd., London (excerpts from Captain Frank Shaw's *The Splendour of the Seas*, 1953),

J. Curwen and Sons, Ltd., London (shanties from *The Shanty Book* by R. R. Terry, 1921, 1926),

Chapman and Hall, Ltd., London (shanty from R. C. Leslie's *Sea Painter's Log*, 1886),

Brown, Son & Ferguson, Ltd., Glasgow (shanties from Capt. Whall's

Sea Songs and Shanties, 1927, and excerpts from Basil Lubbock's *Last of the Windjammers*, 1927–29),

Rupert Hart-Davis Ltd., London, and M. D. Hay (excerpts from *Landsman Hay*, ed. M. D. Hay, 1953),

George Dickinson, ed., *Sea Breezes*, Liverpool (shanties and letters from *Sea Breezes*),

Boosey & Hawkes Ltd., London (shanties from Davis & Tozer's *Sailor Songs or 'Chanties'*, 1887, and from Sampson & Harris' *Seven Seas Shanty Book*, 1927),

Miss Maud Karpeles, International Folk Music Council (shanties collected by Cecil Sharp),

Harvard University Press, Cambridge, Mass. (Negro songs from Newman I. White's *American Negro Folk-Songs*, 1928),

Harcourt, Brace & Company, Inc., New York (songs and shanties from Carl Sandburg's *The American Songbag*, 1927),

Popular Publications Inc., New York (shanties from *Adventure* Magazine),

Swan & Co., Ltd., London (shanties from F. T. Bullen and W. F. Arnold's *Songs of Sea Labour*, 1914),

Miss M. S. Smith, Dorset (shanties from Miss C. Fox Smith's *A Book of Shanties*, 1927),

The Peabody Museum, Salem, Mass. (shanties from F. P. Harlow's *The Making of a Sailor*, 1928),

W. W. Norton & Co., Inc., New York (shanties from J. C. Colcord's *Songs of American Sailormen*, 1938, and from F. Shay's *American Sea Songs and Shanties*, 1948),

The Macmillan Company, New York, and William M. Doerflinger, New Jersey (shanties from Mr. Doerflinger's *Shantymen and Shantyboys*, 1951),

Mrs. George C. Beach, New York (shanties from the collection of Mr. Nathaniel Silsbee of Cohasset, Mass.),

E. H. Freeman, Ltd., Brighton (shanties from *The Shell Book of Shanties*, 1952),

The Liverpool *Daily Post and Echo* Ltd. (shipping advertisement from the *Daily Post*, 1855).

Owing to the fact that I have been collecting shanties for the best part of my life, originally without any intention of publishing them, it is possible that I have forgotten the sources of some of them. If I have therefore inadvertently failed to acknowledge any oral or literary source I hope the source concerned will forgive me.

Finally, I wish to thank my brother, Harold George Hugill, for the many hours he has spent taking down the airs of these shanties from my wild singing, and for his patience in endeavouring to get as exact as possible my very often erratic renderings of the solos. Without him this book would not have been possible.

Oh, it's 'pipe up, Dan', when yer feelin' kind o' blue,
With a half-drowned ship, an' a half-dead crew,
When yer heart's in yer sea-boots 'n the cold is in yer bones,
An' ye don't give a damn how soon she goes to Davy Jones,
When it's dark as the Divil an' it's blowin' all it can,
Oh, he's worth ten men on a rope is Dan!

(From *Sea Songs and Ballads* by C. Fox Smith)

When Ham and Shem and Japhet, they walked the capstan round,
Upon the strangest vessel that was ever outward bound,
The music of their voices from wave to welkin rang,
As they sang the first sea chantey that seamen ever sang.

(From *Chanteys and Ballads*, by Harry Kemp)

STAN HUGILL 1906-1992
A Remembrance

ERHAPS the most appropriate things that can be said of Stan Hugill are that he accumulated friends and admirers everywhere he went, and that he always managed to make a lasting impression—almost wholly favorable—as a singer, raconteur, amateur anthologist, armchair philologist, self-taught artist, and boon companion. His charm was infectious and his energy boundless. He was a truly remarkable fellow. After a hard life of sea labor in peacetime and in war, two devastating shipwrecks, and a retirement career as an Outward Bound boatswain and sailing instructor, he blossomed in his sixties and seventies as an internationally renowned authority on seafaring songs and lore, and became the perpetual mainstay of an international sea-chantey revival for which he was the individual most singly responsible. Before he was done, Stan inspired a generation of folksingers, scholars, and major media to pay closer attention to the intrinsic beauty and historical worth of sailor songs and sailor language, and to the cultural heritage of the seafaring life that he himself had come to personify.

The biographical details are simple and straightforward. His father, Henry James Hugill, was a Royal Navy sailor and Coast Guardsman; his mother, Florence Mary Hugill, was a nurse. Stan remembered both parents warmly and spoke of them often. He was born on 19 November 1906 at the Coastguard Cottages in Hoylake, Cheshire, England, was educated briefly at the Church School, which he never much liked, and went to sea in 1921 at the tender age of 14, serving first in steam and later in square rig. He served as Able Bodied Seaman and sometime chanteyman in British and foreign sailing ships; and in 1929 he was shipwrecked and cast ashore in the *Garthpool*, the last square-rigger in British registry. He spent time "on the beach" in Australia, South America, and Oceania, and four years as a German prisoner of war, studied languages at the University of London, and retired from the merchant service in 1950. Then, for twenty-five years, he was on the faculty at the Outward Bound School in Aberdovey, Wales. He was married in Aberdovey in 1953; and there he and his wife Bronwen

xix

raised their sons, Philip and Martin. Meanwhile, Stan developed his interests and skills as a marine artist and writer. His seminal, comprehensive anthology *Shanties from the Seven Seas* was published in 1961; *Sailortown*, the classic mariner's-eye-view of the waterfront districts of the world, appeared in 1967; and *Shanties and Sailor Songs*, a concise anthology of lyrics and tunes with a most informative text, in 1969. *Songs of the Sea*, a colorful international collection, came out in 1977 and has since been issued in several foreign translations. All of his books but the last one are illustrated with his own engaging drawings, and most of them have been reprinted at least once (sometimes with variations in the title). But it was not until after OpSail 1976, with Stan in his seventieth year, that his charisma and extraordinary gift of gab came to the forefront, and his fame and personal influence began to spread.

At Mystic Seaport we first met Stan in 1977, when the Maine Maritime Museum (known at the time as the Bath Maritime Museum) brought him across the Atlantic to lecture and impart atmosphere in Maine, then generously sponsored him on a singing-and-lecturing mini-tour of maritime shrines in the Northeast. Having enjoyed his books and pillaged them for songs, we were thrilled to meet him face-to-face and discover that he was if anything more colorful and interesting than even his own salty prose had led us to suspect. Stan seemed delighted that most of us already knew who he was, and he gloried in the ships and nautical atmosphere. Stan was particularly impressed with the atmosphere and proximity of New London, Connecticut. We took him over there to see the old whaling port, and he pronounced the little city, after thoroughly exploring its docks and pubs, "the only old-time Sailortown still left in the civilized world," worthy of any real sailor's attention. Meanwhile, there was some terrible error about his motel room back in Mystic, as the Seaport administration was horrified to discover later; but Stan allowed as how he had hardly noticed, being a sailor and all and accustomed to less-than-elegant surroundings. He enjoyed himself thoroughly, and we him. It was the first of many gratifying and mutually informative visits.

From those auspicious beginnings—Stan's first forays into America since deepwater days—there gradually arose a groundswell of chanteying nationwide. At Mystic we had been singing chanteys and demonstrating their use at the halyards, capstan, and windlass on a daily basis since 1972; and even before that, a handful of hearty Yankee singers and a few British imports were thundering out the old sea songs in folk concerts and coffeehouses on both coasts. Most of the songs that we had learned from one another or from recordings could be traced back to Louis Killen. who had gotten many of them from Stan; and even half the songs we knew from books had been lifted from Stan, or had been enhanced and informed by versions in *Shanties from the Seven Seas*. Now was our opportunity to learn some songs where Louis had learned so many, directly from Stan, who billed himself as the last English chanteyman.

Through the years he proved to be a generous friend and advocate as well as a star, reveling in the attention he was receiving – and increasingly cultivating the image and the look of the Retired Old Salt – but also reveling in the rejuvenation of grassroots shipboard culture through the songs and lore he loved. From modest chantey concerts and jamborees at Mystic and South Street Seaport emerged a mini-festival in Seattle, a larger, one-time festival in San Francisco in 1979, and the annual Sea Music Festival and Symposium at Mystic Seaport, first held in 1980. Stan was a mainstay of all of these, and his influence inspired a galaxy of others. He also exported inspiration and talent to festivals in Scandinavia, the Netherlands, Britain, France, Canada, and Poland; he recorded songs and yarns and voice-over narrations for the BBC, the Cutty Sark Society, dozens of radio and television documentaries in a half-dozen countries, and countless miles of oral-history tapes at Mystic Seaport; and he continued to accumulate shipmates wherever he went.

Stan stories are legion. He spoke fondly of the substantial repertoire of nautical songs that his Coast Guardsman father would sing at home with button-accordion accompaniment. Stan himself was no instrumentalist, but when pressed he could sing and play bits of parlor songs, sea ballads, and windlass chanteys learned at his father's knee, accompanying himself on the melodeon.

Many were the times at concerts and festivals that Stan would suddenly recall something to memory—or would whip out his little black notebook of lyrics—and rattle off some song or chantey or version that none of us had ever heard, and which Stan had never got around to publishing or recording. As often as not, he expected everyone to join in the choruses right off the bat, and seemed genuinely surprised at the breadth of his esoteric knowledge of songs. Of course, he knew very well all of the legendary, unexpurgated, shipboard versions of the chanteys, and could occasionally be induced to sing them for small, private audiences of colleagues and friends. But these "original Liverpool versions," as he sometimes called them, always turned out to be far less interesting than Stan's clever expurgations created for popular consumption.

Only reluctantly, late in life, could Stan be brought to narrate his harrowing experiences as a German prisoner of war during World War II; but he often reminisced about his brief career after the war as a specially-selected student at the University of London's School of Oriental and African Languages. Understandably, he found it ironic that a lad who had fled school at earliest opportunity to spend his youth on a heaving deck, who never sat for Britain's fearsome A Level and O Level qualifying examinations, and who did not have so much as a high school equivalency diploma, could proceed by official invitation to matriculate at one of the world's most prestigious postgraduate institutions. Stan did have a remarkable facility for languages. He claimed to be able to converse easily in a dozen tongues, and to understand the philology of two or three dozen more. It seems that His Majesty's Government somehow came to recognize this uncanny ability and its potential usefulness in the postwar world. So Stan was duly enrolled at University, and was eventually given a diploma for Japanese Studies.

Stan was perpetually rattling on in what he claimed were actual languages—including pidgin English and the sailortown patois of the entire Asian seacoast and the whole Pacific Basin—and making self-assured pronouncements about linguistics and etymology. However, as he spoke Low German only haltingly and seemed not to be able to deliver an understandable sentence in anything recognizable as Spanish, French, Italian, or Norwegian—the European languages one expects would have been the easiest for him to pick up—many of us held his purported linguistic accomplishments in doubt. This all changed for me one summer evening when we took Stan to one of the festive Japanese Tea Garden parties that the Peabody Museum of Salem used to hold every year. Bevies of chefs and sushi masters were in action everywhere, throngs of people of all races and colors were milling about in hapi coats and kimonos, and the sake and beer flowed freely—a perfect occasion for gregarious Stan to wander into the crowd and meet some of the folks. We lost track of him for an hour or so; and when we found him again, he was standing in a corner of the garden, arms akimbo, surrounded by elderly Japanese women in full-dress kimonos who were weeping openly and profusely. Turned out Stan was singing songs, telling stories, and recalling half-forgotten places of old Japan that they hadn't heard of in decades, nostalgically recalling their childhood memories of a generation before. And, according to the women, all sweetly rendered by Stan in an archaic form of the Japanese language that they understood perfectly but which none of the young folks knew nowadays. Methinks he could probably have done as well in Chinese and Hawaiian.

For all his historical opinions, his engaging prose, his charming pictures, his host of subtle and not-so-subtle street-wise aphorisms about deepwater life, and his trustingly oblivious, sailor-like ways that, one-on-one, made him a natural friend to all until given reason to think otherwise—for all the strange and wonderful human qualities for which he was likeable and admirable as a friend, colleague, and companion—Stan was nevertheless at his best on stage, with the spotlights bright upon him, weaving an audience into rapt approbation. He could work his magic under the bigtop at Mystic Seaport as easily as in a cozy British pub or California coffeehouse, or a crowded civic auditorium in the Dutch provinces, or aboard a Finnish square-rigger, or in a circle of sentimental Japanese matrons in a sedate New England museum, or with acres of swaying teenagers screaming affirmation in Krakow. Stan was the quintessential showman, a larger-than-life character who by re-creating himself in his own Sailortown image persistently taught us something about the sea and, more poignantly, perhaps something about how to live. He caught our attention and captured our imagination. He anchored a host of festivals and reached the people on a surprisingly large scale. He provided encouragement and inspiration for an entire generation of singers, almost singlehandedly precipitating the revival of old deepwater chanteys and sailor songs. And when he slipped his anchor in May of 1992 after a mercifully brief illness, we lost our saltiest sailor—a singer, mentor, writer, painter, raconteur, favorite world-class curmudgeon, and genuine, world-renowned authority on sailor lore. He was an extraordinarily colorful old salt with great panache, and we can hold dear to our hearts the precious, enduring legacy of song and *joi de vivre* he bequeathed to us. By virtue of his having been Stan we have inherited and can pass along to future generations greater insights into our collective past and, perhaps, may find it a bit easier to navigate into the future. Thank you, Stan. And farewell.

STUART M. FRANK, Ph.D.
The Kendall Whaling Museum
Sharon, Massachusetts

INTRODUCTION

~~~~~~

THE ART OF THE SHANTYMAN

~~~~~~

SHANTIES were the work-songs of the sailing-ship man; the staves John Salt, Huw Puw, Jean Mat'lot, and Jan Maat tipped at capstan, halyard, sheet, and pumps. In the Trades or off the pitch o' the Horn, in hail and snow, in doldrum and calm, the not un-melodious voices of Yankee, Nigger, Limey, Squarehead, Johnny Crapoo, and Dutchie would oft-times be raised to cheer the soul, curse the afterguard and owner, mark the beat, and lighten the labour.

To the seamen of America, Britain, and northern Europe a shanty was as much a part of the equipment as a sheath-knife and pannikin. Shanties were always associated with work—and a rigid tabu held against singing them ashore. When the sailor caroused ashore, or sang at sea in the dog-watches, his choice would invariably be a popular ballad, love song, or the like. To sing a shanty when there was no heaving or hauling would be courting trouble—and the sailing-ship man was superstitious to a degree.

The aged mariners who are still with us must groan inwardly as they hear the smooth attempts of a trained radio singer declaring some of their Rabelaisian favourites to a receptive audience without the harmony(?) of the Cape Stiff gale and the cursing mates. The day of the shanty as a work-song is done, and now it is left to the Oriental —the Japanese and Chinese junk seamen, the Moslem and Indian coolie, the African Negro—to carry on the tradition of singing at labour. It is quite possible that one of the many origins from which the art of shantying and even some of the shanties themselves developed is that of the age-old Oriental coolie method of chanting when doing a job of work.

Early shantying was, from what we know, little more than primitive chanting and wild aboriginal cries to encourage the seamen to keep time and work harder, and the fierce elemental yells on a rope known as 'sing-outs' were to be heard even in modern times aboard

I

sailing vessels and occasionally aboard steamers while some sailing-ship shellbacks still remained to sail in them.

*　　*　　*

Many research workers have delved into the past endeavouring to find ancient references to seamen singing at their work, but their efforts have produced little. Undoubtedly early seamen *did* sing at their work, but I rather fancy that in Greek and Roman galleys, triremes, and whatnot any singing that was done would be at the oars—rowing songs rather than heaving and hauling chants. Miss Lucy E. Broadwood, in the *Journal* of the Folk Song Society, writes in similar vein. Sir Maurice Bowra, who has kindly waded through many existing Greek texts on my behalf, has produced two sailor songs only, both from the Oxyrhynchus Papyri, and of these he writes: 'It is not certain that either of these pieces is a sea-chantey in the strict sense of the word, but the first looks as if it were sung by a group of sailors competing and the second is clearly a sailor's song.'

I believe there is a book in existence called *Chanties in Greek and Latin* by Rouse, but I have been unable to locate a copy.

*　　*　　*

The earliest reference to a sing-out—the wild yell seamen would raise when hauling a rope hand-over-hand, a sort of embryo shanty—is to be found in a manuscript of the time of Henry VI, recording the passage in 1400 of a ship loaded with pilgrims towards the port of the shrine of St. James of Compostella.[1]

> Anone the master commaundeth fast,
> To hys shyp-men in all the hast,
> To dresse hem sone about the mast,
> Theyr takelyng to make.

> With 'howe! hissa!' then they cry,
> 'What howte! mate, thou stondyst to ny,
> Thy felow may nat hale the by';
> Thus they begyn to crake.

> A boy or tweyne anone up-styen,
> And overthwarte the sayle-yerde lyen;—
> 'Y-how! taylia!' the remenaunte cryen,
> And pull with all theyr myght.

This in modern English would read something like:

> Now the Old Man gives the order for the crowd,
> To get to their stations (about the mast) and make sail,
> 'Haul away! Hoist 'er up!' they cry,
> 'Hey mate, keep clear o' me!

[1] *The Early Naval Ballads of England*, edit. J. O. Halliwell. The Percy Society, 1841 (Library of Trinity College, Cambridge).

2

Can't haul with you blowin' down me bleedin' neck!'
Croaked the older shellbacks.
A couple of deckboys climb aloft,
And overhaul the buntlines,
'Yo ho! Tail on the fall!' the rest sing out,
And pull with all their beef.

Coming to the period when Venetian galleys ploughed their way beyond the Pillars of Hercules we find, in the work of a Dominican friar, Felix Fabri, who made a passage to Palestine aboard such a craft in the year 1493, references to the duties of her crew:

Under these again there are others who are called mariners who sing when work is going on, because work at sea is very heavy, and is only carried on by a concert between one who sings out orders and the labourers who sing in response. So these men stand by those who are at work, and sing to them, encouraging them, and threaten to spur them with blows. Great weights are dragged by their means. They are generally old and respected men. . . .[1]

This is probably the earliest mention in literature of shantying. The earliest work giving the words of shanties is the *Complaynt of Scotland* (1549), wherein a ship is described getting under way in the Firth of Forth and the following heaving and hauling songs are given:[2]

An Anchor Song:

Vayra, veyra, vayra, veyra,
Gentil gallantis veynde;
I see hym, veynde, I see hym,
Porbossa, porbossa,
Hail all and ane, hail all and ane;
Hail hym up til us,
Hail hym up til us.

Vayra, veyra are words probably related to the Spanish word 'Vira!'— 'Heave' or 'Hoist'—heard from ports of the Mediterranean to those of the Far East.

Another *Anchor Song*:

Caupon, caupona, caupon, caupona,
Caupon hola, caupon hola,
Caupon holt, caupon holt,
Sarabossa, sarabossa.

[1] *The Book of the Wanderings of Brother Felix Fabri*, translated by Aubrey Stewart, Library of the Palestine Pilgrims Text Society VII, 1893.
[2] These verses are taken from the Introduction to Capt. W. B. Whall's *Sea Songs and Shanties*, Brown, Son & Ferguson, Glasgow, 1927.

THE ART OF THE SHANTYMAN

Bowline Shanty (the bowline was a very important rope in these early vessels and much use was made of it in a head wind):

> Hou, hou, pulpela, pulpela,
> Boulena, boulena,
> Darta, darta,
> Hard out strif.

And for *hoisting the lower yard*:

> Afore the wind, afore the wind,
> God send, God send,
> Fair weather, fair weather,
> Many prizes, many prizes.

Another *hauling song* or *sing-out*:

> Heisa, heisa,
> Vorsa, vorsa,
> Vou, vou,
> One long pull,
> More power,
> Young blood,
> More mud.

And:

> Yellow hair, hips bare,
> To him all,
> Vidde fulles all,
> Great and small, ane and all
> Heisa, heisa.

Rowing songs are found, from the fourteenth and fifteenth centuries, in which the word 'rumbelow' frequently appears—the word also appears in songs sung in the water processions which used to be held by the Lord Mayor of London. This has been pointed out by L. G. Carr Laughton and Miss L. A. Smith and others, and D'Israeli in his book *Curiosities of Literature* writes that, 'our sailors at Newcastle in heaving their anchors (still) have their "heave and ho, rumbelow" ', which brings the word down to comparatively recent times. My friend Mr. G. Legman has pointed out that in Skelton's sixteenth-century *Bowge at Court* there is a song 'Heve and how, rombelow, row the bote, Norman, rowe!'

Three shanties often cited as having their origin in Elizabethan times are *Haul the Bowline, A-rovin'*, and *Whisky Johnny. Haul the Bowline* may be Elizabethan or even earlier (Masefield states that it was certainly in use at the time of Henry VIII), but, apart from the fact that the bowline was an important rope in those days, degenerating later into a light line on which no shanty would ever be raised, there is little or no real evidence to go on. *A-rovin'* may date from this period but as a shore-song only. There is not enough evidence to prove that *Whisky Johnny* is an Elizabethan SHANTY, even if some people do think it was sung as *MALMSEY Johnny*!

For the seventeenth century we can produce nothing, and very little for the eighteenth, with perhaps the exception of some evidence given by Falconer in his *Marine Dictionary* (1769). He makes mention of a windlass worked by handspikes which fitted into holes in the barrel and which had to be fleeted (shifted) at each heave, and after each fixing of the bars the mariners would heave and 'give a sudden jerk . . . regulated by a sort of song or howl'. Laughton in *The Mariner's Mirror* writes that he thinks this may mean the singing of an elemental type of shanty such as *Lowlands*, whereas other writers believe it to be nothing more than a sing-out such as 'yo heave ho!'

Although we haven't any real proof that the art of shantying and the shanty itself as we know it existed in the eighteenth century, it is fairly obvious, although unrecorded, that many of the shanties which have survived to the present day must have been 'invented' and circulated towards the end of this century, and this we can judge from the accepted manner in which the earliest writers of the nineteenth century refer to these working songs. They don't introduce them as something new but merely refer to them as one would a well-established custom.

The shanty *Boney* seems to indicate that later eighteenth-century events were used by the shantyman—in all probability the words being taken from existing 'broadsheets'—but whether the shanty was in use at this time it is difficult to say. Another shanty that may hail from this period is the hauling song *Bunch o' Roses* or *Blood-red Roses*, the latter phrase being a name given to the English Redcoats by Napoleon's troops.

From 1739 to 1815 England was engaged in wars with the French. It was a period of the 'Johnny Haul-taut' as opposed to the Merchant John, the days when naval plays were all the rage, and songs and ballads were built around Dibdinian Jack Tars and great sea battles hawked by the sellers of ballad-sheets around the city of London. Aboard naval vessels heaving and hauling was done to the music of the fiddle, to the whistle of the bosun's pipe, and to numbers. The rather peculiar shout of 'Two-six!' used when hauling on a rope, and still heard in naval vessels, has probably been handed down from this period. No shantying was allowed in the Senior Service, although Whall seems to think that it was permitted in small craft and revenue cutters and then the only type of shanty used would be a stamp-'n'-go song suited to big crews who would walk away with married falls. *Cheer'ly Man* was also used at times, but in the main, though they had the aid of the fiddle, the pipe, and the calling of numbers by the bosun's mate, naval seamen worked in silence—hence the disparaging title given them by Merchant John—'Johnny Haul-taut'.

In these days Merchant John carried on without any publicity; he was not in the limelight like his naval brother, and, the times being what they were, even Merchant John was inundated with naval customs and routine. Many merchant ships were armed on account of the preponderance of privateers, pirates, and enemy vessels scouring the high seas. Naval discipline was to be found aboard many merchant ships. The arming of merchant ships left its mark even down to the latter days of sail, when many ships had painted ports along their sides. The Blackwall frigates of the nineteenth century had their gunners, topmen, middies, fiddlers, and other naval hangovers from these stirring times.

All this naval discipline naturally tended to submerge the wild shantying of uncouth Merchant Jack, and furthermore the pressgang tenders which awaited every merchantman offshore, ready to seize him and press him into the service of the King's Navee, robbed the commercial ship of good shantymen, their place being taken by landsmen and foreigners who knew nothing about, and cared less for, these traditional work-songs. Obviously shantying *did* exist, but only as a trickle; and even mention of this trickle has been omitted from the nautical works of the period.

From 1815, the Year of Peace, onwards a new and prosperous era at sea and ashore rapidly developed, but there is very little concrete reference to shantying to be found in literature until the eighteen-thirties. In the eighteen-thirties reference to shanties and shantying entered literature, and for several years most authorities thought that Dana[1] (1834) was the first writer to mention the subject and to give the title of several work-songs. (Nevertheless he did not call them SHANTIES.)

Doerflinger[2] however discovered an interesting reference to shanties in a little volume called *The Quid* (London, 1832). I came across two copies of this rather rare book—one in the British Museum Library and one in the Greenwich Maritime Library. It is the work of an anonymous steerage passenger who sailed to the Far East in a ship of the Honourable John East India Company, and its secondary title is 'Ditties, Quid-ditties, and Od-ditties'. On page 222 there is a woodcut portraying heaving at the capstan, which has a Negro fiddler perched on its crown,·together with a description of the singing which runs:

. . . (a) motley group man the bars. . . . It is a time of equality; idlers, stewards and servants, barbers and sweepers, cooks and cooks' mates,

[1] Dana, R. H., *Two Years Before the Mast*, Harper and Bros., New York, 1840.
[2] Doerflinger, W. M., *Shantymen and Shantyboys*, Chap. IV. The Rise of Shantying. The Macmillan Co., N.Y., 1951.

ministers, doctors' mates and loblolly boys; every man runs the same road and hard and impenetrable is that soul that does not chime in with the old ditties. . . .

The words of two of these ditties sung at the capstan are then given.

Quite recently I discovered an even earlier reference to shantying, although it is not called by this name and the workers were long-shoremen not seamen, but nevertheless to my way of thinking the given songs are undoubtedly shanties as distinct from Negro work-songs; their wording and refrains speak for themselves. The book I quote is *Landsman Hay*—Memoirs of Robert Hay, 1789–1847.[1] The work is about the life of a merchant seaman who at times was pressed into the King's Navee, and the life at sea of a Merchant Jack and of a Naval Tar is described in rather quaint but very readable English. References to the use of the fiddle and fife in men-o'-war when heaving at the anchor and the tunes that were played are many. Here are some extracts, the first from page 80:

(Sailing of H.M.S. *Culloden* towards the East Indies, July 1804.)
'Are you ready there forward?'
'All ready, Sir.'
'Heave away. What kind of a drawling tune is that you Fifer? Strike up *Off She Goes* or *Drops of Brandy*. Aye, that is the tune. Keep step there, all of ye, and stamp-and-go. Light round the messenger there, aft, hand forward the nippers, you boys.'

This must be the first time in print the expression 'stamp-and-go' is to be found. Two capstans were used in naval vessels of this time to heave the anchor—a messenger of rope linking the two. At the larger (which was placed aft of the smaller), the seamen manned the bars, causing the smaller to revolve as well. The anchor cable was a nine-stranded cable-laid rope which came through the hawse-pipe, ran alongside the two capstans (on the main-deck), and was stowed down in the cable tier beneath the main deck. 'Nippers' were short pieces of rope (stoppers) one end of which would be fastened to the 'messenger', the other end to the cable, and as the cable was hove in, and the 'nippers' reached the barrel of the larger capstan, small boys would 'fleet' them (i.e. untie and move them) and fasten them on again near the small capstan. It was from such circumstances that the word 'nipper' entered our language as the name for a small boy.

Page 162:

In the early February 1809 we met at Point de Galle with the home-ward bound Indiamen, which we had appointed to rendezvous there, and 14th we found ourselves dancing round the capstan to the tune of *Off She Goes.* . . .

[1] Edited by M. D. Hay, Rupert Hart-Davies, 1953.

7

Page 286:

Heaving up and sailing after waiting for water at the Bar off Shields aboard a merchant brig, Oct. 1811 . . . the stentorian voices of the pilots, the nautical heave O of the mariners as they braced their yards and hauld their bowlings. . . .

On the voyage to Jamaica in the *Edward* merchantman, in the year 1811, the crew cleared out and Negroes from ashore worked the cargo. The following I feel must be the earliest reference to shanties, such as we understand them, in print (page 201):

Our seamen having left the ship, the harbour work was performed by a gang of Negroes. These men will work the whole day at the capstan under a scorching sun with almost no intermission. They beguiled the time by one of them singing one line of an English song, or a prose sentence at the end of which all the rest join in a short chorus. The sentences which prevail with the gang we had aboard were as follows:

Two sisters courted one man,
Ch. Oh, huro, my boys,
And they live in the mountains,
Ch. Oh, huro boys O.

And the second:

Grog time of day, boys,
Grog time of day,
Ch. Huro, my jolly boys,
Grog time of day.

Note that this reference to singing at the capstan is in the period before 1815, a period all writers on the subject of shantying declare to be void of any tangible proof of shantying.

Although the West Indian is rarely referred to by writers on shantying, I feel that he was responsible for producing far more seamen's work-songs than any Negro of the Southern States of America. West Indian Negroes have shipped as seamen and cooks in our merchant ships and naval vessels from earliest times and were ever to the fore as shantymen. Bullen seems to be the only writer who looks towards the Caribbean and the Guianas as a source of shanties, although Terry does state that he heard many shanties in 'West Indian seaports . . . one of the few remaining spots where shanties may still be heard'. I endorse this, as I have heard them sung at work in the Windward Islands as late as the thirties. In *The Sea Made Men* (Memoirs of a Yankee Sea Captain, 1826–1840) the author, G. P. Low, mentions on page 31 darkies singing as they hoisted aboard his ship hogsheads of tobacco at James River, Virginia, but otherwise no mention is made of shantying.

The two shanties given in *The Quid* (already mentioned on page 7) are capstan songs, although they do not have the saltiness or the ring of true shanties as have those I quote from *Landsman Hay*. They were probably forebitters used as shanties, although the second one could be a Negro song.

> Oh her love is a sailor,
> His name is Jemmy Taylor,
> He's gone in a whaler
> To the Greenland Sea.

and

> Oh! if I had her,
> Eh then if I had her,
> Oh! how I would love her
> Black although she be.

This latter is more than likely a variant of the folk-song called *Still I love him*, the verse of which has the same tune as *Villikins and his Dinah*, and the chorus of which runs:

> Oh I love him,
> How I love him,
> Still I love him, [I'll forgive him,]
> Wherever he be!

It *was* sung at sea, but usually by fishermen when hauling in their catches. Here is how it usually starts:

> He gave me a nice shawl which I always wore,
> I wore it until I could wear it no more,
> Oh I love him, *etc.*
> He bought me a nice handkerchief, red, white, and blue,
> I had it until I had torn it in two,
> Oh I love, *etc.*

Doerflinger notes that a Scottish folk-song *Were you ever in Dumbarton?* has lines similar to the above:

> Oh if I had her,
> If I had her,
> Oh if I had her,
> Happy would I be.

Another shanty given in this little book, by name only, is *Pull away now, my Nancy O !* which is obviously a true hauling song. This may be the same shanty as that mentioned by Dana in his *Two Years Before the Mast*[1] which he calls *Nancy Oh*.

Dana's shanties (he calls them 'songs for capstan and falls') are ones which were sung aboard the American ships *Pilgrim* and *Alert* between the years 1834 and 1836. He lists:

Heave to the Girls.
Cheerily Men.

[1] See page 319.

Round the Corner.
Hurrah, Hurrah, My Hearty Fellows.
Nancy O!
Captain's Gone Ashore.
Heave Round Hearty. .
Jack Crosstree.
Roll the Old Chariot.
Neptune's Raging Fury.
Cheer Up, Sam.

Laughton[1] writes that Dana gives no Negro shanties, but is this quite correct? *Round the Corner, Cheer Up, Sam,* and *Roll the Old Chariot* are all of Negro extraction. These and *Cheerily Men* are the only ones of Dana's work-songs that have survived until the present day. But then again, as we know nothing of his shanties beyond their titles, what is to prevent many of them from being Negro songs? For example, in this book I have produced several 'new' shanties, the titles of three are *Heave Away, Boys, Heave Away* (a), *Heave Away, Boys, Heave Away* (b), and *Haul Away, Boys, Haul Away.* With the aid of the titles only who would know these were Negro shanties? And yet that is what they are.

And then again, to further an idea presented by the author of the *Seven Seas Shanty Book,* many of the shanties that appear to be developed from Negro sources may be white men's ditties taken to the West Indies by the slaves of the Monmouth Rebellion and, after being altered by the Negroes to suit their tastes, turning up again as Negro work-songs aboard sailing ships.

Sally Brown is mentioned by Captain Marryat as having been sung in 1837 by seamen aboard the packet he sailed in from England to America. This shanty is of Negro extraction, if it is not a pure Negro song.

I am rather inclined to think that Negro shanties or shanties developed from Negro songs were more common about this period than the authorities seem to suggest. And why not? From just prior to the end of the Napoleonic Wars the Cotton Trade between the Southern States of America and England advanced steadily until, in about 1836–7, the amount of cotton carried to England reached more than 500 shiploads.

Laughton states that in the 1830s the loading of cotton on to the ships gave seamen many opportunities to listen to slave songs, the result being that the white sailors picked up Negro work-songs and took them to sea as shanties, ousting the old favourites; but he does admit too that the 1840s produced *Western Ocean* and *Blow the Man Down.* I believe that Negro songs were being sung in British ships earlier than is usually accepted. Even *Blow the Man Down* is now

[1] Laughton, L. G. Carr, 'Shantying and Shanties', *The Mariner's Mirror,* 1923.

believed to have come from an earlier Negro version *Knock a Man Down*, and *Western Ocean* (*Leave Her, Johnny*) in its earliest form *Across the Rocky Mountains* is probably a Negro–Irish mixture. Incidentally, it would appear that shanties of unmistakable Negro parentage were rarely heard aboard British Tea Clippers or East Indiamen.

Some American writers suggest that shantying—an art of peace—was developed by white Americans during the period when England was at war with France and her allies and therefore an unfruitful field for the growth of work-songs. I agree that in British ships, on account of the pressing of merchant seamen into the Navy and the very fact that merchant ships were in themselves semi-naval, the art of shantying during these eventful years was at a low ebb, but then again America had her War of Independence from 1775 to 1783, followed by the war of 1812—hardly a very peaceful period! It seems reasonable enough to suppose that in both countries shanties *did* develop in a minor fashion, but it was not until 1815, the rebirth of the British Merchant Service and the renewed growth of the young American Merchant Marine, that shantying really came into its own in both countries. By the 1820s shantying was on a fairly equal footing in both English and American ships, but as the new merchant service of the younger country advanced with its smart packet ships of hitherto unseen design—ships much faster than those of Britain—shantying must obviously have developed to a greater degree aboard such ships than in the more cautious, slower water-pushers of the Old Country. But then again, apart from the afterguard, the crews of such ships were in the main seamen from Britain, it being a known fact that from 1830 onwards many Americans 'swallowed the anchor' and went west in search of employment, leaving the packets and later clippers in the hands of Irishmen and seamen from Liverpool and Scandinavia.

Captain Frank Shaw writes in Chapter 12, 'Shipsavers', of his book *Splendour of the Seas*:

My own theory is that the sea-shanty first began really to flourish in the days of the hard run Yankee clippers. Many of the songs are undoubtedly of American origin and some of plantation origin, down to a fine point.

Take *Roll the Cotton Down* . . . (it) goes on to describe the dreary life of a plantation slave more than that of a seaman . . . the reason is not hard to seek. American and West Indian slave owners were not philanthropists. . . .

The trouble with slave-owning was that the human cattle must eat, no matter whether they worked or not.

(And here he mentions the fruitless expedition of Bligh to bring back breadfruit to grow as slave food, which if it had succeeded would have conferred a benefit on slave-owners.)

After harvest . . . slaves were most costly to support in the winter months. The owners found a solution to this recurring problem. They hired them out as crews for America's growing mercantile marine.

This practice, he writes, was especially common in coastwise ships, but I rather feel, historically, it was not such a common practice as he implies. He then goes on to say:

To lighten labour and solace woe, the Negroes sang their nostalgic plantation songs, using them as their free forbears had used them in the Gambia jungles to induce combined effort. Then an occasional white man would sign on . . . and hear these songs, and when he joined another ship he would sing them and his new shipmates found them attractive and helpful. . . .

Since the blacks used their own jabber . . . the borrowers fitted their own words to the catchy tunes . . . (often) ribald, obscene and a means of administering reproofs to the little liked afterguard.

Even in Dana's journal the crews of American ships mentioned seem very mixed. Apart from a few Boston and Cape Cod boys the older seamen were English, Scotch, German, Frenchmen, African Negroes, and South Sea Islanders.

Cheerily Men, sung repeatedly aboard the ships Dana sailed in, is a hundred per cent British shanty of fair antiquity.

From the eighteen-twenties to the eighteen-sixties was the 'great constructive period of shanties'—a phrase used by Laughton. In ships such as the Western Ocean Packets, the Indiamen, the California Hide Traders, the Timber Droghers, the Cotton Traders, the Australian Traders, and the Cape Horners carrying thousands of people to the Gold Rush of the Sacramento River (1849), new shanties were produced and earlier ones developed and altered for the better. Strangely enough the clippers (American and British) of the China Tea Trade produced little if anything new in the way of shanties, and it can be safely said that from 1860 onwards the production of new shanties ceased entirely. The Crimean War (1854), the American Civil War (1861-5), and the Boer War (1900) produced marching songs which Seamen of the Sail took, altered, and adapted as shanties to suit their own needs at the capstan. However, as I have shown elsewhere, foreign seamen did devise 'new' shanties, from older English sea-songs, for some time after this.

Doerflinger, the most painstaking shanty research worker of recent times, gives a certain Francis Allyn Olmstead as the first man to publish shanties with their tunes. Searching through Olmstead's book—*Incidents of a Whaling Voyage* (1839–40); Scenery, Manners and Customs and Missionary Stations of the Sandwich and Society Islands[1]—I found on page 115 a few paragraphs referring to shantying aboard the author's ship, the *New America*:

. . . there are many songs in common use among seamen of a very lively character, which though bereft of all sentiment and sense in many instances are performed with very good effort when there is a long line of men hauling together. Mr. Freeman usually officiates as chorister and with many demisemiquavers strikes up the song, while all the rest join in the chorus.

The two shanties he gives with tunes are *Drunken Sailor* and *Nancy Fanana*. On page 182 Olmstead mentions another shanty *Oh, Hurrah My Hearties O!* which he says was sung when pulling out the teeth from the jaws of a sperm whale by means of a watch-tackle. It was obviously a bowline or foresheet shanty, now unfortunately lost for ever.

As Bone[2] remarks, instead of diminishing shantying grew stronger as sail competed with steam. Ashore, as mechanization grew apace, the work-songs of the folk naturally died, but at sea the arrival of engines was an incentive to the men of the poorly manned, larger sized windbags to haul and heave all the harder to help their outmoded ships keep their position, and this meant more shantying than ever.

Alden(?) (*Harper's Magazine*) mentions a shanty—'pulling, with two different choruses'—used in a steamship in 1882, so it would appear that shanties were still sung even in the sail-carrying steamers of the 'transition period'. Captain Robinson and other competent observers have pointed out that steam-power was never used for setting sail aboard such steamers, and, as long as the old Packet Rat survived to man the ship-, barque-, and brig-rigged steamers of the Cunard, Union, Inman, White Star, and National Steamship Lines, shanties were still to be heard on their decks.

Whence came these working-songs of the sea?

Many writers have tried to solve this puzzle. I have worked unceasingly in this direction, and in the main body of this work I have included as much information as I have been able to find regarding the origin of each shanty; but here I will deal with this question in a general way.

As already pointed out, Negroes, those of the West Indies and the Southern States of America, were responsible for quite a number of these songs. Sampson has voiced an opinion that many of the Negro

[1] New York, 1841.
[2] *Capstan Bars* by Capt. D. W. Bone, Porpoise Press, Edinburgh, 1931.

work-songs and shanties were nothing more than English folk-songs taken out to the West Indies and Southern States by white P.O.W.s transported after the Monmouth Rebellion to the Caribbean.[1] Often in these matters the question is which came first, the chicken or the egg?

R. W. Gordon (*Adventure*: 'Old Songs That Men Have Sung'), writing about songs that have 'authors', points out that occasionally a certain song has an 'author' version and a version partly composed by the folk. Sometimes the work of an author has been taken and altered by the folk, and sometimes an author has taken as his basis a genuine folk-song altered to suit himself. Many minstrel songs were based upon or contained folk material; but sometimes, to make matters more complicated, such material returns to the folk and 'exerts an influence on true folk-song'. He points out that maybe a 'modern folk text and a modern "author" text' come from a common source. 'It is never safe to be dogmatic in any case unless all the evidence is in.' The great folk-song collector Cecil Sharp found many 'genuine' American folk-songs to have old English roots. The job of tracing folk-songs may be difficult, but the arduous task of tracking down the origins of shanties is infinitely more so.

The influence of the 'nigger minstrel' on shantying is plainly emphasized by Doerflinger, who points out that the Sailors of the Sail would naturally frequent the 'melodeons' and 'concert saloons' of both America and England, where they would hear many nigger minstrel ditties suitable for use at capstan and halyard—the ditties of Pompey Smash, Gumbo Chaff, and Liza Lee, all noted nigger minstrels. Also he would more than likely buy the cheap song-books of the period known as 'Ethiopian Songsters'. Many of these minstrel songs, as well as being pseudo-Negro ditties, were traditional Negro folk material, and both the real Negro songs and the adapted ones would be appropriated by the seamen. Doerflinger gives *Do Johnny Boker*, *A Long Time Ago*, and *De Camptown Races* as minstrel choruses which the seaman took to sea with him and turned into 'genuine' shanties.

The following couplets are to be found both in the shanties and Negro and minstrel song, and in some cases in English and American folk-song and 'hobo' songs.

> Where there ain't no snow,
> And the winds don't blow.

> What d'you think we had for supper?
> Possum tails and a donkey's crupper.

> If whisky was a river and I could swim,
> I'd take a jump and dive right in.

[1] *The Seven Seas Shanty Book*, John Sampson. Boosey & Co., Ltd., London, 1927.

We dug his grave with a silver spade,
And lowered him down with a golden chain.

Who's bin here since I've bin gone?
A nice little gal wid bootees on.

There once was a farmer in Sussex did dwell,
Now he is dead and he's gone to Hell.

And there are countless others.

In Negro spirituals and revivalist songs too, wording similar to that found in shanties often appears. Arnold in *Songs of Sea Labour* states that many of the Negro slave-songs sung during the revival meetings of the Jubilee Singers touring Great Britain bore striking resemblance to both the shanty tunes and those of the Sankey and Moody collection. Many of the Negro slave-songs were *work*-songs—digging, planting, cane-cutting, peanut-picking, corn-shucking, cotton-picking, and cotton-stowing songs—as were the songs sung by Negroes employed in the railway gangs of Young America. Many of these songs have been made popular on the radio under the collective name of skiffle. Gordon in *Adventure* gives a song sung by Negro gangs as they drove the spikes in the railroad ties formed like and used in a similar manner to the sailor's shanty:

Ole Aunt Dinah,
Bumpy ditty bump-bump!
Settin' in de co'nah,
Bumpy ditty bump!

In the main body of this work many instances are given of the railway gang songs of Negroes adapted by seamen as shanties. Then we have the labour songs of the Negro stevedores and wharf workers. These in the main came from the cotton stowers of the Gulf Ports—New Orleans, Mobile, and so on. Bone, Laughton, Doerflinger, and others have shown how white seamen picked up these ditties from the cotton stowers or 'hoosiers' and made use of them at capstan and halyard. But, apart from Bone, Doerflinger is the only writer who has discovered in literature the fact that *white men* as well as Negroes were engaged in this cotton-stowing business. He points out that these white men were in the main seamen from the North Atlantic Packet Ships, and the job of stowing cotton down the dark holds of ships, forcing the cotton bales in tightly by means of jackscrews—a job requiring much shantying—was done just as ably by the whites as by the darkies. He cites Charles Erskine (*Twenty Years Before the Mast*[1]) on the fact that many of these white men were seamen from Boston, and E. I. Barra (*A Tale of Two Oceans*[2]), who describes how the seamen from the Liverpool Packets would dodge the Winter North Atlantic by jumping their ships and heading south to the

[1] Boston, 1890.   [2] San Francisco, 1893.

Gulf Ports to work at stowing cotton until the summer. He also quotes Charles Nordhoff—the author of *Nine Years a Sailor*,[1] who gives a good example of the type of life these white 'hoosiers' led in the late 1840s. I was lucky enough to come across a later edition of the same book—*The Merchant Vessel, A Sailor Boy's Voyages*.[2] Nordhoff refers to singing when heaving on jackscrews and he calls the singing 'chanting' and the foreman of the gang of singers the 'Chantyman'. On page 36 ('Songs of the Gangs') he writes:

The chants as may be supposed have more rhyme than reason in them. The tunes are generally plaintive and monotonous as are most of the capstan tunes of sailors, but resounding over the still waters of the Bay, they had a fine effect.

He gives the words of 'four typical capstan or cotton songs or chants'. Of the first, *Stormalong*, he writes:

There was one in which figured that mythical figure 'Old Stormy', the rising and falling cadences of which, as they swept over the Bay on the breeze, I was never tired of listening to.

Of the second one, which he writes is in praise of the Dollar, he gives two stanzas:

> Oh, we work for a Yankee Dollar,
> *Ch.* Hurrah, see-man-do,
> Yankee Dollar, bully dollar,
> *Ch.* Hurrah, see-man-dollar.
>
> Silver dollar, pretty dollar,
> *Ch.* Hurrah, see-man-do,
> I want your silver dollars,
> *Ch.* Oh, Captain, pay me dollar.

The tune of this shanty is unfortunately lost; it seems to be of Negro origin.

His third one, for encouraging the gang, is *Fire, maringo, fire away*:

> Lift him up and carry him along,
> Fire, maringo, fire away.
> Put him down where he belongs,
> Fire, maringo, fire away.
> Ease him down and let him lay,
> Fire, maringo, fire away.
> Screw him in, and there he'll stay,
> Fire, maringo, fire away.
> Stow him in his hole below,
> Fire, maringo, fire away.
> Say he must, and then he'll go,
> Fire, maringo, fire away.

[1] Cincinnati, 1857.   [2] Dodd, Mead & Co., New York, 1884.

THE ART OF THE SHANTYMAN

Doerflinger seems to think that *Fire, maringo* is of Negro origin, but I feel that Ireland is as like as not its birthplace. The word 'maringo' is the clue. This quaint word is found in many Irish folk-songs, such as the following:

> As I was going along the road,
> As I was going a-walking,
> I heard a lassie in the shade;
> To a young man she was talking.
> *Ch.* With a maringo do-a-day,
> With a maringo do-a-daddy-o!

The tune of *Fire, maringo* has also been lost.

The fourth chant he gives is *Highland Laddie*, which has remained until fairly recent times as a very popular walkaway and capstan song. Nordhoff continues:

> These samples . . . might be continued to an almost indefinite extent . . .

And how every shanty collector wishes he had continued with samples of others now lost for ever!

Of the men who sang these songs he writes:

> The men who yearly resort to Mobile Bay to screw cotton are, as may be imagined, a rough set. They are mostly English and Irish sailors, who, leaving their vessels here, remain until they have saved a hundred or more dollars, then ship for Liverpool, London, or wherever port may be their favourite. Screwing cotton is, I think . . . the most exhausting labour that is done on shipboard.

It is fairly obvious that the wharves of Mobile and such places were the meeting-ground of white men's songs and shanties and Negro songs and work-songs. Scottish, Irish, and English folk-songs would be brought into the mart by visiting sailors and left the mart after being hammered into shanties by the Negroes, and Negro work-songs from ashore would be taken by white sailors and added to their repertoire for halyard and capstan. And of course regular white men's shanties would be handed over to the Negro and regular Negro shanties would be taken away across the seven seas by the white men. The Gulf Ports could have been called the shanty mart or work-song exchange!

Apart from genuine Negro (Southern States and West Indian), white 'hoosier', and pseudo-Negro (minstrel) sources, shanties had many other origins. C. F. Smith[1] has proposed a theory which I feel has much to justify it—the idea that many shanty tunes are no more than 'loose ends' left over from airs played by the ship's fiddler. At sea the fiddle has constantly been a favourite 'dog-watch' instrument, and in ships of the King's Navee a fiddler was part of the ship's company. Captain Frank Shaw writes that fiddlers were

[1] *A Book of Shanties* by C. Fox Smith, Methuen & Co., Ltd., London, 1927.

carried in the Royal Navy to play for the vigorous dancing of the hornpipe insisted upon daily by the commanders to keep the men's blood circulating so as to prevent that dreaded disease of the days of sail—scurvy. They were a sort of anti-scorbutic like the limejuice of the later sailing ships. But as well as fulfilling this function they also played at the capstan as the men hove the huge wooden-stock anchors to the hawse-pipes. They were first employed as far as we know about the first half of the nineteenth century and even in the East India Company and in the Blackwall frigates which took their place a fiddler was an important cog in the ship's machinery.

My father told me that even in his time, when larger vessels of the Navy carried a marine band, smaller ships still clung to their fiddler. And although the fiddler was ousted from the Navy scene and from the Indiamen, scraps of the tunes they played—jigs and reels, marches and waltzes—were adapted by shantymen for work-songs at capstan, brace, and halyard.

Again, the Irishman—real, Liverpool, and New York—was in no minor degree responsible for a good many shanties and forebitters—the songs seamen sang off watch in the fo'c'sle or on the fo'c'sle-head. As the reader will observe as he wades through this volume, many shanties had Irish tunes—dance, folk, and march—and not only were the words and phrases of many of the shanties of Irish origin but in some cases it was customary for the shantyman to sing the shanties with an imitative Irish brogue. The Packet Rats of the Western Ocean Packets were almost one hundred per cent Irish, either from County this or that, or from Liverpool's Scotland Road or New York's Bowery and West Side, and as these seamen were responsible for many of our finest shanties it was only natural for them to choose tunes and words from Irish sources when they made up these songs. Nearly all the forebitters are of Irish origin and many of these were used as capstan and pump songs on account of their stirring choruses. Doerflinger seems to think that the forebitters were sires to the shanties, but, although this was true in several cases, very often the line of descent was the other way around. Not only is it difficult to state which copied which, but very often neither collectors nor sailors can agree as to which was a shanty and which was a fore-bitter. For instance Bone gives *Liverpool Girls* as a shanty, but *Paddy, Lay Back* (*Mainsail Haul*) as an example of a forebitter. On the other hand Doerflinger gives *Mainsail Haul* (one version) as a shanty and the *Liverpool Girls* (*Roll, Julia, Roll*) as a forebitter. Sampson gives *High Barbaree* as a shanty, other collectors give it as a forebitter. Captain F. Shaw gives *Spanish Ladies* as a shanty, others present it as a forebitter. Most collectors give *Rolling Home* as a forebitter, but C. F. Smith definitely states it to be a capstan shanty. And there are many more examples to be found in the following pages.

It all boils down to the fact that in talking about shanties and shantying one cannot be too dogmatic. It was a common practice too for the tune of one forebitter to be put to the words of another. As to the fitting of words of one shanty to another this was a very common practice—all adding to the difficulty of the collector! It should be noted that the words of most of the hauling songs (and some capstan) can be fitted to one another with comparative ease— *Blackball Line, Roll the Cotton, Santiana, Clear the Track, Bunch o' Roses, South Australia, Blow the Man Down, A Long Time Ago, Whisky Johnny, Mobile Bay, Stormalong, Rio, Hogeye Man, Boney*—and the fitting of words from one shanty to another was often the means by which the shantyman lengthened his shanty to complete a long haul or heave. Gordon, in *Adventure*, points out that work-songs rarely tell a long or consecutive story, since men at work find it difficult to create, recollect, or listen to complicated themes without being distracted from their job of work, and also because such songs are either shortened or lengthened on the spot, according to the time needed in which to execute the work. And he writes that this last process is noticeable in shanties. I agree, but nevertheless most white men's shanties *did* have a narrative, although I doubt if they could be called 'complicated'. Negro shanties, on the other hand, after the first verse or so nearly always called for improvisation. J. Glyn Davies, writing about the 'stringing out' some shantymen indulged in (i.e. the repeating of a solo line), suggests that repeated lines were a certain sign of a defective text. With this I agree.

Other sources from which the shanty came are many. Shore-songs were often taken over holus-bolus; new shanties would be made up from scraps of tunes heard in Oriental and Latin ports; hymn tunes may have sired some, war-songs others.

The following list may give some idea of the many sources from which shanties have, presumably, 'growed':

1. Developed from the hauling cries of Elizabethan seamen.
2. British folk-song and ballad origins (north country, west country, and over the border).
3. Based on fiddler tunes, dance tunes, march tunes, opera and classical music, and war-songs.
4. True Liverpool and New York Irish origins.
5. Afro-American origins.
   (A) Railroad work-songs. Plantation songs from the Mississippi and Deep South. Negro work-songs, in general, from the Gulf Ports. Cotton-hoosiers' chants (Negro and white). Minstrel songs.
   (B) West Indian origins, from Barbadoes, Jamaica, etc.
   (C) Latin-American origins, from Trinidad, Guiana, etc. (some with Asiatic connections).
6. Various northern European folk-song origins, as well as

imitative Dutch, Spanish, etc., and some Mediterranean sources.

7. White American folk-songs; from songs of the backwoodsmen, rivermen, lumbermen, *voyageurs*, army, and mountain men.

8. From the emigrant songs of various countries and, possibly, from hymns sung by these emigrants.

9. From Oriental and Kanaka origins.

And of course shanties resulting from a mixture of any two or more of the foregoing were common—particularly Irish–Negro. To quote an expression of C. F. Smith: 'All was fish to the shantyman's net.' Some shanties are even reminiscent of children's nursery rhymes!

After 1860 few shanties were 'invented'; old ones often had new themes fitted to them, and different methods of singing them by different shantymen brought forth a few new variants, but the great hey-day of shanty-producing was finished. From 1860 to 1880 was the period of their greatest use, and from 1880 onwards a change came about in the tasks for which they were used. The old-fashioned windlass shanties became capstan songs, the stamp-'n'-go choruses were used for hand-over-hand hauling as the crews became smaller, and the up-and-down pump songs had their timing adjusted to suit the 'modern' flywheel pump.

*　　*　　*

Now a little about the word *shanty*, *chanty*, or *chantey*.

Many suggestions have been put forward about the origin of the word and when it was first applied to the work-songs of sailors. Taking the latter problem first, it is pretty certain that prior to the middle or late forties in the last century the term was unknown. As Doerflinger has pointed out, Melville, Olmstead, Dana, and other nautical writers of the thirties and early forties did not use the word. The *Oxford English Dictionary* (which prints it 'shanty') declares that the word never found its way into print until 1869. But this is wrong. Doerflinger's researches prove that the word was used in the fifties. Nordhoff used the word 'chantyman' (the leader of the 'hoosier' gang) in his book *The Merchant Vessel*, a narrative dealing with the life of a seaman in the fifties. Doerflinger also uses G. E. Clark's work, *Seven Years of a Sailor's Life*[1] as further proof. Clark uses 'chanty', 'chanty-man', and 'chanty-gang' (stevedores) many times throughout his work, the latter term apparently being the usual one at this time for the cotton-stowers of the Gulf ports.[2] E. I. Barra,

[1] Boston, 1867.

[2] *Negro Folk Songs* by Natalie C. Burlin (G. Schirmer, Inc., N.Y., 1918) gives some interesting information regarding the singing of 'chants' by Negro wharf gangs in Savannah, etc., when stowing cotton. The title of the leader of the singing is given as a 'header'—the screw-gangs in this case being those of Savannah. The

writing of a voyage in the mid-forties, states that the mate of the Yankee ship he sailed in would often sing out 'Give us a shanter', a word that Doerflinger thinks, and I agree, was an intermediate form between the 'chant' of Nordhoff and the 'chanty' of Clark. It will be noticed that in these early references the word is spelled with a 'ch' and not an 'sh'. The *Oxford English Dictionary* reference is to an article in *Chambers's Journal* (1869) where the writer spells the word 'shanty'. His full title, however, was 'Shanty Songs' and not just 'shanty' alone. Whall told Laughton that in 1861 when he went to sea these work-songs were called 'shanties', and Messrs. James Brown, Whall's publishers, informed Laughton, on what proof I do not know, that still earlier they were called 'shanty songs'. But in my edition of Whall (Preface to the Sixth Edition) the publishers state: 'As to the spelling of shanty, the earliest collection·known to us, published about 1875, calls these ditties "Shanty Songs", meaning, we suppose, songs from the shanties.' In the seventies (Adams *On Board the Rocket*) and early eighties (Admiral Luce) the spelling 'shanty' was popular, and then Davis & Tozer (1887) and L. A. Smith (1888) and others reverted to the 'chanty' spelling. After this both spellings were used equally by seamen-writers and landsmen alike.

It seems fairly obvious that the 'chant', 'chanter', and 'chanty' forms became slurred into 'shant', 'shanter', and 'shanty'—sailors as a race being given to the distorting of words, and in particular to the shortening and softening of nautical words and phrases. And the fact remains that whichever spelling may be deemed 'correct', seamen *always* pronounced it 'shanty'. Of course the defenders of the French origin of the word may say that it was always pronounced with a soft 'ch', being derived from the French verb *chanter* (shontay) 'to sing', and from 'shontay' it is an easy step to 'shanty'.

This brings us to the question of the origin of the word, but before we move on I would like to point out a reference Captain Hayet has made in his book *Chansons de Bord*[1] to the French word *chanter* as given in the dictionary *De Marine à Voiles* published in the year 1847 (Bonnefoux et Paris, M. le vice-amiral baron de Mackau, ministaire de la Marine et des Colonies).

---

songs are called 'cotton-packin' songs' and two examples are given, the tunes of which are little more than chants. One, consisting of nothing more than a repetition of the line 'Screw dis cotton, *heh!*', was sung by a Negro called James Scott, who said that at the grunt 'heh!' the screws would be turned. The word 'header' was also used for the leader of a Negro gang working in the mines (Virginia) where 'hammerin' songs' were sung. These songs, in structure, are all very like my shanty, *Dan-dan* (page 440).

A West Indian word for shantyman is 'lead-man'. It has been heard recently in the West Indian work-song sung by Harry Belafonte in the film *Island in the Sun*: the first line runs: 'Lead-man holler, oh, oh, oh, All men foller . . .'

[1] Edition, Eos. Paris, 1927.

Chanter. To utter certain sounds, words, and rhythmical cries which help sailors, working as a body, to make simultaneous effort in order to obtain the best effect. Sometimes a single sailor sings and then he is called the *Chanteur*; sometimes the *Chanteur* gives voice and the other seamen respond, and sometimes all the seamen sing at the same time.

And now let us tackle the problem as to the origin of the word 'chanty' or 'shanty' by setting forth all the existing theories.

Theory 1. Years ago, in the West Indies, the Negroes, who lived in 'clinker-built' huts called 'shanties', when desirous of shifting domicile, moved their huts intact, by the process of lowering them from the stilts on which they were perched (the space beneath the huts serving as a store-room and chicken-run) on to rollers. As the hut was moved by the men hauling on ropes attached to the hut the after roller would become clear and would then be placed under the for'ard end. A man was seated on top of the shanty—and he was called a 'shantyman'—and he would sing improvised verses whilst the haulers, the 'crew', sang the chorus and hauled on certain words in the chorus. Some writers state a platform on wheels was used. (*R. R. Terry, Captain T. P. Marshall.*)

Theory 2. The word 'shanty' comes from the drinking shanties of Mobile and other Gulf ports where Negroes and white seamen congregated—in particular the white and coloured cotton-stowers or 'hoosiers'. The name for the drinking dens, a shanty, was applied to the working songs of the 'hoosiers' and thence copied by seamen, in the same manner that the music-hall gave its name to music-hall songs. (*L. G. Carr Laughton.*)

Theory 3. The word comes from the boat-songs of the old French *voyageurs* of the New World. These were called *chansons*. (*L. A. Smith, C. F. Smith.*)

Theory 4. The word comes from the French *chantez*, 'sing'; either by way of Norman French, Modern French, or the French *Gumbo* dialect of New Orleans. Norman French gave us many of our seafaring words and phrases. (*Bone, C. F. Smith.*)

Theory 5. The word is merely a derivation of the English word 'chant'. As 'chaunt' this word was often used to designate 'nigger' songs of the Southern States. (*Nordhoff, Doerflinger, Brown, Son & Ferguson Ltd.*)

Theory 6. The shanty has some connection with lumbermen's songs which often start with 'Come-all-ye brave shanty-boys'. (*Colcord.*)

(The authorities and collectors mentioned in brackets do not always agree with these theories: they merely refer to them.)

These are the theories. Let us examine them.

In regard to Theory 1, the West Indies was undoubtedly a breeding ground of shanties. In the thirties when I gained many 'new' shanties from West Indian shantymen it was still possible to hear them being used in places like Tobago, where they hauled sugar boilers ashore by means of tackles through the surf, after they had first been floated shorewards from deep-sea vessels lying in the roadstead. In the West Indies too, particularly in Jamaica, until recent times it was possible to hear shanties sung—such as *Sally Brown* and its variants—while Negro loggers with peevie and handspike rolled the logwood waterwards. 'Roll de mutu!' was a common shout heard when singin' out only. But whether these sailor worksongs started life among these loggers years ago is difficult to say. Doerflinger writes that there is no evidence to prove that seamen acquired their work-songs from lumbermen. He also is emphatic in denying that loggers ever sang at their job—that is in the Maine woods—except perhaps in isolated instances. However modern skiffle has brought to life many old 'axe-cutting' songs from the States such as *July Ann* (*Julian*) *Johnson*. Colcord on the other hand believes that shanties *were* used by lumbermen as *work-songs*.

I am rather inclined to believe that Theory 1 has much in its favour, but it is, I'm afraid, rather difficult to prove.

Theory 3 I feel has little to support it—the only shanty that may have stemmed from the *voyageurs* is *Shenandoah*. Theories 2, 4, and 5 have some stronger claims perhaps, but No. 2 is rather weak. Quite possibly Theory 5 is the right one—that 'shanty' came from the Old English word 'chant', with modified sound as the usage of the word grew. Or perhaps again all these theories are wrong and, like C. F. Smith says, the word 'just growed'! Whatever is the secret of the origin of the word I'm afraid it is lost for all time and we must take it as it stands.

*   *   *

And now a very simplified explanation of the nautical terms used in connection with shantying—to describe all the parts of a square-rigger in detail would turn this work into a seamanship manual!

Taking a single mast of a squarerigged sailing ship we find that normally it consists of three parts—the lower-mast, the topmast, and the t'gallantmast. This mast, like every bit of gear attached to it, is prefaced by the word fore, main, or mizen, depending on its position from the bows. Across each mast are several spars of wood or steel to which the upper edge of the square sail is fastened (or 'bent'). These are called *yards*. The two bottom corners of the square sail have ropes, wires, or chains attached to them called *sheets*, these in every case, except those of the bottom sail, lead through pulleys (blocks) in the end of the yard beneath, then into the middle of the yard and down alongside the mast to the deck.

Starting at the bottom sail (on the front-, that is the fore-, mast) the sails are called *foresail, fore lower tops'l, fore upper tops'l, fore lower t'gans'l, fore upper t'gans'l*, and *fore royal* (usually the highest, although some ships did sport *skys'ls* above the royals). If they are on the second mast from the bow they are called *mainsail, main lower tops'l*, etc., and on the third mast, *mizen-sail* (usually called the *crojik*), *mizen lower tops'l*, etc. The fore- and main-sails are sometimes called *fore course* and *main course*. If it is the yard we are talking about, then it would be the *fore yard, fore lower tops'l yard*, etc. The fore, main, and mizen yards are fixtures and their sails are set by hauling *down* on the *sheets* after the *gaskets* are loosed. *Gaskets* are ropes that confine the rolled-up sails to the yards when they are not being used. If one bottom corner of the *fore-, main-, or mizen-sail* is pulled out towards the bow the rope that pulls it out is called the *tack*; the rope that pulls the other corner of the sail towards the stern of the ship is called the *sheet*. The *lower tops'l yard* is also a fixture and the sail is set by hauling down on the *sheets*, but the *upper tops'l* is set by hauling on the *halyard*, a wire or chain pendant that runs from the yard down to the deck where it has a purchase in the form of two three-fold blocks, the hauling part of which leads through a *lead block* to the *belayin'-pin* in the *pin rail* or *fife rail* and is there made fast. Nearly all the innumerable ropes of a sailing ship lead eventually to the deck and are made fast around belayin'-pins—halyards, sheets, braces, etc.

The *upper tops'l* is one that needs a *halyard shanty* to hoist it. The *lower t'gans'l* is—like the *lower tops'l*—a fixture, and set the same way, but the *upper t'gans'l* and *royal* are set by hauling on a halyard, like the upper tops'l. Strictly speaking a *royal* is partly pulled down and partly hoisted. A *short drag shanty* would often be used on a royal.

The *yards* are turned from one side of the ship to the other, following the direction of the wind, by means of *braces*. These are wires and rope tackles (rope and blocks) which run from the ends of each yard either down to the deck or to the next mast. Other ropes for pulling the sails up to the yards when taking in sail were *buntlines* and *clewlines*, and *downhauls* were used to haul the movable yards down. All these would be hauled on to wild *sing-outs*.

Between the masts supporting them are wire supports called *stays* and on many of them sails called *stays'ls* are hoisted. Other *stays'ls*, along with *jibs*, are set on the wire stays that run from the *foremast* down to the wooden or metal spike that sticks out from the bow of the ship, known as the *bowsprit* or *jibboom*, depending on whether it is in three sections or one. To hoist *stays'ls* or *jibs* either a wild *sing-out* or a *hand-over-hand song* would be raised. *Braces* too, in going *about ship* (i.e. putting the ship from one *tack* to the other, or bringing the wind from one bow to the other), would need a lively sing-out, or a *stamp-'n'-go chorus*.

Every so often the sheets, tacks, halyards, and braces would need a hefty pull to stretch them all the more. This task was called *sweatin' up*, and to aid the job a *foresheet shanty* would be used. In regard to *lower sheets*, however, this only applied in the days when sheets were made of four-inch hemp rope, but in the latter days of sail, in the large 'four-posters', these would be made of wire and then they would be hauled tight by means of *maindeck capstans*. Tops'ls also, and other sails with yards, would be taken to these capstans and hoisted by their semi-mechanical help. A *capstan* was a vertical barrel revolving round a centre 'axle', pushed by men who inserted bars called *handspikes* into the mushroom head of the barrel and stamped around quickly or slowly, depending on the nature of the 'heave'. *Pawls* were fitted so as to prevent the barrel 'walking back'. Whenever a capstan was used a *capstan shanty* would be raised, but for work at the heavier and sturdier *anchor capstan* or *windlass* situated on the *fo'c'sle-head* (the raised part of the deck at the bow) a slower type of capstan shanty or *windlass shanty* would be used.[1]

The pumps of a sailing ship were usually situated by the *fife rail* of the main or mizen masts, and at the back-breaking toil of 'pumping ship' a *pump shanty* would be raised.

In the last of the big squareriggers a new type of semi-mechanical aid was installed—the *Jarvis brace winch* and the *Jarvis halyard winch*. At this type of winch, which lessened the arduous job of setting sail and the dangerous job of hauling on the braces—dangerous, because the brace most often hauled on was the *lee brace*, i.e. that on the side of the ship nearest the water as she heeled over, and often an area smothered in water neck-deep—capstan shanties were sometimes raised, as the handles were turned by four or more seamen.

*　　*　　*

[1] I will here try to clear up the mix-up many shanty collectors appear to encounter with the words *Capstan* and *Windlass*.

Some write that the capstan superseded the windlass, others declare that the windlass is modern and used only in the latter days of sail. Whall, writing about *Goodbye, Fare You Well*, says that the reference to a capstan makes the shanty at least fifty years old and that merchant ships built after this were nearly all fitted with a windlass—' "wilderness", as John always called it'. Doerflinger and others point out that the barrel of a windlass was horizontal, whereas that of the capstan was vertical, and that windlasses were ousted on deep-water ships by capstans from 1870 onwards. Both of these statements are correct but misleading to the reader, and often to collectors as well. The fact is the latter group describe the type of windlass used from the time of Drake and even earlier, one with a horizontal barrel, hove round by means of spokes, and later by 'brakes', whereas the windlass Whall writes about was the new-fangled device, placed beneath the fo'c'sle-head capstan, so that the cable, instead of going round the barrel, as it did in the earlier windlasses and capstans, went over a cable-holder or 'gipsy' as it does in a modern steamer's windlass, straight down into the chain-locker. It was to this type of windlass Masefield refers when he writes: 'It is a glorious thing to be on the fo'c'sle-head, heaving at a capstan bar, hearing the chain clanking in *below* you to the music of a noisy shanty' (italics are mine).

This type of windlass was, at times, connected by a chain 'messenger' to a steam-driven 'donkey' situated in a house abaft the foremast, and the anchor would then be hoisted by steam-power, but owing to the small amount of coal and fresh water windjammers could carry this mechanical aid was rarely used, and Armstrong's Patent was the rule rather than the exception.

A shanty was, in general, of two forms—one with two single solo lines and two alternating refrains, and one with a four-line verse and a four- or more line chorus. Of course exceptions are to be found to these two general descriptions.

The first of these two main types was that used for hauling, the second for heaving, although many heaving songs also had a four-line pattern (i.e. *Sally Brown*).

These two main types were sub-divided into the following:

I. *Hauling Songs*

    (A) Halyard or 'long drag' songs (for tops'ls and t'gallants).

    (B) Short haul or 'short drag' songs (for t'gallants and royals).

    (C) Sweating-up, fore-sheet, or bowline shanties (for boarding tacks and sheets, etc.).

    (D) Bunt shanty (for stowing a sail on the yard).

    (E) Hand-over-hand songs (for jibs, stays'ls, and braces).

    (F) Walkaway or stamp-'n'-go songs (braces, etc.).

II. *Heaving Songs*

    (A) Main capstan or windlass songs (for heaving the anchor).

    (B) Capstan songs (for hoisting sails, etc., by 'mechanical' means, and warping in and out of dock).

    (C) Pump shanties.

The first group were used for an intermittent operation, the second for a continuous process. Taking the latter group first, the reader will notice as he wades through this book that many of them are in 4/4 time, many of them are shore matching songs, and many of them are not sufficiently camouflaged to hide their shore origins. On the other hand, the shanties that come under the hauling-song group are in 6/8 time, usually less musical than the heaving songs and so 'salty' that their shore origins have been long forgotten.

Of course *all* the heaving songs are not marches, although the first tramp around the capstan was usually a march (taking in the slack of the cable, in other words, heaving the ship to her anchor). At the time of the American Civil War many army marching songs such as *John Brown's Body, Dixie, The Battle Cry of Freedom, Maryland,* and *Yeller Rose of Texas* were roared out on the fo'c'sle-head, and Masefield has pointed out how the Crimean War march *Cheer, Boys, Cheer* was used in similar manner. But, as noted by Bone, apart from the early stamp-around, marches were too fast to be used for the entire job of heaving the 'hook'. After the slack chain was aboard the shantyman would, instinctively, alter the tempo, and a slower tune like *Shenandoah* or *Stormalong* would be raised. The quicker capstan songs too were often used at the maindeck capstans for setting sail, when the halyard would be taken to the capstan instead of being handed by the crowd.

The songs sailors sang when off-watch—forebitters or, as the Yanks called them, main-hatch songs—if they had a good chorus were often utilized for capstan and pump, in particular for the pumps. Then again, although in theory there was a strict division between the various types of shanty, in fact, one cannot be too dogmatic about the matter, as many halyard songs were sung at capstan and pump, many windlass and capstan songs were interchangeable, and many pumping songs were used for anchor-heaving. One ruling however held—anchor songs were recognized as outward- and homeward-bounders, and very rarely were they used on the wrong passage.

As well as the above shanty divisions there were also special shanties for special trades. They weren't 'special' in the sense that they were only used in these trades, but in the sense that certain capstan and hauling songs, as used deep-sea, were often singled out for use when working special cargoes in different ports of the world. We have seen how certain shanties were used by the hoosiers—the cotton-stowers—of the American Gulf ports. Another important trade was that of carrying timber. Timber ships were known as 'droghers' (a term also used for sugar-carrying ships in the West Indian Trade) and nearly all these ships had large square ports in their bows through which lengthy logs could be launched. Capstans and tackles were used in the process of loading and discharging the logs and at the work both dockers and seamen (who in many ports in the days of sail had to work the cargo of their ship) raised shanties to lighten the labour. Many shanties, particularly those of the 'Hieland Laddie' family, were used by timber workers. Canadian and North American ports (of both seaboards) were centres of the timber trade, as well as West Indian and Central American ports. Also aboard the Baltic 'onkers', or sailing ships in the pit-prop trade, manned by Scandinavian seamen—Danes, Finns, Norwegians, and Swedes—many shanties and shore-songs were sung when working the cargo.

It is quite possible that this close alliance of lumbermen, stevedores, and seamen did, in this trade, help to infuse new shore-songs, suitable for use at work, into the already extensive repertoire of the shantyman.

As one writer puts it, 'a real seaman of the days of sail wouldn't pick up a rope-yarn without raising a song'. And Rex Clements, in his fine book *A Gipsy of the Horn*,[1] writes:

There was even a shanty for doing nothing at all. It was like the others with solo and chorus and was sometimes started by a discontented crowd who felt they were having their old iron worked up unnecessarily. One of the men would begin: 'I've got a sister nine foot high' and was taken up by the chorus, "Way down in Cuba!" but instead of heaving, the

[1] London (Heath Cranton Ltd.), 1924.

words were followed by three short jumps. It was very infrequently heard and always came to an abrupt end after the first line, in obedience to an angry order from the mate—'Stop that!'

A shanty once used entirely for 'ceremonial'—the only shanty composed for amusement—was the *Dead Horse*, but in later years, as the custom of 'paying off the dead horse' died out, the shanty took its place as a normal hauling song.

In the foregoing classification of the shanties we can see the development of the shanty through the ages, showing how, from the rude, seagull-like cries and yells of the earliest hauling song the shanty grew until it became the musical, 'true' song of the latter-day anchor-shanty.

Shanty Development

Hauling

> 1st stage: *Hey, holly, hilly, oh! Hey, ro, ho, yu!* (sing-out)
> 2nd stage: *Hand, hand, hand-over-hand, Divil run away with a Liverpool man*, etc. (chant)
> 3rd stage: *Cheer'ly Man, Boney, Handy, Me Boys* (rather tuneless short hauls and sweating-up songs)
> 4th stage: *Blow the Man Down, A Long Time Ago*, etc. (tuneful hauling songs)

Heaving

> 1st stage: *Yo ho, heave ho!* (sing-out)
> 2nd stage: *Round come roundy for Liverpool Town* (chant)
> 3rd stage: *Yo heave ho, round the caps'n go*, etc. (rather tuneless heaving song)
> 4th stage: *A-rovin', Shenandoah, Rio* (tuneful heaving songs)

* * *

The wild yells, mentioned several times in the foregoing paragraphs, have always been part and parcel of a sailor's life when working ship, from dim, remote times. And, although others may disagree, I believe that among white men the finest exponents of the art of singing out were German and Scandinavian seamen. Of course the Negro was the singer-out *par excellence*. When hoisting aloft a light jib or stays'l, the shantyman would keep up a running cry of meaningless sounds to time the hand-over-hand movement of the hauling men—'rather to guide the grip of the hand than to encourage the pull' (Bone). This was the sing-out. When stamping away at the braces as a ship was 'put about' a sing-out of slightly different tempo would be used, unless a proper stamp-'n'-go song was raised. Also final pulls on brace, sheet, tack, and halyard would elicit a sing-out, such as *Ho-yu!, Hee-lay-ay!, Fiddle-string 'im!, Two block 'er!,* the pull coming on the final syllable. Of course, here again, a verse or two of a bowline or foresheet shanty would do equally well.

When hoisting a heavier stays'l, after a few sing-outs in hand-over-hand fashion, the final tautening of the luff would be performed by means of a bowline or foresheet shanty or even by a few stanzas of a short haul shanty such as *Boney*. Royals, in some ships, would need no more than a sing-out to set them; in others *Boney* or a similar song would do the job. When it came to t'gans'ls and tops'ls the real hauling song came into its own, although here again the slack of the fall, before the wind filled the sail, would be taken in by a few yells or grunts. Very often this procedure was referred to as a 'dry pull', meaning that a shanty was not used. Once the wind bellied the sail away from its creased and stowed confines the shantyman would raise his halyard song—something in the nature of *Whisky Johnny* if a t'gans'l, or *Blow the Man Down* if a tops'l. Although a division did exist between the shanties used at tops'ls and t'gans'ls, normally they were interchangeable.

The usual method of spilling the wind partly from the sail so as to make the job of hoisting it lighter was for the ship to be 'luffed'—brought closer to the wind. A common line in hauling songs was 'Hey-ho, rock 'n' shake 'er!', a sly dig for the officer of the watch to give the helmsman the order to 'luff' and thereby ease the strain.

In all these better-developed shanties, however, the wild yells still persisted. In fact this yell was the very essence of the shantyman's art. Strangely enough few, if any, of the early collectors mention it in regard to the shanties, referring to it only in connection with singing out. These yells had no real functional value except, in certain cases, to stimulate the crowd for the next pull. Nearly every verse of a hauling song would commence with one, and, although sometimes omitted from the first solo line, it was invariably sung at the commencement of the second. Also in the capstan songs these yells would sometimes be heard in the choruses. The German shanty-book *Knurrhahn* has this yell identified in its title which means both a 'cockerel with a sore throat' and 'a fish which grunts'. One of the reasons why Negro shantymen were so good at their job was because of their ability to handle these wild falsetto 'yodels' (hardly the correct term though!) much better than white men. Sailors called these yells 'hitches' and they were performed either by a break or several breaks in the voice on a certain note, or else by emitting a high yelp at the end of a solo line. Most people find their voice 'breaks' when they don't want it to, but this was a systematized breaking of the voice on definite notes. I don't think 'grace note', used by some collectors, is the right word to describe it. Grace notes, appogiaturas, and demi-semiquavers have been used by some collectors, but one has to hear such a 'hitch' to appreciate it properly. Doerflinger and Miss Colcord, American collectors, both refer to this style of singing, and write of the grace notes, flourishes, and variations with which a good shantyman would embellish his singing.

This peculiar breaking of the voice was also to be found in the lookout's cry of 'Aaaall's well!', and sometimes is to be heard even today in the cry of the leadsman: 'By the dee-ip nine!'

*　　*　　*

In ages long past the shantyman was probably a person of some substance, on a higher level than the seamen (see the extract from Felix Fabri's *Voyage* on page 3), and even in the days of the Blackwall frigates he held a fair post, standing at the knightheads or near the halyards, or else sitting on the capstan crown as he sang his solos, and being relieved of the arduous work of hauling and heaving, ranked with the idlers of the ship—i.e. bosun, carpenter, sailmaker, etc. But in the later sailing ships, and particularly in the latter days of sail when ships got bigger and crews smaller there was no such rank as shantyman—he didn't sign on as such at the shipping office. He was usually an older hand, a good seaman, one with an extensive repertoire, a retentive memory, and a good powerful voice, who would automatically take his position as shantyman on sailing day at the capstan. Sometimes there would be two, one in each watch. He was essential to the easy working of the ship. His song, as Shaw puts it, was the 'war-cry of the non-combatant but ever-fighting seaman of the spacious days of sail'. And the sailor's adage declared, 'A good song was worth ten men on a rope.' But, naturally, there were many voyages and many ships in which a shanty was never raised—black, blood-boat passages when men were hazed from port to port. Of course the 'modern' shantyman didn't always 'pull his weight' on a rope, he merely went through the motions, saving his wind for the song. At the capstan he 'rode the bars'.

On sailing day the capstan would be the first object the half-soused fo'c'sle crowd would come in contact with, either to heave the anchor or warp the vessel out through the locks. Once the cry was raised 'Man the caps'n!' the crowds would lumber up, take the bars from the rack, ship them in the pigeon holes in the head of the capstan, and start heaving. From the mate would come the questioning shout, 'What about a song there?' or 'Who's the bloody nightingale aboard this packet?' And there and then the self-appointed shantyman would roar forth the opening solo of his shanty. From then on he would keep his job until the final tying up of the packet at the end of the voyage. Sometimes he would start the shanty by singing first the chorus of the song to give the gang a clue as to which shanty was to be raised. This was done also when hauling at the halyards, so much so that many shanties now in print are accepted as starting with the chorus. Normally harmony didn't exist, and tenors were rare. In the refrains the bass and baritone voices of the men and the trebles of the boys alone would be heard.

At halyards the shantyman would stand at the 'forehand', i.e. in front of the lead block where the fall of the halyard comes down vertically from aloft. With him would stand the bosun or a leading hand or even the second mate. The rest of the hands would face the shantyman and haul on the part of the halyard beyond the lead block, i.e. they would pull, with their backs bent, on the horizontal part of the rope. The shantyman would, after several 'dry pulls' to stretch the flapping sail, burst forth into a 'hitch', a breaking yelp in his voice, and then roar forth the solo line; before he sang the last note, the crowd would come in with the refrain, and before the last note of the refrain was completed the shantyman would start his next solo. This overlapping of the last note with the first note of the refrain was common in many kinds of folk singing.

At the pumps the shantyman would be at one of the handles, the main part of the crowd tailing on the 'bell-rope', one of each of which would be looped over the handles of the pump's flywheels. 'Roll the water-wheel!' would be the cry, and 'Who wuz drunk last?' would be the query, followed by the shantyman breaking forth into something like *Lowlands* or *Stormalong*. As various suitable shore-songs were often sung at the pumps, to while the weary hours away at this back-breaking job (particulariy in *wooden* ships), others besides the regular shantyman would start a song. This was also true when taking in sail. Here various groups of men would handle the different buntlines, clewlines, and downhauls, and each group would have its singer-out, irrespective of whether he was a shantyman or not. And each group leader would sing his own sing-out, making a tremendous babel of sound rising above the howling of the wind. There was one more job at which the shantyman or any suitable member of the crew would sing out and that was on the yard when furling the sail. After being 'clewed up' from the deck by means of buntlines and clewlines, the men had to fight their way aloft and muzzle the hard still-bellying canvas on the yard. To get the bulk of the sail rolled on to the yard a collective heave was necessary and this was timed by the wild elemental cries of the bunt shanty known as *Paddy Doyle's Boots*. When going ''bout ship' or 'tacking' the men would grasp the braces with their backs to the lead block and stamp away up the deck. The stamp-'n'-go, walkaway, or runaway songs they raised were sometimes sung in chorus. Such, then, were the jobs at which the shantyman sang his songs.

In the solo part strict time was not absolutely necessary, the shantyman could slow down or speed up according to his fancy, and, incidentally, a good shantyman was an expert at putting in far more words than the original notes catered for. But with the refrain strict tempo had to be kept. The pull came on certain words in the refrain (in a hauling song), normally two, although at times the pull would come on one word only. A short space would come between the two pulls sufficient for the crowd to shift their grip on the halyard. In the case of sheet shanties the haul would not come until the last word of the refrain, which was usually shouted out. The method of pulling was 'down and out'—a downward drag of the whole body and then backward fling, a holding of the rope with one hand while the othe sought a fresh grip further for'ard without letting go altogether. Th whole art of pulling was to keep the body low.

All British and American and most Scandinavian, French, anc German shanties had a theme or pattern telling some sort of con-secutive story, only in typical Negro shanties were the first two o1 three verses so-called 'regulation' and the remainder improvised in the manner of calypso singing. Normally in an English-worded shanty the fact that the shantyman improvised, used verses from other shanties, or repeated the solos twice in each stanza, showed that he had an imperfect memory. Of course in a very long hoist the regulation verses would often run out and then stock phrases or verses from such a shanty as *Handy, Me Boys* would be utilized. The process of repeating the solos was referred to as 'stringing out'. Many shantymen would, of course, improvise even if they knew the real words, particularly if the ship was a 'hungry bitch', the voyage a tough one, or the afterguard a set of bullies. Improvising, they would bring out these tribulations in their solos, and, strangely enough, rarely did the afterguard victimize the shantyman or the crowd on account of it—it was an unwritten ruling of the sea that a sailor could 'growl' only through the medium of his shanties. Of course in some ships this unwritten rule was set at naught and it was better to sing the regulation words and leave improvisation for the final shanty of the voyage—*Leave 'er, Johnny, Leave 'er*—sung when tying up or pumping out for the last time.

It was on occasions such as Captain Frank Shaw refers to in his book *Splendour of the Seas*[1] that sly digs at the afterguard would be substituted for the regular words.

Toadying types of mates—those who crept to superior authority—would keep the hands on the run. . . . Sour-souled enthusiasts who would in the Sunday 6 to 8 dog-watch get the hands 'sweating up'. Maybe a dry pull on the royal halyards—which in fine weather could be hauled taut by a man and a boy—would bring out the whole watch plus idlers—cook, carpenter, sailmaker, etc. They would all tail on to the fall . . . and then someone would strike up a shanty. The singing would go on—a direct insult to those aft—until the mate purple-faced would yell from the poop, 'Belay all that! That'll do the hands!'

A shanty would be brought to a full stop by the officer of the watch loudly giving the command, different phrases for different

[1] London (Edward Stanford, Ltd.), 1953.

jobs, very often in the middle of a verse. The cease action order when heaving at the capstan was "Vast Heaving!' For halyards, 'Belay!' or 'Belay that!' or 'Well enough!' And for the pumps—after one of the men had advised the officer that the pumps were dry by a yell of 'Suck-O!'—"Vast pumping there!' And the customary words to stop the end-of-the-voyage shanty, *Leave 'er, Johnny, Leave 'er!*, was 'That'll do, men!' Expressions such as 'Well there, the brace!', 'Up behind!', or 'Belay all!' would bring to a halt sing-outs at brace, tack, and sheet.

*　　*　　*

Much has been written about obscenity in the shanties. Some declare they weren't as dirty as shore folk like to imagine. Clements says: 'Sailor John, I admit, called a spade a spade, but that's a virtue not a vice. The most outspoken of them all is not a whit more indecent than many songs in an Elizabethan book of plays. And these latter are literature; sailors' songs never claimed to be that. . . . Not in the chorus of one single shanty was there anything that would be impermissible in a drawing-room' (*A Gipsy of the Horn*). Victor Slocum in *Cornell's Sea Power*[1] by W. M. Williamson says, 'Contrary to the present impression the words of a chanty were never ribald though they may have been elemental and often uncouth. I have never heard an indecent word or allusion in a chanty on a ship's deck.'

But Bullen writes: 'Many a Chantyman was prized in spite of his poor voice because of his improvisations. Poor doggerel they were mostly and often very lewd and filthy, but they gave the knowing and appreciative shipmates, who roared the refrain, much opportunity for laughter.'[2] Sampson says: 'I think that the alleged coarseness of the Shanties has been greatly exaggerated.' And Whall writes: 'Seamen who spent their time in cargo-carrying sailing ships never heard a *decent* shanty; the words which Sailor John put to them when unrestrained were the veriest filth. But another state of things obtained in passenger and troop ships; here sailor John was given to understand very forcibly that his words were to be decent, or that he was not to shanty at all. (As a rule, when the passengers were landed, and this prohibition was removed, the notorious *Hog-Eye Man* at once made its appearance.)'

Miss Colcord[1] feels that many of the words were gross but not suggestive like many music-hall ditties used to be, and she points out that there was always a decent set of words with one or two exceptions. She writes about the grossness: 'it was jovial, forthright, almost wholesome obscenity. . . .'[3]

[1] 1942.

[2] Frank T. Bullen. *Songs of Sea Labour*, London (Swan & Co.), 1914.

[3] Joanna C. Colcord. *Songs of American Sailormen*, New York (W. W. Norton & Co.), 1938.

A suggestion is also made by many writers that the solos alone were dirty, the choruses being fit for anyone's ears. Terry[1] declares: 'The Rabelaisian jokes of the shantyman were solos, the sound of which would not travel far beyond the little knot of workers who chuckled over them. The choruses—shouted out by the whole working party—would be heard all over the ship and even penetrate ashore if she were in port. Hence, in not a single instance do the choruses of any shanty contain a coarse expression.'

It is fairly obvious that sailor's working songs did contain a great amount of gross obscenity, but many versions of the same shanty were either quite clean by comparison or else the dirt was disguised (even if Miss Colcord and others don't agree) in a nautical *double entendre*. One version of *Blow the Man Down* is a good example of this. Nearly every shanty had its dirty version—there were some exceptions—and two or more shanties had a dirty version only. Some shanties—not a great number—were entirely devoid of anything obscene or even coarse. Some writers believe that all homeward-bound songs were free of filth but this is not true, as I will endeavour to prove elsewhere. Also I disagree with Terry's statement that the shanty choruses were always clean. *Jamboree* had a chorus that was invariably roared out in all its anatomical lustiness, and this was a homeward-bound song. Others were, *The Girls of Chile*, *Hog-Eye Man*, *Saltpetre Shanty*, one version of *Rio*, *Sacramento*, and *Miss Lucy Long*.

For the student who can understand French, proof of the bawdy singing of French shanties can be found in a now out-of-print volume, *Chansons de la voile 'Sans Voile'* by Jean Marie le Bihor (a pseudonym for Captain A. Hayet).

*　　*　　*

Of what did the shantyman sing?

Well, naturally, he sang of the girls; of his kind of love . . . such as was to be found down the Barbary Coast, Schiedamschedyk, Ship Street, the Bowery, San Pauli, Reeperbahn, Schipperstraat, Ratcliffe Highway, and other unsavoury streets and quarters of the ports he visited; of beer and rum and whisky; of tough ships and hungry ships; of bucko mates and shanghaiing. But he also sang of irrelevant things like soldiers and inland waters, of revolutions and railways and huckleberries. And he sang of people, true and otherwise; more often than not about legendary figures like Reuben Ranzo, Lucy Loo and Lucy Anna, Stormalong, Hanging Johnny, Eliza Lee and Susiana, Sally Brown and Shallow Brown, and Johnny Boker; but also of only-too-real figures, like the shanghaiing crimps—Shanghai Brown, Rapper Brown, Mother Shilling, Larry

[1] R. R. Terry. *The Shanty Book* (2 parts), London (J. Curwen & Sons, Ltd.), 1921, 1926.

Marr, etc. Great names like Napoleon, Santiana, General Taylor, Mister Tapscott, and Daniel O'Connell—great and fairly great in their respective fields—all were included in his songs. He sang of places with romantic names like Shenandoah, Rio, the Broomielaw, Mobile Bay, Valparaiso and Essequibo, and Hilo. Strangely enough he rarely sang of a famous ship by name—the *Dreadnaught* was one of the few exceptions.

Peculiar expressions, too, many of them Negro or of minstrel source, dotted his stanzas—Yaller Gals, Bulgines, Round-the-Corner Sallies, Queens-in-the-Forest, and the mysterious Wild Goose Nation.

In fact Sailor John sang of everything and anything.

* * *

For many years several English and American books about shanties have been on the market. In the Yankee ones the shanties have been mainly drawn from the east coast. In the English books, Northumberland and the Tyne, the Bristol Channel ports and London have been the collecting grounds of the writers concerned.

It has always struck me as rather strange that Liverpool, the greatest of all sailing-ship ports, should have contributed so little to the existing data on shanties. The nearest to a Liverpool collection is the work of Professor J. Glyn Davies, but then again he added to the existing tunes words in Welsh which he himself composed and which were never sung at sea; but he gives, in the prefaces to his works, *Cerddi Huw Puw* and *Cerddi Portinllaen*,[1] much valuable information about the shanties as they were sung by Welsh seamen sailing out of the port of Liverpool.

Of course the tunes and words varied among seamen from different ports and even in different ships out of the same port. Glyn Davies declares that the Welsh versions of the shanties were more 'conventional musically' than those in Terry's and Whall's collections, and he rather thinks that the Welsh versions were based unconsciously 'on hymn models', and that the not-so-musical versions of the English were due to the 'bungling of English crews who usually did not know how to sing hymns or anything else'! He believed that there was a greater uniformity of shanty singing in Welsh ships (like in the Swedish 'family ship'), since the crews came from the small area of the three western counties of North Wales. The same men came from the same village, signing on the same ship voyage after voyage, a consistent state of affairs which he contrasts with the

. . . complete stampede of a crew from an English starvation hulk and the signing-on of a new set of riff-raff, who, like the thunder winds, came from all round the compass. . . .

[1] Both published by the Oxford University Press.

35

Such crews would start on the yard halliards with three or four different versions in the chorus, with the evolution of a fifth in progress, bungled out of the total mixture.

He declares that on account of this sort of thing the shanties we have with us today are nothing more than mangled survivors of the original songs. He writes: 'The difference between the comparative uniformity of the North Welsh versions and the confusion on so many English ships is at the bottom the difference between the family party crew and a boarding-house runner's mixed crew.'

I am a Liverpool man, and, although this collection is an international one, I have endeavoured to supply the deficiency of a Liverpool collection by giving as many Liverpool versions as possible. Incidentally, although no *book* collections of Liverpool shanties exist, the recently published record of sixteen sea-songs and shanties called *The Singing Sailor* (Worker's Music Association) could be described as hailing from Liverpool.

In literature odd verses exist of reputed shanties, but, at this late date, it is difficult to ascertain whether they were ever sung at sea, or even genuine, since most of the authors of the works in which they appear are long since dead.

The late Basil Lubbock in many of his books gives snatches of shanties now hard to verify:

> A full-rigged ship is a royal queen,
> *Ch.* Way-hey for Boston town, oh!
> A lady at court is a barquentine,
> A barque is a gal with ringlets fair,
> A brig is the same with shorter hair,
> A topsail schooner's a racing mare,
> But, a schooner, she's a clown-O!

> (Old shanty given in Part III, Chap. I,
> *Last of the Windjammers*)

Another tidbit he gives may have been a forebitter and not a shanty:

> I asked a maiden by my side,
> Who sighed and looked to me forlorn,
> 'Where is your heart?'
> She quick replied—
> 'Round Cape Horn!'

And on page 159 of Vol. II of *The Last of the Windjammers*[1] he writes: 'Seattle began as a sawmill village grouped around Yester's Mill, and, as the old Puget Sound chanty relates, was the "place to have a spree" '. I wonder to which shanty he was referring? Was it one of the rarer timber-droghers' songs for stowing timber?

Anderson, in *Windjammer Yarns*, writes that the crew of his ship, the *Verulam*, 'started singing and gave us the shanty "Soon we'll be in

[1] Pub. by Brown, Son & Ferguson Ltd., Glasgow, 1927–29.

London Town".' This line is to be found in *The Powder Monkey*, which in fact never was a shanty, but a music-hall type of sea-song. Was there a shanty which had this line? (See page 148.)

In the Introduction to *Opsang Fra Seilskibstiden*, D. H. Brockmann writes: 'As a child I found that at sea there were a lot of strange songs with stranger refrains, for example:

> Med skibet Jone Jonas fra Engelland vi gik,
> At gjeste varme Indien for at laere folkeskik,
> > *Ch.* Kom sjung hop falleriora,
> > Ta i mersefald og dra!

> (In the ship *Jone Jonas* from England we went,
> We went as guests to warm India, to teach the folk there manners.
> > *Ch.* Come, sing hop falieri ora,
> > Take a drag on the tops'l halyard!)[1]

> Kong David var en yngling da han til harpen tog,
> Han kjaempede med Goliat og slog ham ned til jord.
> > *Ch.* Kom sjung hop falleriora,
> > Ta i mersefald og dra!'

> (King David was a youth when he began playing a harp,
> He fought with Goliath and knocked him to the ground.
> > *Ch.* Come sing, *etc.*)[1]

And then he goes on to ask . . . 'and what do you make of this?

> Jeg hadde mig di kjerring og hun hedte Sara,
> > *Ch.* Pompa, pompa, falleriollalei!
> Og det var nu mig slik ei h . . . s mara,
> > *Ch.* Pompa, pompa, falleriorei!'

> (I had an ol' cow and her name was Sarah,
> > *Ch.* Pump, pump, falleriollalei!
> And she was such a hell of a nightmare,
> > *Ch.* Pump, pump, falleriorei![1]'

In Ernest Gann's book *Twilight for the Gods* is mentioned a shanty *Miss Bailey's Ghost* which I have not as yet run to earth.

These scraps must tickle the appetite of the genuine collector for more, but who, at this late date, can supply more?

*　　*　　*

I wish to bring to the notice of collectors the use made by northern European seamen of English sea-songs sung ashore in Victoria's time, but usually held in contempt by British seamen. Miss L. A. Smith has written that Dibdin was so honoured by British tars that his songs—'redolent of pitch and tar and oakum'—were sung to 'cheer the tars as they toiled at the capstan'. Now apart from the

---

[1] Translation by B. Streiffert.

fact that Miss Smith got her merchant and naval seamen mixed up somewhat, this statement contains a fallacy. No doubt Dibdin's airs were played in naval vessels by the ship's fiddler, but they were never sung as shanties. And they would be sung by naval tars in the mess-deck, but they were not popular with merchant Jacks off duty.

'These imitations by landsmen,' writes Whall, 'may have been sung in the wardroom but never before the mast.' Bullen writes: 'The grand old songs of Dibdin such as *Tom Bowling*, etc., were tacitly tabooed (in the fo'c'sle).'

No, we know for a fact so-called sailor songs written by landsmen were never popular at sea (in the merchant service), and certainly never sung as shanties. Shore-songs having nothing whatsoever to do with the sea were sometimes, as we have seen, used at capstan and halyard, but never shore sea-songs. But in Scandinavia and Germany, that fine old British sea-song *Nancy Lee*, for example, *was* used at the capstan, in the belief that it was a genuine British shanty. In *Knurrhahn* it is shown in typical shanty fashion with *Vorsänger* (shantyman) printed at the head of each verse. In *Sång under Segel*, the Swedish shanty book, it is described as 'the most popular sailor's song of the sailing ship days', and is given as a *Gångspelsshanty* (capstan shanty). The Victorian sea-song *Sailing, Sailing* also appears to have been used by European seamen, and in Katherine Wood's translation of Roger Vercel's story of the last days of the French Cape Horners—*Ride Out the Storm*—the chorus of this song is given, and it is described as 'the famous sea chantey of the great American sailing ships'. And other examples besides these do exist. I have often, too, expressed my belief that foreigners, in particular Germans and Scandinavians, carried on adapting shore-songs as shanties long after British and American seamen had ceased to 'invent' shanties. A German example I give in the following pages is *Up She Goes*, which is nothing more than the shore-song *Baltimore* or *We Parted on the Shore*. Just before the *Pamir* sailed on her first voyage after the Second World War (1951) an old Hamburg sailor sent to her bosun the words and music of an almost forgotten shanty sung in *plattdeutsch* called *Yo-ho for de Bottel o Rumm* (!). Unfortunately, I have been unable to secure a copy of it. And here is a Swedish example. It is described in *Sång under Segel* as a *Roddarvisa*, a rowing song, and it is nothing more than the well-known revivalist hymn, *Pull for the shore, sailors*:

My old shipmate, Jack Birch of Plymouth, gave me a sailor version of the old song, *Polly Wolly Doodle*, which he said he believed had been used as a shanty—and if this is so, then not only foreigners 'invented' shanties in modern times!

> Oh, we went up Channel with a new main yard,
>   *Ch.* Singing skiddly, winkie, doodle all the day!
> And it fell upon the deck an' it broke the skipper's neck,
>   *Ch.* Singing skiddly, winkie, doodle all the day!
>   Fare-ye-well, fare-ye-well, fare-ye-well, my lady friend,
>   For we're bound to Alabama for to see me Susiana,
>   Singing skiddly, winkie, doodle all the day!

Many of the words in this song—Susiana, Fare-ye-well, doodle—have the genuine shanty touch.

*   *   *

In many parts of the world even today, songs that could be classed as shanties—songs for hauling in tunny nets, for working cargo and coal, for rowing, and so on—are in use among Levantines, Arabs, Malays, Indians, Tamils, Chinese, and Japanese. Among Africans too such songs are to be found. Bill Fuller, a shipmate of mine, collected many from S.E. Africa:

Shantyman	*The Crowd*
U der der-der!	U der der-der!
Already!	Already!
One, two, three!	One, two, three!
Assigo!	Assigo!
Ai-O!	Ai-O!

On the final 'Ai-O!' all hands would either pull or push as the case may be.

A, a, *sisi*-ah! A, a, *sisi*-ah!

This was a chant used by Kaffirs when hauling a whale up the slipway—a scene familiar to anyone visiting Durban some years ago.

Indian coolies are naturally given to chanting when working and it makes me think that there must have been quite a number of real sailor shanties—a mixture of Hindustani and English—originated by the lascaris of sailing ships in the India–Trinidad Trade (like those of James Nourse), but it is rather too late now to seek them. The only example I have, which I honestly believe to be of this origin, is *Eki Dumah*. All seamen, more or less, tend to be cosmopolitan in their outlook, and the mixing of foreign words and phrases with their own language is one of their common characteristics even today, and in the days of sail this was still more pronounced. For example, in all the ports of the East—from Gibraltar to Shanghai—the orders used for working cargo are a mixture of many languages:

Portuguese, Spanish, Hindi, Arabic, and English. Examples are 'Pawl avis!' or 'Avis pawl!' ('Heave a pawl', or 'a little'), 'Vira pawl!' ('Heave a pawl'), 'Vira!' ('Heave' or 'Hoist'), 'Vira vech!' ('Heave away'), 'Aria!' ('Come back', 'Walk back'), 'Aria asti!' ('Slack a little', 'Come back slowly'), 'Asti, asti' ('Slowly', 'Easy'), 'Whoa!' ('Stop'), and 'Leg-go!'

While in the Far Eastern Trade I collected many work-songs of Chinese and Japanese seamen, but, mainly because of the lack of space, I shall have to omit them from this work.

*　　*　　*

In days gone by dwellers in sea ports were only too familiar with the rising cadences of the choruses of the windjammerman's working songs—over the dock sheds, house tops, and even sounding a mile or more away from their source, the deck of some tall ship entering or leaving dock.

Basil Lubbock in his *Last of the Windjammers*, describes on page 97 the arrival of the *Dawpool* (Captain Fearon) at Liverpool after a terrible homeward passage from San Francisco round Cape Horn in 1891:

> The next day, a Sunday, the crews of the *Henry B. Hyde* and the *R. D. Rice* . . . came aboard and chantied her through the three docks. Quite a big crowd of Liverpool shipping people came down to see her dock. . . . It was a calm, quiet Sunday, with the three crews chantying at the capstans. As the lines were hove in, the singing was most impressive. Indeed people said that they heard the capstan chanties on St. James's Mount, where Liverpool Cathedral now stands.

Such scenes have long departed, never to return again, but even in this prosaic age an occasional glimpse of the past is revived in, I'm afraid, a rather ghostly fashion.

In answer to the query 'When was the last shanty sung?' a subscriber in *Sea Breezes* writes:

> As to when the last full-blooded chanty was sung, I remember one occasion on board H.M. destroyer *Foresight* in the Barents Sea . . . on the evening of May 1, 1942. We were trying to steer H.M. cruiser *Edinburgh* after her stern had been blown off by a torpedo, by acting as a drag astern. We had to get fathoms of anchor cable across from the *Edinburgh*'s quarter on to our forecastle with heavy seas running and no steam coming through to the capstan owing to the pipes being frozen. It was 'Out capstan bars and heave away!' and I don't think that the old 'shellbacks' would have been ashamed of our performance!
>
> (Wm. Pritchard, Menai Bridge, N. Wales.)

And ashore, in Britain, even today, almost unbelievably, shanties are still being used as work-songs. This striking information was gained by my friend Peter Kennedy, the well-known B.B.C. folk-song collector. Apparently in the stone quarries of Portland there are many odd corners which mechanization cannot reach. Here the stones are split by metal wedges with men wielding heavy mauls. And, as they swing the mauls—in the manner of Negro railroad gangs of Young America—they sing *sailor* shanties, two men working on one wedge and striking it alternately at different words in the song. *Roll the Old Chariot* is a general favourite. This singing at work has been going on for years, the shanties having been brought ashore by west country seamen who became quarrymen. As well as shanties, hymns and popular songs are used and also chants such as *Now boys! High ho!* One song has a refrain 'Round, round!'

Work-songs, in olden days, were to be found in every country and in almost every trade. From the canoe hauling songs of the New Zealand Maori to the waulking songs of the Hebrides may seem a long traverse, but they all had one thing in common with the sailor shanty, and that is they were used to lighten labour. In *Atlantic*, Vol. 146, p. 28 (August 1930) appears a 'track-lining chantey', in other words a railroad work-song, but the collector, incorrectly, has referred to it as a 'chantey'. Obviously at the back of his mind he classifies all work-songs as 'chanties'—a natural classification, for the shanty was the work-song *par excellence*.

And to conclude our theme, here, where I work, at the Outward Bound Sea School, Aberdovey, we also do our best to keep the shanty alive. We often have 'shanty evenings', but as well as these we sing these old halyard songs in true deepwater fashion whilst hauling cutters up to be scraped and painted, hoisting our lifeboat at the davits, and doing many other 'pulley-hauley' jobs, and when we had the ketch *Warspite* we also made use of capstan songs as the lads stamped round her brass capstan raising the mud-hook. I hope we shall be able to keep these old songs and their spirit alive for many years to come.

PART ONE

~~~~~~

Shanties telling of John's Shore
Activities; of the Gals; of Booze and
Limejuice; Shanghaiing; the Lowlands
Family; the Stormalong Group; Mexico
and Rio; the Sacramento and California;
Goodbyes and Hurrahs

~~~~~~

I FEEL that we cannot do better than start this comparative work on shanties with one which embodies all Sailor John's roving and amorous activities—the shanty in question being that popular capstan song *A-rovin'*.

A-rovin' was originally sung at the pumps and old-fashioned windlass. In both labours—at the pump and at the windlass—two long levers were worked up and down by the men: a back-breaking job. These levers—in the case of pumps they were known as 'brakes' —had a long wooden handle inserted in their outboard ends, enabling three or four men to grasp each brake. Many shanties started life at the pump-brakes or old-fashioned windlass levers. Later, when ships began to use capstans with a large windlass below the fo'c'sle-head and iron ships began to replace wooden ones, thereby doing away with the arduous toil of pumping ship with monotonous regularity, watch and watch, these shanties were adapted for use at the capstan and more modern and not so often used flywheel or Downton pump.

Naturally in their conversion the tune and words remained unaltered, but the rhythm very often had to be adjusted to the new type of job. *A-rovin'* is, I feel, always sung much too fast by modern professional singers. The words 'A-rovin', a-rovin'' should be timed to fit the downward movement of a four-foot-diameter pumpwheel. The flywheel pump handles, like the old-fashioned levers, allowed only three or four men at the most to do the job, but in the case of the former, so that many more hands could be employed,

43

a rope known as a 'bell-rope', with an eye spliced in one end, was looped over the end of each pump-wheel handle, and as the wheel was about to descend the men, first on one side and then on the other, would haul on the rope, lightening the toil considerably.

As a matter of interest the old-fashioned 'up-an'-down' or 'jiggity-jig' windlass for anchor-heaving was used right to the end of the days of sail in the coastal schooners and ketches of Great Britain; I have myself spent many hours at its brakes and know something of the back-breaking labour it must have caused in the larger deepwater ships of a bygone age.

A-rovin' appears to be of fair antiquity; some collectors state that the words are in, or bear certain resemblance to lines in, a song given by T. Heywood in his play *The Rape of Lucrece* (1640). I have spent some time investigating this statement and have discovered that the song alluded to in Heywood's play is of the type known as a 'catch'. It is certainly *not* the shanty *A-rovin'*, and the only thing that can be said about it is that the approach of Sextus to Lucrece bears some resemblance, in sequence, to that of the amorous seaman to his Dutch girl in the full bawdy version of the shanty. But then again this 'sequence' is to be found in other shanties and in folk-songs such as *Gently, Johnny, my Jingalo*, and in the soldiers' song popular during the Second World War—*Roll Me Over in the Clover*.

Some say the tune of *A-rovin'* is Elizabethan; this may be quite true, but as well as the shore folk-song found in Great Britain, Dutch, Flemish, and French versions of this tune exist. An English shore version collected by Cecil Sharp is *We'll go no more a-cruisin'*. And from being a song of fair antiquity it has within recent years reappeared over the radio as *O Women! O Women!* with a touch of the cowboy and hillbilly about it!

In all the versions sung by Sailor John the main theme was frankly Rabelaisian—'coarse and indelicate words wedded to a haunting rhythm', as one writer has expressed it. In my version I have tried to keep as much as possible to the story as it used to be sung at sea, bowdlerizing only at impossible places. The first six verses are unaltered, and in the subsequent verses I have kept the rhyming words at the end of each solo intact. This is the nearest attempt yet made to give the shanty as Sailor John rendered it. I have versions from my father, from Anderson, a Scottish carpenter who had served in many Liverpool sailing ships, and from H. Groetzmann, a German seaman who had sailed for years in English barques in the West Coast of South America trade.

In the chorus very often 'I'll' was sung instead of 'We'll', and other alternatives are 'roamin'' for 'rovin'', 'false maid' for 'fair maid', and 'overt'row' or 'downfall' for 'ruin'.

PUMPING SHIP BY MEANS OF A DOWNTON PUMP
'Since rovin's bin me ru-eye-in!' (Pumping Shanty)

A-ROVIN' (a)

Alternative titles, *Amsterdam* or *The Maid of Amsterdam*

In Am-ster-dam there lived a maid, Mark well what I do say! In Am-ster-dam there lived a maid, An' she wuz mis-tress of her trade, We'll go no more a-ro-o-vin' with you fair maid, A-ro-vin', a-ro-vin', since ro-vin's bin me ru-i-in', We'll go no more a-ro-o-vin', with you fair maid.

2. One night I crept from my abode.
    Ch. Mark well what I do say!
   One night I crept from my abode
   To meet this fair maid down the road.
    Ch. We'll go no more a-rovin' with you, fair maid.
    Full Chorus. A-rovin', a-rovin',
            Since rovin's bin me ru-i-in,
            We'll go no more a-rovin',
            With you, fair maid.

3. I met this fair maid after dark,
   An' took her to her favourite park.

4. I took this fair maid for a walk,
   An' we had such a lovin' talk.

5. I put me arm around her waist,
   Sez she, 'Young man, yer in great haste!'

6. I put me hand upon her knee,
   Sez she, 'Young man, yer rather free!'

7. I put me hand upon her thigh,
   Sez she, 'Young man, yer rather high!'

8. I towed her to the *Maiden's Breast*,
   From south the wind veered wes'sou'west [sou'sou'west].

9. An' the eyes in her head turned east an' west,
   And her thoughts wuz as deep as an ol' sea-chest.

10. We had a drink—of grub a snatch,
    We sent two bottles down the hatch.

11. Her dainty arms wuz white as milk,
    Her lovely hair wuz soft as silk.

46

12. Her heart wuz poundin' like a drum,
    Her lips wuz red as any plum.

13. We laid down on a grassy patch,
    An' I felt such a ruddy ass.

14. She pushed me over on me back,
    She laughed so hard her lips did crack.

15. She swore that she'd be true to me,
    But spent me pay-day fast and free.

16. In three weeks' time I wuz badly bent,
    Then off to sea I sadly went.

17. In a bloodboat Yank bound round Cape Horn,
    Me boots an' clothes wuz all in pawn.

18. Bound round Cape Stiff through ice an' snow,
    An' up the coast to Callyo.

19. An' then back to the Liverpool Docks,
    Saltpetre stowed in our boots an' socks.

20. Now when I got back home from sea,
    A soger had her on his knee.

The last three or four stanzas are fairly modern. Saltpetre, guano, and all kinds of nitrates were shipped from the west coast of South America to British and continental ports mainly in the latter days of sail.

The tune of the following version, given only by Terry and Sharp, is probably the older one—it has the jerkiness of all shanties which were sung at the earlier brake-pumps and lever windlasses.

A-ROVIN' (d)

2. I took this fair maid for a walk.
   Ch. Bless you, young women!
I took this fair maid for a walk.
   Ch. Now mind what I do say!
I took this fair maid for a walk,
An' we had such a lovin' talk.
   Ch. I'll go no more, *etc.*

3. An' didn't I tell her stories true,
   Of the gold we found in Timbuctoo.

4. But when she'd spent me bloomin' screw,
   She cut her cable an' vanished too.

Other stanzas with a genuine ring are:

I met her walking on the Strand,
Dressed up for to beat the band.

In Number One New England Square,
Me Nancy Dawson she lives there.

This last ten months I've bin to sea,
Ah' hell, this gal looked good to me.

Versions which give

I kissed that maid and went away,
Said she, 'Young man, why don't ye stay?'

contrive to bring the shanty to a close without carrying out the true amours of Jack!

Another shanty singing of Jack's amours is the one which I will call *The Girls of Chile*. It was an outward-bound anchor song, and a version is also to be found in Captain Robinson's collection; Miss Colcord also gives it, but she had it from Captain Robinson. He gives it the title of *Hero Bangidero*, his first and third refrains being 'To my Hero Bangidero', but this refrain, on his own admission, was never sung—being bawdy, it had to be camouflaged. In fact both the verses and refrains I have had to alter to make the song printable. Sailors abused 'furrin lingoes' no end—it was quite a pastime in the old days—and the original refrains of this shanty were nothing more than bawdy alterations of Spanish phrases. Here is a typical example —the name sailors of the sail gave for Valparaiso: 'Wallop-me-ass-with-a-razor'! I had my version from Mike O'Rourke, a fine old Irish seaman who had spent much time in the W.C.S.A. trade—that is, in Liverpool Cape Horners which traded to the ports of Peru and Chile to load guano and nitrates.

I think the reason it is rarely found in print is not because it only circulated among seamen in certain trades, as some believe, but because of the difficulty of camouflaging it. This applies to many so-called *rare* shanties.

I have inserted it here since several bars of its third solo are reminiscent of the tune of *A-rovin'*.

THE GALS O' CHILE
Alternative title, *Timme Heave-O, Hang Her, Hilo!*

To.. Chi-le's coast we are bound a-way, Tim me heave-O, hang her Hi-lo! To.. Chi-le's coast we are bound a-way, An' we'll dance an' all drink pis-co! We are bound a-way, at the break o' day, Where the pretty little Spanish gals are so bright an' gay, Tim me heave-O, hang her Hi-lo! Sing o-lay for them Da-go gals!

2. An' when we get to Vallipo,
   Ch. Timme heave-ho, hang 'er hilo!
   An' when we get to Vallipo,
   Ch. We'll dance an' all drink pisco!
   Dance the gals up the street with a roll-'n'-go,
   Grab 'em round the middle an' we won't let go.
   Ch. Timme heave-ho, hang 'er hilo!
   Sing olay for them dago gals!

3. Them gals o' Chile, they are hard to beat.
   Ch. Timme, *etc.*
   Them gals o' Chile, *etc.*
   Ch. We'll dance an' *etc.*
   From truck to keel they are trim an' sweet,
   They're all a-pullin' on the ol' main-sheet.
   Ch. Timme heave-ho, *etc.*

4. Them senoritas, they are smart and gay,
   Them senoritas, *etc.*
   They dance an' drink till the break o' day,
   Then clean ye out an' blow yer pay.

5. Rosita, Anna, and Carmen too,
   Rosita, *etc.*
   They'll greet ye with a hullabaloo,
   An' soon ye'll know what they can do.

6. My trim little frigate is a very smart craft,
   My trim, *etc.*
   She's armed to the teeth both fore 'n' aft,
   Sharp at the bows with a fine view abaft.

49

7. Them ol' senyoras, as we know well,
   Them ol' senyoras, *etc.*
   They're red-hot divils from the other side o' hell,
   An' ye'll niver get a chance for to ring a Chile belle.

8. When the time comes for to sing farewell,
   When the time, *etc.*
   Goodbye to the gals an' our money as well,
   Callyo, Coquimbo, an' ol' Corynel.

A rather curious shanty related in theme to *A-rovin'* is the following. Harlow gives it under the title *Fal-de-lal-day*, and calls it a whistling shanty from the fact that the first refrain was sometimes whistled—a statement I have not been able to verify. It has many shore counterparts in Britain. It is usually called *The Devil's Song*, and sometimes the shore versions have the whistling refrain and sometimes it is omitted; but the second chorus is always the 'Fol-de-lol-day' one. It was often sung by the tinkers and 'trav'ling people' of mid and southern England. Seamus Ennis of the B.B.C. Folk Song Department came across a version in County Leitrim, Ireland, with a different theme, and another in Norfolk. In this latter one the first refrain is 'Right fol-lol, folladdy', and the second, 'Singing right for the loll, tiddy follol, fallay'. The sailor version was always sung at pumps. I also had this from Mike O'Rourke. He said that the first solo was often repeated as the first refrain.

THE GIRL IN PORTLAND STREET

Alternative title, *Fol-de-lol-day*

I met a gal in Portland Street, Fol-de-lol, fol-de lol, fol-de-lol-lol-day, I met a gal in
(I met a gal in Portland Street)
Portland Street, With a fol-de-lol-day, fol-de-lol-day, fol-de-lol-lol-de, lol-de, lol-day!

2. This gal I met in Portland Street,
      Ch. Fol-de-lol, fol-de-lol, fol-de-lol, lol-day [or else *repeat
         solo* or *whistle*]
   Was the sweetest gal I ever did meet.
      Ch. With a fol-de-lol-day, fol-de-lol-day,
         Fol-de-lol-lol-de, lol-de, lol-day!

3. Sez I, 'Me gal, 'Ow do ye do?'
   Sez she, 'The worst for seein' o' you.'

4. 'Now, miss,' sez I, 'I like yer style.'
   Sez she, 'Young man, just wait a while.'

5. 'Just wait until you try an' play,
   And then I'll send ye on yer way.'

6. I took her hand into my own,
   And we headed soon for her old home.

7. And in her room not far away,
   We drank until the break o' day.

8. I pulled her down upon me lap,
   Sez she, 'Young man, your face I'll slap.'

9. On her ankle next I placed my hand,
   Sez she, 'For this, I will not stand.'

10. I pulled her dress above her knee,
    Sez she, 'Young man, please let me be.'

From here onwards the amorous adventures of Sailor John are much the same as those in the bawdy version of *A-rovin'*, but Harlow finishes with a stanza:

> 'And why did I no further go?
> Alas! her leg was cork, you know!'

This was one of the 'anatomical progression' shanties—to quote a friend of mine—sired by the 'catch' in *The Rape of Lucrece*.

Another shanty telling of Jack's shore amusements is *So Early in the Morning*. It was used for both halyards and pumps. Terry calls it an 'interchangeable shanty' and expresses some doubt as to how the first line was manipulated when sung at halyards. This is not really difficult to understand. The first line is the chorus, sung, as many shantymen sang the chorus of other shanties, as an introduction when they were in doubt as to whether a greenhorn crowd knew the refrain or not.

This introduction-chorus became so common that many shanties are now written down in this fashion, e.g. *Shallow Brown*, *Drunken Sailor*, *Lowlands*, etc. Terry got his version mussed up because he started each stanza with the introduction-chorus. C. F. Smith thinks the tune is much like a nursery rhyme which runs, 'Fiddle de dee, The fly has married the bumble-bee', and Sharp likens it to a folksong, *Gently, Johnny, my Jingalo*. My first version is a Liverpool-Irish one.

SO EARLY IN THE MORNING (a)

Alternative titles, *The Sailor Loves, The Sailor Likes his Bottle-O*

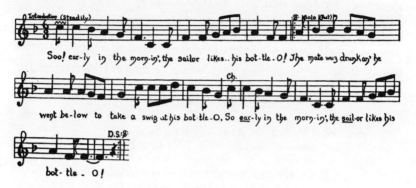

Soo! ear-ly in the morn-in', the sailor likes.. his bot-tle-O! The mate was drunk an' he went be-low to take a swig at his bot-tle-O, So ear-ly in the morn-in', the sail-or likes his bot-tle-O!

2. The bottle-O, the bottle-O, the sailor loves his bottle-O,
   Ch. Soo, *ear*ly in the mornin', the *sail*or likes his bottle-O!

3. A bottle o' rum, a bottle o' gin [beer, brandy], a bottle o' Irish whisky-O [good canary-O].
   Ch. Soo, early, *etc.*

4. The baccy-O, terbaccy-O, the sailor loves his baccy-O.

5. A packet o' shag, a packet o' cut [twist], a plug o' hard terbaccy-O [Faithful Lover-O, Yankee Doodle-O, Bird's-Eye baccy-O].

6. The lassies-O, the maidens-O, the sailor loves the judies-O.

7. A lass from the 'Pool [The lassies o' London], a gal from the Tyne, a chowlah so fine an' dandy-O [the gals across the water-O].

8. A bully rough-house, a bully rough-house, the sailor likes a rough-house-O.

9. A tread on me coat, an all-hands-in, a bully good rough an' tumble-O.

10. A sing-song-O, a sing-song-O, the sailor likes a sing-song-O.

11. A drinkin' song, a song o' love, a ditty o' seas and shipmates-O.

According to my informant this shanty was one in which improvisation was the thing, anything and everything a sailor was likely to 'love' was brought in by a versatile shantyman. The refrain in every case can be the first one about the 'bottle', but sometimes the name of a thing the sailor loves would be substituted for 'bottle':

> The sailor loves the judies-O,
> The sailor likes a sing-song-O.

And the word 'early' was always pronounced 'ear-lye', a common trick even with shore folk-song singers.

Miss C. F. Smith writes that it was a favourite in the old Black-wallers. Its opening solo bears a striking resemblance to the shanty

Miss Lucy Long. Ezra Cobb, a Bluenose (Nova Scotian) seaman of the old school, gave me a variant sung only at pumps, although he did say that "Twere used sometimes at caps'n.'

SO EARLY IN THE MORNING (b)

SO EARLY IN THE MORNING (c)

Another version, sung at the capstan and pumps, and usually heard aboard ships in the West Indian trade, is the following.

2. Now we're bound to Kingston Town,
   Where the rum flows round an' round.
   Ch. So early in the mornin',
       Sailors love the bottle-O!
       Bottle-O! Bottle-O!
       Bottle of very good whisky-O!
       So early in the mornin',
       Sailors like the bottle-O!

3. The Mate wuz drunk an' he went below,
   To take a swig o' his bottle-O.
   Ch. So early, *etc.*

Captain Robinson in his article on Shanties [1] gives a version with the tune almost identical with this, but his one verse runs:

> When you get to Baltimore,
> Give my love to Susanna, my dear.

After these examples of Sailor John's shore activities, our next shanty tells of his food and drink while at sea. It was a forebitter really, but was often used at pumps and sometimes at the capstan.

The Merchant Shipping Act came out in the year 1894, and in it was laid down the amount of food, water, etc., Sailor John was allowed when on shipboard. This doling out of rations was known to John as 'Pound and Pint'. The Act also covered fines and punishments for delinquent mariners, such as 'For concealing Knuckle-dusters, Slung-shot, Sword-stick, etc. 5s. for each day of concealment', and many commandments and regulations in similar strain. But the item around which this sarcastic song was built was also the origin of the Yanks calling English sailors 'Limejuicers'. This was the daily issuing of limejuice to British crews when they had been a certain number of days at sea.

My version of this song is partly that of my father and partly that of a shipmate, Arthur Spencer. The tune is also to be heard in Nova Scotia, the song being one about 'Sauerkraut and bully' sung in the Lunenburg dialect.

THE LIMEJUICE SHIP

Alternative title, *According to the Act*

Now, if ye want a merchant ship to sail the seas at large, Ye'll not have any trouble if ye have a good dis-charge, Signed by the Board o' Trade an' ev'-ry thing ex-act, For there's noth'in' done on a Lime-juice ship con-tra-ry to the Act, So haul boys yer weath-er main brace an' ease a-way yer lee Hoist jibs an' tawp's'ls lads an' let the ship go free, Hur-rah, boys, hur-rah! We'll sing this Ju-bi-lee, Damn an' Leg gur the Nav-y, boys, A mer-chant ship for me!

[1] *The Bellman*, Minneapolis, 1917.

2. Now when ye join a merchant ship ye'll hear yer Articles read.
They'll tell ye of yer beef an' pork, yer butter an' yer bread,
Yer sugar, tea, an' coffee, boys, yer peas an' beans exact,
Yer limejuice an' vinegar, boys, according to the Act.
    [Alternative last line: For what's the use of growlin' when ye know
       yer get yer whack.]
    Ch. So-o! Haul, boys, yer weather main brace, *etc.*

3. No watch an' watch the first day out, according to the Act.
Ten days out we all lay aft to get our limejuice whack.
Fetch out her handy billy, boys, and clap it on the tack,
For we gonna set the mains'l, oh, according to the Act.
    Ch. So-o! Haul, *etc.*

4. It's up the deck, me bully boys, with many a curse we go,
Awaiting to hear eight bells struck that we may go below.
Eight bells is struck, the watch is called, the log is hove exact;
Relieve the wheel an' go below, according to the Act.
    Ch. So-o! Haul, *etc.*

Another version exists, sung to a similar tune as far as the verse is concerned, but with five verses, the fifth one being my chorus. The chorus, however, is:

Shout, boys, shout! For I tell you it's a fact . . .

followed by

    There's nothing done on a limejuice ship contrary to the Act.

sung to bars 13, 14, 15, 16, and 17 of my verse.

    A shanty often used at the capstan and also at the pumps was *Larry Marr* or, as sometimes called, *The Five-Gallon Jar*. In chorus it is related to the second version of *The Limejuice Ship*. H. de Vere Stacpoole in his famous romance *The Blue Lagoon* mentions a snatch of it exactly the same as I give. Mr. Bryce of Sutton Coldfield, in a letter to me, writes: 'I believe Stacpoole got *The Five-Gallon Jar* from a book of old Irish songs. . . .' I had my version from an old Irish sailor, Paddy Delaney, and it is pretty certain that it is of Irish origin. There is also a forebitter of the same name, telling much the same story. J. F. Keane in his *Three Years of a Wanderer's Life* refers to the forebitter and gives the crimp concerned as Larry Meagher, while Doerflinger, who also gives the forebitter, although he calls it a 'ballad', gives Jack Jennings as the crimp. Paddy Delaney, who also knew the forebitter, told me he believed it to be older than the shanty, and that the words of the forebitter, after the first verse, were much the same as those in the shanty. The chorus of the forebitter, however, indicates an American origin.

LARRY MARR

Alternative titles, *The Five-Gallon Jar* or *Sound the Jubilee*

There wuz five or six old drunken shell-backs standin' before the bar, An' Larry he wuz servin' them, from a big five-gallon jar. Then.. hoist up yer flag, long may it wave, long may it lead us to the glory or the grave, Steady boys, steady, we'll sound this Jubilee, For Babylon's a-fallen an' the niggers are set free! (2) In Larry's place 'way on the Coast there lived old Larry Marr, Missus an' Larry did employ such a big five gallon jar.

3. The pair they played the shanghai game, wuz known both near an' far,
   They never missed a lucky chance to use the five-gallon jar.
   Ch. Oooh! Hoist, *etc.*

4. A hell-ship she wuz short o' hands, o' full red-blooded tars,
   Missus an' Larry would prime the beer in their ol' five-gallon jar.

5. Shellbacks an' farmers jist the same sailed into Larry Marr's,
   And sailed away around the Horn, helped by the five-gallon jar.

6. In 'Frisco town their names is known, as is the Cape Horn Bar,
   An' the dope they serve out to ol' Jack, from the big five-gallon jar.

7. From the Barbary Coast steer clear, me boys, an' from ol' Larry Marr,
   Or else damn soon shanghaied ye'll be by Larry's five-gallon jar.

8. Shanghaied away in a skys'l-ship around Cape Horn so far,
   Goodbye to all the boys an' girls an' Larry's five-gallon jar.

Here is Paddy Delaney's rendering of the first verse of the fore-bitter for comparison.

THE FIVE-GALLON JAR
(Forebitter)

The chorus is clearly allied—in words and tune—to those of the following songs of the Lowlands family.

The lilt of the word 'Lowlands' seemed to have a fascination for the shantyman and sailor in general. A very ancient song of the sea sings of the Lowlands of Holland—the Lowlands of Holland, those of Scotland, and even the Lowlands of Virginia were all woven into the songs of the shantyman.

The old song variously known as *Lowlands, The Lowland Sea, The Golden Vanitee,* or *The Lowlands Low* seems to have been based on a ballad of the seventeenth century entitled *Sir Walter Raleigh Sailing in the Lowlands* (see Aston, *Real Sailors' Songs*). The origin of the melody is unknown, but it would never have fitted the words of the older ballad. Captain Davis [1] is the only collector who gives it as a shanty, but I myself and many of my shipmates have sung this old song at both capstan and pumps. My version I had from my father with some added verses from the singing of my shipmate Jack Birch of Plymouth.

[1] Davis & Tozer, *Sailors' Songs or 'Chanties'*, London (Boosey & Co., Ltd.), 1887.

THE LOWLANDS LOW (a)

Alternative titles, *The Golden Vanitee, The Lowland Sea,* or *Lowlands*

There once was a skip-per who was boast-in' on the quay, Oh, I - have a ship - and a gal-lant ship is she, Of all the ships I know, she is far the best to me -, an' she's sail-ing in the Low-lands Low, In the Low-lands, Low-lands, she's sail-in' in the Low-lands Low!

2. Oh, I had her built in the North a-counteree,
An' I had her christened the *Golden Vanitee.*
I armed her and I manned her an' I sent her off to sea,
And she's sailing in the Lowlands Low.
   Ch. In the Lowlands, Lowlands, she's sailing in the Lowlands Low

3. Then up spoke a sailor who had just returned from sea,
'Oh, I wuz aboard of the *Golden Vanitee,*
When she wuz held in chase by a Spanish piratee,
And we sank her in the Lowlands Low.'
   Ch. In the Lowlands, Lowlands, and we sank her, *etc.*

4. 'Oh, we had aboard o' us a little cabin-boy,
Who said, "What will ye give me if the galley I destroy?"
Oh, ye can wed my daughter, she is my pride and joy,
If ye sink her in the Lowlands Low.'
   Ch. In the Lowlands, Lowlands, if ye sink her, *etc.*

5. 'Of treasure and of gold I will give to ye a store,
And my pretty little daughter that dwelleth on the shore,
Of treasure and of fee as well I'll give to thee galore,
If ye sink her in the Lowlands Low.'
   Ch. In the Lowlands, Lowlands, if ye sink her, *etc.*

6. 'So the boy bared his breast and he plunged into the tide,
An' he swam until he came to the rascal pirate's side.
He climbed on deck an' went below, by none was he espied,
And he sank 'em in the Lowlands Low.'
   Ch. In the Lowlands, Lowlands, and he sank 'em, *etc.*

58

7. 'He bore with his auger, he bored once an' twice,
An' some were playin' cards an' some were playin' dice,
An' the water flowed in an' dazzalèd their eyes,
An' he sank 'em in the Lowlands Low.'
    Ch. In the Lowlands, Lowlands, and he sank 'em, *etc.*

8. 'Oh, some were playing cards, oh, an' some were playin' dice,
An' some wuz in their hammocks a-sportin' with their wives,
An' then he let the water in an' put out all their lights,
And he sank her in the Lowlands Low.'
    Ch. In the Lowlands, Lowlands, and he sank her, *etc.*

9. 'Then the cabin-boy did swim o'er to the starboard side,
Sayin' "Capen, take me up, I am drifting with the tide."
"I will sink ye, I will kill ye, if ye claim my child as bride,
I will sink ye in the Lowlands Low." '
    Ch. In the Lowlands, Lowlands, I will sink ye, *etc.*

10. 'Then the cabin-boy did swim all to the larboard side,
Sayin' "Shipmates take me up for I'm drownin' with the tide."
They hauled him up so quickly, but when on deck he died,
And they buried him in the Lowlands Low.'
    Ch. In the Lowlands, Lowlands, and they buried him, *etc.*

11. 'And his shipmates took him up, and when on deck he died,
They sewed him in his hammock which was so strong and wide,
They said a short prayer o'er him, and they dropped him in the tide,
And they sailed from the Lowlands Low.'
    Ch. In the Lowlands, Lowlands, and they sailed, *etc.*

12. 'Here's a curse upon that Captain, wherever he may be,
For taking that poor cabin-boy so far away to sea,
For taking that poor cabin-boy so far away to sea,
And to leave him in the Lowlands Low.'
    Ch. In the Lowlands, Lowlands, and to leave him, *etc.*

For the third line, verse 9, Jack Birch would sing:

I will shoot you, I will kill you, I will knock you in the eye

and for verse 7 he sang:

Then he took up his auger and let the water through,
He sank the pirate Spanish craft an' all her rascal crew.

Another popular tune was one also sung by Birch; after the first verse the above verses were sung, from verse 4 onwards.

LOWLANDS LOW (b)

There was a loft-y ship boys, an' she put out to sea, An' she goes by the name of the Gold-en Van-i-tee, An' we thought she would be tak-en by the Span-ish pi-ra-tee, As we Sailed a-long the Low-lands, Low-lands, As we sailed a-long the Low-lands Low !

Slight variants of these two tunes also exist, and in all versions the words are very similar. Some sing 'they sewed him up in hide'. But the name of the ship differs widely; some versions give the *Gold China Tree* or the *Mary Golden Tree*; others have the *Weep Willow Tree, Golden Willow Tree,* and *Sweet Trinitee.* And the pirate ship has many names: the *Turkish* [or *Spanish*] *Canoe,* the *Turkish Roveree,* and the *Spanish Gahalee* being some. One version makes the cabin-boy threaten:

> 'If it warn't for my love for your daughter an' your men,
> I would do unto you as I did unto them,
> I would use my trusty auger an' do the job again,
> An' I'd sink ye in the Lowlands Low.'

And sometimes the story wound up joyfully:

> 'So we took him up aboard an' we praised him joyfully,
> For he'd saved us from the hands of the Turkish piratee,
> And the skipper gave his daughter, fairest in the North Countree,
> When they sailed upon the Lowlands Low.'

Another shanty with the Lowlands theme was *Lowlands Away.* Originally a pumping song, it was later used at windlass and capstan. It was never too popular, as it was difficult to sing properly—Whall describes it as a 'recitative type' of song. It savours of a shore-ballad with words unusually sentimental for seamen. Some think it is of North Country origin, and the words appear to justify this, but the tune has a Negro touch about it. More than likely it is one of the songs that passed through the shanty mart of the Gulf Ports as referred to in the Introduction. C. F. Smith, who strangely enough gives it as a halyard shanty, declares it was practically extinct by the eighties, and Terry says that after the China clipper era it was seldom heard. However, I have met coloured shantymen who told me they had sung it at a much later period.

Its 'dead lover' theme definitely originated in Scotland or the North of England. Masefield has a very old ballad in his *A Sailor's Garland* telling the same story and one from which the shanty theme probably stemmed.

The 'dead lover' pattern (*a*) is sub-divided into two types:

> i. The dead lover is a male;
> ii. The dead lover is a female.

LOWLANDS AWAY (a) (i)

Alternative title, *Lowlands*

2. I dreamt I saw my own true love,
    Ch. Lowlands, Lowlands, away, my John.
   He stood so still, he did not move,
   [Alternative line: His hair was wet, his eyes above.]
    Ch. My Lowlands away.

3. I knew my love was drowned and dead,
   He stood so still, no word he said.

4. All dank his hair, all dim his eye,
   I knew that he had said goodbye.

5. All green and wet with weeds so cold,
   Around his form green weeds had hold.

6. 'I'm drowned in the Lowland Seas,' he said,
   'Oh, you an' I will ne'er be wed.'

7. 'I shall never kiss you more,' he said,
   'Never kiss you more—for I am dead.'

8. 'I will cut my breasts until they bleed.'
   His form had gone—in the green weed.

9. 'I will cut away my bonnie hair,
   No other man will think me fair.'

10. I bound the weeper round my head,
    For now I knew my love was dead.

11. My love is drowned in the windy Lowlands,
    My love is drowned in the windy Lowlands.

LOWLANDS AWAY (a) (ii)

(Same tune as (a) (i))

Introduction-Chorus

> Lowlands, Lowlands, away, my John,
> Lowlands away I heard them say,
> My Lowlands away.

1. I dreamed a dream the other night,
   Ch. Lowlands, Lowlands, away, my John.
   My love she came dressed all in white,
   Ch. My Lowlands away.

2. I dreamed my love came in my sleep,
   Her cheeks were wet—her eyes did weep.

3. She came to me as my best bride,
   All dressed in white like some fair bride.

4. And bravely in her bosom fair,
   A red, red rose did my love wear.

5. She made no sound—no word she said,
   And then I knew my love was dead.

6. I bound the weeper round my head,
   For now I knew my love was dead.

7. She waved her hand—she said goodbye,
   I wiped the tear from out my eye.

8. And then awoke to hear the cry,
   'Oh, watch on deck, oh, watch ahoy!'

Variations on the chorus are:

> Lowlands, Lowlands, hurrah my Jo,
> Lowlands, high, Lowlands, alay!

> Lowlands, Lowlands, hooraw my John,
> My Lowlands aray!

This was a shanty in which 'stringing out' was carried out—that
is repeating the solo lines to make the song last out. It appears to me

to be the only shanty in which Sailor John allowed 'sob-stuff', indicating, of course, a positive shore ancestry.

We now come to the Southern States version—*A Dollar an' a Half a Day*. Bullen believes it to be of Negro origin, Whall calls it 'American', from the cotton ports. Sampson disagrees and says it is English, having been taken out to the West Indies by the P.O.W.s of the Monmouth Rebellion, and Doerflinger too thinks it a British song, taken to the Gulf ports by the English and Irish packet seamen who worked there loading cotton. Colcord says that this is what happened to the preceding *Lowlands* when the Negroes of Mobile Bay got hold of it. All of these theories have much to support them, but wherever the place of origin the only sure point is that this is a shanty which at some time or other passed through the shanty mart of Mobile and was moulded accordingly.

LOWLANDS or MY DOLLAR AN' A HALF A DAY

2. A white man's pay is rather high.
    Ch. Lowlands, Lowlands, away, my John!
   A black man's pay is rather low,
    Ch. My dollar an' a half a day.

3. Five dollars a day is a hoosier's pay,
   Five dollars a day is a hoosier's pay.

4. A dollar an' a half a day is a matlow's pay,
   A dollar an' a half a day won't pay my way.

5. Oh what shall we poor shellbacks do?
   We've got no money an' we can't git home.

6. I packed me bag an' I'm bound away,
   I'm bound away for Mobile Bay.

7. We're bound away for Mobile Bay,
   We're bound away at the break o' day.

8. Oh, say wuz ye never down in Mobile Bay?
   A-screwin' cotton all the day.

9. Oh, me poor ol' mother, oh, she wrote to me,
   She wrote to me to come home from sea.

10. We'll heave 'er up from down below,
    Oh, heave 'er up an' away we'll go!

11. Oh, I thought I heard the Ol' Man say,
    He'd give us rum three times a day.

(From here onwards livelier words to put life into the otherwise
mournful proceedings were usually inserted. These were much the
same as the stanzas used to enliven *Stormalong*.)

12. I wished I had ten thousand pound,
    I'd steer me ship for miles around.

13. I'd load her up with grub an' gin,
    An' stay in the port where we wuz in.

14. I'd stand ye drinks three times a day,
    An' feed ye well an' raise yer pay.

15. With a bully ship an' a bully crew,
    An' a bucko skipper for to kick her through.

16. Oh, I wished I wuz in Liverpool Town,
    With them Liverpool judies I'd dance around.

17. Wake up, yer bitch, an' let us in,
    Wake up, yer bitch, 'cos we want some gin.

My next shanty is also of the Lowlands family, but this was a
halyard song. I had it from Old Smith of Tobago, a fine old coloured
shantyman who gave me many little-known shanties, in the thirties
when I was shipmates with many West Indian seamen. Sharp gives
a Bristol version very similar to mine—of course it is a West Indian
song, and many of the shanties Sharp collected around the Bristol
channel area he had from seamen who had served in ships in the
West Indian trade (sugar and rum), many of which had chequerboard crews, i.e. one watch white and one watch coloured. Sharp
gives an introductory chorus.

LOWLANDS LOW
(Halyards)

64

2. The Ol' Man hails from Barbadoes,
   Ch. Low*lands, Lowlands, *Low*lands Low.
   He's got the name Ol' Hammertoes,
   Ch. Low*lands, Lowlands, *Low*lands Low.

3. He gives us bread as hard as brass,
   Our junk's as salt as Balaam's ass.

4. The monkey's rigged in the sojer's clo'es,
   Where he gottem from God 'lone knows.

5. We'll haul 'em high an' let 'em dry,
   We'll trice 'em up into de sky.

6. Lowlands, me boys, an' up she goes,
   Git changed, me boys, to yer shore-goin' clo'es.

A fine old shanty was *Stormalong*. Like *Lowlands Away* it was originally used at the pumps and later sung at the capstan. Although there are those who believe it was built around John Willis—the owner of the *Cutty Sark*—there is no doubt at all but that it is of Negro origin, and of much older vintage than the *Cutty Sark* period.

Negro songs are to be found with *Stormalong Stormy* refrains dating back to the thirties and forties in the 'Ethiopian Collections' of Negro folk-song (see Bibliography), and Nordhoff gives one form sung in the thirties by the hoosiers of the Gulf Ports. All the variants of this song have come from, or at some time or another passed through and have been moulded in, the shanty mart of Mobile Bay. Many of the couplets found in *Stormalong* are in other Negro songs. Quite recently I heard the American folk-singer Burl Ives singing over the radio 'Go on Blue, I finally got there too', in which the following lines also found in the shanty were used:

Lowered him down with a golden chain,

and

Dug his grave with a silver spade.

Here is a list of the *Stormalong* family:

(1) *Mister Stormalong.* Pumps; Colcord: capstan; Terry and Sharp: halyards; Doerflinger gives it in his capstan, windlass, and pumps section; C. F. Smith gives it as pumps and capstan.
(2) *Stormy Along, John.* Pumps; Sharp, Terry, and L. A. Smith give it as capstan; Colcord gives pumps; Masefield gives halyards.
(3) *Stormalong, Boys, Stormy.* Halyards.
(4) *Way Stormalong John.* Halyards.
(5) *Walk Me Along, Johnny (Storm an' Blow).* Halyards; cotton stowers' chant.
(6) *Yankee John, Stormalong.* Halyards.

65

In many of the Stormalong songs there were two patterns:

(1) Praising the dead seaman,
(2) Praising the benevolent son of the dead seaman.

The second pattern was usually added after the dirge-like regulation stanzas had run out.

Mister Stormalong has several chorus patterns. The 'Ay, ay, ay' was always yelled out staccato.

> To me, way you, Stormalong,
> Ay, ay, ay, Capen Stormalong.
> Yi, yah, yah, Mister Stormalong,
> To me, way ho, Storm and Blow. (Perry)

(This was an inverse form like that mentioned in the case of *Lowlands*.)

> To me way you Stormalong,
> Fi-i-i, Massa Stormalong.

> To me way yah Stormalong,
> Aye, aye, aye, Mister Stormalong.

> To me way hay hay, we'll stormalong,
> With me a-yo, Stormalong. (John Perring) (Inverse pattern)

> Tibby way you Stormalong,
> Hay, hay, hay, Massa Stormalong.

An inversion of refrains is noted in the *Journal* of the Folk Song Society, sung by John Farr, aged seventy-six, to a collector called Thomas (1926). The singer gave words from another shanty, *Whisky Johnny*.

> Whisky is the life of man,
>   *Ch.* Hi, hi, hi, Mister Stormalong!
> Whisky is the life of man,
>   *Ch.* To me way-O, Stormalong!

MISTER STORMALONG
Alternative titles, *Stormalong, Captain Stormalong*

66

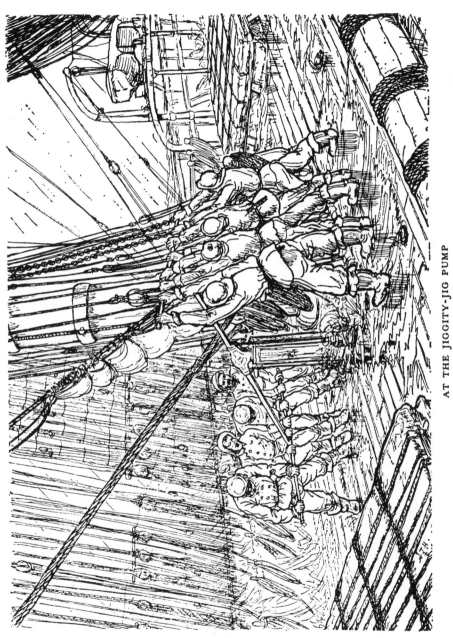

AT THE JIGGITY-JIG PUMP

'Ay! ay! ay! Mister Stormalong!' (Pumping Shanty)

2. Of all ol' skippers [the sailors] he was best,
    Ch. To me way you Stormalong!
   But now he's dead an' gone to rest,
    Ch. Ay! ay! ay! Mister Stormalong!

3. He slipped his cable off Cape Horn,
   Close by the place where he was born.

4. Oh, off Cape Horn where he was born,
   Our sails wuz torn an' our mainmast gorn.

5. We'll dig his grave with a silver spade.
   His shroud of finest silk was made.

6. We lowered him down with a golden chain,
   Our eyes all dim with more than rain.

7. He lies low in his salt-sea [earthen] bed,
   Our hearts are sore, our eyes wuz red.

8. An able seaman bold an' true,
   A good ol' skipper [bosun] to his crew.

9. He's moored at last an' furled his sail,
   No danger now from wreck or gale.

10. Old Stormy heard the Angel call,
    So sing his dirge now one an' all.

11. Oh, now we'll sing his funeral song,
    Oh, roll her over, long an' strong.

12. Old Stormy loved a sailors' song,
    His voice wuz tough an' rough an' strong.

13. His heart wuz good an' kind an' soft,
    But now he's gone 'way up aloft.

14. For fifty years he sailed the seas,
    In winter gale and summer breeze.

15. But now Ol' Stormy's day is done;
    We marked the spot where he is gone.

16. So we sunk him under with a long, long roll,
    Where the sharks'll have his body, an' the divil have his soul.

17. An' so Ol' Stormy's day wuz done,
    South fifty six, west fifty one.

18. Ol' Stormy wuz a seaman bold,
    A Grand Ol' Man o' the days of old.

Some versions say he was buried 'in Sailortown, down Mobile Bay'. Perry calls him 'Old Storm an' Blow', a name found more usually in Negro versions.

The 'livening-up' pattern runs:

    1. I wisht I wuz Ol' Stormy's son,
      I'd build a ship o' a thousand ton.

    2. I'd sail this wide world round an' round,
      With plenty o' money I'd be found.

    3. We'd sail this ol' world round an' round,
      An' get hot rum oh, I'll be bound.

    4. I'd load her up with Jamaicy rum,
      An' all me shellbacks they'd have some.

    5. We'd git our drinks, lads, every man,
      With a bleedin' big bottle for the shantyman.

    6. I'd load 'er up with grub an' gin,
      An' stay in the port that we wuz in.

    7. I'd feed ye well, an' raise yer pay,
      An' stand ye drinks three times a day.

    8. An' whin we git to Liverpool Town,
      We'll dance them judies round an' round.

    9. Oh, Stormalong an' around we'll go,
      Oh, Stormalong through ice an' snow.

Lowlands has a similar livening-up set of verses.
Another fairly popular stanza was:

      When Stormy died he made a will,
      To give us sailors gin to swill.

Sharp gives: Was ye ever in Quebec,
               A-stowing timber on the deck?

               I wish I was in Baltimore,
               On the grand old American shore.

For similar verses see *Tom's Gone to Hilo*, *Highland Laddie*, *A Young Thing, Lately Left Her Mammy-O*, and *Donkey Riding*.

STORMY ALONG, JOHN

Alternative titles, *Stormalong John, Come-along, Git-along,
Stormalong John*

Oh... Stormy's gone that good ol' man, Stormy-a-long boys, Storm-a-long John! Oh, Stormy's gone that good ol' man, Oh-ha! Come-a-long, git a-long, Storm-y a-long John!

2. Oh, poor Ol' Stormy's gone to rest,
   Ch. Stormyalong boys, stormalong, John!
Of all ol' seamen [bosuns] he wuz best,
   Ch. Ah, ha, come-along, git-along, stormy along, John!

3. He slipped his cable off Cape Horn.
Close by the place where he wuz born.

4. We dug his grave with a silver spade.
His shroud o' finest silk wuz made.

and all the verses of *Mister Stormalong,* including the 'livening-up' ones.

I wisht I wuz Ol' Stormy's son,
I'd build a ship o' a thousand ton.

Sometimes the first refrain would be:

To me way-ay Stormalong John!

STORMALONG, LADS, STORMY
Alternative titles, *Oh, Stormalong, Old Stormalong,* or *Wo Stormalong* (Sharp)

Storm-a-long an'a-round we'll go, Ol' Storm-a-long! Oh, Storm-a-long an' a-round we'll go, Storm-a-long lads, Storm-y!

2. If ever you go to Liverpool,
   Ch. Ol' Stormalong!
If ever you go to Liverpool,
   Ch. Stormalong, lads, stormy.

3. To Liverpool that packet school,
   (*Repeat.*)

4. Yankee sailors ye'll see there,
   (*Repeat.*)

5. With red-topped boots an' short cut hair,
   (*Repeat.*)

6. There's Liverpool Pat with his tarpaulin hat,
An' 'Frisco Jim, the packet rat.

7. Wake up, yer bitch, 'n' let us in,
   Get up, yer bitch, 'n' serve us gin.

8. Oh, I wisht I wuz in Liverpool Town,
   Them Liverpool judies I'd dance around.

9. O long Stormy-stormalong,
   O long Stormy-stormalong.

The words of the above shanty are much the same as those in *Across the Western Ocean*. Both *Stormy Along, John* and *Stormalong, Lads, Stormy* I had from a fine old coloured seaman who hailed from Barbadoes. He was called Harding, the Barbadian Barbarian, and having sailed in British, American, and Bluenose (Nova Scotian) ships, as well as West Indian traders, he was a mine of information regarding the shanties, and at times had enacted the role of shanty-man himself. He was a master of the 'hitch'—the singing of wild yelps at certain points in a hauling song. In both the foregoing shanties and in the one which follows—which I also obtained from him—he would give vent to many wild 'hitches', absolutely impossible for a white man to copy, although white sailors did execute a poor shadow of these Negro yelps.

'WAY STORMALONG, JOHN
Alternative title, *Mister Stormalong John*

Oh, Storm-y's gone that good ol' man. 'Way, Storm-a-long John! Oh, Stormy's gone that good ol' man, Way-ay Mist-er Storm-a-long John!

2. A good ol' skipper [bosun] to his crew,
   Ch. 'Way Stormalong John!
   An able seaman bold an' true,
   Ch. 'Way-ay, Mister Stormalong John.

3. We dug his grave with a silver spade,
   His shroud o' finest silk wuz made.

4. Old Stormy heard the Angel call,
   So sing his dirge now one an' all.

5. He slipped his cable off Cape Horn,
   Close by the place where he wuz born.

At this point normally the stanzas about 'Old Stormy's son' would be sung.

> I wisht I wuz Ol' Stormy's son,
> I'd build a ship o' a thousand ton, *etc.*

All the foregoing shanties—the three I had from Harding—savour of Gulf port or West Indian origin. Our next comes from the same part of the world and in all probability has stemmed from a slave song. Nordoff gives this shanty:

> Lower him down with a golden chain,
> *Ch.* Carry him along, boys, carry him along,
> Then he'll never rise again,
> *Ch.* Carry him to the burying ground.
> *Grand chorus.* 'Way-oh-way-oh-way—storm along,
> 'Way—you rolling crew, storm along stormy.

as a cotton stowers' *chant*, but to fit the words the tune must have been slightly different from the one I give.

WALK ME ALONG, JOHNNY
Alternative titles, *Walk Him Along, John, General Taylor*

2. We dug his grave with a silver spade,
   Ch. Walk me along, Johnny, *carry* me along [Walk him, *etc.*, carry him, *etc.*],
   His shroud o' finest silk wuz made,
   Ch. Carry me to the burying ground [carry him, *etc.*],
   Then away-ay-ay-ay-ay O Storm an' Blow [you Stormy].
   Ch. Walk me along Johnny, carry me along,
   Way-ay-ay-ay-ay you Storm an' Blow [Stormy],
   Ch. Carry me to the burying ground.

3. Oh, ye who dig Ol' Stormy's grave,
   Dig it deep an' make it safe.

4. Oh, lower him down with a golden chain,
   Make sure that he don' rise again.

5. Oh, General Taylor died long ago,
   He's gone, me boys, where the winds don't blow.

6. He died on the field of ol' Monterey,
   An' Santiana he gained the day.

7. Dan O'Connell he died long ago,
   Dan he was an Irish boy-O.

8. We'll haul, me boys, an' wake the dead,
   Let's stow him in his little bed.

Many of the ordinary and the 'livening-up' verses of *Mister Storm-along* were used to this tune.

Terry and Sharp, both of whom had it from the same shantyman, Short of Watchet, Somerset, call it 'halyards', but although I also give it as a halyard song, I am inclined to believe that it must have been used as a capstan song or pump shanty at some time or other, since the last two solos and refrains suggest that they were once sung as a full chorus. Nordhoff's version *was* sung in this fashion—at the jackscrews—and Sharp too gives these last four lines as 'chorus'. Of course other halyard shanties do exist with four solos and four refrains—*Cheer'ly Man*, for example—but there were not many, and in all the last solo is sung the same throughout all the verses, e.g. *John Kanaka, Mobile Bay, John Cherokee, Bunch o' Roses*. Sharp gives 'Oo, oo, oo . . . oo you Stormy' instead of 'Away' etc., and his first two bars (*General Taylor*) are a little different from mine.

Gen-er-al Tay-lor gained the day . . .

Several Negro songs exist that point to its origin. N. I. White (*American Negro Folk Song*) discovered in a book called *Journal of Residence Among Negroes of the West Indies*[1] a song about the disposing of dead slaves by the slave-owner which runs:

> Take him to the Gully! Take him to the Gully!
> But bringee back the frock and board.
> 'Oh, Massa, Massa, me no deadee yet!'
> Take him to the Gully! Take him to the Gully!
> Carry him along!

[1] M. G. Lewis, London, 1845.

73

Zora Neale Hurston, in her book *Caribbean Melodies*, gives a humorous dance song from New Providence (West Indies), which may be an ancestor of the shanty:

> Carry him along!
> Carry him if he's dead or live,
> Carry him along!

And for our last of the Stormalong family we have:

YANKEE JOHN, STORMALONG
Alternative title, *Liza Lee*

2. Liza Lee she promised me,
    Ch. Yankee John, Stormalong!
   She promised to get spliced to me,
    Ch. Yankee John, Stormalong!

3. So I shipped away across the sea,
   In a hard-case Down-Easter to Mirramashee.

4. I promised her a golden ring,
   I promised her that little thing.

5. I promised I would make her mine,
   Oh, wouldn't we have a Jamboree fine?

6. Liza Lee she's jilted [slighted] me,
   Now she will not marry me.

7. Oh, up aloft that yard must go,
   Up aloft from down below.

8. Oh, stretch her, boys, and show her clew,
   We're the boys to kick her through!

Other couplets from the 'general utility' shanty *Handy, Me Boys* would often be used to lengthen the haul.

Santiana in many ways resembles *Stormalong*; very often shantymen would bury each hero in a similar burying place, i.e. off Cape Stiff.
Also *Santiana* and *Mister Stormalong*, together with the shanty *Lowlands Away*, started life in the same job—that of being pump

74

shanties. Also they were used at the old-fashioned brake or lever windlasses. Later, as iron ships superseded wooden ones, dispensing with the use of pumps to a very great extent, and upright capstans took the place of the older horizontal barrelled windlasses, these three venerable songs were adapted for capstan work, and so they remained to the end of sail.

Santiana was very popular with whalers, and the fine tune (b) was sung to me by an old Norwegian whaler Captain Larsen of Magallanes (Punta Arenas). The three tunes I give are all much the same, yet each has its own character. Although I give two versions of the words, in actual fact both were used, or some of both, in any singing of this shanty. These patterns were:

(1) The unhistorical story of Santiana,
(2) The Spanish Senoritas (no mention of Santiana),
and sometimes, as in *Stormalong*,
(3) The Benevolent Sailor.

Terry gives a fourth, the verses of *Boney*.

This is another shanty whose origin is veiled in mystery. Probably it has a Negro source, but Bone wonders whether it may have come from a seaman's prayer to Sainte Anne, the patron saint of Breton seamen. In actual fact General Taylor beat the Mexican general Santa Aña at the battle of Molina del Rey (Buena Vista), but only one shantyman seems to have the correct story:

> Santiana ran away . . .,
> General Taylor gained the day . . .,

and

> the Americans make Huerta fly.

Quite a number of British seamen deserted their ships to join Santa Aña's wild and ragged army—Britishers, it would appear, favoured the cause of the Mexicans. Many shanties seem to have been taken by cowboys and made use of as camp-fire songs if we are to believe the many instances given in American cowboy song collections. I doubt if sailors ever got them from the cowboys! And this one—*Santiana*—appears to have been a great favourite with the men of the Wild West! Here is the manner in which *they* sang it:

> Ol' Santiana, ol' Santiana!
> Ol' Santiana! ol' Santiana!
> Ol' Santiana . . .
> Santiana gained the day,
> Hooray Santiana!
> Santiana gained the day,
> Upon the plains of Mexico, Mexico, Mexico.

The refrains of this shanty varied greatly from ship to ship:

First refrain

> Heave and weigh Santiana.
> Hooray Santiana.
> And away Santianno.
> Hooraw boys, hooraw ho.
> Horoo Santy Ana.
> 'Way Santiana.

Second refrain

> Heave away, hurra for roll-an'-go. (*Norwegian source*)
> All on the plains of Mexico.
> Heave an' weigh, we're bound for Mexico.
> All across the plains of Mexico.
> All along [on] the shores of Mexico.
> Along the plains of Mexico.
> On the banks and plains of Mexico.
> Around the Bay o' Mexico.
> All along the coasts of Mexico.
> Upon the plains of Mexico.

Sometimes an inverse order of singing is to be found as in *Lowlands Away* and *Stormalong*:

> Santiana gained the day,
> *Ch.* All on the plains of Mexico,
> Santiana gained the day,
> *Ch.* Hurrah Santianno.

The opening bars of this shanty are similar to those of *Jamboree*, and the second refrain resembles *Clear the Track*. Miss Gilchrist (*Journal* of the Folk Song Society) seems to think that the tunes of *Santiana* and *Clear the Track* are based upon one of the many tunes of *High Barbaree*.

SANTIANA (a)
Alternative titles, *The Plains o' Mexico, Old Santy Ana*

Ch. San-ti-a-na gained the day, A-way San-ti a-na! San-ti-a-na gained the day, all a-cross the Plains of Mex-i-co!

> 2. He gained the day at Molley-del-rey [Monterey],
>   *Ch.* Away Santiana!
>   An' General Taylor ran away,
>   *Ch.* All across the plains of Mexico!

3. All of his men were brave an' true,
Every soldier brave an' true.

4. Oh, Santiana fought for fame,
An' Santiana gained a name.

5. An' Zacharias Taylor ran away,
He ran away at Molley-del-ray [Monterey].

6. Santiana's men were brave,
Many found a soldier's [hero's] grave.

7. 'Twas a fierce an' bitter strife,
Hand to hand they fought for life.

8. An' Santiana's name is known,
What a man can do was shown.

9. Oh, Santiana fought for his gold,
What deeds he did have oft been told.

10. 'Twas on the field of Molley-del-rey,
Santiana lost a leg that day.

11. Oh, Santiana's day is o'er,
Santiana will fight no more.

12. Oh, Santiana's gone away,
Far from the field o' Molley-del-rey.

13. Oh, Santiana's dead an' gone,
An' all the fightin' has bin done.

14. Santiana was a damn fine man,
Till he fouled hawse with Old Uncle Sam.

15. Now Santiana shovels his gold,
Around Cape Horn in the ice an' cold.

16. We'll dig his grave with a silver spade,
An' mark the spot where he was laid.

17. Oh, Santiana now we mourn,
We left him buried off Cape Horn.

18. We left him deep 'way off Cape Horn,
Close by the place where he was born.

THE PLAINS OF MEXICO (b)

In Mex-i-co where the land lies low, Hoo-raw, boys, hoo-raw ho! Where there ain't no snow on' the whale fishes blow, Heave a-way for the Plains of Mex-i-co!

2. In Mexico so I've heard say,
    Ch. Hooraw, boys, hooraw ho!
    There's many a charmin' señorita gay,
    Ch. Heave away for the plains of Mexico!

3. 'Twas there I met a maiden fair,
    Black as night was her raven hair.

4. Her name wuz Carmen so I'm told,
    She wuz a Spanish señorita bold.

5. But she left me there, an' I did go
    Far away from the plains of Mexico.

6. Them gals is fine with their long black hair;
    I found my charmin' senorita there [They'll rob ye blind
        an' skin ye bare].

7. In Mexico I long to be,
    With me tight-waisted gal all on me knee.

8. Them little brown gals I do adore,
    I love 'em all, each sailor-robbin' whore.

9. In Mexico where I belong,
    Them gals all sing this rousin' song.

10. Why do them yaller gals love me so?
    Because I don't tell 'em all I know.

11. Them Dago gals ain't got no combs,
    They comb their hair with whale-fish bones.

12. When I wuz a young man in me prime,
    I courted them yaller gals two at a time.

13. Oh, Mexico, my Mexico,
    Oh, Mexico where the land lies low [where the wind don't
        blow].

SANTIANA or *THE PLAINS OF MEXICO* (c)
(The benevolent sailor version)

2. I'd build a ship of a thousand ton,
    Ch. Hooraw, Santiano!
   An' load her up with Jamaicy rum,
    Ch. All along the plains of Mexico!

3. I'd give ye whisky an' lots o' gin,
   An' stay in the port where we wuz in.

4. Though times is hard an' the wages low,
   'Tis time for us to roll 'n' go!

5. When I leave this ship I'll settle down,
   An' marry a tart called Sally Brown.

These three tunes I give were not necessarily ones to which the given words were sung. The three versions of the words were sung to all three of the tunes, either as complete versions, or as a mixture, taking a few verses from each. This was entirely up to the individual shantyman. The words of the refrains too were not especially the property of the individual versions as given here. The combination I prefer is: some of the verses of version (a) and some of version (b), sung to the tune, and using the words of the refrains, of version (c).

Terry's shantyman gives Santiana as having fought the special enemies of Napoleon!

> He beat the Prussians fairly,
> He whacked the English nearly.
>
> He was a rorty gineral,
> A rorty, snorty gineral.
>
> They took him out and shot him,
> Oh, when shall we forget him?
>
> (*The Shanty Book*, Part I)

These of course are stanzas from *Boney*.

A different form of *Santiana* commonly known as *Round the Bay of Mexico*, in which there is no reference at all to Santiana either in the solos or refrains, is probably the older hoosier version as was once sung round the Gulf ports.

ROUND THE BAY OF MEXICO

Heave a-way me bul-ly boys, Way-ay, heave a-way! Heave a-way, why dan't ye make some noise boys? Round the Bay of Mex-i-co!

2. Heave away an' around goes she,
   'Way-ay, heave away!
   Six for you an' seven for me-e,
   Ch. Round the Bay of Mexico!

3. Heave around an' with a will,
   If she don't go she'll stay there still.

4. Heave away for she's trimmed tight,
   Bend yer backs if yer wanner sleep ternight.

Rio Grande naturally makes one think of Mexico, and although one of the most popular shanties in the days of sail was *Rio Grande* it was not the Mexican Rio Grande about which they were singing but the one further south in Brazil; not Rio Grande del Nord but Rio Grande do Sul. It has even been suggested that the Rio Grande referred to in the shanty may have been the one in West Africa, but I doubt this very much. The reference in some versions of the song to 'golden sand', whether taken literally or symbolically, applies to the southern Brazilian river and port, for both banks of the Brazilian Great River (it is a lagoon really) are heaped high with sand dunes, as many seamen are aware, and also in the past gold was a commodity found in this district. In the eighteenth century gold was found in southern Brazil and hordes of seekers flocked to this then-new Eldorado, and, as C. F. Smith has pointed out, it would be the natural thing for seamen to compose a new shanty about a new trade. Gold *was* discovered in the Mexican Rio Grande district but not until the sixties of the last century, by which time the shanty had been well aired. In origin it has the distinct flavour of a shore ballad —from either side of the Border I should say.

Rio Grande was always sung at the anchor capstan or windlass, and was an outward-bound song.

Captain P. Tayluer in Doerflinger's work says that this shanty was usually sung aboard the little Baltimore coffee barques running down to São Paolo and Rio Grande. But from my own researches I should say that this song was heard more on the decks of ships leaving the West Coast of England and Wales than in any other vessels. From the Salthouse Dock, Liverpool, and from Welsh ports like Portmadoc full-rigged ships, barques, brigs, and all types of schooners ran down to the Brazils. Sometimes they sailed to Newfoundland first, to load salt cod, and Cadiz too was another port of call where the salt used for salting the fish was loaded.

I've often felt that the popular version of the chorus now sung in British schools, etc.—'Sing fare-ye-well, my bonnie young girls', and the bit about 'away, love, away'—savours too much of a Scottish ballad and hardly the sort of thing one would expect from robust, tarry seamen, but maybe this is something left over from the days when it was a shore ballad. I don't know whether the Scottish ballad which starts 'I've been a wanderer all my life' has any age to it, but if it has, taking into account several bars of its melody, it *could* be a possible shore origin. The chorus I give is the one I always sang myself and which I learnt from older Liverpool seamen.

Of all the versions of the tunes in print Bullen's is the only one which differs—and the difference is really too slight to be worth noting—yet Terry writes that the 'variants of this tune are legion'. This I am sure is an unjustifiable statement. This shanty of all the work-songs of the sea is the one with the least variation in tune. Some versions give three notes to the final 'Rio', others give two— the only difference worth recording.

Ri - o Grande!

The main patterns are:

(1) Leaving Liverpool,
(2) Gold Rush Version,
(3) The Milkmaid,
(4) Leaving New York,
(5) The Fishes,
(6) The Mail ('Gam').

Chorus variants:

Then away, bullies, away,
Away for Rio!
Sing fare-ye-well, me Liverpool girl,
An' we're bound for the Rio Grande.

Then away, love, away,
Away down Rio!
Sing fare-ye-well, my bonnie young girl,
We're bound for the Rio Grande.

81

Then away, my love, away,
Away for Rio!
The biscuits is weevily,
An' the salthorse is tough,
An' we're bound to the Rio Grande.

Then away, boys, away,
'Way for Rio!
Instead of milking her cow
She was courtin' her boy,
An' we're bound to the Rio Grande.

Hurrah you Rio!
Rolling Rio!
So fare-ye-well, you Liverpool gals,
For we're bound to the Rio Grande.

'Way Rio!
Rolling Rio!
Then sing fare-ye-well, to me pretty young gel,
We're bound to Rio Grande. (*Norwegian source*)

Some also started, 'And away Rio, away Rio!' or 'Heave away
Rio! Heave away Rio!' or else 'Aaaaawaaaay Rio, Oh Rio!', and in
the singing of the word 'away' fancy trills were the order. In fact
wherever the word 'away' is to be found in the refrain of a shanty
usually it was sung in a certain wavering manner. If there was a
Negro cook among the crowd then this 'warbling' was something to
wonder at. A Yank I once knew aboard the American barquentine
Forest Friend was a splendid 'yodeller' of this shanty.

RIO GRANDE (a)
Alternative titles, *Away for Rio, Bound for the Rio Grande*

Oh, a ship went a-sail-in' out o-ver the Bar, 'Waaay for Ri - o ! They've
point-ed her bow to the Southern Star, 'An' we're bound for the Ri-i-o Grande ! Then a-
waay, bul-lies, a-way ! 'Waaay for Ri-o ! Sing fare-ye-well .. me
Liv-er-pool gels, an' we're bound for the Ri-i-o Grande !

2. Oh, say wuz ye never down Rio Grande?
    Ch. 'Way for Rio!
Them smart señoritas they sure band the band,
    Ch. An' we're bound for the Rio Grande,
        Full Chorus. Then away, bullies, away!
            Away for Rio!
            Sing fare-ye-well, me Liverpool gels,
            An' we're bound for the Rio Grande!

3. We wuz sick o' the beach when our money wuz gone,
    So we signed in this packet for to drive 'er along.

4. There's some o' us sick, aye, there's some o' us sore,
    We've scoffed all our whack an' we're lookin' for more.

5. Our anchor we'll weigh an' the rags we will set,
    Them Liverpool judies we'll never forget.

6. Ye Parkee Lane judies we'll 'ave ye to know,
    We're bound to the southard, Oh, Lord let us go!

7. Oh, pack up yer donkeys an' get under way,
    Them judies we're leavin' will git our half-pay.

8. Cheer up, Mary Ellen, an' don't look so glum,
    On white-stockin' day ye'll be drinkin' hot rum.

9. We're a deep-water ship with a deep-water crew;
    Ye can stick to the coast, but I'm damned if we do.

10. It's goodbye to Ellen an' sweet Molly too,
    Ye Parkee Lane chowlahs [An' the judies of Bootle], 'tis goodbye to
        you.

11. Now blow, ye winds westerly, long may ye blow,
  We're a starvation packet—Good God let us go!

12. Saltfish an' lobscouse for the next 'alf year,
  She's a Liverpool packet an' her Ol' Man's the gear.

13. Them Liverpool judies they never use combs,
  They comb out their locks with a haddock's [kipper's] backbone.

14. Heave only one pawl, then 'vast heavin', me sons,
  Sing only one chorus—it's blowin' big guns.

Many of the verses used in the 'Leaving New York' version were sung in the former and vice versa. Other Liverpool stanzas often sung to the above version run:

> An' now we are leavin' the sweet Salthouse Dock,
> An' soon we'll be oh a-roundin' the Rock.
> We're a Liverpool ship wid a Liverpool crew,
> Wid a Liverpool mate an' an Old Man too.
> We're Liverpool born, an' Liverpool bred,
> Oh, thick in the arm, an' thick in the head!

RIO GRANDE (b)

1. Oh, say, wuz ye ever down Rio Grande?
  It's there that the river flows down golden sands.

2. So heave up the anchor, let's get it aweigh,
  It's got a good grip, so heave, bullies, 'way-ay!

3. Oh, where are yiz bound to, me bully boys all?
  An' where are yiz bound for to make yer landfall?

4. We're bound to the south'ard, me bully boys all,
  Bound out to the Brazils, me bully boys all.

5. An' what'll ye do there, me bully boys all?
  What job will ye do there, me bully boys all?

6. We'll dig for red gold, oh, me bully boys all,
  We'll dig for a fortune, me bully boys all.

7. Or die o' the fever, me bully boys all,
  Or die o' the fever, me bully boys all.

8. Heave with a will, boys, oh, heave long an' strong,
  Sing a good chorus, for 'tis a good song.

Patterson gives a version similar to this.

RIO GRANDE (c)

1. Oh, where are ye goin' to, my pretty maid?
   I'm going a milkin', kind sir, she said.

   Full Chorus. Then away, bullies, away,
       'Way for Rio,
       'Stead o' milkin' her cow,
       She wuz courtin' her boy,
       An' we're bound for the Rio Grande!

For other verses, see *Blow the Man Down*, page 210.

Doerflinger gives a Milkmaid version without mentioning the milkmaid. This is from the singing of Captain Patrick Tayleur of New York. His second refrain is a sort of answer to the solo line, a method of singing which would not be in general use, e.g. 'Because I'm bound to the Rio Grande!'

RIO GRANDE (d)

1. A ship went a-sailing out over the bar,
   They've pointed her bow to the southern star.

2. Oh, farewell to Sally an' farewell to Sue,
   An' you on the pierhead it's farewell to you.

3. You Bowery ladies we'd have ye to know,
   We're bound to the south'ard—O Lord, let us go!

4. We've a bully good ship an' a bully good crew,
   But we don't like the grub, no I'm damned if we do.

5. Oh fare ye well, all ye ladies o' town,
   We've left ye enough for to buy a silk gown.

6. We'll sell our salt cod for molasses an' rum,
   An' get back again 'fore Thanksgivin' has come.

7. Oh, New York town is no place for me,
   I'll pack up me sea-chest an' git off to sea.

8. Oh, man the good caps'n an' run her around,
   We'll heave up the anchor to this bully sound.

9. To the Brazils we're bound an' we hope ye don't mind,
   We soon will return to the Molls left behind.

10. The chain's up an' down now the Bosun did say,
    It's up to the hawse-pipe, the anchor's aweigh!

RIO GRANDE (e)

1. Oh, a ship she wuz rigged, an' ready for sea,
   An' all of her sailors wuz fishes to be.
   [*or* There wuz once an ol' skipper I don't know his name,
   Although he once played a ruddy fine game.]

The remainder of this version is the same as that sung to the 'Fishes' version of *Blow the Man Down*, page 209.

RIO GRANDE (f)

1. Oh, Capitan, Capitan, heave yer ship to,
   For we've got some mail to be carried home by you.

2. Oh, Cap'tan, you're sailin' to England away,
   An' we will not see it for many a day.

3. Oh, Cap'tan, you've weathered full many a gale,
   So heave yer ship to for to pick up our mail.

4. Oh, Cap'tan, ye'll pick up our letters for home,
   To carry a letter from us who do roam.

5. Oh, Capitan, Cap'tan, our ensign we'll dip,
   Pray tell 'em at home that you've spoken our ship.

Another shanty singing of *Rio* is *Oh, Aye, Rio!* This is the first time this one has been in print. I learnt it from an old sailor in Port Adelaide, South Australia. It is a capstan song, entirely ribald, so I have had to camouflage it somewhat, keeping to the original theme as much as possible. In L. A. Smith's collection the shanty *Slapandergosheka* (which, incidentally, I feel should read 'Slap an' go shake 'er') obviously has the same theme.

> Oh, lady, have you a daughter fine?
> *Ch.* Slapandergosheka!
> Fit for a sailor that's crossed the Line?
> *Ch.* Slapandergosheka!

Unfortunately Miss Smith does not give the tune.

Probably the earliest song with this theme is of 1815 vintage:

> Three Prussian officers crossed the Rhine,
> *Ch.* Skiboo.
> (See R. Nettel, *Sing a Song of England*, London, 1954)

A later version of the late 1800s is:

> A little Dutch soldier crossed over the Rhine,
> *Ch.* Snapoo!
> Oh, a little Dutch soldier crossed over the Rhine,
> And he stopped at an inn to have some wine,
> *Ch.* Snapeeta, snapoota, filanda, gosheeta, fidam snapoo!

86

Miss Colcord seems to think this song was used as a shanty. It was sung by seamen even in recent times but, so far as I know, as a fo'c'sle song only. And of course the most recent song using this theme is that of the First World War:

> Oh, lady have you a daughter fine,
> Fit for a soldier just up from the Line?
> *Ch.* Inky pinky parley vous!

Miss Colcord in her second book, *Songs of the American Sailormen*, has given much space to the origin of this type of song.

OH, AYE, RIO

2. Oh, yes I have a daughter fine,
    Ch. Oh, aye, Rio!
   Oh, yes I have a daughter fine,
   Fit for a sailor that's crossed the Line.
       Ch. To me way, hay, ho, high, a long, long time ago!
       To me way, hay, ho, high, a long, long time ago!

3. But madam, dear madam, she is too young,
   But madam, dear madam, she is too young,
   She's never been courted by anyone.

4. Oh, sailor, oh, sailor, I'm not too young,
   Oh, sailor, oh, sailor, I'm not too young,
   I've just been kissed by the butcher's son, *etc.*

A shanty which had refrains similar to the final one of *Oh, Aye, Rio* was the halyard song *A Long Time Ago*. This was very popular in both English and American ships. Probably of American Negro origin, it became, by the nineties, the most-used halyard song of them all. Even the Germans and Scandinavians popularized versions in their own tongues. There exist an old minstrel song and a Negro

spiritual with this title but the tunes are not the same. Another
shore-song which may have some connection is:

> The little black bull came down the meadow,
> *Ch.* Hoosen Johnny, Hoosen Johnny.
> The little black bull came down the meadow,
> *Ch.* A long time ago.

According to C. Sandburg, this was often sung by the lawyers of
Illinois in the fifties while awaiting a court case.

The shanty sometimes was sung in lively fashion, other times
slow and melancholy, depending on the shantyman. Sometimes it
was used at the capstan and then a full chorus would be added
which was nothing more than a repeat of the two solos and refrains:

> A long, long time, an' a very long time,
> To me 'way hay, ho, high, ho.
> A long, long time, and a very long time,
> A long time ago.

The various patterns sung to this shanty are:

(1) *The 'Frisco Ship* (from an A.B. of the New Zealand tops'l schooner
   Huia);
(2) The *If* version (Captain Kihlberg, ex-Scots barque *Fasces*);
(3) The *Noah's Ark* version (Bosun Chenoweth, ex-*Mount Stewart*);
(4) A *Roll the Cotton Down* version (this version was very popular);
(5) A *Blow the Man Down* version (from the singing of Paddy
   Delaney);
(6) An *A-rovin'* version (mainly bawdy);
(7) A *Time for us to go* version; and
(8) A *China Clipper* version (from the singing of Jock Anderson).

A LONG TIME AGO (a)
Alternative title, *The 'Frisco Ship* or *In 'Frisco Bay*

O-ho, three ships they lay in Frisco Bay, Tim-me way, hay, ho, high
ho! Three ships they lay in Frisco Bay, Oh a long time a-go!

2. These smart Yankee packets lay out in the Bay,
   Ch. Timme *way*, hay, *ho*, high ho!
   All a-waiting a fair wind to get under way,
   Ch. Oh, a *long* time *ago*!

3. With all their poor sailors so weak an' so sad,
   They'd drunk all their limejuice, no more could be had.

4. With all their poor sailors so sick an' so sore,
   They'd scoffed all their whack an' they couldn't get more.

5. Oh, I sailed out of 'Frisco in a full riggèd ship,
   I sailed out o' 'Frisco in a full-riggèd ship.

6. Her masts wuz of silver an' her yards wuz of gold,
   Her masts wuz of silver an' her yards wuz of gold.

7. We wuz bound for New York with a cargo o' gold,
   Bound south 'round the Horn through the ice an' the cold.

8. In eighteen hundred and ninety-four,
   We shipped in a drogher bound for Singapore.

9. An' I fell in love with young Malay [Japanee] maid,
   She swiped all me money, an' then she did fade [before I wuz
   paid].

10. My ol' mum she wrote to me,
    She wrote to me to come home from sea.

11. Says she 'Me son, ye'll rue the day,
    When the girls have blown, lad, all yer pay
    [or When off to sea ye go away].'

12. She sent me some money, she sent me some clothes,
    But I spent all the money an' pawned all the clothes.

13. An' ever since then I have thought of her word,
    'Twas the finest advice that a man ever heard.

14. An' as soon as I gits me feet on shore,
    I'll ship as a bosun of a little rum store.

15. An' if ever I gits me feet on land,
    I'll ship as some young lady's fancyman.

16. Oh, a long, long time, an' a very long time,
    'Tis a very long time since I first made this rhyme.

The ships in the first and second verses are sometimes given in the
singular—'A ship she lay', etc., 'This smart Yankee packet', etc.
Taylor Harris gives a verse (after my verse 9):

> The banns they were read and the wedding day near,
> I hove up my anchor and home I did steer.[1]

A LONG TIME AGO (b)

1. A ship lay becalmed off Portland Bill,
   If she hasn't a fair wind she's layin' there still.

---

[1] *Six Sea Shanties*, Whitehead & Harris, Boosey & Co., Ltd., London, 1925.

2. There once wuz a family which lived on a hill,
   If they're not dead they're livin' there still.

3. There once wuz a sailor shipped in a balloon,
   An' if he's still floatin' he's now reached the moon.

4. There once wuz a farmer in Norfolk did dwell,
   If he went off an' died, oh, he's sure bound to hell.

5. There wuz an ol' woman that lived in a shoe,
   If she'd had ten brats more, oh, she'd have forty-two.

6. There wuz an ol' lady who lived in Dundee,
   If she hadn't been sick she'd have gone off to sea.

7. There wuz an ol' yokel in Sussex did dwell,
   He had an ol' wife an' he wished her in hell.

A LONG TIME AGO (c)

1. Three ships they lay in 'Frisco Bay,
   Three ships they lay in 'Frisco Bay.

2. An' one o' these packets wuz ol' Noah's Ark,
   All covered all over with hickory bark.

3. They filled up her seams with oakum an' pitch,
   Her sails wuz badly in need o' a stitch.

4. Her bow it wuz bluff an' her counter wuz round,
   Her knees wuz so thin, an' her timbers unsound.

5. Her fo'c'sle wuz low, an' her starn wuz too high,
   The hold for the animals never wuz dry.

6. Her pumps they wuz jammed and her fores'l wuz torn,
   She looked like an ol' Spanish galley-eye-orn.

7. Now this is the gangway the animals went down,
   An' this is the hold where they walk round an' round.

8. Ol' Noah of old he commanded this Ark,
   His cargo wuz animals out for a lark.

9. He boarded the animals, two of each kind,
   Birds, snakes, an' jiggy-bugs, he didn't mind.

10. The animals rolled up, oh, two by two,
    The elephant chasin' the kangaroo.

11. The bull an' the cow they started a row,
    The bull did his best to horn the cow.

12. Then Ol' Noah said with a flick o' his whip,
    'Stop this bloody row, or I'll scuttle the ship.'

13. An' the bull put his horns through the side o' the Ark,
    An' the little black doggie, he started to bark.

14. So Noah took the dog, put his nose in the hole,
    An' ever since then the dog's nose has been cold.

15. The animals came in three by three,
    The elephant ridin' the back o' the flea.

16. The animals came in four by four,
    Ol' Noah went mad an' he hollered for more.

17. The animals came in five by five,
    Some wuz half-dead, an' some half-alive.

18. The animals came in six by six,
    The hyena laughed at the monkey's tricks.

19. The monkey was dressed up in soger's clo'es;
    Where he got 'em from, God only knows.

20. The animals came in seven by seven,
    Sez the ant to the elephant, 'Who are yer shovin'?'

21. The animals came in eight by eight,
    A drunken big chimp an' a scabby big ape.

22. The animals came in nine by nine,
    The sea-lions havin' a bloomin' fine time.

23. The animals came in ten by ten,
    The Ark with a shriek blew her whistle then.

24. An' Noah while working at loading her stock,
    Had anchored the Ark with a bloody great rock.

25. Ol' Noah he then hove the gang-plank in,
    An' then the long voyage it sure did begin.

26. They hadn't the foggiest where they wuz at,
    Until they piled right up on ol' Ararat.

27. The ol' Ark with a bump landed high an' dry,
    And the bear give the turkey a sailor's goodbye.

28. I thought that I heard Ol' Noah say,
    Give one more pull lads, an' then belay!

A LONG TIME AGO (d)

1. I'll sing ye a song of the Blackball Line,
   That's the Line where ye can shine.

2. In the Blackball Line I served me time,
   That's the Line where I wasted me prime.

3. It's when a Blackballer hauls out of the dock,
   To see them poor 'Westers', how on deck they flock.

4. There's tinkers an' tailors, an' fakirs an' all,
They've all shipped as A.B.s aboard the Blackball.

5. It's fore tops'l halyards the Mate he will roar,
It's lay along Paddy, ye son-o-a-whore!

(See *Blow the Man Down* and *The Blackball Line.*)

A LONG TIME AGO (e)

1. In 'Frisco Town [Amsterdam] there lived a maid,
An' she wuz mistress of her trade.

2. One night I crept from my abode,
To meet this fair maid down the road.

3. I placed my arm around her waist,
Sez she, 'Young man yer in great haste.'

4. I put me hand upon her knee,
Sez she, 'Young man yer rather free,' *etc.*

(See *A-rovin'*.)

A LONG TIME AGO (f)

1. Old Bully John from Baltimore,
Old Bully John from the Eastern Shore.

2. Old Bully John I knew him well,
But now he's dead an' gone to hell.

3. A bully on land an' a bucko at sea,
Old Bully John wuz the boy for me, *etc.*

(See *A Hundred Years Ago.*)

A LONG TIME AGO (g)

1. There wuz an old lady in Greenock did dwell,
She had three fine sons an' their story I'll tell.

2. One was a sailor an' one was a Mate,
The third got his Master's a little bit late.

3. He shipped as the Master of a big clipper ship,
An' out to far China he made a smart trip.

4. The ship he commanded was no ruddy [bulgin'] Ark,
But a dandy fine clipper as fast as a shark.

5. When he reached far Foochow oh he there met his fate,
He found him a Chink gal to serve him as mate.

6. He spliced this young Chink gal with a pigtail so long,
But later he wished he had not met Miss Fong.

7. Oh, she wore the trousers an' he wore the skirt,
   He was down on his luck an' his pride it was hurt.

8. The passage to England was a hell o' a show,
   One hundred an' eighteen long days for to go.

9. Oh he roused up his Chink wife an' cursed loud an' long,
   Oh, you are the bastard that's caused all this wrong.

10. 'You're a bloody big Jonah, yer a hoodoo to me,
    I've had nought but bad luck since ye came to sea.'

11. But when he reached London, the owners did say,
    'You've made a smart passage you've earnt your pay-day.'

12. So he kissed his young Chink wife, gave rum to the crowd,
    The hands gave a cheer, boys, so strong an' so loud.

13. An' this is the end of my salty story,
    Just think o' the luck o' the heathen Chinee.

Tayluer, Doerflinger's shantyman, gives a rather broken-down version of this, and names the ship concerned as *Cutty Sark*, but I rather think this is shantyman's licence, as no known shanties sing about *Cutty Sark*, or in fact any named clipper of the Tea Trade. In fact the Tea Trade and the Wool Trade—both using clipper ships—produced no shanties, strangely enough, and very few shanties refer to these Trades, their ships, or their men.

Cecil Sharp[1] gives three versions of this halyard song, one much like mine, one crossed with *Sally Brown* and one which I give here:

A-way down south where I was born; To my way-ay-day, ha! a-way down south where I was born, A long time a-go, 'Twas a long, long time and a very long time, a long time a-go.

The last five bars of this version are unusual and make it a possible capstan shanty. Here is a very fine and rather different tune given in the *Shell Book of Shanties*:

[1] *Journal* of the Folk Song Society.

93

a long, long time and a long time a-go, To me way, hay, o - hi - o! a

long, long time and a long time a-go, a long time a - go!

(By permission, E. H. Freeman, Ltd., Brighton)

Another well-known work-song is *Sacramento*. This shanty was always sung at the capstan and especially when raising the 'mud-hook'. Its origin has been the cause of many controversies. Naturally, on account of its tune, form, and 'Hoodah' or 'Doodah' chorus, it has been associated with Stephen Foster's *Camptown Races*. C. F. Smith seems to think that if the shanty came after the minstrel ditty is is curious that a new set of words should have been fitted to the chorus of *Camptown Races* while it was still a new song.

Sacramento came into being aboard the great ships *Sea Witch*, *Flying Cloud*, *Romance of the Seas*, etc., at the time of the California Gold Rush (1849). Now Foster's song *Camptown Races* was made copyright in February 1850, but it was not published until 1856. Did Foster copy his song from the shanty or did the seamen take his ditty and alter it to suit themselves, or did both songs, as Sampson seems to think, have a common Negro origin? It is difficult to say. Colcord definitely states that this shanty is the 'nigger minstrel' song *Camptown Races*. I feel we have insufficient evidence to make such a statement. Terry, although he doesn't say so outright, seems to think that the shanty came first.

One big question is—was the shanty sung in 1849 or did it come into being in 1850? The answer if known would settle the matter. Doerflinger seems to think that seamen took Foster's verses and their 'hoodahs' and added a new grand chorus, that of the following gold rush song (introduced by the Hutchison family, a well-known concert troupe).

CALIFORNIA

When formed our band, we are all well-manned, To journey a-far to the promised land, The gold-en ore is rich in store, on the banks of the Sac-ra-men-to shore, Then ho, boys, ho, To Cal-i-for-nia go, There's plenty of gold in the world I'm told, On the banks of the Sac-ra-men-to shore.

(From *The American Songbag*, compiled by Carl Sandburg, published by Harcourt, Brace & Co., N.Y.)

Howard, the biographer of Stephen Foster, states that the tune of the chorus of *Camptown Races* is that of the English ballad *Ten Thousand Miles Away*. There is a faint resemblance, but this suggests to my mind that *seamen* took the tune of this old sea song—which was often used as a shanty—and added its chorus to some existing Negro song, the resultant mixture being *Sacramento*, from which Foster on hearing it sung at the time of the '49 Gold Rush derived his *Camptown Races*. Maybe, too, the Hutchison family took the words of their song *California* from those of the chorus of the sailor shanty about the same time. But this, of course, is all supposition and we really don't know which came first, the chicken or the egg. According to Doerflinger, O. T. Howe relates in *Argonauts of '49* that when the ship *La Grange* crowded with goldseekers left Salem for 'Frisco everybody on board joined in the singing of 'Then ho! Brothers ho!', but could this not have been an early version of the shanty?

The chorus variants of this shanty are many. An American version given to me by Arthur Spencer runs:

> Blow, boys, blow, for Californ-eye-O!
> There's plenty of Spicks in that land o' sticks,
> On the banks o' Sacramento.

A Rabelaisian version, slightly camouflaged, popular in British ships was:

> Blow, boys, blow, for Californi-O,
> There's plenty o' grass, to wipe yer moustache,
> On the banks of the Sacramento.

95

F. W. Wallace's Gloucester fisherman's version runs:

> Blow, boys, blow, blow down to old Increau,
> There's lots o' gold, so I've bin told,
> On the banks o' the Bacalhao!

L. A. Smith gives:

> Steer, boys, steer, for Californ-i-o!

Some collectors give 'Blow, *bullies*, blow!' and 'Blow, me lads, high ho!' In the refrains of the verse the words 'hoodah' and 'doodah' are both to be found, although seamen preferred the heavily aspirated 'hoodah' to the latter.

My first version is a bawdy version common in British ships. The last line of verses 2, 4, and 7 have been camouflaged, and verse 3 has been composed by the writer to keep the theme; of course the real accident in this song was 'damage sustained whilst on a voyage to Cytherea', to quote Bone!

SACRAMENTO (a)

Alternative titles, *Banks of the Sacramento, Californi-O, Blow, boys, blow for Californi-O*

As I wuz rol-lin' down the Strand, Hoo-dah! Hoo-dah! I met two fair-ies hand in hand, Hoo-dah, hoo-dah day! Blow, boys, blow! For Cal-i-forn-eye-O! There's plen-ty o' gold, so I've bin told on the banks o' the Sac-ra-men-to!

2. I chose the one with the curly locks,
 Ch. Hoodah! Hoodah!
 She let me chase her o'er the rocks,
 Ch. Hoodah, hoodah, day!
 Full Chorus. Blow boys, blow!
 For Californ-eye-O!
 There's plenty o' gold so I've bin told,
 On the banks o' the Sacramento.

3. I chased her high, I chased her low,
 I fell down an' broke me toe.

4. Off to the doctor I did go,
   An' I showed him my big toe.

5. In came the doctor with a bloomin' big lance,
   'Now, young sailor, I'll make you dance!'

6. In came the nurse with a mustard poultice,
   Banged it on, but I took no notice.

7. Now I'm well and free from pain,
   I'll never court flash gals again.

SACRAMENTO (b)

This version is a rather more respectable form of the preceding one.

1. Oh, as I was walkin' down the street [on the quay],
   A charmin' gal I chanct to meet [see].

2. The gal was fair an' sweet to view,
   Her hair so brown an' her eyes so blue [her lips were red, so sweet and new].

3. I raised me hat an' said 'How do?',
   Sez she, 'Quite well, no thanks to you' [She bowed an' said, 'Quite well, thank you'].

4. I asked her if she'd take a trip [then to come with me],
   A-down the docks to see my ship [my ship to see].

5. She quickly answered, 'Oh, dear, no.
   I thank you but I cannot go.

6. 'My love is young, my love is true,
   I wouldn't leave my love for you.'

7. So quickly then I strode away,
   I'd not another word to say [Although with her I longed to stay].

8. An' as I bade this gal adieu,
   I said that gals like her were few.

The most popular version was the Cape Horn one. It was probably the original one, and the words could be sung to either tune, or to a mixture of both tunes, depending on the number of syllables in the verses.

SACRAMENTO (c)

Oh a-round Cape Horn we are bound for to go, To me hoo-dah, To me hoo-dah! A-round Cape Horn through the sleet an' the snow, To me hoo-dah, hoo-dah day! Blow, boys, blow, for Cal-i-forn-eye O! There's plenty o' gold so I've bin told, On the banks of the Sac-ra-men-to!

2. Oh around the Horn with a mainskys'l set,
   Around Cape Horn an' we're all wringin' wet.

3. Oh, around Cape Horn in the month o' May,
   Oh, around Cape Horn is a very long way.

4. Them Dago gals we do adore,
   They all drink vino an' ask for more.

5. Them Spanish gals ain't got no combs,
   They comb their locks with tunny-fish bones.

6. To the Sacramento we're bound away,
   To the Sacramento's a hell o' a way.

7. We're the buckos for to make 'er go,
   All the way to the Sacramento.

8. We're the bullies for to kick her through,
   Roll down the hill with a hullabaloo.

9. Starvation an' ease in a Yankee ship,
   We're the bullies for to make 'er rip.

10. Santander Jim is a mate from hell,
    With fists o' iron an' feet as well.

11. Breast yer bars an' bend yer backs,
    Heave an' make yer spare ribs crack.

12. Round the Horn an' up to the Line,
    We're the bullies for to make 'er shine

13. We'll crack it on, on a big skiyoot,
    Ol' Bully Jim is a bloody big brute.

98

14. Oh, a bully ship wid a bully crew,
    But the mate is a bastard through an' through.

15. Ninety days to 'Frisco Bay,
    Ninety days is damn good pay.

16. Oh, them wuz the days of the good ol' times,
    Back in the days of the Forty-nine.

17. Sing an' heave an' heave an' sing,
    Heave an' make them handspikes spring.

18. An' I wish to God I'd niver bin born,
    To go a-ramblin' round Cape Horn.

When the wool clippers made their appearance this shanty had a face lift and although many of the foregoing verses were sung, new ones singing of the Australian Trade were added. This Blackball line is not the Western Ocean Packet Ship one but a line of colonial clippers.

> In the Blackball Line I served me time,
> (*Repeat*)
>
> From Limehouse Docks to Sydney Heads,
> (*Repeat*)
>
> We wuz never more than seventy days,
> (*Repeat*)
>
> An' home again in eighty days,
> (*Repeat*), *etc.*

And of course the verses of *Camptown Races* were also sung:

SACRAMENTO (d)

1. Camptown ladies sing this song,
   Camptown race-track's five miles long.

2. Go down dar wid me hat caved in,
   Come back home with me pockets full o' tin.

3. De long-tailed filly an' de big black hoss,
   Dey fly de track an' dey both cut across.

4. De blind hoss stickin' in a big mud hole,
   Can't touch bottom wid a ten-foot pole.

5. Ol' muley cow come out on de track,
   De bob he fling her ober his back.

6. Den fly along like a railroad car,
   Runnin' a race wid a shootin' star.

7. De sorrel hoss he's got a cough,
   An' his rider's drunk in de ol' hay-loft.

8. Dere's fourteen hosses in dis race,
   Ah'm snug in de saddle an' got a good brace.

9. De bobtail hoss she cain't be beat,
   Runnin' around in a two-mile heat.

10. Ah put me money on de bob-tail nag,
    Somebody bet on de one-eyed lag.

11. I win me money on de bobtail nag,
    An' carry it home in de ol' tow-bag.

Some shantymen would sing the 'Milkmaid' theme to *Sacramento*, the same as was sung to *Blow the Man Down* and *Rio*. In Doerflinger's first version of this shanty the singer[1] improvises in true sailor fashion, singing, in repeated solos, of the ship's passage round the Horn, through the Trades, Doldrums, etc., and also of the type of canvas set to suit the zone through which she is passing. In his second version the singer has stanzas from the *Dead Horse* shanty.[2] Terry (and some other 'purists') tend to look upon this purloining of the words of other shanties as the work of old, ignorant sailors whose memories have gone. This of course is ridiculous. Sharp, Doerflinger, and others have accepted this transferring of the words of one shanty to the tune of another, and of course all sailormen of the days of sail *know* it to be true. It was the rule and not the rare exception. Strangely enough, Terry, after condemning this sort of thing, gives the words of *Boney* to his *Santiana*, and of *Sally Brown* to his *Sacramento*!

Other stanzas sometimes met with are:

I came to a river an' I couldn't get across,
So I jumped upon a nigger 'cos I thought he was a horse.

We came to the land where the cocktails flow.

Both of these, of course, are from nigger minstrelsy.

Patterson's version is like all Patterson's shanties, unusual. Since he has not given the music with his shanties it is difficult to see how they were sung. In almost every shanty he inserts short refrains

---

[1] Captain Patrick Tayleur, N.Y.
[2] Ritchard Maitland, Sailors' Snug Harbor.

where normally no refrain existed. And he calls his version of *Sacramento* a 'hauling song'!

> Now my lads, get yer beds and lie down,
>   *Ch.* With a hoodah!
> Now my lads, get yer beds and lie down,
>   *Ch.* With a hoodah, hoodah day!
> Blow, boys, blow, for Californi-o,
>   *Ch.* With a hoodah!
> There's plenty of gold, so I've been told,
>   *Ch.* On the banks of Sacramento!

> (From *The Sea's Anthology*, J. E. Patterson, published by
> W. Heinemann Ltd., London, 1913)

Another capstan shanty of the Gold Rush Period is *Bound to California* of which C. F. Smith has found but a fragment. Her informant, Captain J. L. Vivian Millet, remembers hearing it sung aboard a big ship weighing anchor in Algoa Bay, but he could only give her the chorus.

BOUND TO CALIFORNIA

(C. Fox Smith, *A Book of Shanties*, Methuen & Co., Ltd., London, 1927)

Whether the hauling song *Goodbye, My Love, Goodbye* has any connection with the preceding shanty is doubtful. Tozer and Colcord give a version, the former giving a set of very sentimental verses which I feel sure have been made up. C. F. Smith sees in it a resemblance to *Shallow Brown*. It is probably a Negro shanty and like most Negro shanties after the first three or four regulation verses relied entirely on improvisation. Sly skits at the ability of the afterguard as seamen, kicks at having to work in the dog-watches, or disparaging remarks about the ship, owners, and grub were the usual insertions produced by a versatile shantyman.

GOODBYE, MY LOVE, GOODBYE

2. I'll leave you my half-pay, Sue,
   Ch. Good*bye* my love good*bye*!
   White-stocking Day soon will be due.
   Ch. Good*bye* my love good*bye*!

3. Have a drink on me, my dearie,
   For waiting's mighty weary.

4. We're bound away to 'Frisco,
   Oh, cut her strings an' let 'er go!

Another hauling song resembling this latter somewhat is *Hurrah, Sing Fare Ye Well!* Whall calls it *O Fare Ye Well, My Bonnie Young Girl.* Sampson's tune is a little different from the usual one, and Whall says it was a favourite in London ships. As in the previous shanty, after a few verses the shantyman would improvise, since there was no regular story as a rule. My version, with perhaps a few more regular verses than usual, I obtained from an old Liverpool seaman now dead. Normally there was one pull in the refrain on the second syllable of 'Hurrah'.

HURRAH, SING FARE YE WELL
Alternative titles, *Goodbye, Sing Fare You Well, Fare Ye Well, My Bonnie Young Girl*

2. We're bound away to Callyo,
    Ch. Hu*rrah* sing fare ye well!
  Oh, fare ye well, me Liverpool gal,
    Ch. Hu*rrah* sing fare ye well!

3. I may come back to ye some day,
   With a spankin' big fat pay-day.

4. But when we get to Callyo,
   I'll git me a nice bit o' Dago.

5. As I walked out one mornin' fair,
   I met a puta standin' there.

6. She winked at me I do declare,
   Black as night was her raven hair.

7. She was a Spanish beauty bold.
   Her name was Carmen, so I'm told.

8. Oh, fare ye well, we're bound away,
   We're bound away this sailing day.

Sampson gives 'Hobson's Bay', a common anchorage for ships in the Australian Trade. The verses of *Handy, Me Boys* were ideally suited for fitting to this sort of shanty when the regulation pattern ran out. Sometimes, instead of 'Hurrah' or 'Hooraw', the word 'Goodbye' was sung.

This brings us to the most popular homeward-bound shanty of them all—with, perhaps, the exception of *Rolling Home*—*Goodbye, Fare-ye-well*. This was sung at the windlass or capstan when raising the anchor, and I know of four versions common to seamen the world over. The first version I learnt from an A.B. known as 'Archie', ex New Zealand brigantine *Aratapu*.

(a) Usual homeward-bound sentiments;
(b) Verses taken from the old forebitter *Homeward Bound*;
(c) The 'Milkmaid' (see *Blow the Man Down*);
(d) Verses from *The Dreadnaught*.

GOODBYE, FARE-YE-WELL (a)
Alternative title, *Homeward Bound*

103

GOODBYE, FARE-YE-WELL

We're homeward bound to Liverpool Town,
    Ch. Goodbye, fare-ye-well, goodbye, fare-ye-well!
Where them judies they will come down,
    Ch. Horraw, me boys, we're homeward bound!

3. An' when we gits to the Wallasey Gates,
Sally an' Polly for their flash men do wait.

4. An' one to the other ye'll hear them say,
Here comes Johnny with his fourteen months' pay!

5. Them gals there on Lime Street we soon hope to meet,
Soon we'll be a-rollin' both sides o' the street.

6. We'll meet these fly gals an' we'll ring the ol' bell,
With them judies we'll meet there we'll raise merry hell.

7. I'll tell me old mammy when I gets back home,
The gals there on Lime Street won't leave me alone.

8. We're homeward bound to the gals o' the town,
Stamp up me bullies an' heave it around.

9. An' when we gits home, boys, oh won't we fly round,
We'll heave up the anchor to this bully sound.

10. We're a fine flashy packet an' bound for to go,
With the gals on the towrope we cannot say no!

11. We're all homeward bound for the old backyard,
Then heave, me bullies, we're all bound homeward.

12. I wrote to my Kitty, she sez she is well,
She rooms at the *Astor* and dines at the *Bell*.

13. Heave with a will, boys, oh, heave long an' strong,
Sing a good chorus for 'tis a good song.

14. We're homeward bound, we'll have yiz to know,
An' over the water to England must go!

Other verses sometimes sung are:

Oh, the anchor we'll weigh and the sails we will set,
The gals we are leaving we'll never forget.

An' when we git to the ould Mersey Bar,
The gulls [girls]'ll be flockin' from near an' from far.

We're homeward bound don't ye hear the Mate say.
Hook on the ol' catfall an' run her away.

We'll spend all our money in one week a shore,
An' then pack our bags—go to sea for some more.

We're homeward bound don't ye hear the sound?
Man the good capstan an' breast [run] 'er around.

We're homeward bound an' the wind's blowin' fair,
Our friends will be waiting to spend our pay-day.

We're homeward bound for home, sweet, home,
Our sails are set, the wind has come.

GOODBYE, FARE-YE-WELL (b)

1. We're homeward bound I heard them say,
   We're homeward bound to Liverpool Bay.

2. We're homeward bound to Liverpool Town,
   Where them gals they will come down.

3. An' when we gits to the Salthouse Dock,
   Them pretty young gals on the pierhead will flock.

4. An' one to the other ye'll hear them say,
   Here comes Johnny with his three years' pay.

5. Then we haul to the *Bull an' the Bell*,
   Where good liquor they do sell.

6. In comes the landlord with a smile,
   Saying, 'Drink up, lads, while it's worth yer while!'

7. But when the money's all spent an' gone,
   Not even a cent for to call yer own,

8. In comes the landlord with a hell o' a frown,
   It's 'Get up, Jack—let John sit down.'

9. Then poor ol' Jack must understand,
   There's ships in port all wanting hands.

10. An' he'll pack up his sea-chest and get under way,
    The gals he has left they can take his half-pay.

11. We're homeward bound don't ye hear the Mate say?
    We're homeward bound—the anchor's aweigh!

GOODBYE, FARE-YE-WELL (c)

1. Oh, as I wuz a-rollin' down Ratcliffe Highway,
   A pretty young maiden I chanct for to see.

2. Oh, where are ye goin' to, my pretty maid?
   'I'm goin' a milkin', sir,' she said.
   (For the other verses, see *Blow the Man Down*.)

At this point I must disagree with collectors and writers who hold
a theory that homeward-bound songs were never debased by Sailor
John. Here is the exception to this theory (the 'Milkmaid' version

was entirely obscene) and there are many others. *Rolling Home* was perhaps the one and only exception.

GOODBYE, FARE-YE-WELL (d)

1. 'Tis of a flash packet—a packet o' fame,
   She's a rorty flash packet an' the *Dreadnaught*'s her name.

2. She's bound to the west'ard where the salty winds blow,
   Bound away in the *Dreadnaught* to the west'ard we'll go.

3. It's now we are leavin' the sweet Salthouse Dock,
   Where the boys an' the girls on the Pierhead do flock.

4. They give three loud cheers while the tears freely flow,
   Bound away in the *Dreadnaught* to the west'ard we'll go.

5. It's now we are sailin' on the wild Irish shore,
   Our passengers all sick, and our new mates all sore.

6. Oh, it's now we've arrived on the Banks o' Newf'n'land,
   Where the bottom's all fishes an' fine yeller sand.

7. Where the fishes they sing as they swim to an' fro,
   She's a Liverpool packet—O Lord let 'er go!

8. Now we're a-runnin' down the Long Island shore,
   Where the Pilot will board us as he's done oft before.

9. Then back yer main tops'l, raise yer main tack also,
   Bound away to the west'ard in the *Dreadnaught* we go.

10. It's now we've arrived in ol' New York once more,
    Where I'll see my dear Sal, oh, the gal I adore.

11. I'll call for strong liquors an' married we'll be,
    Here's a health to the *Dreadnaught* where'er she may be.

12. Here's a health to her Ol' Man an' officers too,
    Here's a health to the *Dreadnaught* an' all her bold crew.

13. This song was composed when the watch went below,
    Bound away in the *Dreadnaught*, to the west'ard we'll go!

Before we pass on to the next shanty I must make mention of the fact that the homeward-bound song *Goodbye, Fare-ye-well* was invariably heard at its best in South American ports like Iquique, where the saltpetre and nitrate traders would lie, often as many as two hundred ships at a time, awaiting or loading their cargoes. When at last a ship was ready to sail crews of the other ships in port would, as Captain F. Shaw relates in his book *Splendour of the Seas*, board the homeward-bounder to help raise the anchor and swell the song. 'That was when a capstan shanty was really sung . . . as many as two hundred voices chorusing heartily.' A sight and sound now gone for ever . . . ah me!

We've had *Hurrah, Sing Fare-ye-well* and *Hurrah, Me Boys We're Homeward Bound!*, and now we have *Hurrah for the Blackball Line*, followed by *Hooraw an' Up She Rises!*

These shanties with the word 'Hurrah', 'Hooray', or 'Hooraw' in the refrain or chorus were known to seamen as 'hooraw choruses' and it was very often said that 'our wild hooraw chorus soon raised the mudhook (or hoisted the tops'l)'. It is a perfect expression—'our wild hooraw chorus'—much better than 'shanty' or 'chanty' or any other title that one could think of. It speaks of the Pitch o' the Horn, of blowing great guns, of skinning a sail in a black nor'-easter's roar, of the savage haul or heave that beat Old Boreas every time. . . .

And so our next 'hooraw chorus', and one of the best of the bunch, is:

HOORAW FOR THE BLACKBALL LINE

In the Black-ball Line I served me time, To me way, hay, hoo. ro, yah! In the Black-ball Line I served me time, Hoo-raw for the Black-ball Line!

2. Blackball ships are good an' true [Blackball ships they make good time],
   To me way, hay, hoo, ro, yah!
   They are the ships for me an' you [Wid clean long runs an' entrance fine],
   Ch. Hooraw for the Blackball Line!

3. That's the Line where ye can shine [I've sailed in the Line full many a time],
   That's the Line where I wasted me prime.

4. If yer wish to find a real goldmine,
   Just take a trip on a Blackball ship [in the Blackball Line].

5. Just take a trip to Liverpool,
   To Liverpool that Yankee school [packet school].

6. Yankee sailors ye'll see there,
   With red-topped boots an' short-cut hair.

7. There's Liverpool Pat with his tarpaulin hat,
   An' Paddy Magee the Packet Rat.

8. There was once a Blackball ship,
   That fourteen knots an hour could slip.

9. They'll carry ye along through the ice an' snow,
   They'll take ye where the winds don't blow.

10. I've seen the Line both rise an' shine,
    An' crossed the line in 'em many a time.

11. Oh, drink a health to the Blackball Line,
    Their ships are stout an' their men are fine.

The Blackball Line of packet ships started in 1816, an American line running between New York and Liverpool. The ships were small, of about 300 to 400 tons, until 1850, when larger ships, over a thousand tons, were added to the fleet. They ran to an almost regular timetable across the Western Ocean, splendid ships for the early passengers to America, but hell for the men who worked them under the hard-case officers in command. Their seamen were known as 'packet rats', and a tough lot they were, but excellent seamen one and all, as were their bucko afterguards.

I learnt my version of this old song from an ancient seaman who had sailed in the Blackball Line. His name was Paddy Delaney, and he was an old man when I was shipmates with him in my early days at sea. He always stated that this shanty was sung at the capstan or windlass, and I note that the majority of collectors give it as heaving and not hauling. Miss Colcord, however, includes it in her chapter on halyard shanties. When one looks at the *shape* of this shanty it seems quite feasible that it may have been used at times as a halyard song. I don't agree with the type of collector who rigidly lists a shanty under a certain job of work and never allows that it may have been used for another task. Miss Colcord—a woman, but a regular seaman if ever there was one—is not so rigid in her cataloguing and states that halyard shanties were often used at pumps, as were capstan songs, and that sometimes they were used at the capstan to liven things up a bit. With all this I heartily agree.

Our next 'hooraw chorus' is the now well-known *Drunken Sailor*. This is a typical example of the stamp-'n'-go song or walkaway or runaway shanty, and was the only type of work-song allowed in the King's Navee. It was popular in ships with big crews when at halyards; the crowd would seize the fall and stamp the sail up. Sometimes when hauling a heavy boat up the falls would be 'married' and both hauled on at the same time as the hands stamped away singing this rousing tune. In later days, in bigger ships with smaller crews, it was mainly used at braces when 'going about' or to hand aloft a light sail such as a stays'l—in this latter case it would then be used as a hand-over-hand song. The chorus without any verses I have often used in fore-'n'-afters as a chant to send aloft a jib or stays'l or even a gaff-sail. Fleetwood Stileman told Sharp that he often used the chorus to tramp up a yard at the beginning and easier part of the operation of setting a tops'l.

It was one of the very few shanties to be sung in quick time. Occasionally it was sung in unison, verses and choruses. Normally only two or three verses were used, but there were many more, some of them obscene and even sacrilegious, the Virgin Mary being referred to in one version.

It is a very old shanty, having been sung in the Indiamen of the John Company. Olmstead gives a version with its tune in his book *Incidents of a Whaling Voyage* (1839) differing very little from the modern accepted one.

The air is from a traditional Irish dance, as well as a march tune. The word 'early' was always pronounced 'earl-eye'. Sailormen liked this sound, as can be seen from his pronunciation of 'California' in *Sacramento*—'Californ-eye-O'.

Normally it started with the chorus, and it was usual to repeat the words of the first line three times, the ''Way hay' being nothing more than a savage yell hard to put in print. Some collectors give 'Hooray' or ''Way aye yah'.

DRUNKEN SAILOR (a)
Alternative title, *Hooray an' up she rises*

2. Put him in the long-boat till he gets sober. (*Three times*)
   Ch. 'Way-hay, etc.

3. Keep him there an' make him bale her. (*Three times*)

4. Trice him up in a runnin' bowline.

5. Tie him to the taffrail when she's yard-arm under.

6. Put him in the scuppers with a hose-pipe on him.

7. Take him an' shake 'im, an' try an' wake 'im.

8. Give him a dose o' salt an' water.

9. Give him a taste o' the bosun's rope-end.

10. Stick on his back a mustard plaster.

11. What'll we do with a Limejuice Skipper?

12. Soak him in oil till he sprouts a flipper.

13. Scrape the hair off his chest with a hoop-iron razor.

14. What shall we do with a drunken soldier?

15. Put him in the guard [barrack] room till he gets sober.

16. What shall we do with the Queen o' Sheba?

Terry is the only collector who gives this stamp-'n'-go song as being used at windlass and capstan.

Harlow in his *Making of a Sailor* calls it a hand-over-hand shanty and gives non-rhyming lines about what to do with a drunken chief mate, steward, 'doctor' (cook), boy, etc., with alternate stanzas singing of their punishments.

Trying to call to mind other shanties with the word 'Hurrah' prominent in them I have just remembered that fine old capstan song *The Girls o' Dublin Town*, or, as it was sometimes called *The Harp without the Crown* or *The Shenandoah*. Miss Colcord gives it as a forebitter or *Come-all-ye* and she says it was sung to a tune almost the same as that of *The Banks of Newf'n'land*. However, the version I give here is a *shanty*, and a very popular one it was too, especially with Liverpool Jacks. The tune of the verse is similar to that of the *Wearing o' the Green*, but the chorus bears a marked resemblance to the American Civil War march *The Bonnie Blue Flag*:

Hurrah! Hurrah! For our civil rights, hurrah!
Hurrah for the bonnie blue flag that bears a single star!

a resuscitated version of which has been heard over the radio in recent years as *The Bonnie Blue Gal*. It seems as though the seaman borrowed from the Texan song, but then again both march and shanty may have stemmed from a common Irish source. *The Harp without the Crown* is a phrase hearkening back to rebellious times in Ould Ireland. Sometimes 'Limerick' was sung instead of 'Dublin', or so my old shipmate Paddy Delaney, ex-Blackball Line, told me. He gave me both versions. In the first version sometimes two of my stanzas were sung before the chorus. This is the form Miss Colcord gives. According to her, Captain Jim Murphy of the *Shenandoah*, in

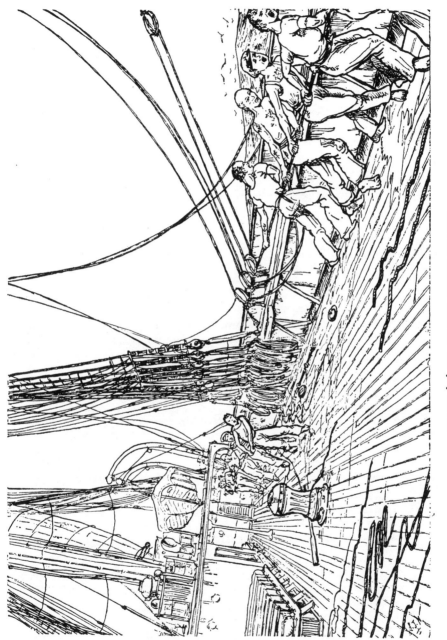

STAMP-'N'-GO AT THE AFTER BRACES
'Way-hay an' up she rises!' (Runaway Chorus)

actual fact, flew the Irish flag beneath the American one aboard his ship. I fail to understand why such a popular capstan shanty as this was should have been omitted from all collections. It must have been popular in Yankee ships (with Irish crews) as well as aboard Liverpool ones.

THE GALS O' DUBLIN TOWN (a)

Alternative titles, *The Harp without the Crown, The Shenandoah*

2. An' when he gazes on that land, that town of high renown,
   Oh, it's break away the green burgee and the Harp without the Crown.
   Ch. Hurrah! Hurrah! for the gals o' Dub-a-lin Town,
   Hurrah for the bonnie green flag an' the Harp without the Crown!

3. 'Twas on the seventeenth o' March, we arrived in New York Bay,
   Our Capen bein' an Irishman must celebrate the day.

4. With the Stars an' Stripes 'way high aloft, an' flutterin' all around,
   But underneath his monkey-gaff flew the Harp without the Crown.

5. Now we're bound for 'Frisco, boys, an' things is runnin' wild,
   The officers an' men dead drunk, around the decks they pile.

6. But by termorrer mornin', boys, we'll work widout a frown,
   For on board the saucy *Shenandoah* flies the Harp without the Crown!

THE GALS O' DUBLIN TOWN (b)

1. Sometimes we're bound for Liverpool, sometimes we're bound for France,
   But now we're bound to Dublin Town to give the gals a chance.
   Ch. Hurrah, Hurrah, *etc.*

2. Sometimes we're bound for furrin' parts, sometimes we're bound for home,
   A Johnny's always at his best wherever he may roam.

3. Sometimes the weather's fine an' fair, sometimes it's darn well foul,
   Sometimes it blows a Cape 'Orn gale that freezes up yer soul.

4. Sometimes we work as hard as hell, sometimes our grub it stinks,
   Enough to make a sojer curse, or make a bishop blink.

5. Sometimes we wisht we'd niver jined, sometimes we'd like to be
   A-drinkin' in a pub, me bhoys, a gal sat on each knee.

6. Sometimes we are a happy crowd, sometimes we'll sing a song,
   Sometimes we wish we'd niver bin born, but we do not grouse for long.

7. An' when the voyage is all done, an' we go away on shore,
   We'll spend our money on the gals, 'n' go to sea for more!

PART TWO

*Runaway Choruses; Young
Things and their Mammies;
the Roll Family; Rolling Rivers
and Rolling Homes and Rolling
Kings; Fishes; the Blow Family; Pigs
—Human and Otherwise; the Ranzo Group*

*L*ET us now go back to the walkaway or stamp-'n'-go
songs. We'll take as our first the famous *Hieland
Laddie*. It is based on an old Scottish march and dance
tune and was very popular both as a walkaway and
capstan song in the old Dundee whalers and according
to Davis & Tozer it was also used at halyards, without the final
grand chorus. It is of fair age; Nordoff mentions it as having been
used by the cotton stowers of Mobile Bay (in the thirties and forties
of the last century). He gives it without the grand chorus (like Davis
& Tozer) and his refrain runs 'Bonnie laddie, Highland laddie!'

HIELAND LADDIE (a)

There was a lad-die came from Scot-land, Hie-land lad-die! Bon-nie lad-die! Bon-nie lad-die

from fair Scot-land, The bon-nie Hie-land lad-die O! Way, hay an' a-way we go! Hie-land lad-die,

bon-nie lad-die! Way, hay, an' a-way we go! The bon-nie Hie-land lad-die O!

2. Where have ye been all the day?
   Hieland laddie! Bonnie laddie!
      Ch. Where have ye been all the day?
         Me bonnie Hieland laddie O! [*or* A-huntin' Hieland laddie!]
       Full Chorus. Way hay an' away we go!
           Hieland laddie, bonnie laddie!
           Way hay an' away we go!
           Me bonnie Hieland laddie O![*or* A-huntin' Hie-
           land laddie!]

3. I did not see ye doon the glen,
   Hieland, *etc.*
   I did not see ye near the burn,
     Me bonnie, *etc.*

4. 'Nay, I wuz no doon the glen,
   Nay I wuz no near the burn.

5. But I went to seek a road to fortune,
   Thought I'd find a road to fortune.

6. I joined a ship an' went a-sailin',
   Sailed far north an' went a-whalin'.

7. Shipped far north on a Dundee whaler,
   Shipped far north as a whalin' sailor.

8. Bound away to Iceland cold,
   Found much ice but not much gold.

9. Greenland is a cold country,
   Not the place for you and me.

10. Thought it was a way to fortune,
    But whalin's not the road to fortune.

11. Wisht meself in Bonnie Scotland,
    Back agen in Bonnie Scotland.

12. We caught some whales an' boiled their blubber,
    Oil an' fat choked every scupper.

13. We'll soon be homeward bound to Scotland,
    Homeward bound to Bonnie Scotland.

14. I'll be glad when I get hame,
    I'll give up this whalin' game.

15. Oh, Hieland Laddie went a-sailin',
    Oh, Hieland Laddie went a-whalin'.

I learnt the above version from Bosun Chenoworth who had
sailed for years in the hard-bitten whaling ships of Dundee. With so

many verses this was obviously the capstan version—when used for stamp-'n'-go normally the whole song would be sung in unison and only half the number of verses needed.

The following version when sung with the full chorus was used by the timber drogher's crews at the capstan when working cargo, heaving in and out through the great bow ports cumbersome logs, in the timber ports of Canada and nor'-east America. When sung without the grand chorus it was used at halyards or, as Nordhoff shows, at the 'screws' used to ram tight bales of cotton down the holds of the Cotton Traders.

HIELAND LADDIE (b)

(Same tune as (a))

1. Wuz ye ever in Quebec,
    Ch. Hieland Laddie, bonnie laddie!
   Launching timber on the deck?
    Ch. Me bonnie Hieland Laddie O!
       Way-ay, an' away we go,
       Hieland Laddie, Bonnie Laddie!
       Way-ay, heels an' toes, me bonnie Hieland Laddie O!

2. Wuz ye ever in Mobile Bay,
   Screwin' cotton on a summer's day?

3. Wuz ye ever off Cape Horn,
   Where the weather's niver warm?

4. Wuz ye ever in Mirramashee,
   Where ye tie up to a tree?

5. Wuz ye ever in London town,
   Where them gals they do come down?

6. Wuz ye ever in Bombay,
   Drinkin' coffee an' bohay?

7. Wuz ye ever in Vallipo,
   Where the gals put up a show?

8. Wuz ye ever in 'Frisco Bay,
   Where the gals all shout 'Hooray'?

A shanty with words similar to this latter version and the same or almost identical tune is that known as *Donkey Riding*. This was also very popular among the timber droghers both in Liverpool and Canadian ports, and was used as both a capstan and runaway song when working cargo. I had my version from an old shipmate called

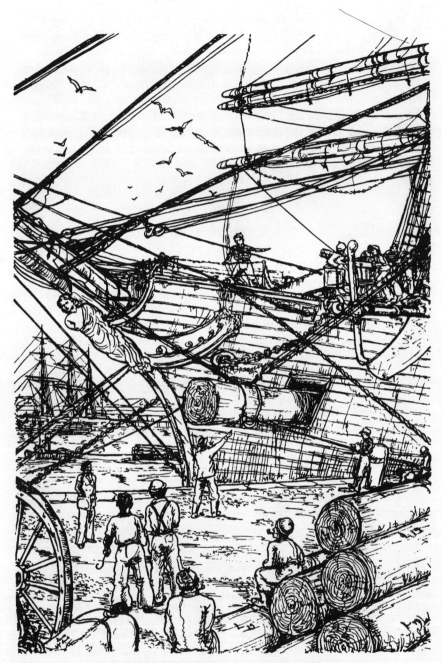

STOWING LOGS THROUGH THE BOW-PORT

Wuz ye ever in Quebec? (Capstan Shanty)

Spike Sennit, who said it was just as popular at sea as in port. The compiler of the *Oxford Song Book (II)*, who gives a version very similar to mine, states that it was 'not a shanty . . . but . . . a song which helped the ship's company stow deck cargo'. I'm afraid this is tying the meaning of the word shanty down a bit too tightly! Many work-songs used by seamen and dockers to stow cargo (in particular lumber and cotton) were the same as those used for capstan and other jobs at sea. And vice versa. Both Bullen and Doerflinger tend to show this, as well as do shanty books in Scandinavian languages. Many Scandinavian shanties used at capstan and pumps were also sung when stowing timber aboard Baltic barques and timber droghers. Much improvisation was given to this song and many indecent lines found in the regulation verses.

DONKEY RIDING

2. Wuz ye ever in Timbucktoo,
    Where the gals are black an' blue,
    An' they waggle their bustles too,
       Ch. Riding on a donkey?
          Full Chorus. Way hay an' away we go,
             Donkey riding, donkey riding!
             Way hay an' away we go,
             Riding on a donkey!

3. Wuz ye ever in Vallipo,
    Where the gals put on a show,
    Waggle an' dance with a roll 'n' go?
       Riding, *etc.*

4. Wuz ye ever down Mobile Bay,
    Screwin' cotton all the day,
    A dollar a day is a white man's pay?
       Riding, *etc.*

119

5. Wuz ye ever in Canton,
   Where the men wear pigtails long,
   And the gals play hong-ki-kong?

6. Wuz you ever in London town,
   Where the gals they do come down,
   See the king in a golden crown?

7. Wuz ye ever in Mirramashee,
   Where ye tie up to a tree,
   An' the skeeters do bite we?

8. Wuz ye ever on the Broomielaw,
   Where the Yanks are all the go,
   An' the boys dance heel an' toe?

9. Wuz ye ever down 'Frisco Bay,
   Where the gals all shout, hooray,
   Here comes Johnny with his three years' pay!

10. Wuz ye ever off Cape Horn,
    Where the weather's niver warm,
    When ye wish to hell ye'd niver bin born?

The *Oxford Song Book* gives for line 3 of the last verse: 'Seen the lion and the unicorn?'

A related shanty to both of the foregoing is the following ditty, once well known to timber droghers. I had this version from my friend Seamus Ennis of the B.B.C. Folk-Song team. He collected it in Ireland, from the McDonagh family, Feanish Island, Carna, County Galway. It was used both for anchor work and for hauling logs through the timber ports of the droghers. The Irish air is redolent of the bagpipes. Words from both the preceding shanties can be (and were) fitted to this fine song.

MY BONNIE HIGHLAND LASSIE-O

Were you ev-er in Round-stone Town? Bon-nie las-sie, high-land las-sie,

Were you ev-er in Round-stone Town, My bon-nie high-land las-sie O? I was

often in Round-stone Town, drink-ing milk and eat-ing flour, Al-though I am a

young maid, that late-ly left my mam-my-O!

2. Were you ever in Galway Bay [Bombay]?
   Ch. Bonnie lassie, highland lassie!
   Were you ever in Galway Bay,
   Ch. My bonnie highland lassie-O?
   I was often in Galway Bay,
   Drinking coffee and bohay,
   Ch. Although I am a young maid,
   That lately left my mammy-O!

3. Were you ever in Quebec?
   Bonnie, *etc.*
   Were you ever in Quebec?
   My bonnie, *etc.*
   I was often in Quebec,
   Throwing timber up on deck,
   Although I am, *etc.*

4. Are you fit to sweep the floor?
   Are you fit to sweep the floor?
   I am fit to sweep the floor,
   As the lock is for the door.

Another well-known runaway chorus was *Roll the Old Chariot*. Doerflinger says that it is based on the words of a Salvation Army revivalist hymn and that the tune is a Scottish reel. In N. I. White's *American Negro Folk-Songs* are several reports of this song. One he gives from the Dismal Swamp in North Carolina was sung by whites at corn-shuckings and log-rollings. Also he gives a version sung by students of Trinity College in 1911 and 1912 as a 'pep' song at base-ball games. The chorus is slightly different since it gives 'we won't drag on behind' for the final line. Also it gives the sinner, drunkard, gambler, harlot, and devil as all 'being in the way' and the idea being to 'stop and take him in', although in the case of the 'devil' we 'run it over him'. On page 300 he gives a Negro version in which instead of a chariot it is a 'golden wheel' that's doing the rolling. It seems without doubt that the shanty is of Negro origin. Doerflinger gives a version in which his shantyman sings the words of 'Roll the Golden Chariot' to the tune of *Drunken Sailor*. In the *Oxford Song Book* a sailor version is given with 'Hot scouse', 'Fresh sea-pie', 'New plum duff', and 'A glass of whisky hot' being the things which 'wouldn't do us any harm'.

Here is my version:

ROLL THE OLD CHARIOT

2. Oh, a plate of Irish stew wouldn't do us any harm,
   Oh, a plate of Irish stew wouldn't do us any harm,
   Oh, a plate of Irish stew wouldn't do us any harm,
   And we'll all hang on behind!
   Ch. So we'll . . . ro-o-oll the old chariot along!
      And we'll roll the golden chariot along!
      Oh, we'll ro-o-oll the old chariot along!
      An' we'll all hang on behind!

3. Oh, a nice fat cook wouldn't do us any harm. (*Three times*)

4. Oh, a roll in the clover wouldn't do us any harm.

5. Oh, a long spell in gaol wouldn't do us any harm.

6. Oh, a nice watch below wouldn't do us any harm.

7. Oh, a night with the gals wouldn't do us any harm.

Now that we have come to a shanty with the word 'roll' prominent, we may as well carry on with others in which this word figures largely. As a matter of fact it vies with 'blow' and 'hilo' as the most popular word in sailor work-songs.

Our first in this series is *Roll the Cotton Down*, a halyard shanty and a very popular one too. At tops'l halyards it was a hardy perennial, although it suited t'gallant halyards even more so, being of a fairly lively march time. I have a version which I obtained from A. Macmillan, Master Mariner, which was used at the capstan, having a grand chorus like most capstan shanties. According to King, during the First World War, the refrain was often sung— 'Roll the Kaiser down!'

ROLL THE COTTON DOWN (a)
(Same tune as (c) without the grand chorus)

1. Oooh, roll the cotton down, me boys,
     Ch. Roll the cotton *down!*
   Oh, roll the cotton down, me boys,
     Ch. Oh, *roll* the cotton *down!*

2. I'm goin' down to Alabam',
   To roll the cotton down, me boys,

3. When I lived down south in Tennessee,
   My old Massa, oh, he said to me.

4. Oh, the nigger works for the white man boss,
   He's the one who rides on the big white hoss.

5. If the sun don' shine, then the hens don' lay,
   If the nigger won't work, then the boss won't pay.

6. Away down south where I was born,
   That's where the niggers blow their horn. [I worked in the
     cotton and the corn *or* Where the niggers work in the
     golden corn.]

7. Oh the nigger works the whole day long,
   The Camptown ladies sing this song.

8. When I was young before the war,
   Times were gay on the Mississippi shore.

9. When work was over at the close of day,
   'Tis then you'd hear the banjo play.

10. While the darkies would sit around the door,
    And the piccanninies played upon the floor.

11. But since the war there's been a change,
    To the darkey everything seems strange.

12. No more you'll hear the banjo play,
    For the good ol' times have passed away.

13. And now we're off to New Orleans,
    To that land of Nigger Queens.

14. Oh, in Alabama where I was born,
    A-screwin' cotton of a summer's morn.

This version speaks aloud of Negro nostalgia.

ROLL THE COTTON DOWN (*b*)
(Same tune as (*c*) without the grand chorus)

1. Come rock an' roll me over,
   Roll, *etc.*
   Let's get this damned job over.
   Oh, roll, *etc.*

2. Was ye ever down in Mobile Bay,
   Screwin' cotton by the day?

3. Oh, a black man's pay is rather low,
   To stow the cotton we must go.

4. Oh, a white man's pay is rather high,
   Rock an' shake 'er is the cry.

5. Oh, so early in the mornin', boys,
   Oh, afore the day is dawnin', boys.

6. Five dollars a day is a white man's pay,
   So bring yer screws an' hooks this way.

7. And bring yer sampson posts likewise,
   Oh, bear a hand, get a curve on, boys.

8. We'll floor her off from fore to aft,
   There's five thousand bales for this 'ere craft.

9. Lift her up an' carry her along,
   Screw her down where she belongs.

10. Oh, tier by tier we'll stow 'em neat,
    Until the job is made complete.

11. Oh, Mobile Bay's no place for me,
    I'll pack me bags an' go to sea [I'll sail away on some other sea].

12. We'll screw him up so handsomely,
And roll him over cheerily.

13. A white man's pay is rather high,
An' a black man's pay is rather low.

14. Oh, come hither, all you nigger boys,
An' come hither, all you bigger boys.

This hoosier version probably stemmed from the Negro one. The white cotton-stowers used it for screwing the huge bales of cotton into place down in the dark holds of the cotton droghers, heaving at the levers of the screws on the same words of the refrains as sailors would at halyards. Once the cotton season was over these men would ship 'foreign', taking these 'cotton chants' with them for use at halyard and capstan, hence a new infusion of shanty blood—coloured blood—entered into the field, which perhaps up till then had been dominated mainly by Irish-shaped work-songs.

In *Adventure* magazine are to be found many of the above stanzas as well as ones from *Johnny Bowker, Dollar-and-a-Half, Sacramento,* and *Handy, Me Boys,* all fitted to *Roll the Cotton Down* with the typical inconsequentiality of the shantyman.

ROLL THE COTTON DOWN (c)

Oh! a-way down south where I wus born, Roll the cot-ton down! Oh! a-way down south a-round Cape Horn, We'll roll the cot-ton down! Roll the cot-ton Roll the cot-ton Mos-es! Roll the cot-ton, oh! roll the cot-ton down!

2. Oh, away down south around Cape Horn,
    Ch. Roll the cotton down!
  Oh, we wisht to Christ we'd niver bin born!
    Ch. We'll roll the cotton down!
      Full Chorus. Roll the cotton,
                Roll the cotton, Moses!
                Roll the cotton,
                Oh, roll the cotton down!

3. Oh, away down south one winter's [summer's, frosty] morn,
  Oh, away down south around Cape Horn.

4. We're bound away to Mobile Bay,
We're bound away at the break o' day.

5. Oh, around Cape Horn we're bound to go,
Around Cape Stiff midst the ice [frost] an' snow.

6. Oh, 'Frisco town is far behind,
An' the gals down south are free an' kind.

7. Oh, fare-ye-well we're bound to go,
Never let it be said we'll forget you.

From here onward the verses are halyard ones only.

8. So stretch it aft an' start a song,
A bloody fine song and it won't take long.

9. Oh, stretch yer backs an' haul away,
An' make yer port an' take yer pay.

10. I'll sing ye a song if ye'll git me some gin,
That'll bouse this block right down to the pin.

11. Oh, rock 'n' shake 'er is the cry,
The bloody topm'st sheave is dry.

12. Oh, haul away when she takes the next roll,
Why don't the Mate shake 'er, oh, Gawd blast his soul.

13. Oh, I wisht Johnny Slite would keep his luff,
The bastard thinks we've hauled enough.

14. Oh, sweat that yard the Mate do say.
Give one more pull, lads, then belay!

Another halyard shanty also similar in tune is *Roll, Alabama, Roll.*
I had my version from an elderly New Zealand lady whose husband
had been a seaman in the *Alabama.* I met her in Gisborne, New
Zealand, in 1925. This shanty tells the story of the Confederate ship
Alabama and its fight with the U.S. sloop of war *Kearsarge.* The
incident took place on Sunday, 19 June 1864. A Negro folk-song
which seems related is *Roll, Jimmy Jenkins, Roll.*

ROLL, ALABAMA, ROLL!

Oh, in eight-een hun-dred an' six-ty one, Roll, a-la-ba-ma, roll! This
ship her build-ing wuz be- gun., Oh roll, a-la-ba-ma, roll!

2. When the *Alabama*'s keel was laid,
    Ch. Roll, Alabama, *roll!*
'This ship her building was begun.
    Ch. Oh, *roll, Alabama, roll!*

3. Oh, she was built in Birkenhead,
    Built in the yard of Jonathan Laird.

4. And down the Mersey she rolled one day,
    An' across the western she ploughed her way [Bound to Fayal she].

5. With British guns, oh, she was stocked,
    She sailed from Fayal—in Cherbourg she docked.

6. To fight the North, Semmes did employ,
    Any method to kill an' destroy.

7. But off Cherbourg, the *Kearsarge* lay tight,
    Awaiting was Winslow to start a good fight [spoiling to fight].

8. Outside the three-mile limit they fought,
    An' Semmes escaped on a fine British yacht.

9. The *Kearsarge* won—*Alabama* so brave,
    Sank to the bottom to a watery grave.

Dick Maitland, Doerflinger's shantyman, gives it as having been sung at the pumps. Here is one of his verses.

> At first she was called the Two-Ninety-Two,
> For the merchants of the city of Liverpool.

On the stocks prior to commissioning she was known as 'Number 290'.

Another shanty partly related to *Roll the Cotton Down* is *Roll the Woodpile Down*. This was the sea version of the Negro song *Haul the Woodpile Down*. It was popular right to the end of sail, for Taylor Harris told me he met an old shantyman in Jack's Palace (The Sailors' Home), London, who had sung it aboard the four-masted barque *Archibald Russell* at the capstan in 1920, on a voyage to Mejillones. The shantyman, called Woodward, I believe, could not remember many verses, so Taylor Harris improvised. His first verse runs—'The white folk larfed as the coon pass'd by'.

I had my version from a West Indian seaman, and it is fairly obvious it originated in either the West Indies or the Southern States of America, most probably in the latter, being, perhaps, one of the many rivermen songs that reached deep-water.

ROLL THE WOODPILE DOWN

'Way down south where the cocks do crow, 'Way down in Flo-ri-da! The gals they all dance to the ol' ban-jo, An' we'll roll th' wood-pile down! Rol-lin'! rol-lin'! oh, rol-lin' th' whole worl' round! That brown gal o' mine's down th' Geor-gia Line, an' we'll roll th' wood-pile down!

2. When I was a young man in me prime,
   Ch. 'Way down in Florida!
   I chased them yaller gals two at a time,
   Ch. An' we'll roll the woodpile down!
   Rollin'! rollin'! rollin' the whole worl' round,
   That brown gal o' mine's down the Georgia Line,
   An' we'll roll the woodpile down!

3. We'll roll him high an' we'll roll him low,
   We'll heave him up and away we'll go.

4. O rouse an' bust 'er is the cry,
   A black man's wage is never high.

5. O Curly goes on the ol' ran-tan,
   O Curly's jist a Down-East Man.

6. O one more heave an' that'll do,
   We're the bullies for to kick 'er through.

A Negro shore version starts:

> Old Aunt Dinah had a farm,
> Way down in Florida!
> Old Aunt Dinah had a farm,
> Haul the woodpile down!

Sailors sometimes sang the Negro refrain 'Haul the woodpile down!' Taylor-Harris gives 'Trav'ling, trav'ling' for 'Rollin', rollin!' This shanty was sung at both capstan and pumps.

Our next 'roll' shanty is the most famous *Roll an' Go!* or *Sally Brown*. Invariably sung at the capstan, this shanty had only one theme—all about Sally and her daughter. There were many obscene verses, which probably accounts partly for the fact that its popularity never waned!

Variants of the refrains:

First refrain.

> Way-hay, roll 'n' go!
> Waaaaay yah!
> Way high, Sally Brown!
> Aye, aye, roll an' go!
> Way ho, a-rollin' go!

Second refrain.

> For I spent me money 'long wid Sally Brown!
> I spend my money with my Sally Brown!
> I spend my money with the gals in town!
> Bet me money on Sally Brown!
> Spend my money on Sally Brown!

Nearly always this shanty starts off with a reference to Sally being a 'bright mulatter' or a 'coloured lady'. Doerflinger gives a version (b), with the first solo line repeated in each verse, which makes no mention of a coloured lady, in fact some shantymen sing about her 'blue eyes' and 'lily-white hands'! Of course a creole could be white—the word really meaning a native, white or coloured, of the West Indies or countries round about, but a 'mulatto' is never *quite* white even in the 'highest brown' examples.

Shantymen with their usual inconsistency get creoles and mulattoes mixed up somewhat. Also sometimes it is Sally herself they're singing about and sometimes her daughter! Some say 'your cheeks are brown and your hair is golden', and that she is 'a white man's daughter' and she usually has a 'nigger baby'.

To me this shanty seems to hail from the West Indies—probably from Jamaica. Some shantymen sang 'Oh, Sally Brown of Kingston City!' Miss Gilchrist mentions the fact that the song was often sung by Negroes ashore in Jamaica. The West Indian seaman Harding, from whom I had many verses, informed me that this and other variants telling of Sally Brown were still used (in 1930) in Jamaica to 'roll de logs' around Black River and other logwood ports of the West Indies and Honduras. The coloured lads also used sing-outs to roll the huge logs, one such shout being, 'Rooooll de mutu!', whatever 'mutu' meant! Doerflinger declares that to his knowledge no lumberman ever used a work-song, although Miss Colcord, on the other hand, states that American lumbermen *did* use work-songs, and very often shanties. This tallies with the statements my West Indian friends have given me in regard to log-rolling in the West Indies. 'Axe-cutting songs', thanks to skiffle, have turned up recently on disc and radio.

The *shape* of this shanty is undoubtedly that of a halyard song, but only one collector, Cecil Sharp, gives it as such. The singing of the last bar of the second refrain varied among sailormen. Terry thinks the difference depended on whether the singers were old or young seamen. My friend, the late Professor Glyn Davies, once wrote me a letter in which he suggested that seamen used to sing these shanties in parts, and many of the so-called 'variations' are nothing more than 'hangovers' from this part-singing. Although I myself have never heard seamen singing in this fashion it is quite possible at one time this did occur.

One of the earliest references to this shanty in literature is in one of Captain Marryat's works describing a passage to America aboard a packet ship in the eighteen-thirties. The mysterious 'Wild Goose Nation' crops up in this shanty although it is a phrase more usually associated with *Sing Hilo Me Ranzo Way*. Who was Sally Brown? A real person or a symbol of shore delights—we will never know, no more than we will ever discover the origins of Ranzo, Stormalong, Johnny Bowker, and other heroes and heroines of shantydom.

SALLY BROWN (a)
Alternative title, *Roll 'n' Go!*

Ooh! Sal-ly Brown she's a bright mulatter, Way-ay—, roll an' go! She drinks rum an'
chaws ter-back-er, Spend my mon-ey on Sal-ly Brown!

The last bar was often sung:

Sal-ly Brown!

Bar 7 was some-times sung in this fashion:

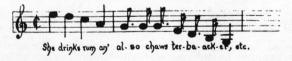

She drinks rum an' al-so chaws ter-ba-ack-er, etc.

2. Sally lives on the old plantation,
   Ch. Way-hay, roll an' go!
   She is a daughter of the Wild Goose Nation [She is a member of the U.S. Nation].
   Ch. Spend my money on Sally Brown!

3. Seven long years I courted Sally,
   But all she did was dilly-dally.

SALLY BROWN

4. Sally Brown's a big buck nigger,
   Her bow is big, but her starn is bigger.

5. I bought her gowns an' I bought 'er laces,
   Took her out to all the places.

6. Sally's teeth are white an' pearly,
   Her eyes are black an' her hair is curly.

7. Sally lives in ol' Jamaica,
   Sellin' rum an' growin' terbacker.

8. I call her my ol' Queen of Faces,
   Bought her coral beads an' laces.

9. The sweetest flower in the valley,
   Is my own my pretty Sally.

10. Sally Brown, what is the matter?
    Pretty gal, but can't git at her.

11. Sally Brown, I love ye dearly,
    Ye had me heart, or very nearly.

12. Sally Brown's a wild ol' lady [creole lady],
    Sally's got a creole [nigger] baby [I guess she's got a yaller
    baby].

13. Sally Brown she wouldn't marry,
    An' I no longer cared to tarry.

14. Sally Brown, I love yer daughter,
    I love yer farm beside the water [For her I'll sail across the
    water].

15. Sally Brown, I kissed yer daughter,
    Stopped her rum an' gave her water.

16. She wouldn't have a tarry sailor,
    So I shipped away in a New Bedford whaler.

17. Sally Brown, I took a notion,
    To sail across the flamin' ocean.

18. I shipped away in a New Bedford whaler,
    When I got back she wuz courtin' a tailor.

19. Now me troubles they are over,
    Sally's married to a nigger soldier.

20. He beat her up an' stole her money,
    Then left her with a nigger baby.

21. Sally Brown, I'm bound ter leave yer,
    Sally Brown, I'll not deceive yer [Heave a pawl, oh, pawl an'
    heave 'er]!

When bar 7 was sung as indicated by the third set of music then
added words would be used, like this:

> She drinks rum and *always* chaws terbacker.
> Her eyes are black and her *lovely* hair is curly.
> I guess she's got *another* nigger baby, *etc.*

The late Stanley Slade, a famous Bristol shantyman, always sang
Sally Brown in this fashion.

Robbins, Cecil Sharp's shantyman, sang the following rather
interesting tune. He said he always used it at halyards.

SALLY BROWN (b)

And after the usual verses Robbins winds up with: 'And now we're
married and we're living nice and comfor'ble.'

Another version of the tune, very popular at halyards among
coloured seamen, is one I had from 'Tobago' Smith, a fine coloured
West Indian shantyman I once knew—a veritable mine of information concerning shanties as sung by the seamen of the Antilles. The
words are the same as for Sally Brown (a).

SALLY BROWN (c)
Alternative title, *Walkalong, You Sally Brown*

A variant of *Sally Brown* I picked up in the West Indies is *Tommy's on the Tops'l Yard*. This was used for halyards, but mainly for quick light pulls on the royal halyard—one pull in each refrain. I have been told that it was also used for tacks and sheets. Masefield gives it as halyards, without the tune.

TOMMY'S ON THE TOPS'L YARD
Alternative title, *Roll an' Go!*

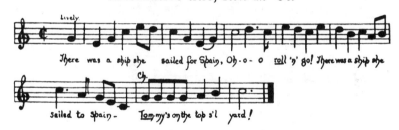

Alternative final refrain:

2. There wuz a ship came home again,
   Ch. Oh-o-o! *Roll* an' go!
   There wuz a ship came home again,
   Ch. Tommy's on the tops'l yard!
   [*or* Oh-o-o! *Roll an'* go!]

3. An' wha' d'yer think wuz in her hold? (*Repeat*)

4. She had diamonds, she had gold.

5. An' what wuz in her lazareet?

133

6. Good split peas an' bad bull meat.

7. An' who d'yer·think wuz her Old Man?

8. Why Slimy Joe, the Squarehead Man.

9. An' who d'yer think wuz her chief mate?

Another shanty with a 'Roll and go!' refrain is the following, which was sung to Cecil Sharp by the shantyman called Short of Watchet, Somerset, who said it was used at the capstan. It is a combination of *Sally Brown* and *A Long Time Ago*:

ROLL AND GO

2. Oh, Sally Brown's the girl for me,
   Ch. A long time ago.
   Oh, Sally Brown she slighted me,
   Ch. Way-ay, roll and go!
   Oh, Sally Brown she slighted me,
   Ch. A long time ago!

3. As I walked out one morning fair,
   It's then I met her I do declare.
   (*English Folk-Chanteys*, C. J. Sharp)

Leaving the immortal Sally Brown behind we now pass on to another 'Roll and go', that of *Randy Dandy O!*, a capstan and pumps song heard mainly aboard the old Cape-Horners. I had this from Harding, who declared it was very popular aboard of a small Nova

Scotian barque he once shipped in. The tune is reminiscent of *The Raggle Taggle Gipsies*. Miss Colcord gives a version from Captain Robinson's collection (*The Bellman*) with a similar tune. This has one verse only and the original bawdy refrain has been camouflaged. I likewise have had to camouflage, but I have left mine a little nearer to the original suggestive word found in one refrain. Two or three of the verses have had to be altered slightly also.

RANDY DANDY O!

Now we are ready to head for the Horn, Way, ay, roll an' go! Our boots an' our clothes, boys, are all in the pawn, Timme rol-lick-in' ran-dy dan-dy O! Heave a pawl, oh, heave a-way, Way, ay, roll an' go! The an-chors on board an' the cable's all stored, Timme rol-lick-in' ran-dy, dan-dy o!

2. Soon we'll be warping her out through the locks,
   Ch. Way, ay, roll an' go!
   Where the pretty young gals all come down in their flocks,
   Ch. Timme rollockin' randy dandy O!
   Full Chorus. Heave a pawl, O heave away!
   Way ay, roll an' go!
   The anchor's on board an' the cable's all stored,
   Timme rollockin' randy dandy O!

3. Come breast the bars, bullies, an' heave her away,
   Ch. Way, ay, *etc.*
   Soon we'll be rollin' her 'way down the Bay,
   Ch. Timme, *etc.*

4. Sing goodbye to Sally an' goodbye to Sue,
   For we are the boy-os who can kick 'er through.

5. Oh, man the stout caps'n an' heave with a will,
   Soon we'll be drivin' her 'way down the hill.

6. Heave away, bullies, ye parish-rigged bums,
   Take yer hands from yer pockets and don't suck yer thumbs.

7. Roust 'er up, bullies, the wind's drawin' free,
   Let's get the glad-rags on an' drive 'er to sea.

8. We're outward bound for Vallipo Bay,
   Get crackin', m' lads, 'tis a hell o' a way!

Captain Robinson gives this capstan shanty with alternating solos and refrains, four solos, four refrains, but Harding sang it in the way I have given. The former calls it *Galloping Randy Dandy O!*—the word 'galloping' being the camouflaged one!

Then we have *Oh, Come Roll Me Over!* This was given me as a halyard shanty, but I feel it would have been more likely used at tacks and sheets. Masefield however gives it as halyards. I had it from my coloured friend Harding, who declared it was still being sung (in 1932) for rolling logs in the West Indies—the roll coming on the word where the drag would be on a rope. Masefield gives 'Aha, come roll him over' for the refrain, and I have seen another version in print with a single solo and refrain only.

HIGH O, COME ROLL ME OVER!

2. One man to strike the bell,
    Ch. High-O! Come roll me over!
   One man to strike the bell,
    Ch. High-O! Come roll me over!

3. Two men to man the wheel.

4. Three men, to'gallant braces.

5. Four men to board the tack.

6. Five men to heave the lead.

7. Six men, to furl t'g'ns'ls.

8. Seven men to bunt-a-bo.

Another 'Roll' halyard shanty I leant from Harding is *Where am I to go, me Johnnies?* He sang it with many wild yelps and 'hitches'. This is the first time it has been in print.

WHERE AM I TO GO, M' JOHNNIES?

Where am I to go, me Johnnies? O, where am I to go? To me way, hay, hay, high, roll an' go! O, where am I to go me Johnnies? O, where am I to go? For I'm a young-sail-or-boy, an' where am I to go?

2. 'Way up on that t'gallant yard, that's where yer bound to go,
   Ch. To me *way* hay, hay, high, *roll* an' go!
   'Way up on that t'gallant yard, that's where yer bound to go,
   Ch. For *I'm* a young sailor boy, an' *where* am I to go?

3. 'Way up on that t'gallant yard an' take that gans'l in,
   'Way up on that t'gallant yard an' take that gans'l in.

4. Yer bound away around Cape Horn, that's where yer bound to go.

5. Yer bound away through ice an' snow, that's where yer bound to go.

Another of Harding's halyard shanties in which Sally Brown
again crops up is *Roll, Boys, Roll!* Definitely originating in the West
Indies, it was popular in ships which carried 'chequerboard crews',
i.e. one watch white and one watch coloured. When Harding sang
it it had its full complement of grace notes and yells. This also makes
its appearance in print for the first time.

ROLL, BOYS, ROLL!

Oh! Sal-ly Brown she's the gal for me, boys, Roll, boys, roll boys, roll! Sal-ly Brown she's the gal for me, boys, Way, high, Miss Sal-ly Brown!

2. We're bound away—'way down south, boys,
   Ch. Roll, boys, *roll*, boys, roll!
   We're bound away—'way down south, boys,
   Ch. Way, high, Miss *Sally* Brown!

137

3. We're rollin' down to Trinidad to see Miss Lucy Loo,
   We're rollin' down to Trinidad to see Miss Lucy Loo [Sally Brown].

4. Oh, she's lovely up aloft, an' she's lovely down below. (*Repeat*)

5. She's lovely on the foreyard, boys, she's lovely down below,
   She's lovely 'cos she loves me, boys, that's all I want ter know.

6. Ol' Capen Baker, how do yer stow yer cargo?
   Some I stow for'ard, boys, an' some I stow arter.

7. Forty fathoms or more below, boys,
   There's forty fathom or more below, boys.

8. Oh, way high ya, an' up she rises,
   O way high ya, an' the blocks is different sizes.

9. One more pull—don't yer hear the mate a-bawlin'?
   One more pull, dat's the end of all our haulin'.

Bullen's version of *Run, Let the Bulgine Run* uses the words of verse 4.

Leaving the West Indies we will get back to Old England for another 'Roll' tune, and this is the Old English ballad *The Fire Ship*, which recently became a popular radio number. At sea it was often sung at the pumps. In the radio version modern words have been fitted to this seventeenth-century ballad; no seaman would ever have sung about taking his inamorata for 'fish and chips'! Being a sailor-song many of the verses are unprintable! Jimmy Sexton (Sir James) declared it to be a very popular pumping song in his day, and I have heard it sung like this and also as a version of *Can't Ye Dance the Polka?*, in which case one verse of *The Fire Ship* would make two verses of the shanty.

THE FIRE SHIP

2. Kind sir, ye must excuse me, for being out so late,
   For if me parents knew o' it, then sad would be me fate.
   Me father he's a minister, a true and honest man,
   Me mother she's a dancin'-gal [Methodist], an' I do the best I can.
      Ch. Oh, she'd a dark an' rollin' eye,
         An' her hair hung down in ring-a-lets [*or* like glow-worms].
         She wuz a nice gal—a decent gal but . . .
         One of the rakish kind.

An older version gives: 'a rare sort, a rakish sort, she's one for a fireship's crew.'

3. I eyed that wench full warily, for talk like this I knew,
   She seemed a little owerbold, she lied for all I knew,
   But still she wuz a comely wench, her lips a ruby red,
   Her bosom full, her hips so slim, she coyly hung her head.

4. I took her to a tavern an' treated her to wine,
   Little did I think that she belonged to the rakish kind.
   I handled her, I dangled her, an' found to my surprise,
   She wuz nothin' but a fire ship, rigged up in a disguise.

5. And so I deemed her company for a sailorman like me.
   I kissed her once, I kissed her twice, said she, 'Be nice to me'.
   I fondled her, I cuddled her, I bounced her on me knee.
   She wept, she sighed an' then she cried, 'Jack, will ye sleep wi' me?'

(*Two verses omitted.*)

6. Now all ye jolly sailormen that sail the Western Sea,
   An' all ye jolly 'prentice lads a warnin' take from me,
   Steer clear o' lofty fire ships, for me they left well-spent.
   For one burnt all me money up, an' left me broke an' bent.

Having got from 'roll' to 'rolling' we will take that now famous 'rolling river' shanty *Shenandoah* as our next item. It was one of the most popular of all capstan and windlass shanties, but I feel that a better title for it would be either *Rolling River* or *Missouri*, since many versions don't even mention Shenandoah. In the mouths of different shantymen the line 'Oh . . . I love yer daughter . . .' could contain any of the following names: Shenandoah, Sally Brown, Polly Brown, Darby Doyle, Paddy Doyle, or Dan O'Shea (Shay).

This last version was always sung by a Scottish carpenter I once knew who had been shantyman in Vicker's big four-posters out of Liverpool.

Another point about this shanty is the fact that no two shantymen ever sang the same pronunciation of the word 'Shenandoah'. Shenadoar, Shannadore, Shanandar, and Shanidah were all used, but the shantyman L. A. Smith obtained her version from what must have been the king-pin at mispronunciation, as she gives this shanty as *Oceanida*! Miss Gilchrist's seaman sang it as 'Shangadore'.

This is one of the shanties collectors have always thought to be 'clean', but when crossed, as it often was, with *Sally Brown* (owing to her having a daughter like Shenandoah), not even the most broad-minded collector could call it 'clean'!

My first version—of Negro origin—I obtained from the coloured cook (doctor) of the *Birkdale*. He had sailed for many years in the *Dales*, and in the *Invers* of the Milne Line of sailing ships.

SHENANDOAH (a)
(Same tune as version (b))
Alternative titles, *The Rolling River*, *The Wide Missouri*

1. Shenandoah, I long ter hear yer.
   Ch. Away [Hooray], you rollin' river!
   O Shenandoah, I cain't git near yer,
   Ch. Ha, ha! [High-ya!] I'm bound away,
   On the wide Missouri.

2. Shenandoah, me daddy's near yer,
   O Shenandoah, I seem ter hear yer.

3. Shenandoah, me mudder's near ye,
   O Shenandoah, for ye I'm weary.

4. Can the piccanninies hear ye?
   O Shenandoah, me heart's a-dreary.

5. Shenandoah, again I'll hear ye.
   O Shenandoah, in dreams I'm near ye.

The next version, about an Indian chief, was very popular at sea. Doerflinger says that the chief's name was Skenandoah and he was of the Oneida tribe, and he also writes that the song was an old cavalry one known as *The Wild Mizzourye*. Whall, who says it used to figure in old school collections, believes it to have belonged originally to the American or Canadian *voyageurs*. Others think it came from the 'mountain men' or traders of the early West. But it may have been nothing more than a river-song—one of the songs used by boatmen of the great American rivers (like the Ohio). We do know that a very popular Ohio boatman-song—*Dance the Boatman, Dance*—became a deep-water shanty, and *The Hog-eye Man* is another one originating with river men. Alan Lomax gives the following 'cavalry version'. He calls it *The Wild Mizzourye*:

SHENANDOAH

1. For seven long years I courted Nancy.

2. She would not have me for a lover.

3. And so she took my fifteen dollars.

4. And then she went to Kansas City.

5. And there she had a little sh-sh baby.

6. She must have had another lover.

7. He must have been a –th Cavalry Soldier.

8. I'm drinking rum and chawin' tobacco.

9. I learnt this song from Tommy Tompkins.

First refrain—

> Hi, oh, the rolling river.

Second refrain—

> Ho, ho, I'm bound away,
> For the wild Mizzourye!

> (From *American Ballads and Folk Songs* by J. A.
> Lomax & Alan Lomax, published by The
> Macmillan Co., N.Y., 1934)

SHENANDOAH (*b*)
(Use this tune with all my versions)

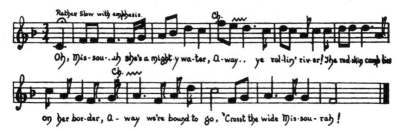

2. O Shenandoah wuz a redskin maiden,
      Ch. Away ye rollin' river!
   And a white man loved that redskin maiden,
      Ch. An' away we're bound to go,
         'Crosst the wide Missourah!

3. Oh, the white man loved the Indian maiden,
   With trade-goods [notions] his canoe was laden.

4. The chief refused the trader's dollars [the white man's offer],
   My daughter ye shall never follow [And vowed the white man should
      not have her].

141

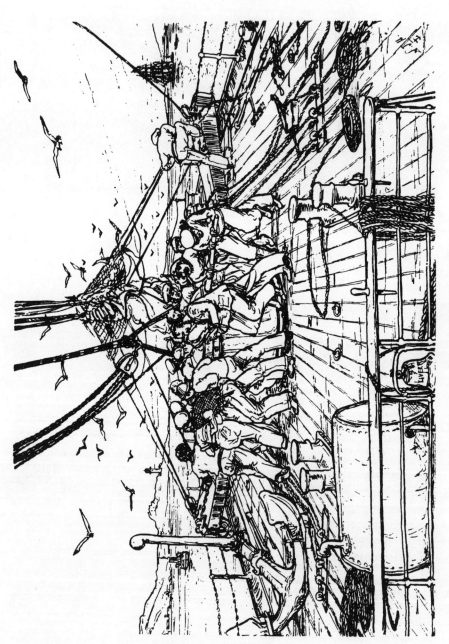

HEAVING AT THE ANCHOR CAPSTAN
'Oh, an' awaaay, ye rollin' river!' (Anchor Shanty)

5. At last there came a Yankee skipper [One day a ship sailed up the river],
    Who winked his eye and flipped his flipper [And brought the chief strong fire-water].

6. He sold the chief some fire-water,
    And stole the gal across the water.

7. O Shenandoah, I love yer daughter,
    I'll take her sailing cross yon rollin' water.

Now we come to the love of Shenandoah as a geographical location. Of this version Captain F. Shaw (in his *Splendour of the Seas*) writes: '. . . the Shenandoah River flowed through the slave-states below the Mason and Dixon Line and whoever sang it first was obviously pining for the delights of that considerable stream. . . .'

SHENANDOAH (c)

1. O Shenandoah, I long ter hear yer,
    O Shenandoah, I long ter hear yer.

2. O Shenandoah, I took a notion,
    To sail across the stormy ocean.

3. O Shenandoah, I'm bound ter leave yer,
    O Shenandoah, I'll not deceive yer.

4. O Shenandoah, I love yer daughters,
    I love the music of yer waters.

5. 'Tis seven long years since last I seed yer,
    But, Shenandoah, I'll never grieve yer.

6. O Shenandoah's my native valley,
    Beside her waters I love to dally.

7. O Shenandoah she's a lovely river,
    An' I shall never forget you ever.

And now we come to another shanty with the name *Shenandoah*— a Negro capstan song given only by Bullen.

SHENANDOAH

Oh, Shen-an-doh, my bul-ly boy, I long to hear you hol-ler; Way ay, ay ay ay, Shen-an-doh, I lub ter bring er tot er rum en see ye make a swol-ler, Way, ay, ay, ay, Shen-an-doh.

(Copyright, F. T. Bullen & W. F. Arnold, *Songs of Sea Labour*, Swan & Co., Ltd., 1914)

Bullen says it wasn't used so much at sea, but he heard it sung by Negroes heaving at the winches when working cargo in, I think, Georgetown, Demerara.

Another 'rolling river' shanty is the following, sung at capstan and pumps:

A-ROLLING' DOWN THE RIVER
Alternative title, *The Saucy Arabella* (*Shenandoah, Davy Crockett,* etc.)

Oh, the A-ra-bel-la set her main top-s'l, The A-ra-bel-la set her main top-s'l, The A-ra-bel-la set her main top-s'l, A-rol-lin' down the riv-er.. .., A-rol-lin' down, a-rol-lin'down, A-rol-lin' down the riv-er.. a-rol-lin' down, A-rol-lin' down, Said the Buck-o Mate to the Greaser's wife, Oh, a pump-kin pud-den an' a bul-gine pie, A pump-kin pud-den an' a bul-gine pie, A pump-kin pud-den an' a bul-gine pie, a-board the A-ra-bel-la!

144

2. So the *Arabella* set her main gans'l,
   The *Arabella* set her main gans'l,
   The *Arabella* set her main gans'l,
   A-rollin' down the river.
    Ch. A-rollin' down, a-rollin' down,
     A-rollin' down the river,
     A-rollin' down, a-rollin' down.
   Said the bucko mate to the greaser's wife,

  Full Chorus. Oh, a pumpkin pudden an' a bulgine pie,
      A pumpkin pudden an' a bulgine pie,
      A pumpkin pudden an' a bulgine pie,
      Aboard the *Arabella*!

3. So the *Arabella* set her main roy-al, *etc.*

4. So the *Arabella* set her main skys'l.

5. So the *Arabella* set her main stays'l.

And so on, naming all the sails of a full-rigged ship. This merry jingle is probably Negro in origin—and certainly American as the reference to 'Bulgine' shows. 'Bulgine' was an American slang name for a railway engine. On page 248 of *American Negro Folk-Songs* (White) will be found a song with the line 'Ginger pudding and a pumpkin pie'.

The tune of this shanty, in parts, is similar to *So Early in the Morning*, the minstrel song.

Now we've had a 'rolling-home' song we will give the most famous homeward-bound song of them all—*Rolling Home*. And a *shanty* is undoubtedly was, although some collectors give it as a forebitter. It was popular in both English and American ships and even in German vessels. Its origin is a bit doubtful, but most collectors seem to think it is based on a poem of Charles Mackay, written on board ship in 1858. On the other hand it may have been that Mackay heard sailors heaving at the capstan and singing the shanty, which gave him the idea of writing his poem, utilizing many portions of the original shanty. It amounts to: which came first, the chicken or the egg? No one has discovered as to whether it is mentioned in any books prior to 1858; if this was the case it would more or less prove that the shanty came first.

Whall, Sampson, Terry, and others give it as a song, but when it is so given two verses of it as a shanty equal one verse as a song. C. F. Smith is the only collector who gives it shanty fashion. My versions are derived from those of my father H. J. Hugill, Charlie Evans, Arthur Spencer, 'Scottie', and the Sailmaker and the Bosun of the *Garthpool*. The song versions usually have a naval touch and start the first verse with '*Pipe* all hands'. Of course the pipe was unknown in merchant vessels, although I believe it was used in the Blackwallers and East Indiamen. Even nowadays this tune is played

by the ship's band on foreign stations when a naval vessel is leaving
for home at the end of a commission.

ROLLING HOME (a)

2. Let us all heave with a will, boys,
   Soon our cable we will trip,
   An' across the briny [southern] ocean,
   We will steer our gallant ship.
       Ch. Rollin' home—rollin' home—
       Rollin' home across the sea,
       Rollin' home to dear Old England,
       Rollin' home, fair land, to thee.

3. Man the bars with perfect will, boys,
   Let all hands that can clap on;
   And while we heave round the capstan,
   We will sing that well-known song.
       Ch. Rolling, *etc.*

4. To Australia's lovely daughters,
   We will bid a fond adieu.
   We shall ne'er forget the hours,
   That we spent along with you.

5. We will leave ye our best wishes,
   We will leave yer rocky shores,
   For we're bound to dear Old England,
   To return to ye no more.

6. Up aloft amongst [amidst] the rigging
   Blows the wild and rushin' gale,
   Strainin' every spar and backstay,
   Stretchin' stitch in every sail.
   [There are lovin' hearts awaitin' in the land to which we
       sail.]

7. Eighteen months away from England,
   Now a hundred days or more,
   On salt-horse and cracker-hash, boys,
   Boston beans that made us sore.

8. Eastwards, ever eastwards,
   To the risin' o' the sun,
   Homewards, ever homewards,
   To the land where we were born.

9. Ten thousand miles now lays behind us,
   Ten thousand miles or more to roam,
   Soon we'll see our native country.
   Soon we'll greet our dear old home.

10. Round Cape Horn one winter's mornin',
    All among the ice and snow,
    Ye could hear them shellbacks singin',
    Sheet 'er home, boys, let 'er go!

11. Heave away, ye sons-o'-thunder,
    For the nor'ard we will steer,
    Where the gals and wives are waiting,
    Standin' there upon the pier.

12. Cheer up, Jack, bright smiles await you,
    From the fairest of the fair,
    There are lovin' hearts to greet you,
    An' kind welcomes everywhere.

13. An' the gal you love most dearly,
    She's been constant, firm, and true,
    She will clasp ye to her bosom,
    Saying, 'Jack, I still love you.'

14. An' we'll sing in joyful chorus,
    In the watches of the night,
    And we'll greet the shores of England,
    When the grey dawn breaks the light.

Other verses sometimes heard in this version are:

And the wild waves cleft behind us,
Seem to murmur as we go,
Loving hearts and hands await us,
In the land to which we go.

New-born breezes swiftly drive us,
Back to childhood's bonnie skies,
To the light of loving faces,
And the gleam of kindly eyes.

All the versions of *Rolling Home* that I have heard have Australia as the country which the singers are leaving, and the following version, given me by an Australian sailmaker, is no exception. Doerflinger has a similar version, but his is in forebitter fashion, with eight lines to a verse, although his seventh verse has only four lines.

ROLLING HOME (*b*)

1. Call all hands to man the capstan,
   See yer cable flaked down clear,
   Now we're sailin' homeward bound, boys,
   For the Channel we will steer.
     Ch. Rollin' home, *etc.*

2. See yer tacks an' sheets all clear, boys,
   Lead down now yer buntlines all,
   Clear all gear upon the sheerpoles,
   Stand by to haul on the catfall.

3. Now Australia we are leavin',
   For Old England give a cheer,
   Fare-ye-well, ye dark-eyed damsels,
   Give three cheers for English beer.

4. Goodbye, Heads, we're bound to leave you,
   Haul the towrope all in-board.
   We will leave Old Aussie starnwards,
   Clap all sail we can afford.

5. A west wind now does blow behind us,
   Fills our sails so full and free,
   Not for the Cape we're steering this time,
   But for the Horn far easterly.

6. Mister, set yer stuns'ls quickly,
   Set all flyin' kites yer can,
   Mollyhawks and chickens meet us,
   Souls of long-drowned sailormen.

7. Round Cape Horn on a winter's mornin'
   Now among the ice an' snow,
   Ye will hear our shellbacks singin',
   Sheet her home, boys, let 'er go!

8. Bullies, sweat yer weather braces,
   For the wind is strength'ning now,
   Now we're roundin' Digger Ramrees,
   To the North our ship will plough.

9. Eighteen months away from England,
   Only fifty days, no more,
   On salt horse an' cracker-hash, boys,
   Boston beans that make us sore.

10. Now we're in the ol' Atlantic,
    With the royals no longer stowed,
    With our lee cathead a-divin',
    To the land—Lord let 'er go!

11. Now we're close to the Western Islands,
    The lee riggin's hangin' slack,
    She's a-rollin' [reelin'] off her knots, boys,
    Hear the main t'gallant crack.

12. Now the Lizard Light's a-shinin',
    And we're bound up to the Nore,
    With the canvas full an' drawin',
    Soon we'll be on England's shore.

13. We'll pass the Start in dandy fashion,
    Eddystone and grim Portland,
    By the Bill we'll roll along, boys,
    Sing this song, oh, every hand.

14. Now we're passin' Dover Point, boys,
    Bullies, get yer cable clear,
    Give her thirty on the windlass,
    For the tugboat next we'll steer.

In *Adventure* magazine (R. W. Gordon) is a unique verse:

I have traded with the Indians,
With the Negroes and Chinee,
I have traded with the Spaniards,
In the dark and southern sea;
Many countries have I travelled,
Many strange sights have I seen,
But give to me the English maiden,
Softly tripping o'er the green.

I remember an unforgettable scene when the four-masted barque *Gustav* was making fast in Belfast after a 142-days' passage from Geelong, Australia, round Cape Stiff. The anchor cable was unshackled from the anchor and hove ashore around a bollard and back aboard again. All hands manned the anchor capstan. I sang one verse of *Rolling Home* in English and all hands sang the chorus in English, then a German shantyman sang a German verse and all hands sang the chorus in Low German, and so on, alternating English and German verses and choruses until the long job was done. And then from the crowd of onlookers on the dockside a rousing cheer rang out.

Our next on the list is *Rolling King* or *Ruler King*, or as some call it *South Australia*. This is a shanty which probably made its appearance during the emigrant days, when thousands travelled by sailing ship to Semaphore Roads, Port Adelaide, South Australia. L. A. Smith gives a version, as also do Doerflinger and Miss Colcord. It was usually sung at capstan (anchor) and pumps.

ROLLING KING
Alternative titles, *Ruler King, South Australia*

2. My wife is standin' on the quay,
   Ch. Heave away! Heave away!
   The tears do start as she waves to me,
   Ch. An' I'm bound for South Australia [We're bound, *etc.*]
   Full Chorus. Heave away! Heave away!
   Heave away you Rolling King [Ruler King]
   [For] I'm [we're] bound for South Australia!

3. An' when I'm on a foreign shore,
   I'll think o' me darlin' that I adore.

4. There ain't but one thing grieves me mind,
   To leave my wife an' child behind.

5. There ain't but one thing grievès me
   An' that's me wife an' dear ba-bee.

6. An' as I stand on a foreign shore,
   I'll drink to the wife that I adore.

7. Now I'm on a foreign strand,
   With a glass o' pisco [samshu, sakee, vino, *etc.*] in me hand.

8. I'll drink a glass to my own shore,
   I'll drink to the gal that I adore.

9. I'll tell ye now, it ain't no lie,
   I'll love that gal until I die.

10. This cross ye see at the bottom of the line,
    Is only to keep ye in my mind.

11. Now we're homeward bound again,
    I'll soon be seeing Sarah Jane.

12. Oh, fare-ye-well, now fare-ye-well,
    Oh, fare-ye-well, I wish ye well.

This was a shanty which had a rather poor regulation pattern and all shantymen had to improvise to make it see the job through. Harlow in his book *The Making of a Sailor*[1] gives the version sung aboard his ship. A shipmate of his declared that it was a very popular anchor song aboard the famous clipper ship *Thermopylae*. Doerflinger's shantyman (William Laurie of Sailors' Snug Harbor) sings this in real sailor fashion:

Oh, in South Aus-tra-lia where I was born, Heave a-way, haul a-way! In South Aus-tra-lia round Cape Horn, I'm bound for South Aus-tra-lia! Heave a-way, you rul-er king, Heave a-way, haul a-way! Heave a-way, don't you hear me sing? We're bound for South Aus-tra-lia!

(W. M. Doerflinger. *Shantymen & Shantyboys*, The Macmillan Co. (New York), 1951)

At the pumps the chorus 'Heave away! Haul away!' would not be out of place, as some would be 'heaving away' at the pump handles and others 'hauling away' at the 'bell-ropes'. Normally the words 'heave' and 'haul' are not mixed in shanties, the former being found only in capstan songs, the latter in halyard shanties.

---

[1] Marine Research Society, U.S.A., 1928.

Another version of this shanty popular in Yankee ships was the following. Several American collections give it, but it was also heard aboard British ships, when the place-names would be changed. For example:

> Liverpool gals ain't got no combs,
> They comb their hair with kipper back bones.

On account of the prominence of the codfish in this shanty it was often referred to as the *Codfish Shanty* (Colcord, Sandburg, etc.). The version I give is one of Harding's, and Paddy Delaney was the old-timer who told me about its British alternatives. One or two verses have had to be camouflaged.

SOUTH AUSTRALIA
Alternative title, *The Codfish Shanty*

2. Yankee gals don't sleep on beds,
    Ch. Heave away! Heave away!
  They go to sleep on codfish's heads,
    Ch. An' we're bound for South Australia.

>   *Full Chorus.* Heave away, me bully-bully boys,
>   Heave away! Heave away!
>   Heave away, why don't ye make some noise?
>   An' we're bound for South Australia!

3. Cape Cod gals have got big feet,
  Codfish's rows is nice an' sweet.

4. Quaker gals don't wear no frills,
  They're tight an' skinny as a halibut's gills.

5. Glou'ster gals make damn fine cooks,
  They're good at catching sprats on hooks.

6. Nantucket gals are very fine,
  They know how to bait a codfish line.

American collections have:

> Cape Cod girls are very fine girls,
> With codfish balls they comb their curls.

> Glou'ster boys they have no sleds,
> They slide down hills on codfish heads.

Our last shanty being sometimes called *The Codfish Shanty*, we will next give a shanty in which the codfish and many other fishes figure. This song is called *The Fishes*, and although the original was undoubtedly a Scottish fishermen's song, it was sung aboard square-riggers at the capstan and often at the pumps as well. The Scottish version of the chorus runs:

Blaw ye winds southerly, southerly, southerly, Blaw bonnie breeze, blaw my lover to me.

Another place of origin may have been the Tyne, as there does exist a 'keelman' version. Miss Colcord has pointed out that it was popular with the Gloucester fishermen of the nor-east coast of America, and that they sang the Scottish air, whereas Whall, who was a Scot, has given a version entirely different in tune from the usual Scottish one. Whall says that sometimes each member of the crew would sing a verse and, if one of them couldn't think of a fish, all hands would chip in with the chorus and thus save the situation. Sharp gives his two versions as capstan shanties. All the sea-going and many of the shore versions describe the duties and antics of various fishes. As a shanty, although all the versions about the fishes were very similar, tunes varied, as did the words of the chorus.

I learnt my version from an old seaman who had sailed in the copper ore barques of the Bristol Channel. He gave me an alternative starting verse:

> Oh, a ship she was fitted out ready for sea,
> And fishes she had for her ship's company.

THE FISHES (a)

Oh a ship she was rig-ged, and ready for sea, and all of her sail-ors were fish-es to be. Then

blow ye winds west-er-ly, west-er-ly, blow. Our ship she's in full sail, now stead-y she goes!

2. First came the Herring sayin', 'I'm King o' the Seas'.
He jumped on the poop, 'Oh, the Capen I'll be!'
Ch. Then blow ye winds westerly, westerly blow,
Our ship she's in full sail,
Now steady she goes!

Another rather good tune, popular in the south of England, was the following; I believe I had it from a Devonshire seaman.

THE FISHES (b)

I'll sing you a song of the fish of the sea, An' I'll trust that ye'll join in this chor-us with me, Wi' a wind-y old weath-er! Storm-y old weather! When the wind blows, we'll all heave to-ge-ther!

Since the words of this shanty were often sung to the tune of *Blow the Man Down*, and as this famous tops'l halyard shanty is next on our list, to save repetition, I will give the verses common to both in *Blow the Man Down* (4), verses 1-24.

Blow the Man Down originated in the Western Ocean Sailing Packets; it was the war-cry of the Packet Rats. The word 'blow' was a Packet Rat production meaning 'to knock' or in a broader sense 'to knock a man down by means of fist, belayin'-pin, or capstan-bar'. Chief Mates in the Western Ocean Packets were known as 'Blowers', Second Mates as 'Strikers', and Third Mates as 'Greasers'. The Western Ocean Law was a rule of the Fist with a capital F. A man could even work his way up to be Mate without a ticket, so long as he could handle himself and a tough crew. The toughest of the gangs of Packet Rats that manned these ships was the famous 'Bloody Forty' mentioned in one of Lubbock's books. 'Handspike Hash' and 'Belayin'-pin Soup' were the order of the day. C. Fox Smith gives a very fine description of a Mate of one of these Packet Ships:

He's a man that's shipped for fightin' 'cos his fists is iron-bound,
An' generally speakin' you'll find his wind is sound;
He's a dandy with a slung-shot, and you'd have to travel far
Before ye'd find his equal with a heavy capstan bar.
(Sea Songs and Ballads)

Some collectors think that the air of *Blow the Man Down* bears some resemblance to the German carol *Stille Nacht, heilige Nacht*, and that it is possible that the Packet Seamen picked up the tune from the German emigrants who were flocking to the New World at this time. But a more feasible theory is that the shanty was nothing more than an old Negro song *Knock a Man Down*. This song, a not so musical version of the later *Blow the Man Down*, was taken and used by the hoosiers of Mobile Bay, and at a later date carried by white seamen to the Packet Ships, the crews of which altered the work 'knock' to 'blow', made the tune more musical and invented many new themes to fit the tune. Briggs in his book *Around Cape Horn to Honolulu in the Barque 'Amy Turner'* gives an early, probably hoosier version, with the refrain as 'Way, hay, knock a man down!', and also two other versions with the usual 'Blow the man down' refrains. Sharp gives a good example of an early *Knock a Man Down* shanty, probably the hoosier version.

KNOCK A MAN DOWN

(*English Folk-Chanteys*, London, 1914)

As to the words of *Blow the Man Down* as sung by the Packet Seamen and the sailors of latter-day windjammers, well, they came from everywhere. Those of our first version were lifted more or less as they were from the old forebitter *Ratcliffe Highway*—itself used as a capstan shanty and pumping song, so my informant old Paddy Delaney, who had sailed in Packet Ships, told me.

RATCLIFFE HIGHWAY

155

2. Her flag wuz three colours, her masthead wuz low,
She wuz round at the counter an' bluff at the bow.
From larboard to starboard an' so sailed she;
She wuz sailing at large, she wuz runnin' free.
    Ch. Singin' too-relye-addie, too-relye-addie,
      Singin' too-relye-addie, aye, too-relye-ay!

3. She wuz bowlin' along wid her wind blowin' free;
She clewed up her courses an' waited for me.
I fired me bow-chaser, the signal she knew,
She backed her maintops'l an' for me hove to.
    Ch. Singin', *etc.*

4. I hailed her in English, she answered me clear,
I'm from the Black Arrow, bound to the Shakespeare,
So I wore ship an' with a 'What d'ya know?'
I passed 'er me hawser an' took 'er in tow.

5. I tipped her me flipper an' took her in tow,
An' yard-arm to yard-arm away we did go,
She then took me up her lily-white room,
An' there all the evening we drank and we spooned.

(Verses 6 and 7 omitted.)

8. Soon the evening did pass, boys, I lashed up an' stowed,
I gave her some shillings 'fore I left her abode,
But it 'twarn't quite enough, boys, she wanted some more,
She cursed me an' called me a son-o'-a-whore.

9. She blazed like a frigate, at me she let fire,
An' nothing could stem, boys, that Irish tart's ire,
She kicked me an' cursed me an' stove in me jaw,
An' I beat retreat through her open back-door.

10. I've fought wid the Russians, the Prussians also,
I've fought wid the Dutch, an' wid Johnny Crapo,
But of all the fine fights that I ever did see,
She beat all the fights [sights] o' the heathen Chinee.

11. Now all ye young sailors take a warnin' I say,
Take it aisy, me boys, when yer down that Highway,
Steer clear of them flash gals, on the Highway do dwell,
Or they'll take up yer flipper an' yer soon bound ter Hell!

Many of these Western Ocean songs and shanties were sung in an Irish accent.

Much of the wording of this forebitter points to a naval origin, and that of the censored bawdy parts even more so. However it is also possible that nauticalisms such as 'stern-chasers', 'lash up an' stow', etc., may point merely to an East Indiaman origin, since many of these ships carried gunners and topmen, and carried out manoeuvres in true naval fashion. If this is so then the song is of fair antiquity, being extant long before the days of the Western Ocean Packets. Of course *Ratcliffe Highway* was known to the East Indiaman long before the Packet Rat or the Southspainer came into existence.

An alternative way of singing verse 5 is:

> In a snug little tavern, oh, soon we did moor,
> I bought me some rum for this young Highway whore,
> She told me her fancyman wuz at sea for a spell,
> So I gave her me flipper an' we wuz both bound to Hell.

Doerflinger gives an unusual verse from the singing of Captain Patrick Tayluer:

> I'll bring you silk dresses and all that I know,
> Fine gold rings and stones from the Islands, you know,
> I'll bring you home plenty of money to spend,
> If you'll only wait till I do return.

The pubs Doerflinger's other shantyman (William Laurie oı Sailors' Snug Harbor) gives are the 'Blue Anchor' and 'Brown Bear'.

Ratcliffe Highway, in the old days, was a tough quarter, full of pubs and 'dives', its pavements cluttered with drunks, pimps, crimps, and prostitutes, but to the sailorman its garish delights were something to look forward to when on an upper tops'l yard sail-clawing off the pitch of old Cape Stiff. Just the place to spend a pound— and there were many Pollies and Sallies awaiting to help Sailor John spend it with gusto. Nowadays, this famous highway is still there, but under another name. It is called, merely, The Highway.

Getting back to the halyard shanty *Blow the Man Down* we find that as well as London's Ratcliffe Highway other streets of various sailor-towns are sung about in most versions. Paradise Street and Great Howard Street were both in Liverpool and still are, although since being bombed during the war there is not much left of Paradise Street as such. Paradise Street was to the sailor another earthly Paradise, where after a long voyage he would stroll ashore, no man his master, money in his pockets to burn, and heading for one of the 'dives' would sort out, or rather be sorted out by, a fancy woman, who would help him spend his hard-earned wages in double-quick time. Great Howard Street was the home of the illustrious crimp and boarding-master Paddy West, of whom more anon. Winchester Street, which is in South Shields, was a different kettle of fish according to Terry, for here, 'in the old days was the aristocratic quarter where only persons of high distinction—such as shipowners and "Southspainer" skippers—lived.'

The six major versions of *Blow the Man Down* are as follows:

(*a*) The Flash Packet (from *Ratcliffe Highway*).
(*b*) The Sailing of the Blackballer.
(*c*) The Flying Fish Sailor or Policeman Version.
(*d*) The Fishes.
(*e*) The Milkmaid.
(*f*) Bungyereye.

Our first version although based on *Ratcliffe Highway* gives Paradise Street as the thoroughfare where Sailor John meets his fate.

I have had to camouflage this a great deal, as the original version was decidedly obscene, but I have kept to the theme as much as possible.

BLOW THE MAN DOWN (a)

Oh, as I wuz a-rollin' down Pa-ra-dise Street, Timme way, hay, blow the man down! a sas-sy, flash clip-per I chanct for to meet, Ooh! give us some time to blow the man down!

2. Of the port that she hailed from I cannot say much,
    Ch. Timme *way*, hay, *blow* the man down!
But by her appearance I took her for Dutch,
    Ch. Oooh, *give* us some time ter *blow* the man down! [or *Gimme* some time, *etc.*]

3. Her flag wuz three colours and her masthead wuz low,
    Ch. Timme, *etc.*
She wuz round in the counter an' bluff at the bow,
    Ch. Oooh, give, *etc.*

4. From larboard to starboard an' so sailed she,
    She wuz sailin' at large—she wuz runnin' free.

5. I fired my bow-chaser the signal she knew,
    She backed her maintawps'l an' for me hove to.

6. She wuz bowlin' along with the wind blowin' free,
    She clewed up her courses an' waited for me.

7. I hailed her in English she answered me clear,
    'I'm from the Black Arrow bound to the Shakespeare.'

8. I tipped her me flipper an' took her in tow,
    An' yard-arm to yard-arm away we did go.

HAULING ON THE TOPS'L HALYARDS

'Oh, as I wuz a-rollin' down Paradise Street . . .' (Halyard Shanty)

9. She then took me up to her lily-white room,
   An' there all the evening we danced and we spooned.

10. Me shot-locker's empty, me powder's all spent,
    I've plenty o' time, boys, to think and repent.

From here onwards other couplets of *Ratcliffe Highway* were used.
This and most other versions of *Blow the Man Down* usually start with
either one of the following two stanzas:

Come all ye young sailors that follow the sea,
Come list to me story, I'll sing it to ye.
I'll sing ye a song all about the high sea [a good song o' the sea],
An' trust that ye'll join in the chorus with me.

Version (*b*) is the sailing of a Blackballer from Liverpool, although
some shantymen sang of the London Ratcliffe Highway as being the
street where the 'flash packet' coerced the young seaman to join the
Blackballer. Of all the Western Ocean Packets the most famous (or
infamous) were those of the Blackball Line. The company started
in the year 1818 with small ships of a few hundred tons, later, about
the fifties, building larger vessels for the run across the Atlantic—
a run they made in defiance of the weather, sailing regularly on the
first and sixteenth of each month with all the regularity of steamers,
from New York, as well as from Boston and Philadelphia, towards
Liverpool, London, and the French port of Le Havre. About the
year 1878 they wound up, but not before they had put the name of
Yankee ships well to the top not only in regard to speed, regularity,
and good seamanship but also to the infamous methods of their hell-
and-be-damned skippers and the toughness of their hard-case crews.
Many earned the name of 'blood-boat' and 'red-hot Yank', but
they were also the fertile field in which the shanty, in many cases,
originated and developed. The seamen before the mast were mainly
New York or Liverpool-Irish, although in later days many other
nationalities drifted into their employ. By 1880 the Packets had been
ousted by the growing number of steamers and many of them
entered other trades or were sold foreign, and the crimson swallowtail flag with its black ball (which was also shown on the fore topsail)
of the Blackball Line, the red cross on a white background of the
Red Cross Line, the blue and white swallowtail flag of the Swallowtail Line, the black cross of the Black Cross Line, and other famous
and notorious house-flags were no longer to be seen flying from
the gaffs of those hard-case breeding grounds of the Packet Rat.

The verses of Version (*b*) I had from old Paddy Delaney, with two
or three from Bill Fuller who sang similar verses in his version of
Bound Away. There were two ways of starting this shanty.

BLOW THE MAN DOWN

First Method.

    1. In the Blackball Line I served my time,
        Ch. Timme way, hay, blow the man down!
    In the Blackball Line I wasted me prime,
        Ch. Ooh! gimme some time to blow the man down!

    2. Blackball ships are good an' true,
    They're the ships for me an' you.

    3. There wuz once a Blackball ship,
    That fourteen knots an hour could clip.

    4. 'Twas when this Blackballer wuz ready for sea,
    'Tis then that you'd see such a hell o' a spree
    [*or* The sights in the fo'c'sle is funny to see].

(*Continue at verse 5.*)

Second Method.

    1. Oh, as I wuz a-rollin' down Great Howard Street,
    A handsome flash packet I chanct for to meet.

    2. This spankin' flash packet she said unto me,
    'There's a dandy full-rigger [Blackballer] just ready for sea.'

    3. This dandy full-rigger to New York wuz bound,
    She wuz very well rigged an' very well found.

    4. So I packed up me sea-bag [sea-chest] an' signed on that day,
    An' with this flash packet I spent me half-pay.

(*Now sing verse 4 of the First Method and then continue at verse 5.*)

    5. There's tinkers an' tailors an' sogers an' all,
    All ship as prime seamen aboard the Blackball.

    6. Oh, muster ye sojers an' fakirs an' sich,
    An' hear yer name called by a son-o'-a-bitch.

    7. An' when the Blackballer hauls out o' the dock,
    To see these poor barstards, how on deck they flock.

    8. 'Lay aft here, ye lubbers! Lay aft one an' all,
    I'll have none o' yer dodges [dodging] aboard this Blackball!'

    9. Now see these poor barstards how aloft they will scoot,
    Assisted along by the toe o' a boot.

  10. The second mate stands 'em all up in a row,
    A seam in the deck he sure makes 'em all toe.

  11. It's 'Fore tawps'l halyards!' the mate he will roar,
    'Oh, lay along smartly, ye son-o'-a-whore!'

12. It's 'way aloft, lubbers, shake them tawps'ls out,
    The last man in the riggin' he clouts on the snout.

13. Oh, lay along smartly each lousy recruit,
    Or 'tis lifted ye'll be by the greaser's sea-boot.

14. 'Tis larboard an' starboard on deck ye will sprawl,
    For Kickin' Jack Williams commands this Blackball.

15. An' when the Blackballer is leavin' the dock,
    All the pretty young gals on the pierhead do flock.

16. An' now when she's leavin' the ol' Merseyside,
    All hands are now ordered to scrub the ship's side.

17. An' now when she's clear over ol' Mersey Bar,
    The mate knocks 'em down with a big caps'n-bar.

18. An' when the Blackballer hauls clear o' the land,
    The bosun roars out the hoarse words o' command.

19. Yes, soon as the packet is well out to sea,
    'Tis cruel, hard treatment o' every degree.

20. Ye've handspike hash every day for yer tea,
    An' belayin'-pin soup many times will ye see.

21. Now we are sailin' the Western so wide,
    An' the green rollin' seas run along our black side.

22. Soon, bully boys, we'll be back round the Rock,
    An' then, bully boys, we'll be snug in the dock.

23. An' then all the hands they will bundle ashore,
    To ship in a Blackballer we'll niver do more.

(*The following three verses were used to wind up the Second Method.*)

24. So I'll give ye a warnin' afore we belay,
    Don't take it for Gospel what spankin' gals say.

25. Don't ye go a-strollin' down Great Howard Street,
    Or else such a chowlah ye'll happen to meet.

26. For she'll spin ye such lies an' they'll sign ye away,
    On a hardcase Blackballer where there's hell every day.

27. So we'll blow the man up, bullies, blow the man down,
    Wid a crew o' hard cases from Liverpool town.

It must be explained that the Packet Rats rarely made a round trip in these ships, therefore men had to be signed on on both sides of the Atlantic. They would freely boast that they never made more than a 'passage', i.e. a one-way trip, and would never work in port, work beneath the dignity of a sailor, only fit for longshoremen. Later when the Western Ocean Packets began to be ousted by steam this version was altered slightly so far as the ports were concerned. Baines, who bought many famous American ships such as *Lightning* and *Flying Cloud*, also had a Blackball Line, which carried on the emigrant trade to Australia for many years after steam had entered the Western Ocean Trade, and so the shantyman would sing the same theme, but Sydney, Adelaide, and Melbourne would be the ports sung about. In Sharp's version of the *Blackball Line* the shantyman sends a Blackballer on an impossible run—down to Mobile Bay for cotton. This altering of a 'run' by the shantyman was common, and very often he would sail her with cheerful inconsequence to some port never thought of by her owners. The shantyman didn't worry, so why should we? Some collectors reject this sort of thing on the grounds of historical inaccuracy, but I feel this is being too pedantic. Such versions *were* sung, and that's all that matters.

Our next version is the famous one about the 'flying-fish sailor' who was mistaken for a Blackball seaman. A 'flying-fish sailor' was a John who preferred the lands of the East and the warmth of the Trade Winds to the cold and misery of the Western Ocean.

BLOW THE MAN DOWN (c)

1. I'm a deepwater sailor just home from Hong Kong.
   If ye give me some whisky I'll sing ye a song.

2. As I was a-walkin' down Paradise Street [Great Howard Street],
   A handsome fat policeman I happened to meet.

3. Sez he, 'Yer a Blackballer by the cut o' yer hair,
   An' the long, red-topped seaboots that I see yer wear.

4. 'Ye've sailed in some packet that flies the Blackball,
   Ye've robbed some poor Dutchman o' boots, clothes an' all.'

5. 'O mister, O mister, ye do me great wrong,
   I'm a flyin'-fish sailor, just home from Hong Kong.'

6. So I spat in his face, an' I stove in his jaw [gave him some jaw].
   Sez he, 'Here, young feller, yer breakin' the law!'

7. They gave me six months, boys, in ol' Walton town,
   For bootin' an' kickin' an' blowin' him down.

8. Now all ye young fellers what follow the sea,
   Put yer vents on the wind an' just listen to me.

9. I'll give ye a warnin' afore we belay,
   Steer clear o' fat policemen, ye'll find it'll pay.

Doerflinger seems to think that the foregoing is a parody of the Scottish song *Erin-go-Bragh* in which an Edinburgh man is rounded up as being a 'straggler' from Ireland.

Our next version is that of *The Fishes* already referred to. I had this from Bosun Chenoworth, ex-Dundee whalers.

BLOW THE MAN DOWN (d)

1. I'll sing ye a song o' the fish o' the sea [Come all ye young sailormen, listen to me],
   An' I trust that ye'll join in the chorus with me [I'll sing ye a song o' the fish o' the sea].

2. There wuz once an old skipper, I don't know his name,
   But I know that he once played a ruddy smart game.

3. When his ship lay becalmed in a tropical sea,
   He whistled all day but he could get no breeze.

4. But a seal heard his whistle an' loudly did call,
   'Just stow yer light canvas, jib, spanker, an' all.

5. I'll send ye some fish to consult if ye please,
   The best way to get ye a nice whistling breeze.'

6. Oh, first came the herring, sayin', 'I'm King o' the Seas',
   He jumped on the poop: 'Oh, the Capen I'll be!'

7. Next came the flatfish, they call him a skate:
   'If ye'll be the capen, why then I'm the mate.'

8. Then next came the hake, he wuz black as a rook,
   Sez he, 'I'm no sailor, I'll ship as the cook.'

9. Next came the shark with his two rows of teeth,
   'Cook, mind you the cabbage, an' I'll mind the beef!'

10. Then came the eel with his slippery tail,
    He climbed up aloft an' he cast off each sail.

11. Next came the codfish with his chuckle-head,
    He jumped in the chains an' began heavin' the lead.

12. Next came the flounder that lies on the ground,
    Sayin', 'Damn yer eyes, chucklehead, mind how ye sound!'

13. Then came the conger, as long as a mile,
    He gave a broad grin an' continued to smile.

14. Then came the porpoise with his pointed snout,
    He went to the wheel shoutin', 'Ready about!'

15. Then came the mackerel with his pretty striped back,
    He hauled aft each sheet, an' he boarded each tack.

16. Then came the whale, the biggest in the sea,
    Shoutin', 'Haul in yer head sheets, now, hellums a lee!'

17. Then came the sprat, he wuz smallest o' all,
    He jumped on the poop cryin', 'Maintawps'l haul!'

18. The mackerel the skipper did scoff for his tea,
    The herring he salted, the seal harpooned he.

19. He baited a hook, an' he thought it a lark,
    To catch as he did that hoary ol' shark.

20. The eel it wuz tasty, the hake it wuz strong,
    The flounder he speared with a lance o' three prongs.

21. The skate he speared next, but the porpose wuz fast,
    The conger it grinned an' it grinned to the last.

22. He caught the ol' whale, which wuz no simple task,
    An' soon with whale-oil he had filled up each cask.

23. With the head o' the codfish he made a fine pipe,
    The sprat then he salted, but 'twas only a bite.

24. The breeze it blew merrily, an' merrily sailed he,
    But what an' ol' barstard that skipper must be!

Alternative verses:

Shark. The first fish to come wuz a hoary old shark,
    Saying, 'I'll chew ye up if ye play me a lark.'

Whale. Next came the whale which wuz biggest o' all,
    He climbed up aloft an' he let each sail fall.

Lobster. Next came the lobster with his prickly back,
    He said, 'I'll go for'ard an' board the main-tack.'

Herring. Last came the herring, the King of the Sea,
    Sayin', 'Haul in yer head sheets, now, hellums a-lee!'

Thrasher. Then came the thrasher, a-slashin' his tail;
    He climbed up aloft an' he loosed every sail.

Our fifth version is the Milkmaid one. This is distinctly Rabelaisian and had to be camouflaged quite a lot. It is based on the old
folk-song *Where are ye going to, my pretty maid?* This version was also
sung to the tune of *Rio Grande, Goodbye, Fare-ye-well,* and others.

BLOW THE MAN DOWN (e)

1. Oh, where are ye goin' to, my pretty maid?
   'Oh, I'm goin' a milkin', kind sir,' she said.

2. Oh, have ye a sweetheart, my pretty maid?
   'I'm lookin' for one, kind sir,' she said.

3. Then may I come wid ye, my pretty maid?
   'Well, yes, since ye axed me, sir,' she said.

4. 'But I guess yer a bad one, kind sir,' she said.
   'Yer want for to love me, but yer don't want ter wed.'

5. Jack took her in tow, an' away they did go,
   The bulls did a grunt, an' the cows did a low.

6. They came to a haystack but the maid she wuz shy,
   They backed and they filled an' heaved many a sigh.

7. The haystack capsized an' Jack got all bent,
   With hay in his gaff-tops'l, his breeches all rent.

8. So he left her a-sittin' a-lookin' forlorn,
   An' shipped to the south'ard away round Cape Horn.

9. Now all ye young sailors that round the Horn sail,
   Don't take a young milkmaid away from her pail.

10. Or else ye'll regret it an' wish ye were dead,
    So don't go a-courtin' in a haystack for a bed.

('Gaff-tops'l' was the sailor's name for a top-hat.)

The sixth version of this famous tops'l halyard shanty I learnt
from my old shipmate Paddy Griffiths. He told me that 'Bungyereye'
was a slang term for a certain kind of whisky popular towards the
end of the last century.

BLOW THE MAN DOWN (f)

1. Jack bein' a sailor, he walked London town,
   She bein' a damsel that walked up an' down.

2. She came over to Jack and axed if he'd buy,
   'I have here in me basket some young Bungyereye.'

3. 'Be-damn me,' sez Jack, 'Oh, what can this be?'
   'The finest o' whisky from far German-ee.

4. 'Smuggled over in a basket an' sold on the sly,
   An' it goes by the name o' the Young Bungyereye.'

5. Jack slipped her a pound an' he thought nothing strange.
   'Hold the basket, young man, while I goes for the change.

6. 'An' ax all them sailors, as they pass you by,
   Would they care for to purchase some young Bungyereye.'

7. Jack waited an hour an' he thought it wuz strange,
   'Tis a hell o' a time fer to wait fer me change!

8. He waited all evening but the maid she had flown.
   Then out of the basket there came a low moan.

9. Jack opened the basket, the strings did untie,
   Rolled up in brown paper wuz a fat little boy!

10. To git this babe christened young Jack was intent,
    So he steered a straight course, to the passon he went.

11. 'What name shall I call it?' the passon did cry.
    'What name shall ye call it?' says Jack. 'Bungyereye!'

12. 'Bungyereye?' sez the passon. 'Well, that's a queer name.'
    'Be damned me,' sez Jack. ''Tis the queer way it came.

13. 'For instead of strong whisky that I chanct to buy,
    Rolled up in brown paper wuz young Bungyereye.'

14. Oh, a warnin', boys, take now, afore we belay,
    Don't ever take heed of what pretty gals say.

15. They'll leave ye a-holdin' a fat baby boy,
    Instead of a bottle of strong Bungyereye.

Paddy Griffiths said he had sung this version aboard both the ships *Birkdale* and *Bidston Hill*.

Les Nickerson, of Freeport, Nova Scotia, sang for Doerflinger the following version, which appears to have come from the Anglo-Scottish ballad *The Three Crows* or *Twa Corbies*:

1. There were three crows sat on a tree,
       Ch. Way, *etc.*
   And they were black as black could be,
       Ch. Gimme, *etc.*

2. Says one old crow unto his mate,
   'Where shall we go for something to eat?'

3. 'There is an old horse on yonder hill,
   And there we can go and eat our fill.

4. 'There is an old horse on yonder mound,
   We'll light upon to his jawbone.' ·

5. Says one old crow unto the other,
   'We'll pick his eyes out one by one.'

Getting back to shanties with the word 'blow' in·them we have *Blow Ye Winds in the Morning*, although the 'blow' in this case had not the meaning of that used by the Packet Rats. Whall says it was a song of the midshipmen's berth rather than that of the fo'c'sle. Miss Colcord gives it as a whalers' song, but Terry has it as a capstan shanty, and as such I give it here. Terry also says that in his opinion it is the only instance of a sea-song being sung as a shanty. But what about *Rolling Home, Home, Home, High Barbaree*, and many others? They were all sea-songs which became popular at sea as shanties. Sharp also gives it as a shanty and I think he had it from the same shantyman as Terry—Mr. Short of Watchet, Somerset.

BLOW, YE WINDS (a)

As I walked out one morning fair, to view the meadows round, 'Tis there I spied a pretty lass come

trippin' o'er the ground, Singing blow ye winds in the mornin', Blow ye winds high ho! See all clear yer

runnin' gear an' blow, me bully boys, blow!

2. My father has a milk-white steed an' he is in his stall,
   He is a clever circus horse, he can balance on a ball,
   Ch. Singin' blow, ye winds, in the mornin',
       Blow, ye winds, high-ho!
       See all clear yer runnin' gear,
       An' blow, me bully boys, blow!

3. When we goes in a farmer's yard an' sees a great big duck,
   We catch him an' we wring his neck, if we have any luck.
   Ch. Singin', *etc.*

4. As I wuz out a-walkin', close by the riverside,
   'Tis there I spied a naked lass a-swimmin' in the tide.

5. Oh, as I wuz out a-walkin' all in the pale moonlight,
   'Tis there I spied a yaller gal, her eyes they shone so bright.

6. As I wuz out a-walkin' down Paradise's Street,
   It's there I met a flash chowlah, who said, 'Will ye stand treat?'

7. She took me arm an' I took hers an' off we rolled away,
   We steered into the Dewdrop Inn, where I could blow me pay.

BLOW, YE WINDS (b)

1. 'Twas on a Sunday mornin', down 'cross the Southern Sea,
   Our ship she lay at anchor, while awaitin' for a breeze.
   Ch. Singin', blow ye winds in the mornin',
       Blow, ye winds, high-ho!
       Clear away yer runnin' gear [See all clear yer runnin' gear],
       An' blow, me bully-boys, blow!

2. The cap'n he wuz down below, the men at their work about,
   When under our bow we heard a splash, an' then a lusty shout.
   Ch. Singin', *etc.*

3. 'Man overboard!' the lookout cried, an' for'ard we all ran,
   An' hangin' to our larboard chains wuz a bluff, ol' green merman.

4. His hair wuz blue, his eyes wuz green, his mouth wuz big as three,
   An' the long green tail that he sat on wuz wigglin' in the sea.

5. 'Hello!' cried the Mate as bold as brass, 'What-ho! shipmates,' cried he.
   'Oh, I want ter speak ter yer Ol' Man, I've a favour to ask, ye see.

6. 'I've bin out all night on a ruddy sea-fight at the bottom of the deep
     blue sea,
   I've just come home and find that ye have caused a hell o' a spree.

7. 'Oh, ye've dropped yer anchor afore me house, an' blocked me only
     door,
   An' me wife's blocked in an' she can't git out, nor me babes who
     number four.'

8. 'The anchor shall be hove at once, an' yer wife an' yer babes set free,
   But I never saw a scale from a sprat to a whale till now that could
     speak to me.

9. 'Yer figgerhead is a sailor's bold, an' ye speak like a human man,
   But where did yer git such a ruddy big tail, answer me that if yer
     can.'

10. 'A long time ago from the ship *Hero* I fell overboard in a gale,
    An' away down below where the seaweeds grow, I met a gal with a
      tail.

11. 'She saved me life, an' I made her me wife, an' me legs changed
      instantly,
    An' now I'm married to a sweet mermaid at the bottom of the deep
      blue sea.

12. 'So I'll stay here for the rest o' me life, with never a worry nor care.
    Goodbye to the trade of a sailor bold—my lot with the fishes I'll share.'

Sharp's shantyman has a starting verse:

> As I walked out one morning fair, all in the month of June,
> I overheard an Irish girl a-singing this old tune.

However, when sung as a shanty our next version was even more
popular. Miss Colcord gives a version calling it a forebitter, but
Harlow gives it as a shanty. My version, obtained from a shipmate—
'Taff' Davies of Anglesey—is closely allied to both. It was sung at the
capstan and pumps to the same tune as version (*a*).

Here is the whaler version given only by Miss Colcord, who
obtained it from an old logbook in the New Bedford Public Library:

BLOW, YE WINDS (c)

1. 'Tis advertised in Boston, New York, and Buffalo,
   Five hundred brave Americans a-whaling for to go.
   Ch. Blow, ye winds, in the morning,
   And blow, ye winds, high-O!
   Clear away your running gear,
   And blow, ye winds, high-O!

2. They send you to New Bedford, that famous whaling port;
   And give you to some land-sharks for to board and fit you out.

3. They send you to a boarding house, there for a time to dwell,
   The thieves they there are thicker than the other side of hell!

4. They tell you of the clipper ships a-going in and out,
   And say you'll take five hundred sperm, before you're six months out.

5. It's now we're out to sea, my boys, the wind comes on to blow,
   One half the watch is sick on deck, the other half below.

6. But as for the provisions, we don't get half enough,
   A little piece of stinking beef and a blamed small bag of duff.

7. Now comes that damned old compass, it will grieve your heart full
   sore,
   For theirs is two-and-thirty points and we have forty-four.

8. Next comes the running rigging, which you're all supposed to know,
   'Tis 'Lay aloft, you son-of-a-gun, or overboard you go!'

9. The cooper's at the vise-bench, a-making iron poles,
   And the mate's upon the main hatch, a-cursing all our souls.

10. The Skipper's on the quarter-deck, a-squinting at the sails,
    When up aloft the lookout sights a school of whales.

11. 'Now clear away the boats, my boys, and after him we'll travel,
    But if you get too near his fluke, he'll kick you to the devil!'

12. Now we have got him turned up, we tow him alongside;
    We over with our blubber-hooks and rob him of his hide.

13. Now the boat-steerer overside the tackle overhauls,
    The Skipper's in the main-chains, so loudly he does bawl!

14. Next comes the stowing down, my boys; 'twill take both night and
    day,
    And you'll all have fifty cents apiece on the hundred and ninetieth
    lay.

15. Now we are bound into Tonbas, that blasted whaling port,
    And if you run away, my boys, you surely will get caught.

16. Now we are bound into Tuckoona, full more in their power,
    Where the skippers can buy the Consul up for half a barrel of flour!

17. But now that our old ship is full and we don't give a damn,
    We'll bend on all our stuns'ls and sail for Yankee land.

18. When we get home, our ship made fast, and we get through our
    sailing,
    A winding glass around we'll pass and damn this blubber whaling!

     (*Songs of American Sailormen*, W. W. Norton & Co., N.Y., 1938)

Another shanty with the word 'blow' in it is that fine old tops'l
halyard chorus *Blow, Me Bully Boys, Blow!*
This shanty has three patterns:

   (*a*) The Guinea Slaver;
   (*b*) The Bucko Ship (A Yankee China Clipper);
   (*c*) The Harry Tate Ship (English skit on Yankee Packets).

This shanty has in its different versions humour and much hard
fact. The fact that many of the Yankee clippers were hell-ships,
albeit much good seamanship was to be found aboard them, is now
well established. Doerflinger writes that the verse about the 'masts
and yards they shine like silver' or, as his shantyman, Captain
Tayluer of New York gives it, 'Her spars were of gold and her
masts were of silver' is nothing more than a reference to the custom
of painting the lower masts white and the yards some light colour,
'whereas the usual British practice had been to paint the masts
and yards in dark colours'. In fact in all British clippers the lower
masts, bowsprit, and doublings were painted white and many ships
had light-coloured yards, even pink! But the shanty has nothing to
do with the light *paint* of the masts and yards. To quote Terry:
'spotless decks and "masts and yards that shone like silver" were the
distinguishing marks of a Yankee Packet, and this immaculate
condition was the result of a terrible discipline, in which the belaying-
pin was a gruesome factor.' And sand and canvas, and the holystone,
and suji-muji (soda-water)!
The masters and mates who drove these tough ships had various
names in the mouths of different shantymen, some humorous and
made up, some real 'buckos' of the old-time hell-ships.
First I will give the fine old version of the Guinea Slavers. I
obtained this from an Australian seaman, ex-*Manurewa* and *Silver
Pine*.

BLOW, BOYS, BLOW (a)

Say, wuz ye niver down the Con-go Riv-er? Blow, boys, blow! Ooh! yes I've bin down the

Con-go Riv-er, Blow me bul-ly boys, blow!

2. Congo she's a mighty river,
    Ch. Blow, boys, blow!
  Where the fever makes the white man shiver,
    Ch. Blow me bully boys, blow!

3. A Yankee ship came down the river,
  As she rolls down her tops'ls shiver.

4. Yonder comes the *Arrow* packet,
  She fired her guns an' I heard the racket. [Don't ye hear the racket?]

5. Yonder comes a Creole lady,
  I guess she's got a nigger baby.

6. Who d'yer thinks the skipper of her?
  Why, ol' Bully Pete, the nigger lover.

7. Who d'yer thinks the chief mate of her?
  Why, Saccarappa Joe wuz the chief mate of her.

(Verses about *second mate, meals*, etc.—same as Bucko Ship version (*b*))

> What d'yer think they had for carger?
> Why, black sheep that have run the Embarger.
>
> Blow me, boys, an' blow for ever [together],
> Blow me down to the Congo River.

This was a shanty in which the singer often repeated the solo lines, to string out on a long haul. I raised this shanty once at eight bells in the middle watch when our Old Man decided to set the main t'gallant after a bit of a blow. Both watches tailed on the fall, and the helmsman later told me that, from his position aft, the singing of this shanty was one of the finest things it had ever been his privilege to enjoy at sea.

BLOW, BOYS, BLOW (b)

1. Blow, me boys, I long ter hear yer,
    Ch. Blow, boys, etc.
  Oooh, blow, me boys, an' I long ter hear yer,
    Ch. Blow, me bully, etc.

172

2. A Yankee ship came down the river,
   Her masts and yards they shine like silver.

3. How d'yer know she's a Yankee clipper?
   By the blood an' guts that flow from her scuppers.

4. How d'yer know she's Yankee liner?
   By the stars an' bars streamin' out behind her.

5. How d'yer know she's a Yankee packet?
   She fired her guns an' we heard the racket.

6. She's a Yankee ship an' she's bound to China,
   And a bunch o' barstards they have signed her.

7. How d'yer know she's bound for China?
   By the flyin'-fish sailors what 'ave gone an' joined her.

8. Who d'yer thinks the skipper of her?
   Why, Ol' Bully Forbes [Waterman] is the skipper of her.

9. Who d'yer thinks the chief mate of her?
   Some ugly case what 'ates poor sailors.

10. Who d'yer think wuz second mate of her?
    Saccarappa Jim was the second mate of her.

11. Saccarappa Jim he's a rocket from hell, boys,
    He'll ride yiz down like yiz ride a spanker.

12. What d'yer think they had for breakfast?
    Why, the starboard side o' an ol' sou'wester.

13. What d'yer think they had for dinner?
    Belayin'-pin soup an' a squeeze through the wringer.

14. What d'yer think they had for supper?
    Oh, handspike hash an' a roll in the scuppers.

15. What d'yer think they had for carger?
    Five hundred whores from Yokohammer.

16. Ye'll wish ye all wuz dead an' buried,
    An' cross the river lets all git ferried.

17. Six days work as ye are able,
    On the seventh day, bullies, ye will [shall] chip the cable.

18. On this bloodboat there ain't no laybacks,
    Get haulin', all ye lazy shellbacks.

19. Blow today an' blow termorrer,
    Blow for this hell-ship all in sorrer.

The last version is the story of the Harry Tate ship.

BLOW, BOYS, BLOW (c)

1. Oh, blow, me boys, I long ter hear yer,
   Oh, blow, me boys, I can't git near yer.

2. Oh, a Yankee ship came down the river,
   Her masts all bent, her sails a-shiver.

3. How d'yer know she's a Yankee clipper?
   By the Stars an' Bars that fly above her.

4. Who d'yer think wuz skipper of her?
   Why, Slimey Joe wuz the skipper of her.

5. An' who d'yer think wuz chief mate of her?
   Why, Boss-eyed Bill the Bowery Bastard [One-eyed Kelly the
   Bowery Runner].

6. Who d'yer thinks the second greaser?
   Why, Santander Jim the 'Frisco bludger.

7. The Third wuz Sam the Slippery Dodger,
   He'll ride yiz down like yiz ride a spanker.

8. The bosun wuz a big buck nigger,
   His handle wuz Joe the 'Frisco Digger.

9. The sails wuz just a jobbin' tailor,
   The chips wuz not a Blackwall sailor.

10. The cook wuz Jack the Boston Booty,
    The steward had to learn his dooty.

11. Her sides wuz old an' her sails wuz rotten,
    His charts the Old Man had forgotten.

12. Irish pennants in her riggin' [Scotchmen hangin' in her riggin'].
    Oh, can't yiz hear them banjoes [backstays] pingin'?

13. The crew wuz anything but frisky,
    They'd never crossed the Bay o' Biscay.

14. What d'yer think they had for dinner?
    Nanny goat's horns an' a Chinaman's liver.

15. She sailed away for Kingston City,
    Never got there, the more's the pity.

16. Blow today an' blow termorrer,
    Blow for that ol' ship in sorrer.

Doerflinger writes that sometimes the words of the shanty called
The Dead Horse were sung to this halyard song. He also points out
that the verse about what they had for supper, etc., is to be found in
many nigger minstrel songs and gives an example from *Zip Coon*:

174

What do you tink now Sukey had for supper,
Why chicken foot and possum heel widout any butter.

This shanty, as Miss Colcord has pointed out, is one of the famous Western Ocean Packet trio—*Blow, Boys, Blow, Blow the Man Down*, and *The Blackball Line*, and, although some authorities seem to think it started its career in the Guinea Slaving Trade, the possibility that it started in the Packet Trade (about 1813) is stronger, and the reference to the Slaving Trade was probably in connection with certain disreputable skippers and shipowners who allowed their vessels to do a spot of slaving, and even piracy, prior to the year 1825, when the slavers and pirates of the West Indies and Guinea Coast were partly cleaned up by the joint effort of America and several European powers. The verse about 'black sheep that have run the Embargo' points to latter-day slaving, as the Embargo was not enforced until about 1800. A Scandinavian pumping song called *Svineper* is all about a 'dirty old pig' and the story told is very like that of the Harry Tate ship and her crew in *Blow, Boys, Blow* (c).

And while we still have 'pigs' in mind we will next give a shanty built around the dirtiest 'sailor' who ever shipped—Reuben Ranzo.

Ranzo was one of the most rousing of all the halyard shanties, the name *Ranzo* beating even the word 'blow' as a savage shout on which to pull—a man just *had* to pull when he roared out 'Rrranzo!' This song was very popular amongst whalers. Who Reuben Ranzo was 'tis hard to say. Here are some of the theories already offered by collectors.

(1) He was a native of the Azores, of Portuguese descent, who shipped in a whaler like many of the Azores Islanders used to do—mainly as harpooners. This may explain the name 'Ranzo'—an abbreviation of 'Lorenzo' a common Portuguese name—but the name 'Reuben' I don't think fits into this picture.

(2) He was a famous Danish hero of the sixteenth century, a certain Daniel Rantzau. Apparently this character is often referred to in Danish sea-songs. He was the hero of Denmark's Seven Years' War with Sweden, but I doubt if he had any connection with whalers!

(3) C. F. Smith thinks he must have been a Russian or Polish Jew with a name like Ronzoff—his 'Christian' name of Reuben would certainly suit the bill. Not often found at sea (in the past), Jews also have the supposed characteristic of not liking soap and water. Also our Ranzo was a 'tailor', a common occupation of Jews, and he shows, too, the national trait of desiring to get on in the world.

(4) He was an American Latin, a 'greenhorn', hence his first name of 'Reuben'—'Reub' or 'Rube' is still used in the States to mean a yokel or farmer.

Many shantymen sang 'Renzo' which would seem to indicate a 'Lorenzo' origin. Briggs gives:

Now he sails the South Seas over,
Orenso, boys, Orenso. . . .

also bearing out this theory. 'Rubin' and 'Robin' too have been sung for 'Reuben'. '*Rovin*' Ranzo' was also sung.

Bone says of this shanty that it was a 'favourite song with the fo'c'sle, for in it there lay opportunity for many a sly innuendo directed aft to the officers. It holds the story of an indifferent fellow who could not learn much of the handcraft and seamanship in a whaler, but who, by account of "book larnin' ", attained some proficiency in the sister (but gentler) art of navigation and attained to the high post of Captain.'[1]

Terry writes that this shanty had many endings and he gives four known to him:

(1) Ranzo marries the captain's daughter.
(2) Crew throw him overboard on account of his dirty habits.
(3) He receives a good lashing for stealing the captain's turkey.
(4) He has further adventures at the bottom of the sea after being thrown overboard.

The tune varies but little in the mouths of different shantymen. A rather common way of starting this shanty was for the shantyman to sing the chorus first. The shantyman would throw his arm out in an unconsciously dramatic gesture and at the same time burst forth with the refrain. With some shanties such as *Lowlands, Shallow Brown*, etc., this was done invariably; with others it was done when the shantyman had some doubt as to whether the crowd knew the song in question. Whall says that there was rarely any attempt to improvise after the regulation story had been told. Incidentally this is one of the many shanties in which, in a long hoist, the shantyman would repeat the solo lines. A sacrilegious but nevertheless very popular way of starting *Ranzo* was:

Ooooh! Jesus Christ Almighty!
Ranzo, boys, Ranzo!
Ooooh! Jesus Christ Almighty!
Ranzo, boys, Ranzo!

My version is a combination of verses given me by A. Spencer, ex-American barque *Monongohela* and the Bosun of the *Garthpool*.

REUBEN RANZO

Ooob! poor ol' Rua-ben Ran- zo, Ran-zo, boys, Ran-zo! O-ob! poor ol' Rua-ben Ran-zo, Ran-zo, boys, Ran-zo!

2. Oh, Ranzo wuz no sailor,
     Ch. Ranzo, boys, *Ranzo!*
He wuz a New York [Boston] tailor,
     Ch. Ranzo, boys, *Ranzo!*

[1]Captain D. W. Bone, *Capstan Bars*, published by the Porpoise Press, 1931.

3. Though Ranzo wuz no sailor,
   He shipped aboard of a whaler.

4. The *Pierre Loti* wuz a whaler,
   But Ranzo wuz no sailor.

5. Ranzo joined *Pierre Loti*,
   Did no' know his dooty.

6. Shanghaied aboard of a whaler,
   They tried to make him a sailor.

7. Ranzo couldn't steer 'er—
   Did ye ever know anything queerer?

8. The mate he wuz a dandy,
   Far too fond o' brandy.

9. Put him holystonin',
   An' cared not for his groanin'.

10. They said he wuz a lubber,
    And made him eat whale-blubber.

11. He washed once in a fortnight,
    He said it wuz his birthright.

12. They took him to the gangway [then rigged up the
    gangway],
    An' gave him lashes twenty.

13. They gave him lashes twenty,
    Nineteen more than plenty.

14. They gave him lashes thirty,
    Because he wuz so dirty.

15. Reuben Ranzo fainted,
    His back with oil wuz painted.

16. The Capen gave him thirty,
    His daughter begged for mercy.

17. She took him to the cabin,
    An' tried to ease his achin'.

18. She gave him cake an' water,
    An' a bit more than she oughter.

19. She gave him rum an' whisky,
    Which made him feel damn frisky.

20. She taught him navigation,
    An' gave him eddication.

21. They gave him an extra ratin',
    An' made him fit for his station.

22. They made him the best sailor,
    Sailin' on that whaler.

23. Ranzo now the skipper
    Of a Yankee whaler [Blackball *or* Yankee Clipper *or*
    China Clipper].

24. An' when he gets a sailor,
    Who's iggerant on a whaler,

25. He takes him to his cabin,
    An' larns him navigatin'.

26. He married the Old Man's daughter,
    An' still sails on blue water.

27. He's known wherever them whalefish blow
    As the toughest barstard on the go.

28. Hurrah for Reuben Ranzo,
    Hurrah for Captain Ranzo!

Another version states that 'when he got his square-rig papers'
he became 'a terror to all whalers'. Doerflinger's singer sends him to
South Georgia, which I fear is an anachronism, since Antarctic
whaling didn't commence until between the two World Wars, after
the South Sea cachalot became nearly extinct and the new-fangled
whalers began to search for the blue whale! Some shantymen would
'take him to the gratin' ' or 'Rig up a fine gratin' ' and some gave
him lashes 'five an' thirty' or 'nine an' twenty'. Cecil Sharp has:

> He shipped with Captain Taylor,
> The man who shot a sailor,
> He couldn't boil coffee,

and:

> The cap'n had a daughter,
> Who cried, 'Father do have mercy.'

And one version runs:

> He went to school on Monday,
> An' learnt to read on Tuesday.

> He learnt to write on Wednesday,
> An' how to fight on Thursday.

> On Friday he licked the master,
> On Saturday came disaster.

> He shipped aboard a whaler,
> He was a hopeless failure.

Our next shanty is another one with the word Ranzo in its chorus.
This is *Ranzo Ray*, or as some call it *Rando Ray*. It is also referred to
as *The Bully Boat*. Terry gives it as halyards, but Sharp, who had it

from the same shantyman as Terry, gives it as being used at the capstan. The seaman I learnt my version from said it was a hauling song, and I think it was more popular at halyards than at the capstan. Terry says that some seamen sang 'paddles roaring'. Sharp writes that Short of Watchet always sang 'rodelling' for 'rolling'— this is the old way of singing 'double l's' referred to by Whall in his Preface. There were three ways of singing this shanty, the first two being popular with white seamen, the third being the Negro way of singing it, although in actual fact all versions of this shanty are of Negro origin, it being one of the many shanties stemming from the cotton hoosiers of Mobile, who may in turn have had it from the rivermen of the Mississippi and Ohio.

RANZO RAY (a)
Alternative titles, *Rando Ray*, *The Bully Boat*

Ooh, the bul-ly boat's a-com-in', Don't ye hear the pad-dles rol-lin'? Ran-jo, Ra-an-jo, hur-ray, hur-ray! Oh the bul-ly boat's a-com-in', down the riv-er she's a-bow-lin'. Ran-jo, Ran-jo ray!

2. Ooh, the bully boat's a-comin', down the Mississippi floatin',
   *Ch. Ranzo, Ranzo, hur*ray, hurray!
   Ooh, the bully boat's a-comin', an' the gals is all a-waitin',
   Ch. Ranzo, Ranzo, ray!

3. Ooh, I'm bound away ter leave yer, but I never will deceive yer,
   I'm bound away ter leave yer, my half-pay I'm gonna leave yer.

4. Ooh, we're bound for Yokohammer, with a load o' grand pianners [an'
      our carger's grand pianners].
   (*Repeat*)

5. Oh, we're bound for Giberralter an' our carger's bricks an' morter.

6. Ooh, we're bound for Valparaiser with a load o' rusty razors.

7. Oh, we're bound for Bonas Airees with a bunch o' green canaries.

8. Oh, we're bound for Santianner and we're loaded down with lager
   [with a load o' German lager].

9. When I come again ter meet yer, it's with kisses I will greet yer.

10. Oh, we'll tie 'er up in London, an' we'll all go on the ran-tan.

Other verses sometimes sung are:

> Oh, as I roved out one mornin' I could see the steamboat rollin'.
> Oh, 'tis there I met a maiden, an' with bundles [baskets] she was laden.
> Oh, we've ploughed the ocean over, an' now soon we'll be off Dover.

Tune (*b*) uses similar words. I learnt both this and the foregoing version from Liverpool Irish seamen. There is an almost identical version given by Miss A. G. Gilchrist in the *Journal* of the Folk Song Society from the singing of W. Bolton of Southport. Miss Gilchrist suggests that this is the air upon which *Off to Philadelphia in the Mornin'* was based. Her singer gives it as a capstan song. It was the tune usually sung by Liverpool crews, whereas the former was, I believe, the Bristol Channel version. My informant gave it as a halyard song.

RANZO RAY (b)

The bul-ly boat's a-com-in', don't ye hear the pad-dles rol-lin'? Ran-zo, Ran-zo, a-way—, a-way! The bul-ly boat's a-com-in', down the riv-er she's a-float-in', Ran-zo, Ran-zo 'ray!

Version (*c*) I learnt from my Barbadian friend Harding—its Negro influence can be plainly seen. Any of the previous verses can be fitted to it. Harding gave it as halyards.

RANZO RAY (c)

Rather fast

We're home-ward bound from Chi-na, oh, a-board a Lim-ey li-ner—, Ran-zo, Ra-an-zo, a-way! a-way! We're get-tin' out our long-tail blues ter waltz the gals a-round, Tim-me Hi-lo, me Ran-zo ray!

2. We've ploughed the whole world over an' now soon we'll be off Dover.

   Ch. Ranzo, Ranzo, away, away! [*or aray,* aray!]

We've ploughed the ocean over, like a proper deepsea rover,
Ch. Timme *H*ilo, me Ranzo *ray!*

3. We'll pass the cliffs of Dover, oh, an' soon we'll be in clover,
We'll anchor in the Downs, for we're bound for London Town.

4. We're loaded down with curios from China an' the Indias,
We'll soon be seein' all the gals, the gals we do adore.

5. We'll drink an' sing an' have our fun, sez every jolly Johnny,
The gals are waitin' on the pier—they soon will have good fun [our money].

Another shanty which mentions our hero Ranzo is the one variously known as *We'll Ranzo Way*, *The Wild Goose Shanty*, or *Huckleberry Hunting*. This was sung at windlass and capstan, but Doerflinger gives it as halyards and pumps—in other words it appears to have been used for every shipboard job with perhaps the exception of tacks and sheets, and hand-over-hand! My version is as follows:

WE'LL RANZO WAY
Alternative titles, *Sing Hilo, Me Ranzo Ray, Huckleberry Hunting, The Wild Goose Shanty*

2. I'm shantyman of the Wild Goose nation,
Ch. Timme *way*, timme hay, timme *hee* ho hay!
Got a maid that I left on the big plantation,
Ch. An' *sing*, Hilo me *Ranzo* way!

3. Oh, the sassiest gal o' that Wild Goose nation,
Is her that I left on the big plantation.

4. Oh, the boys an' the gals went a huckleberry huntin',
The gals began to cry an' the boys they dowsed their buntin' [stopped their huntin'; stopped their courtin'].

5. Then a little gal ran off an' a little boy ran arter,
The little gal fell down an' he saw her little garter.

6. Said he, 'I'll be yer beau, if ye'll have me for yer feller,'
But the little gal said, 'No, 'cos me sweetheart's Jackie Miller.'

7. But he took her on his knee, an' he kissed her right an' proper,
She kissed him back agen, an' he didn't try to sto-o-p'er.

8. An' then he put his arm all around her tight an' waspy waist,
   Sez she, 'Young man, you're showin' much too great a haste!'

The remaining verses are mainly obscene and much the same as those used in the bawdy version of *A-rovin'*.

Davis & Tozer give a theme about 'Minnie and the Wild Geese' which has not an authentic ring, appearing to me as being entirely composed and not merely camouflaged.

Bullen gives one verse only, 'Oh, what did yer give for yer fine leg o' mutton?' Terry says that the verse about 'huckleberry hunting' was rarely omitted, but he never heard this theme further developed. Whall, Sharp, Doerflinger, and Miss Colcord all give this verse. Terry gives the shanty as windlass and capstan, Whall doesn't state its usage, Sharp gives it as capstan, but Miss Colcord, like Doerflinger, gives it as halyards. Bullen also presents it as windlass and capstan.

Most forms indicate a Negro origin, as far as the tune and refrains are concerned, but the words of the solos savour of a Down East or Nova Scotian source.

Most versions refer to the 'Wild Goose nation'. This mysterious race of people often crops up in shantydom and also in nigger minstreldom, and many theories have been put forward regarding its origin, none, I'm afraid, very convincing. Doerflinger maintains that in minstreldom the phrase refers to Southern or Indian-inhabited country. Miss Colcord rather fancies Ireland as the source, since she has discovered that the phrase 'Wild Goose nation' was used as a poetical name for the Irish, in particular for the Irish Guards who fought the French in the wars of 1748, and refers the reader to Kipling's poem, 'The Irish Guards'. Then again the Irish connection with the phrase may come from an historical incident which happened when George III, I believe, desired the Irish regiments to swear allegiance to the English flag. The flag was hoisted on a hill and the regiments had two alternatives—either to pass the flag on the left and thereby swear allegiance, or to march to the right and downhill to the waiting French frigates which were to carry them to France and exile. Many regiments accepted the latter course and became mercenaries in Europe, never being allowed to return to their wives and children or their native heath. This going into exile is often referred to as 'The Flight of the Wild Geese'. But all this is rather far removed from the sailor's shanty—unless it came to the shanty by way of an Irish forebitter, and to my knowledge no forebitter, Irish or otherwise, includes such a phrase.

Some authorities seek further afield and suggest that it may mean Ashanti or some other Guinea Coast locality, homeland of the original Negro slaves of America.

PART THREE

~~~~~~

The Hilo Group; Gals with
Blue Dresses and Hogs-eye
Men; Johnnies of all Kinds; the
Heaving Group and Cheerily Man
Items; Paddy Doyle and all His
Relations; Shanties of Railroad Origin
and Banjoes; Good Mornin', Ladies All

~~~~~~

EAVING behind Ranzo and the shanties which immortalize him we will now run through those work-songs woven around the word 'Hilo'. Hilo is a port in the Hawaiian group, and, although occasionally shell-backs may have been referring to this locality, usually it was a port in South America of which they were singing—the Peruvian nitrate port of Ilo. But in some of these Hilo shanties it was not a port, either in Hawaii or Peru, to which they were referring. Sometimes the word was a substitute for a 'do', a 'jamboree', or even a 'dance'. And in some cases the word was used as a verb—to 'hilo' somebody or something. In this sense its origin and derivation is a mystery. Furthermore, since shanties were not composed in the normal manner, by putting them down, it is on paper quite possible many of these 'hilos' are nothing more than 'high-low', as Miss Colcord has it in her version of *We'll Ranzo Ray*. Take your pick!

Our first in this series is the halyard shanty of Negro origin, *Hilo, Johnny Brown*. The usual verses of *Sally Brown* were sung to it.

183

HILO, JOHNNY BROWN
Alternative title, *Stand to Yer Ground!*

2. Sally she'm the gal that I spliced nearly,
    Ch. 'Way, sing, *Sally*!
Her lips is red an' her hair is curly,
    *Ch. Hi*lo, Johnny Brown, *stand* to yer ground!

3. Sally she'm a Badian beauty,
Sally-gal she'm know her dooty.

4. Sally she'm a bright mulatter,
Pretty gal but Ah cain't git at her [She drinks rum an' chaws ter-backer].

5. Seven long years Ah courted Sally,
But Ah doan care ter dilly-dally.

(*Continue with other* 'Sally Brown' *verses*)

Stand to yer ground an' we'll walk her up, boys,
Stand to yer ground an' we'll make a bit o' noise.

Never mind the weather, boys, keep yer legs tergether,
Haul away, me bully boys, an' bust the chafin' leather.

The mate he goes aroun', boys, dinging an' a-dangin',
Fair land o' Caanan soon be a-showin'.

Terry and Whall give a tune similar to mine, except that Whall gives G sharp in bars 2 and 3.

Our next 'Hilo' shanty is *Hilo, Boys, Hilo*. This is a Negro shanty used at halyards, although Terry gives it as 'interchangeable'. He makes mention of the figure of speech often found in shanties 'blackbird and crow', although he himself gives 'blackbird and crew'. On page 533 I give a shanty referring to the 'blackbird and the thrush'. In fact, for some unknown reason, shantymen seemed partial to our feathered friends blackbirds, crows, and thrushes. In English folk-songs too one finds many ditties singing of birds, for example, Sharp's *Blackbirds and Thrushes*.

Like in most Negro and cotton-hoosier's songs, after the first few regulation verses the shantyman would have to extemporize, since such shanties told no familiar story; but in my version, which comes from Old Smith of Tobago, a one-time shipmate, a short tale is told.

HILO, BOYS, HILO
Alternative titles, *Hilo, Somebody, Below, Hilo, Somebody, Hilo*

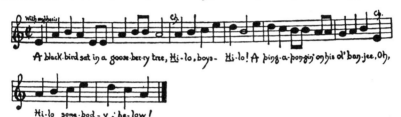

A blackbird sat in a goose-ber-ry tree, Hi-lo, boys- Hi-lo! A ping-a-pong-in' on his ol' ban-jee, Oh, Hi-lo some-bod-y :be-low!

2. The blackbird sang unto the crow,
    *Ch. Hi*lo, boys, *Hi*lo [below]!
   I'll soon be takin' you in tow,
    Ch. Oh! *Hi*lo, some*bod*y below [Hilo]!

3. Said the blackbird to the crow,
   Come down below with yer blackfaced crew [the whole 'yer crew].

4. The crow flew down to Mobile Town,
   Met a high yellar gal called Sally Brown.

5. Them yaller gals we do adore,
   They'll drink ye skint an' ask for more.

6. The blackbird sang [an'] the crow said 'caw'.
   Got ter set this sail by half pas' four.

7. High an' dry we'll hoist her high,
   Hoist her high for a bulgine pie.

A closely related shanty is *Hilo, Come Down Below*. This also was used at halyards and is obviously of Negro origin. Bullen's is the only other version in print. I had mine from Harding, who sang words much the same as in the foregoing shanty.

HILO, COME DOWN BELOW

A blackbird sat in a wal-nut tree, Hi-lo, come down be-low! A ping-a-pong-in' on his ol' ban-jee, Hi-lo! come down be-low!

185

2. Said the blackbird to the crow,
   *Ch. Hi*lo, come *down* below!
  Come down below wid the whole 'yer crew,
   *Ch. Hi*lo, come *down* below!

3. The crow flew down to Mobile Town,
  Met a high yaller gal called Sally Brown.

4. Said the blackbird to the crow,
  Don't tell them yaller gals all yer know.

5. The blackbird sang, the crow said 'caw',
  Gotter set this sail by half pas' four.

6. The blackbird flapped his wings an' crowed,
  Why does a chicken cross the road?

7. If the sun don' shine, then the hens don' lay,
  If we don' haul, we git no pay.

8. One more pull, the ol' crow cried,
  We got to hurry for to catch the tide!

Another relation of the foregoing two hauling songs is *Hello, Somebody!* also used at halyards. Captain J. P. Barker of the American ship *Tusitala* gives a verse on page 40 of *Log of a Limejuicer*. Harding gave me my version and he said it was very popular in ships with coloured crews. It cannot be of any great age, since I believe the word 'hello' was not in use much before the seventies. Doerflinger gives a three-verse example with an introductory chorus from the singing of Captain Barker, who in turn had learnt it from an American coloured seaman, 'Lemon' Curtis, aboard the ship *Dovenby Hall*. The tune is obviously a variant of *Whisky Johnny*.

HELLO, SOMEBODY!

2. Somebody's knockin' with a bloody big stick,
   *Ch. He*llo, somebody, *he*llo!
  It's Dirty Dick from New Brunswick,
   *Ch. He*llo, somebody, *he*llo!

3. Somebody's knockin' at the Gates o' Hell.
   It's Bully John an' we knows him well.

4. Somebody's knockin' at the Gates o' Heaven,
   There wuz eight little nigger boys an' now there's seven.

5. Saint Peter's knockin' on the fo'c'sle door,
   Guess I ain't ready for the Golden Shore.

6. Somebody's hangin' on to this 'ere line,
   The blighter oughter rise an' shine!

7. Haul away an' make yer pay,
   Haul away for Saccarappa Bay.

8. She's knockin' up the miles, reelin' off the knots,
   When we get to Boston, we'll drink lots.

Doerflinger gives 'Nigger Dick' in verse 2.

Before we pass on to our next Hilo shanty I would like to point out that one of Sharp's versions of *Shallow Brown*, although it has the refrain of *Shallow Brown*, has in fact the solo words of *Blow, Boys, Blow* and the solo *tune* of *Hilo, Boys, Hilo*. This is how it goes:

SHALLOW BROWN (Sharp)

Sharp gives four more verses taken from *Blow, Boys, Blow*.

And now to the usual version of *Shallow Brown*. This shanty started life as a pumping song. It is I feel of West Indian origin, some singers giving the refrain of 'Challo Brown'—'Challo' being a West Indian word of Carib extraction meaning a 'half-caste', and heard as far afield as the ports of Chile. In the latter days of sail it was usually sung at halyards, although Doerflinger and others give it as being used to bowse down tacks and sheets. This was one of the shanties in which it was the normal thing to start off with the chorus as an introduction.

SHALLOW BROWN (*a*)
Alternative title, *Challo Brown*

Ooh! Shal-low, Ooh! Shal-low Brown! Oh! Shal-low in the morn-in', Ooh! Shal-low, ooh!

Shal-low Brown! Just as the day wuz dawn-in', Ooh! Shal-low, ooh! Shal-low Brown!

2. She is a bright mulatter,
   Ch. Shallow—oh, *Shallow Brown!*
   She hails from Cincinatter [Saccarappa, Antiguer],
   Ch. Oh, Shallow—oh, *Shallow Brown!*

3. Come put me clothes in order,
   The packet sails termorrer.

4. Once ye wuz sweet and cheery [like a fairy],
   But now ye are contrary.

5. For ye are fat an' lazy,
   Ye nearly drive me crazy.

6. My half-pay ye've spent like chaff,
   Ye'd like the other half.

7. Ye boozed me pay away,
   But ye've had yer last pay-day.

8. The packet sails termorrer,
   I'll leave yer without sorrer.

9. Me clothes are all in pawn,
   I'm bound around the Horn.

10. She won't miss me when I've gone,
    She'll hook some other bum.

A more sentimental version gives:

4. I'm bound away to leave yer,
   I never will deceive yer.

5. I long ter look upon yer,
   I spend me money on yer.

188

6. Ye are me only treasure,
I love ye to full measure.

7. The packet sails termorrer,
I'll leave ye with much sorrer.

8. In the cradle is me baby,
I want no other lady.

9. My wife an' baby grieves me,
'Tis pain for me ter leave ye.

10. Be on the pier ter meet me,
With kisses I will greet thee.

Both versions can wind up with a similar last verse:

Goin' away termorrer,
Bound away termorrer.

A slightly different tune used by some shantymen I had from Harding.

SHALLOW BROWN (b)

Oh, Shallow in the morn-ing, Shal-low, oh, Shallow Brown! Oh, Shallow in the morn-ing, Shal-

low, oh, Shallow Brown!

Davis & Tozer present another tune:

SHALLOW BROWN (c)

Come get my clothes in or-der.., Shallow - Shallow- Brown! I'm off a-cross the

bor-der, Shallow, Shallow, Brown !

(From *Sailor Songs and Chanties*, by permission of Boosey & Co., Ltd., London.)

And Sharp's other version has a different tune still. His repeated solos show true Negro influence.

SHALLOW BROWN (d) (OH, I'M GOING TO LEAVE HER)

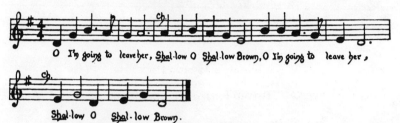

O I'm going to leave her, Shal-low O Shal-low Brown, O I'm going to leave her,

Shal-low O Shal-low Brown.

2. Ship on board a whaler,
   Ch. Shallow, O Shallow Brown,
   Ship on board a whaler,
   Ch. Shallow, O Shallow Brown.

3. Bound away to St. George's.

4. Love you well, Juliana.

5. Massa going to sell me.

6. Sell me to a Yankee.

7. Sell me for the dollar.

8. Great big Spanish dollar.

This version tells a story reminiscent of Captain Frank Shaw's paragraphs, quoted in my Introduction, which describe the life of a slave sold to a Yankee shipowner. At some time or other this Negro song passed through the shanty mart and was used by the cotton-hoosiers of Mobile as a cotton-screwing chant. Sometimes the wording would be that of *Sally Brown*, and 'Oh, Sally Brown' would be substituted for 'Oh, Shallow Brown' in the refrains. An interesting verse is given by Piggott in the *Journal* of the Folk Song Society:

> I'll cross the Chili mountains,
> To pump the silver fountains, . . .

which means that a sailor deserted his ship in some West Coast port and went working in the silver mines of Chile.

And now we have a 'link' which will bring us back to our Hilo series; this is a fragment given by Bill Adams in one of his books. Unfortunately, we have no tune. It is a version of what appears at first glance to be *Shallow Brown* but which in actual fact is a variant of *Tom's Gone to Hilo*:

SHILOH BROWN

Oh, Johnny's gone, what shall I do?
Ch. Shiloh, Shiloh Brown,
Oh, Johnny's gone, what shall I do?
Ch. Johnny's gone to Rio!

It is fairly certain that the tune of this would be *Tom's Gone to Hilo*.

Tom's (or *John's*) *Gone to Hilo* was a tops'l halyard song, and one which never found favour with the afterguard, as it took too long to hoist a yard to it on account of the slow and lethargic way in which it was sung by a good shantyman. It was rather difficult to sing correctly, but even so it was popular with the crowd, particularly for heavy lifts.

TOM'S GONE TO HILO
Alternative title, *Johnny's Gone to Hilo (Ilo)*

2. Tommy's gone to Hilo town,
      Ch. Away you *hilo*-o-o!
   Where all them gals they do come down.
      Ch. Tom's gone to *Hilo*!

3. Hilo town is in Peru,
   It's just the place for me an' you.

4. Tommy's gone to Liverpool,
   To Liverpool, that packet school.

5. Yankee shellbacks ye'll see there,
   Wid red-topped boots an' short cut hair.

6. He signed for two pound ten a month,
   No more than two pound ten a month.

7. Tommy's gone to Baltimore,
   To dance upon a sandy floor.

8. Tommy's gone to Mobile Bay,
   A-screwin' cotton all the day.

9. Tommy's gone to far Quebec,
   A-stowin' timber on the deck.

10. Tommy's gone to Cally-o,
    He won't come back from there, I know.

11. Tommy's gone to Vallipo,
    He'll dance them Spanish gals, y'know.

12. Tommy's gone to 'Frisco Bay
    In a Cape Horner the other day.

13. Tommy's gone to Pernambuck,
    He's gone to get a nip an' tuck.

14. Tommy's gone to Montreal,
    In a packet ship wid skys'ls tall.

15. Tommy's gone to Rye-o Grand,
    He's rollin' in the yellar sand.

16. Tommy's gone to Singapore,
    Oh, Tommy's gone for evermore.

17. Oh, haul away, me bully boys.
    Oh, haul away, kick up some noise.

18. Now hoist 'er up an' show 'er clew,
    Oh, we're the barstards to kick 'er though!

19. One more pull, lads, then belay,
    Ooh! One more pull an' then belay.

The game played by the shantyman was to take Tom (or John) to as many ports of three syllables as he could think of. Harlow gives a couplet:

> To Hilo Town we'll see her through,
> For Tom has gone with a ruling crew. . . .

in which the phrase 'ruling crew' smacks of *South Australia*. Terry has an unusual pair of stanzas:

> Tommy fought at Trafalgar (*Repeat*),
> Brave old *Victory* led the way. (*Repeat*)

Another common theme was the following, from the singing of Bill Dowling of Bootle:

1. Tommy's gone on a whalin'-ship,
   Oh, Tommy's gone on a damn long trip.

2. He never kissed his gal goodbye,
   He left her an' he told her why.

3. She'd robbed him blind an' left him broke,
   He'd had enough, gave her the poke.

4. His half-pay went, it went like chaff,
   She hung around for the other half.

5. She drank an' boozed his pay away,
   With her weather-eye on his next pay-day.

6. He shipped away around Cape Horn,
   His clothes an' boots wuz in the pawn.

7. This tart will get another flame,
   Aye, she will git him just the same [she will treat him just the same].

8. Steer clear, me boys, of flash chowlahs,
   They'll make ye wiser than ye are!

9. Oh, Tommy's gone an' left her flat,
   Oh, Tommy's gone an' he won't come back.

The place name 'Hilo'—whether in Hawaii or Peru—is pronounced with a soft 'i', but seamen always pronounced these soft 'i's'—in songs—as 'eye', e.g. Rio—'Rye-O', California—'Californye-O', etc. Therefore 'Hilo' was sung 'High-low', that is in the second refrain and in the solos, but in the first refrain I feel that I am right in saying that the soft sound was used—'hee-lo-o-o', in this case it being a sort of yodel aimed at by good singers of shanties. Whall spells this first refrain 'Hilo' as 'Hee-lo', in the same way as I do. The tune has an oriental touch to it. Bone, a good authority, states that Sailor John often sang 'Tom's gone to Hell-O'—particularly fitting if he had shipped in a vessel bound to the Chinchas, or some other unsavoury place, to load guano!

A variant of this shanty is the halyard song *Tommy's Gone Away*. Apart from myself Terry is the only collector who gives it. I learnt my version of the tune from a South Wales seaman who had served in the Bristol Channel copper ore trade. The words are the same as those of the preceding shanty.

TOMMY'S GONE AWAY

Tom-my's gone an' I'll go too, My Tom-my's gone a-way...! Oh, Tom-my's gone, an'

I'll go too, My Tom-my's gone a-way!

If the shantyman managed to reach the last verse it was usually:

> Tommy's gone for evermore,
> *Ch.* My *Tommy's* gone *away*!
> Oh! Tommy's gone for evermore,
> *Ch.* My *Tommy's* gone *away*!

But the strangest variant of this Hilo shanty is one given by F. W. Wallace. It appears to be a capstan song, but no music is given. It runs:

> Hilo town is far away,
> *Ch.* Tom's gone to Hilo!
> Hilo town is in Haway. [Hawaii]
> 'Way down, you Mobile hoosier,
> 'Way down, 'way down I tell you,
> *Ch.* Tom's gone to Hilo.

A fine hauling song in this series is *Can't Ye Hilo?* This is West Indian in origin, and it was from my West Indian friend Harding that I learnt it. Captain Robinson (in *The Bellman*) gives a version. I don't know Captain Robinson's background, but judging from his shanties I should say that he spent most of his time in the West Indian, Gulf Ports, and West Coast of South America Trades, since all his shanties are those common to the crews of ships in such trades. Sharp too had many of his shanties from an old shellback of Bristol who had spent many years in the West Indian sugar and rum trade. Robinson's tune and words are similar to mine.

CAN'T YE HILO?

2. Young gals, good gals, bad gals, O!
   Ch. Young gals can't ye *Hilo*?
   I will take 'em all in tow,
   Ch. Young gals can't ye *Hilo*?

3. Love 'em all both old an' young,
   Thin gals, fat gals, let 'em all come.

4. When I wuz a young man in me prime,
   I chased them coloured gals all the time.

5. Dance, gals, dance, till the break o' day,
   Let's all dance our cares [woes] away.

6. High brown, dark brown, yeller gals, O!
   Let's all go on a big Hilo!

7. Young gals, young gals, young gals, O,
   Rouse 'er up an' let's Hilo!

Here the word 'Hilo' seems to indicate some sort of dance, or else a 'jamboree'.

Now we come to the last of our Hilo series, one well known nowadays, thanks to Terry's making it popular in schools, and so on. This is *Johnny, Come Down to Hilo*. Sharp gives it as *Johnny, Come to Hilo*, and Doerflinger has *Johnny, Walk Along to Hilo*. And I once knew an old sailor who sang it as *Johnny, Come Down the Backstay*. The tune is Irish in origin and the wording is a mixture of Negro catch-phrases, of lines from Negro and nigger minstrel ditties, and odd bits from other shanties, e.g. *Poor Old Man* and *The Gal With the Blue Dress*. The reference to the 'big buck nigger with his seaboots on' has its counterpart in nigger ditties such as:

Walk, Jawbone, Jenny come along,
In comes Sally wid de bootees on . . .

and similar couplets are to be found in English folk-songs. In Bullen's *Ten Stone* there is a starting solo reminiscent of the first verse of this shanty:

I nebber seen de like since I've been born,
Nigger on de ice an' a-hoein' up corn.

A piece of music, frequently heard over the air, called *The Man from the Sea*, vividly shows how this shanty is very akin, in tune, to the children's rhyme 'Three Blind Mice'!

The normal use of *Johnny, Come Down to Hilo* was at the capstan when a steady march round was needed. Pieces from *Hand Me Down Me Walkin'-cane*, *Poor Old Ned*, and *Camptown Races* are included in it, and the bawdy version of *Hog-eye Man* was also made use of.

JOHNNY, COME DOWN TO HILO

Alternative titles, *Johnny, Come to Hilo, Johnny, Walkalong to Hilo, Johnny, Come Down the Backstay*

2. I love a little gal acrosst the sea,
   She's a big buck nigger an' she sez to me [She's a 'Badian beauty, *etc.*],
   Ch. Oh, Johnny come down to Hilo,
   (Oh) poor old man!
   Oooh! wake her!
   Oh, shake her!
   Ooooh! wake that gal wid the blue dress on!
   When Johnny comes down to Hilo,
   (Oh) Poor old man!

3. Wuz ye never down in Mobile Bay,
   A-screwin' cotton for a dollar a day?
   Ch. Oh, Johnny come down, *etc.*

4. Ooh, there once wuz a nigger an' his name wuz Uncle Ned,
   An' he had no yarns on the top o' his head.

5. Did ye ever see the ol' plantation boss,
   An' his long-tailed filly, an' his big, black hoss?

6. Oh, go fetch me down me riding cane,
   For I'm off to see me sweetheart Jane.

7. Ooh, Sally [Jinny] in the garden, pickin' peas,
   An' the hair of her head hangin' down to her knees.

Cecil Sharp gives a slightly different air to his verse:

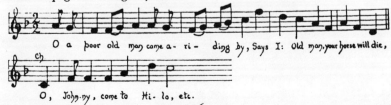

The following hauling song, *The Gal With the Blue Dress*, is the one from which a similar line in *Johnny, Come Down to Hilo* was probably taken. I had it from Harding, who considered it one of the best in his repertoire for halyards. It is essentially a Negro song, probably one used by cotton hoosiers. I feel that L. A. Smith's *Slapandergosheka* is a similar or related song. Davis & Tozer give a version, calling it 'pumps', which of course it could have been, but this appears to be a rather too poetical effort for hairy shellbacks or Negroes to have sung. There does exist a nigger minstrel song called *The Girl With the Blue Dress On*.

THE GAL WITH THE BLUE DRESS
Alternative title, *Shake Her, Johnny, Shake Her!*

2. This gal she did look good to me,
  Ch. Shake her, Johnny, *shake* her!
 'Cos I had bin ten months at sea,
  Ch. Shake her an' we'll *wake* her!

3. She's a Down East gal wid a Down East style,
 For a dollar a time it's all worth while.

4. Roust an' shake her is the cry,
 The bloody topmast sheave is dry!

5. A big wind comes from the Wes'-nor'-west,
 This gal ain't gonner git no rest.

6. Shake 'er, bullies, oh, helm's a-lee,
 She'll git washed out wid a big green sea.

7. Her oilskins they are all in pawn,
 It's wet an' draughty round Cape Horn.

8. So roust 'er up from down below,
 An' haul away for yer Uncle Joe.

9. This gal she is a high-brown lass,
 High-brown lass in a flash blue dress.

10. So roust 'er up be quick I say,
 An' make yer port an' take yer pay.

11. Soon we'll be down Mobile Bay,
 Screwin' cotton for to git our pay.

Next we have a windlass song given only by Bullen & Arnold. This is *Ten Stone*, a shanty of pure Negro origin, heard by Bullen himself being sung by Negroes working a dolly-winch on his ship in Georgetown, Demerara. Its opening lines are very similar to those of *Johnny, Come Down to Hilo*.

TEN STONE

I nebber seen de like sence I bin born! Way, ay ay ay ay! Digger on de ice on' a-
hoe-in' up corn, Way, ay, ay ay ay, Ten stone! ten stone! ten stone de win' am o-ber,
Jen-ny git a-long, Jen-ny blow de horn, As we go march-in' o-ber!

(*Songs of Sea Labour*, by permission of Swan & Co., Ltd., London)

And now we come to a shanty usually spoken of in hushed tones by collectors—I don't know why; many other shanties were just as obscene, and even worse! This is the 'notorious' *Hog-eye Man* which is supposed to rank with *Abel Brown the Sailor* in infamy. Terry devotes several paragraphs trying to explain why it wasn't decent, and what the hidden meaning of the term 'Hog-eye' was in the minds of dirty old sailors, but with all his verbosity and hinting he doesn't explain a thing. As a matter of fact Whall, 'Seaman of the Old School', gives an explanation of the word 'Hog-eye' without any obscene entanglements. He plainly states that it was a type of barge invented for the newly formed overland trade which used the canals and rivers of America at the time of the Gold Rush (1850 onwards). A 'Ditch-Hog' was a sarcastic phrase used by American deep-watermen to denote sailors of inland waterways such as the Mississippi and Missouri as opposed to foreign-going Johns. I rather think Terry got his words mixed—he was thinking of 'Dead-eye' and not 'Hog-eye', the former having both a nautical and an obscene significance. Nevertheless the solo parts *were* indecent, and a large amount of camouflaging was necessary before this song could be made public.

Davis & Tozer give it as a pumping song with a shortened chorus:

Heigh ho for the ox-eyed man!

Normally however it was used at the capstan.

THE HOG-EYE MAN

Alternative Titles, *The Hogs-eye Man*, *The Ox-eye Man*, *The Hawks Eye Man*

Fairly fast with emphasis.

The hog-eye man is the man for me, he came a-sail-in' from o'er the sea, An' a hog-eye! Rail-road nigger wid his hog-eye! Row the boat a-shore wid her hog-eye-oh! She wants the hog-eye man!

2. He came to a shack where his Sally [Jinny] she did dwell,
And he knocked on the door and he rang her bell.
   Ch. An' a hog-eye [Oh, hog-eye O]!
     Railroad nigger wid his Hogeye [Row the boat ashore for her
     hogeye]!
     Row the boat ashore wid her hogeye O!
     She wants the hog-eye man!

3. Oh, Jinny's [Sally's] in the garden, pickin' peas,
An' the hair of her head hangin' down to her knees.

4. Oh, who's bin here since I've bin gone?
Some big buck nigger wid his sea-boots on.

5. If I cotch him here wid me Jinny [Sally] any more,
I'll sling me hook an' I'll go to sea some more.

6. Oh, Jinny [Sally] in the parlour a-sittin' on his knee,
A-kissin' of the sailor who'd come o'er the seas.

7. Sally [Jinny] in the garden siftin' sand,
An' the hog-eye man sittin' hand-in-hand.

8. Oh, Sally [Jinny] in the garden shellin' peas,
With her young hog-eye all a-sittin' on her knee.

9. Oh, I won't wed a nigger, no, I'm damned if I do,
He's got jiggers in his feet an' he can't wear a shoe.

10. Oh, the hog-eye man is the man for me,
He wuz raised way down in Tennessee [For he is blind an' he cannot
see].

11. Oh, go fetch me down me ridin'-cane,
For I'm off to see me darlin' Jane.

12. Oh, a hog-eye ship an' a hog-eye crew,
A hog-eye mate an' a skipper too.

199

Sometimes stanzas from *A-rovin'* would be used. The tune and the theme of this shanty varies but little, but there are several forms of the chorus:

Chorus variants—

1. An' a hog-eye O!
   Blow, me bully boys, wid a hog-eye,
   Blow, me bully boys, blow the boat ashore,
   For she wants her hog-eye man.

2. An' a hog-eye O!
   Row the boat ashore for a hog-eye,
   Steady on a jig wid her hog-eye O!
   All she wants is the hog-eye man.

3. Hog-eye! Pig-eye!
   Oh, I once knew a nigger wid a hog-eye,
   Steady on a jig wid a hog-eye O!
   Bully for de hog-eye man.

4. (*C. Sharp*)

And a hog-eye, steady up a jig and a hog-eye, steady up a jig, and all she wants is her hog-eyed man.

5. (*Bullen & Arnold*)

Hog-eye, Pig-eye! Row de boat a-shore fer de hog-eye O! An' all she wants is de hog-eye man.

(*Songs of Sea Labour*, by permission of Swan & Co., Ltd., London)

In the *Journal* of the Folk Song Society there are two choruses sung by Mr. Bolton of Southport to Miss Gilchrist (1906):

1. With his hawk's eye,
   And when he comes ashore,
   Roll the boat ashore and the hawk's eye,
   Roll the boat ashore and the hawk's eye oh!
   She wants the hawk's-eye man.

2. With his hawk eye—
   And when he comes ashore,
   He rattles at the door,
   Oh, Johnnie is my hawk's-eye man.

Both *Johnny, Come Down to Hilo* and this shanty were more popular when there was a Negro shantyman aboard, since both contained, when sung properly, many 'hitches' and wild yelps. This shanty probably started life as a railroad work-song (many railroad navvies were Negroes), then taken over by the 'river boys' and finally, by way of the cotton hoosiers of the Gulf Ports, passed into the hands of deep-water sailormen.

The phrase 'Johnny, come down the backstay' which I have stated was sometimes sung instead of 'Johnny, come down to Hilo' was a rather popular expression among seamen and is even used today by steamboatmen. It has the suggestion of 'Stand clear, here we come!', ''Way for a sailor!', or 'Let 'er go!' A variant—'May the Lord come down the backstay!'—is a sort of epithet, related to 'May the Lord look sideways through the porthole at yiz!' This brings us to the shanty variously known as *Johnny, Come Down the Backstay* or *John Damaray*. It was a stamp-'n'-go chorus, and a favourite in Yankee ships according to my coloured shipmate Harding. Doerflinger gives a version from the MS. of a certain N. Silsbee where it bears the notation 'braces'.

Here is Harding's version:

JOHNNY, COME DOWN THE BACKSTAY
Alternative Title, *John Damaray*

2. Hoist her from down below,
   Ch. Johnny, come down the backstay!
   Through wind an' rain an' sno-ow,
   Ch. Johnny, come down the backstay, John Damaray-ay,
   Johnny, come down the backstay, John Damaray-ay,
   Johnny, come down the backstay, John Damaray-ay!

3. Oh, shake her as she ro-olls,
   For John's a bully so-oul.

4. 'Tis time now for our smoko,
   The Ol' Man he's gone loco.

201

5. When I gits me feet ashore,
   To sea I won't go mo-ore.

6. From sea I will steer cle-ear,
   An' stick to drinkin' beer.

Now having come to a shanty singing of 'Johnny' it is opportune to commence a 'Johnny' series.

The name John was used from the time of the Packet Ships to denote a merchant seaman, and even today it is sometimes used by older mariners, particularly if they hail from Liverpool. The name Jack was also used but mainly to denote a naval tar, except when it was coupled with a word not used in the best circles, and then it had a ring of being real Merchant Service! A ship's company in the old days would often be referred to as 'the Johns' and hence it is an ever-recurring name in the shanties.

For the first of our 'John' series we give that famous halyard shanty *Whisky Johnny*. It was used at either t'gallant or tops'l halyards, and at times it would even be sung while stamping round the caps'n. One cannot lay any hard-and-fast rules as to when or where a certain type of shanty was sung. A native of the Welsh village of Aberdovey once told me that when she was a girl the locals would man the capstan at the head of the lifeboat slip and heave the lifeboat up to the strains of *Whisky Johnny* and *Haul the Bowline*, which isn't a capstan shanty either. Clark in his book *Seven Years of a Sailor's Life* (Boston, 1867) refers to the singing of *Whisky Johnny* at the windlass. But it was usually sung at t'gallant halyards, and often, in ship-rigged vessels, at the mizen tops'l halyards—the hands in this case being strung out across the poop, the idea being to give the Old Man a gentle hint from the very nature of the words sung to issue a tot of rum. Some authorities seem to think that this shanty is of great antiquity, dating back to Elizabethan times. Patterson claims that the original words were 'Malmsey Johnny', but whether this was so is difficult to tell, as sufficient proof is lacking.

Most of the verses of my first version I obtained from a certain Mr. Butcher, while those of the other two versions are from Jimmy Sexton, Arthur Spencer, and other seamen.

The versions may be grouped under:

(*a*) The advantages and disadvantages of whisky drinking,
(*b*) Shanghaiing version,
(*c*) The limejuice skipper, and
(*d*) Crabfish, crayfish, or lobster version.

WHISKY JOHNNY (a)

Ooh, whis·ky is the life of man, Whis·ky John·ny, Ooh! whis·ky for an old tin can, Whis·ky for my John·ny!

2. Whisky here, whisky there,
   Ch. Whisky Johnny!
   Oooh! whisky almost everywhere,
   Ch. Whisky for me Johnny!

3. Whisky up an' whisky down,
   Oooh! whisky all around the town.

4. I'll drink it hot, I'll drink it cold,
   I'll drink it new, I'll drink it old.

5. Whisky made me sell me coat,
   Whisky's what keeps me afloat.

6. Whisky fills a man with care,
   Whisky makes a man a bear.

7. Whisky gave me many a sigh,
   But I'll swig whisky till I die.

8. Whisky made me mammy cry,
   Whisky closed me stabbud eye.

9. Whisky killed me poor ol' Dad,
   Whisky druv me mother mad.

10. Whisky made me pawn me cloes,
    Whisky gave me this red nose [a broken nose].

11. Whisky made me shun the booze,
    Put me in the calabooze.

12. Whisky gave me a big, fat head,
    But I'll drink whisky till I'm dead.

13. If I can't have whisky, then I'll have rum,
    That's the stuff to make good fun.

14. Whisky killed me Sister Sue,
    Whisky killed me brother too.

15. I had a sister an' her name wuz Lize,
    She puts whisky in her tea.

16. My wife an' I could never agree,
    She'd put whisky in her tea.

17. Some likes whisky, some likes beer,
    I wisht I had a barrel here.

18. Oh, the mate likes whisky an' the skipper likes rum,
    The sailors like both but we can't git none.

19. Oh, a tot of whisky for each man,
    An' a bloody big bottle for the shantyman.

20. If whisky wuz a river an' I could swim,
    I'd say here goes an' I'd dive right in.

21. If whisky wuz a river an' I wuz a duck,
    I'd dive to the bottom an' never come up [suck it all up].

22. I wisht I knew where whisky grew,
    I'd eat the leaves an' the branches too.

23. The Divil came from the worl' below,
    That is where bad whisky do grow.

24. Oh, whisky straight an' whisky strong,
    Gimme some whisky an' I'll sing ye a song.

25. If whisky comes too near me nose,
    I tip it up an' down the hatch she goes.

26. Here comes the cook with the whisky-can,
    A glass o' grog for every man.

27. Whisky made me scratch me toes,
    Whisky makes me fight me foes.

28. I say Ol' Man it is a sin,
    To make us work widout any gin.

29. Whisky made the bosun call,
    Hang tergether one an' all!

30. Whisky stole me brains away,
    The bosun shouts, so I'll belay!

WHISKY JOHNNY (b)

1. Now if ye ever go to 'Frisco town,
   Ch. Whisky Johnny!
   Mind ye steer clear o' Shanghai Brown,
   Ch. Whisky for me Johnny!

2. He'll dope yer whisky night an' morn,
   An' then shanghai ye round Cape Horn.

3. Two months' wages they are dead,
   An' a donkey's breakfast for yer bed.

4. Ol' Shanghai Brown an' Larry Marr,
Their names are known both near an' far.

5. Ol' Larry Marr an' Shanghai Brown,
They robbed me up an' robbed me down.

6. They fit ye out wid bumboat gear,
That's got ter last yer 'alf-a-year.

7. Carpet slippers made o' felt,
An' a nice, clean rope-yarn for a belt.

8. A suit o' oilskins made o' cotton,
An' an ol' sea-chest wid bricks in the bottom.

9. Oh, the Barbary Coast is no place for me,
Ye have one drink then wake up at sea.

10. Ol' Shanghai Brown he loves us sailors,
Oh, yes he does like hell 'n' blazes.

11. All ye young sailors take a warnin' from me,
Keep an eye [watch] on yer drink, lads, when ye come from
sea.

12. Or else ye'll awake on a cold frosty morn,
On a three-skys'l yarder bound round the Horn.

13. On a skys'l yarder all bound round the Horn,
Ye'll wish ter hell that ye'd niver bin born.

14. Oh, I thought I heard the Ol' Man say,
Just one more pull, lads, then belay!

WHISKY JOHNNY (c)

1. There wuz a limejuice skipper of the name of Hogg,
    Ch. Whisky, etc.
Once tried to stop his sailor's grog,
    Ch. Oh, whisky, etc.

2. Which made the crew so weak an' slack,
That the helmsman caught her flat aback.

3. An' ever after so they say,
That crew got grog three times a day.

4. So we'll boost her up an' bowl along,
An' drink that skipper's health in song.

5. We'll keep closehauled without a breach,
With just a shiver in the weather leach.

6. Now if this ship wuz the ol' James Baines,
That yard would never be lowered again.

7. The halyards they would rackèd be,
   We'll drive along through a big green sea.

8. Oh, hoist the yard from down below,
   To the sheave-hole she must go.

9. Up aloft with tautened leach,
   Hand over hand, lads, ye must reach.

10. Whisky made the Ol' Man say,
    One more pull, lads, then belay!

WHISKY JOHNNY (d)

1. 'Mornin', Mister Fisherman'; 'Good mornin',' sez he,
   Whisky, *etc.*
   'Have ye got a crayfish [crabfish, lobster] ye can sell to me?'
   Whisky for my, *etc.*

2. 'Oh, yes,' sez he, 'I have got two,
   One for me an' the other for you.'

3. I took the crayfish home, but I couldn't find a plate.
   I put it in the place where me Missus always ate.

4. Early next mornin' as ye may guess,
   The Missus got up for an early breakfast.

5. The Missus gave a howl, a groan, and a shout,
   She danced around the room with the crayfish on her snout.

6. I grabbed a scrubber, the Missus grabbed a broom,
   We chased the bloomin' crayfish round an' round the room.

7. We hit it on the head, we hit it on the side,
   We hit the bloomin' crayfish, until the blighter died.

8. The end of my story—the moral is this,
   Always put yer specs on before ye eat yer fish.

A stamp-'n'-go song singing of whisky is *Rise Me Up From Down Below!* This was very popular in Yankee ships with coloured crews, so my informant Harding told me. According to Harding the tune is a Jamaican work-song taken to sea by West Indian seamen and altered to suit their needs. Doerflinger, who also gives it, says that it used to be sung by Captain J. P. Barker of the ship *Tusitala*, and he in turn had learnt it from an American Negro called 'Lemon' Curtis. Harding told me it was the usual type of stamp-'n'-go song, but Doerflinger was informed by Captain Barker that two pulls would be taken on the rope (at '*Whisky O, Johnny O*') prior to the crowd stamping away with it. At the end of the chorus the grip would be shifted and another two pulls given before stamping away again. If this was so then it was the only shanty ever used in this fashion. The words Harding gave me have some connection with a certain Victorian ditty my father used to sing:

> I'm the ghost of John, James, Christopher, Benjamin Binns.
> I was cut down right in the midst of me sins.

RISE ME UP FROM DOWN BELOW

2. I am the ghost of Bertie Binns,
   Cut down wuz I for me 'orrible sins.
   Ch. Whisky O, Johnny O!
       Rise me up from down below,
       Down below, Oh, Oh, Oh, Oh!
       Rise me up from down below, boys,
       Rise me up from down below!

3. Me only home is down below,
   They've let me out for an hour or so.

4. An' when the cocks begin to crow,
   'Tis time for me to roll 'n' go.

5. Back in a hurry to the southern shore,
   That is where the fires do roar.

6. I'll tell yuh, boys, 'tis hot in hell,
   An' I should know the place damn well.

7. An' now the bleedin' sail is set,
   Back to me hole I'll have ter get.

Doerflinger gives for the fourth line of the chorus: 'Up aloft this yard must go, John.'

Carrying on with the 'Johnny' type of shanty, next we have one of the most famous, *Hanging Johnny*. Was *Hanging Johnny* the noted eighteenth-century hangsman Jack Ketch, as some suggest? Who can say? In spite of its somewhat melancholy tune and macabre wording its rhythm lent itself to being one of the best of all the halyard shanties. The word 'hang' was often used when 'swigging'. In this manoeuvre—when a buntline or clewline or light halyard had to be given a few final strong pulls—one man took a part turn with the line around the portion of the belayin'-pin beneath the pin-rail, while two or three other seamen with their hands as high as they could place them gripped the line and fell backwards heavily, then 'giving in' the resultant slack to the chap at the pin. The sing-out at such times would be:

> Hang, me bullies, heavy arses!
> Hang, ye sons o' whores, hang!
> Hang heavy!

Hanging Johnny was usually sung at t'gallant halyards and it had one theme only. Stringing-out was common in a long hoist. Sentimental verses like some collectors give were never sung—Sailor John hanged any person or thing he would think about without a qualm!

HANGING JOHNNY

Oh, they calls me Hang-in' John-ny, A-way, boys, a-way! They sez I hangs fer
mon-ey, So-o hang-boys-hang!

2. They sez I hangs for money,
   Ch. Away, boys, a*way!*
   But hangin' is so funny,
   Ch. So hang, boy-oys, *hang!*

3. At first I hanged me daddy,
   An' then I hanged me mammy.

4. Oh, yes, I hanged me mother,
   Me sister, an' me brudder.

5. I hanged me sister Sally,
   I hanged the whole damn family.

6. An' then I hanged me granny,
   I hanged her up quite canny.

7. I'd hang the mate and skipper,
   I'd hang 'em by their flippers.

8. I'd hang a ruddy copper,
   I'd give him the long dropper.

9. I'd hang a rotten liar,
   I'd hang a bloomin' friar.

10. I'd hang to make things jolly,
    I'd hang Jill, Jane, an' Polly.

11. A rope, a beam, a ladder,
    I'd hang yiz all tergether.

12. We'll hang an' haul tergether,
    We'll hang for better weather.

For the second line of verse 6 Terry gives 'sae canny' since his is a Northumbrian version.

The first refrain has several ways of singing it:

Hooraw, boys, hooraw!
Hooray, boys, hooray! (*Whall*)
Away—I—oh! (*Sampson*)
Hooway—ay hay ay! (*Doerflinger*)
.Hooway-ay hay ay! (*Doerflinger*)

A fine description of the singing of this shanty off Cape Horn is given by Masefield in one of his works.

Mr. Doerflinger sent me a letter in which he makes mention of a certain Mr. Charles H. Wexler of Pittsburgh, Pa., who had written to him calling attention to the fact that the shanty *Hanging Johnny* appears in an old book on army life published in America. Unfortunately, this information came just as my book was going to the press, so I have not had time to find a copy of the book myself.

Mr. Wexler writes:

In a book entitled *Army Life in a Black Regiment* by Thomas W. Higginson, the author, who commanded a regiment of Federal troops raised among the ex-slaves of the sea islands of the Carolina coast, devotes a full chapter to the songs sung by the men of this regiment. As one of the two songs he remembered which were not in the religious or spiritual class, he quotes two verses of *Hanging Johnny*, and speaks of a third verse whose words apparently had some relation to men's enlistment in the army during the Civil War. The quotation is on pp. 220–1 of my edition, which was published by Fields, Osgood & Co., in Boston in 1870.

Another popular 'Johnny' shanty was that known as *John, Come Tell Us As We Haul Away*. It was often sung at pumps when the word 'pump' would be substituted for the word 'haul', although in the more modern flywheel type of pump where a bell-rope was used both words were equally appropriate. It probably started life as a cotton hoosiers' song down in the Gulf Ports. It was one of the very few shanties that had two singers for the solo lines. *Billy Boy* too was sung in this fashion. It was also used at halyards by some shantymen. I have given the line 'Aye, aye, haul away' as a solo and marked the hauling words in the refrains on account of this. It was also used at the windlass and capstan when the word 'heave' would be substituted for 'pump' or 'haul'. Ex-shantyman Stanley Slade of Bristol, who has recorded this for H.M.V., puts the regular shantyman's 'yodel' into the line 'Hay-ey-ey haul-ey!' (third solo), his version of the shanty being a hauling one.

JOHN, COME TELL US AS WE HAUL AWAY
Alternative title, *Mobile Bay*

From Liv-er-pool Town we sailed a-way, John come tell us as we *haul* a-way! Out-ward bound at the break of day, John, come tell us as we *haul* a-way! Aye, aye *haul* aye, John come tell us as we *haul* a-way!

2. *First Shantyman:*

 Wuz ye never down in Mobile Bay?
  Ch. John come tell us as we *haul* away!
 A-screwin' cotton all the day,
  Ch. John come tell us as we *haul* away!
 Aye, aye, haul, aye,
  Ch. John come tell us as we *haul* away!

3. *Second Shantyman:*

 Oh, yes, I've bin down Mobile Bay,
  Ch. So he *tells* us as we *haul* away!
 A-screwin' cotton all the day,
  Ch. So he *tells* us as we *haul* away!
 Aye, aye, *etc.*

4. *First Shantyman:*

What did yer see down in Mobile Bay?
John, *etc.*
Were the gals all free an' gay?
John, *etc.*

5. *Second Shantyman:*

Oh this I saw in Mobile Bay,
So he tells, *etc.*
A spankin' gal in a hammock lay [a-making hay],
So he tells, *etc.*

6. *Second Shantyman:*

An' this flash gal wuz Saucy May,
She wuz tall an' fine an' had lots to say.

7. *First Shantyman:*

An' what did yer do in Mobile Bay?
Did yiz give that flash tart all yer pay?

8. *Second Shantyman:*

Oh, this I did in Mobile Bay,
I courted this gal whose name was May.

9. *Second Shantyman:*

I married her in Mobile Bay,
An' lived there happy many a day.

Like many other shanties this had several non-drawing-room verses.
A very fine halyard shanty closely related to *Mobile Bay* is *John Kanaka*. This is the first time it has been in print. I learnt it from that wonderful shantyman, Harding of Barbadoes. He sang it with many falsetto yelps and hitches almost impossible to imitate. The chorus is of Polynesian origin and I should say the words 'tulai ē' were Samoan. It has the not so common form of three solos and three refrains.

Dana in his *Two Years Before the Mast* often refers to the singing of work-songs by the Kanaka (Hawaiian) crews of ships loading hides on the Californian coast. In particular he mentions the singing-out of a certain Hawaiian called Mahana (page 120). It seems feasible that these Kanaka songs would be adapted for use by the white seamen, who would give them white men's solos and keep the Polynesian refrains. If this did occur, then, unfortunately, they have all been lost—unless our *John Kanaka* is the one survivor.

JOHN KANAKA

I heard, I heard the Old man say, John Ka-na-Ka-na-ka tu-lai-ē! To-day, to-day is a hol-i-
day, John Ka-na-Ka-na-Ka tu-lai-ē! Tu-lai-ε, ooh! tu-lai-ε, John Ka-na-Ka-na-Ka tu-lai ē!

2. We'll work termorrer, but no work terday,
   Ch. John Kanaka-naka, tulai-ē!
   We'll work termorrer, but no work terday,
   Ch. John Kanaka-naka, tulai-ē!
   Tulai ē! ooh! tulai-ē!
   Ch. John Kanaka-naka, tulai-ē!

3. We're bound away for 'Frisco Bay,
   We're bound away at the break o' day,
   Tulai ē, *etc.*

4. We're bound away around Cape Horn,
   We wisht ter Christ we'd niver bin born.

5. Oh, haul, oh haul, oh haul away,
   Oh, haul away an' make yer pay.

Our next 'Johnny' shanty is the fore-sheet song *Johnny Bowker*. It was used for 'sweating up', i.e. to give a final drag on a halyard to gain the last inch, at tacks and sheets and sometimes for bunting a sail, although this latter job was considered the prerogative of *Paddy Doyle*. My friend Mr. T. E. Elwell told me that in ships in which he served it was usually sung when there was an 'all-hands' job at the fore, main, or crojik sheets. Instead of 'do' he always sang 'haul'. This final 'do' was grunted out staccato, or rather the word was sung to its correct note and then a rising, gasped-out 'ugh' would follow as the pull came.

Doerflinger believes it to be related to Negro and minstrel ditties since the name Johnny Bowker, Booker, or Boker often appears in such songs, and he refers to a minstrel song with a refrain which ran:

O, Jonny Boker, help dat nigger, do, Jonny Boker, do!

Miss Colcord writes that the words of an American song *Aunt Jemima's Plaster* were sometimes sung to this tune, but to my knowledge these were more usually found in another fore-sheet shanty *Haul Away, Joe!* In the recent story of the 'Great Eastern'—*The Iron*

Ship—reference is made to the singing by her seven-foot bosun of 'Adieu, my Johnny Boker', to which the crew roared out responses, many unfit for the ears of the ladies in the Grand Saloon! A version once used in Newfoundland to help haul portable huts across the ice and also to move boats on the land is to be found in *Ballads and Sea Songs of Newfoundland* (Greenleaf and Mansfield):

> And it's o my jolly poker,
> And we'll start this heavy joker,
> And it's o my jolly poker-O!

JOHNNY BOWKER
Alternative titles, *Johnny Polka, Johnny Poker*

Ooh! do me Johnny Bowker, Come rock 'n' roll me o-ov-er, Oh do me Johnny Bow ker do!

2. O do, me Johnny Bowker, come roll me down to Dover,
Ch. Oh, do me Johnny Bowker *do*!

3. O do, me Johnny Bowker, let's all go on a Jamboree.

4. O do, me Johnny Bowker, the watches are cala-la-shee.

5. O do, me Johnny Bowker, the chief mate he's a croaker.

6. O do, me Johnny Bowker, the Old Man he's a soaker.

7. O do, me Johnny Bowker, the bosun's never sober.

8. O do, me Johnny Bowker, I bet ye are a rover.

9. O do, me Johnny Bowker, the sails he is a tailor.

10. O do, me Johnny Bowker, the chips he ain't no sailor.

11. O do, me Johnny Bowker, come roll me in the clover.

12. O do, me Johnny Bowker, come rock an' roll 'er over.

13. O do, me Johnny Bowker, from Calais down to Dover.

14. O do, me Johnny Bowker, in London lives yer lover.

15. O do, me Johnny Bowker, the packet she is rollin'.

16. O do, me Johnny Bowker, come haul away the bowline.

17. O do, me Johnny Bowker, we'll either break or bend it.

18. O do, me Johnny Bowker, we're men enough to mend it.

19. O do, me Johnny Bowker, get round the corner, Sally.

20. O do, me Johnny Bowker, let me an' you live tally.

21. O do, me Johnny Bowker, we'll haul away an' bend 'er.

22. O do, me Johnny Bowker, me sweetheart's young an' tender.

23. O do, me Johnny Bowker, one more pull then choke 'er.

Of course very few of these lines would be used in actual fact—any sweatin'-up would not take more than three or four verses at the most.

Captain Whall gives a verse and chorus called *Ooker John* in his book *Sea Songs and Shanties*. From my Barbadian friend Harding I learnt a similar capstan shanty, but he sang *Hooker John*, and he said that it was still popular in the West Indies (1931). It probably originated as a cotton-stower's song. Whall gives:

> O my Mary she's a blooming lass,
> *Ch.* To my Ooker John, my Oo-John,
> O my Mary she's a blooming lass,
> *Ch.* To my Ooker John, my Oo-John.
> > *Full Chorus.* Way, fair lady, O way-ay-ay-ay-ay,
> > My Mary's on the highland,
> > O yonder's Mary—yonder. . . .

and judging from these words it looks as though, in spite of the Negro tune and the way the refrains are worded, some Scotsman or North Countryman had a hand in this version. The tune of the solo lines is similar to that of *Roll the Cotton Down*.

HOOKER JOHN

Oh! me Ma-ry she's a sail-or's lass, To me Hook-er John, me Hoo-john! Oh, we court-ed all day on the grass, To me Hook-er John, me Hoo-john! 'Way Su-zan na - Oh, way, hay, high, high ya! John-ny's on the fore-yard, Yond-er, 'way up yond-er!

2. Oh, my Susie she's a nigger's gal,
> *Ch.* To me Hooker John, me Hoojohn!
She's nine foot high—that gal's so taall.
> *Ch.* to me Hooker John, me Hoojohn!
> > *Full Chorus.* 'Way Susanna—oh, way, hay, high, high ya!
> > Johnny's on the foreyard,
> > Yonder, way up yonder.

3. Oh, my Flora she's a hoosier's frien',
   She's beamy round the ol' beam-end.

4. Oh, Sally Brown she's the gal for me,
   She courts a bit when her man's at sea.

And now we come to the 'Johnny' song that usually ended the voyage—*Leave Her, Johnny, Leave Her!*

Collectors give pumps and halyards alike as the job it was used for. Terry and Whall call it a hauling song; Miss Colcord and Doerflinger give it for pumps. I think they are all right. It was probably sung at halyards with two solos and refrains, and when a full chorus was added then it was used at the pumps and even capstan. I learnt it partly from my mother's father, and he always sang the full chorus, and partly from an old Irish sailor, who also used the final chorus. It probably came to life about the time of the Irish potato famine, in the forties, and was originally sung in the Western Ocean Packets in this fashion:

ACROSS THE ROCKIES

Oh, a young girl said to me one day, A young girl goes a-weepin', I've got no money an' I can't get home, A- cross the Rock-y Mountains!

2. Oh, what shall we poor shellbacks do?
   A *young* gal goes a-*weepin'*,
   We've got no money and we can't get home,
   Ch. Across the Rocky *Mou*ntains!

3. I thought I heard the Ol' Man say,
   If ye git no money, oh, ye'll niver git home.

4. Oh, my poor ol' mother she wrote to me,
   She wrote to me to come home from sea.

5. Oh, I've got no money an' I've got no clothes,
   I've joined a bunch of tough hoboes.

This would be a hauling song, although C. F. Smith gives both this and the next as being used at pumps. Whall gives the next one as being a halyard song. C. F. Smith gives evidence that the former was sung in ships of the Blackball Line at the brake-pumps. This

next version probably grew out of the former and in its turn fathered
the later song *Leave Her, Johnny*.

ACROSS THE WESTERN OCEAN (1)
(Same tune as above)

1. Oh, though times are hard and the wages low,
   Ch. Amelia (O'Melia) whar yer *bound* to?
   The Rocky Mountains is me home,
   Ch. Oh, *across* the Western *Ocean*!

2. A land of promise there ye'll see,
   I'm bound away across that sea.

3. To Liverpool I'll make [take] my way,
   To Liverpool that Packet [Yankee] School.

4. There's Liverpool Pat wid his tarpaulin hat,
   An' Yankee John ['Frisco Jim], the Packet Rat.

5. Beware them Packet Ships I pray,
   They'll steal yer gear [stores] an' clothes away.
   [They'll steal yer hide an' soul away.]

6. We are bound away from our friends and home,
   We're bound away to seek for gold.

7. Mothers and sweethearts don't ye cry,
   Sisters an' brothers say goodbye.

Some singers sang:

> Say, sailor, where yiz bound to?

or

> O say where yer bound to?

for the first refrain. And Whall gives as a final refrain for the second
verse only—'To join the Irish Army'.

Clark Russell often mentions this shanty in his novels.

The later version *Leave Her, Johnnies* or as some sang it *Leave Her,
Bullies* was sometimes sung during the voyage—at the pumps—but
its better-known function was that of airing grievances just prior to
the completion of the voyage either when warping the vessel in
through the locks or at the final spell of the pumps (in wooden ships)
after the vessel had docked. Many unprintable stanzas were sung,
directed at the afterguard, the grub, and the owners. Bullen writes
that: 'to sing it before the last day or so was almost tantamount to
mutiny.' C. Sharp sees a resemblance in the tune to the old folk-
song from Somerset, *I'm Seventeen Come Sunday* and he also believes
it to have hymn connections; and Doerflinger notes that it is like
the ballad called the *Two Sisters*. I give the pumping and capstan

216

WARPING THE SHIP ALONGSIDE BY CAPSTAN

'. . . An' it's time for us to leave 'er!' (Capstan Shanty)

version, but have put the hauling marks in the refrains of the verse. In the case of hauling, of course, the full chorus would not be sung.

LEAVE HER, JOHNNY, LEAVE HER
Alternative titles, *Time for Us to Leave Her, Leave Her, Bullies, Leave Her*

Oh, the times wuz hard, an' the wa-ges.. low, Leave her, Johnny, leave her! But now once more a-shore we'll go, An' it's time for us to leave her! Leave her Johnny, leave her, Ooh! leave her, Johnny, leave her! For the voyage is done, an' the winds don't blow, An' it's time for us to leave her!

2. Oh, I thought I heard the Ol' Man say,
    Ch. Leave her, Johnny, *leave* her!
  Tomorrow ye will get your pay,
    Ch. An' it's *time* for us to *leave* her!
      Full Chorus. Leave her, Johnny, leave her,
        Oooh! leave her, Johnny, leave her!
        For the voyage is done and the winds don't blow
        [Ye may go ashore an' touch yer pay, *or* Come ashore
            an' grab yer pay],
        For [An'] it's time for us to leave her!

3. The work wuz hard an' the voyage wuz long,
  The sea wuz high an' the gales wuz strong.

4. The wind wuz foul an' the sea ran high,
  She shipped it green an' none went by.

5. The grub wuz bad an' the wages low,
  But now once more ashore we'll go.

6. Oh, our Old Man he don't set no sail,
  We'd be better off in a nice clean gaol.

7. We'd be better off in a nice clean gaol,
  With all night in an' plenty o' ale.

8. She's poverty-stricken an' parish-rigged,
  The bloomin' crowd is fever-stricked.

9. Oh, sing that we boys will never be
  In a hungry bitch the likes o' she.

10. The mate wuz a bucko an' the Old Man a Turk,
    The bosun wuz a beggar with the middle name o' Work.

11. The Old Man swears an' the mate swears too,
    The crew all swear, an' so would you.

12. It's growl yer may an' go yer must,
    It matters not whether yer last or fust.

13. The winds wuz foul, all work, no pay [play],
    To Liverpool Docks from 'Frisco Bay.

14. The ship won't steer, nor stay, nor wear,
    An' so us shellbacks learnt to swear.

15. She will not wear, nor steer, nor stay,
    Her sails an' gear all carried away.

16. We wuz made to pump all night an' day,
    An' we half-dead had beggar-all to say.

17. We'll leave her tight an' we'll leave her trim,
    We'll heave the hungry barstard in.

18. Oh, leave her, Johnny, an' we'll work no more,
    Of pump or drown we've had full store.

19. Leave her, Johnny, an' we'll leave her with a grin,
    There's many a worser we've sailed in [She's the hungriest barstard
        we ever shipped in].

20. The sails is furled an' our work is done,
    An' now ashore we'll have our bit o' fun.

21. We'll make her fast an' stow our gear,
    The gals are a-waitin' on the pier.

22. Leave her, Johnny, ye can leave her like a man,
    Oh, leave her, Johnny, oh, leave her while yer can.

23. Now I thought I heard the Old Man say,
    One more good heave [pull, pump] an' then belay.

Other verses:

No Liverpool bread, nor rotten crackerhash,
No dandyfunk, nor cold an' sloppy hash.

A rantin' mate an' a bully skipper too,
Oh, a leakin' ship an' a rotten, harping crew.

Come sing, me bullies, this farewell song,
A bully ol' song an' it won't take long.

We're all of us old an' we're weak an' sad,
Since first we joined this ruddy wooden-clad [iron-clad].

Now it's time for to say goodbye,
The old Pier Head is quickly drawin' nigh.

Mahogany beef an' weevils in our bread,
We wisht old Crackerhash Joe wuz dead.

The rain it rained the whole day long,
The nor'east wind wuz blowin' strong.

No more Cape Horn, no more stand-by,
We'll pump her out, an' leave her dry.

We swear by rote for want o' more,
But now we're through so we'll go on shore.

Leave her, Johnny, we'll leave her now for good,
In a ruddy short time we'll be out o' the wood.

Oh, Capen, now ye are gonna lose yer crew,
We've had enough of the ship, the grub an' you.

A slightly different tune is the following, sung to me by a Liverpool
seaman. It is a halyard version.

LEAVE HER, JOHNNY
(Halyards)

Oh I thought I heard the Old Man say. Leave her John-ny, leave her! Oh, I thought I heard the
Old Man say, It's time for us to leave her!

And now I will give the pumping version sung during the voyage.
It goes to the same tune as the first one.

LEAVE HER, JOHNNY, LEAVE HER
(Pumps)

1. Oh, a dollar a day is a Jack Sprite's pay,
     Ch. Leave her, *etc.*
   To pump all night an' to work all day,
     Ch. An' it's time, *etc.*

       Full Chorus. Leave her Johnny, leave her,
                    Ooh, leave her Johnny, leave her,
                    For the winds do roar an' we wish we wuz
                    ashore,
                    An' it's time for us to leave her!

2. Though times is hard an' the wages low,
There's a fathom o' water down in the hold.

3. The Old Man shouts, the pumps stand by,
Oh, we can never suck her dry.

4. Heave one more turn an' around she goes,
Or else we'll be kickin' up our toes.

5. Leave her, Johnny, we can pump no more,
Of pump or drown we've had full store.

6. It's pump or drown, the Old Man said,
Or else damn soon ye'll all be dead.

7. Heave around or we shall drown,
Hey! don't yiz feel her settlin' down?

8. Heave around them pump-bowls bright,
There'll be no sleep for us this night.

9. The rats have gone an' we, the crew,
It's time be damned that we went too.

10. Oh, pump away in merry, merry strife,
Oh, heave away for to save dear life.

11. Oh pump her out from down below,
Oh, pump her out an' away we'll go.

12. The starboard pump is like the crew,
It's all worn out an' will not do.

13. Leave her, Johnny, we can pump no more,
It's time we wuz upon dry shore.

The last of our 'Johnny' series is *Heave Away, My Johnnies* or
We're All Bound To Go. This shanty, very popular in the days of the
Packet Ships, in spite of its fine tune (my brother reckons it the best
of the lot), was rarely heard in the latter days of sail. It was essentially
an outward-bound song used at the windlass, although at times it
would also be sung at the pumps, and came into being about the
thirties of the last century. It is Irish to its very bones and the tune is
reminiscent of a jig. As to the words they were pronounced in Irish
fashion, giving rise to the belief that the ship concerned was carrying
'mail' and therefore a packet of some standing, whereas, in actual
fact, these ships which used to carry emigrants across to the New
World were very often real third-raters, and the food the poor Irish
emigrants had daily was 'meal'—the Irish pronunciation of which
was 'male', hence the error. Herman Melville in *Redburn* gives a fine
description of the plight of these early Irish emigrants and their
hellish crossings in rattletrap emigrant ships to the Land of Promise
in the New World. Doerflinger, seeking an Irish song from which

this shanty may have stemmed, came across a song called *Yellow Meal* which he says is to be found in many old American songsters. While up at Cecil Sharp House, London, giving a talk on shanties, I made the acquaintance of Patrick Shuldam-Shaw, and being on the look-out for some personal evidence of this song *Yellow Meal*, I mentioned the matter to him. He said that in one of his visits to the Shetland Islands collecting folk-songs he had taken down such a song from the singing of a certain John Stickle of Balla Sound, but he called it *Lay Me Down*. Here is his transcription:

LAY ME DOWN

2. 'I have a packet, a packet or two,
    The one, the *Georgie Walker*, and the other, the *Kangaroo*.
    The one, the *Georgie Walker*, on Friday she'll set sail,
    And all the provisions she's got on board is a thousand bags of meal.'
        Ch. Lay me down, lay me down,
            Lay me down dead,
            Lay me down, ay-jer-bup, Mrs. McQuale,
            Lay me down, ay-jer-bup, Mrs. Mahoölichan,
            Jeannie go 'hooch'!
            Fire away, Bridget, I'm dying for thee.

3. Now I'm landed in New York, and working in a canal,
   For me to go back in a packet ship, a thing I never shall,
   I'll go back on one of the White Star Lines, they carry both steam
       and sail,
   And there I'll get plenty of beef and soft tack, and none of your yellow
       meal.
   Ch. Lay me down, *etc.*

In the nautical magazine *Sea Breezes* I came across a letter in
reference to three songs popular in Liverpool 'free-'n'-easies' during
the middle of the last century, and one of these was a ditty called
Across the Western Ocean. I contacted the writer of the letter (Mr. T. E.
Elwell of the Isle of Man, with whom I corresponded frequently
afterwards on the subject of shanties) and he gave me this:

ACROSS THE WESTERN OCEAN (2)

'Have you got an emigrant ship that's bound for Amer-i-kay?'
'Oh, yes! I have an emigrant ship,
I have got one or two;
I've got the *Georgie Walker* and I've got the *Kangaroo.*
   Ch. Oh! here we go, there we go,
       Lay me down do;
       Here we go, there we go,
       Mrs. O'Halligan, too,
       Jenny, hooroo!
       Fire away, laddie, I'll bully for you!

Mr. Elwell could not remember any more verses, but I then was
lucky enough to meet an old Irish friend of mine, a native of Wexford
who turned up the full version of this song, which he called *The Irish
Emigrant*:

THE IRISH EMIGRANT

1. As I walked out one morning down by the Clarence Dock,
   I heard a bully Irish boy conversing wid Tapscott;
   'Good morning, Mister Tapscott, would ye be arter telling me,
   If ye've got a ship bound for New York in the state of Amerikee?'
   Ch. Lay me down, lay me down,
       Lay me down do!
       Lay me down, here we go, Mrs. McQuale,
       Here we go to, lay me down, Mrs. O'Halligan,
       Jinny hooraw!
       Fire away, Bridget, I'll bully for you!

2. 'Yes, yes, me handsome Irish boy, I've got a ship or two,
   One's laying at the wharf there, awaitin' for her crew,
   She is a handsome packet and on Friday she will sail,
   And now she's takin' her on board a thousand bags o' meal.'
   Ch. Lay me down, etc.

3. So then I paid me passage down in solid Irish gold,
   And when the packet sailed, boys, 'twas on the yellow grog road;
   There was roars of milly murder, the loikes wuz never known,
   An' ev'ry mother's son, me bhoys, did wish himself at home.

4. On the day on which we set out, 'twas on the first o' May,
   The Capen came upon the deck, these words to us did say,
   'Cheer up, me beefy Irish bhoys, now we have set all sail,
   We'll give ye a feed o' pork an' beans, tomorrow—yellow meal!'

5. Next day when we was sailin' down the channel right as rain,
   A nor'west wind began to blow, an' druv us back again.
   Bad luck to the Joey Walker and the day that we set sail,
   For them packet sailors broken open me chest, an' stole me yellow
   meal.

6. Now that I am in Amerikee, a-working on a canal,
   I'll niver go home in a packet ship, I know I niver shall,
   But I'll ship in a darn big National boat, that carries both steam an'
   sail,
   With lashin's o' beef, an' plenty to eat, an' none of yer yellow meal.

This is much the same as the song Doerflinger calls *Yellow Meal* with a few verbal differences—'Sligo' instead of 'Clarence' dock; 'Channel of St. James' instead of 'channel right as rain' and *Josh. A. Walker* as the name of the ship—but he does not give any chorus at all. Nevertheless, all the foregoing songs under different names and Doerflinger's *Yellow Meal* are one and the same song. But did the shanty stem from this song or vice versa? Since both date from the thirties or forties it is difficult to say.

In the shanty *Henry Clay* is often given as the name of the packet ship concerned.

As Terry points out *Heave Away, Me Johnnies* has a definite narrative and varies but little in the hands of different shantymen, although the name of the ship varied considerably. *Josie, Joshuay, Joseph* or *Jinny Walker* was the most usual, but *Henry Clay, Dreadnaught*, and *Kangaroo* were sometimes substituted. Tapscott was a Liverpool emigrant agent operating in the middle of the nineteenth century.

This shanty, being a genuine brake-windlass shanty, I may as well describe here the difference between the movements at the brakes of windlasses and those at the pumps. At the latter the brakes or levers were pushed up and down in one movement each time,

TAPSCOTT'S AMERICAN PACKET OFFICES,
GENERAL OFFICE....OLDHALL, OLDHALL-STREET.
PASSENGER OFFICE................ST. GEORGE'S-BUILDINGS,
REGENT'S-ROAD.
The following
FIRST-CLASS PACKETS
Will be despatched on their appointed days,
as under:
FOR NEW YORK.

	Tons.	To sail.
DE WITT CLINTON. FUNK	2000	This Day.
ALBION, (new) WILLIAMS	2500	18th June.
ANDREW FOSTER, SWIFT	2500	26th June.
A. Z. CHANDLER	1800	To follow.
WEST POINT, WILLIAMS	2000	—
FRANCIS A. PALMER (new,) RICHARDSON	2500	—
EMERALD ISLE (new) CORNISH	2500	—
KOSSUTH, DAWSON	2500	—
WM. TAPSCOTT, BELL	2500	—
PROGRESS, CRACE	2500	—
EMPIRE, A. ZEREGA	2000	—
CENTURION, COOMES	2000	—
NORTHAMPTON, REED	2500	—
ANTARCTIC, STOUFFER	2500	—
BENJAMIN ADAMS, DRUMMOND	2500	—
ROCK LIGHT (new) DRUMMOND	3000	—
W. NELSON, CREEVER	2000	—
SHAMROCK, DOANE	2000	—
CAMBRIA, BERRY	2000	—
CONSTELLATION, ALLEN	3000	—
DRIVER, HOLBERTON	3000	—

And succeeding Packets every five days.

FOR PHILADELPHIA.

TONAWANDA, JULIUS	1223	19th June.
TUSCARORA, TURLEY	1000	12th July.
SARANAK, ROWLAND	1000	12th Aug.
WYOMING, DUNLEVY	1100	12th Sept.

The above Ships are of the largest class, and commanded by men of experience, who will take every precaution to promote the health and comfort of the passengers during the voyage.
Private Rooms for Families, or persons who wish to be more select, can at all times be had, and deposits of £1 each, to secure berths, should be remitted, which shall have due attention.
Surgeons can have free Cabin Passages by the above Ships.
Persons proceeding to the interior of the United States can know the actual outlay, and make the necessary arrangements here, to be forwarded, on arrival at New York, without one day's delay, and thereby avoid the many annoyances Emigrants are subject to on landing at New York.
Drafts and Exchange for any amount, at sight, on New York, payable in any part of the United States, can at all times be furnished to those who prefer this safer mode of taking care of their funds.
For further particulars apply, post-paid, to
W. TAPSCOTT and Co., Liverpool, and 7, Eden-quay, Dublin,
Agents for TAPSCOTT and Co, New York.
TAPSCOTT'S EMIGRANT'S GUIDE, fifth edition, can be had by remitting six postage stamps.

(From *The Liverpool Daily Post and Echo Ltd.*, with permission)

An original shipping advertisement of the Tapscott's Agency, inserted in the first
Liverpool Daily Post, 1855.

but in the case of the windlass brakes the work was too heavy for one movement up and one down. The windlass brakes were dragged down from the up position to the level of a man's waist in one movement and then pushed down to knee level in a second movement, hence two movements were needed at the windlass to one at the pumps. This naturally timed the song and it seems that shanties needed for this kind of work were usually sung in 2/4 or 6/8 time, whereas latter-day capstan songs were often in 4/4 time, the operation being more of a march rhythm. In the second verse of my version of this shanty I have shown in brackets how the shantyman would sing the solos.

HEAVE AWAY, ME JOHNNIES (a)
Alternative title, *We're All Bound To Go*

2. (*Slow*) 'Good mornin', Mister Tapscott, sir,'
   (*Quicker*) 'Good-morn, me gal,' sez he,
   > Ch. Heave away, me Johnnies [Bullies, Bonnies, Jollies], heave
   > away-away!
   (*Slow*) 'Oh, it's have yiz got a packet-ship,
   (*Quicker*) All bound for Amerikee?'
   > Ch. An' away [Heave away], me bully boys [jolly boys, bonnie
   > boys, Johnnie boys],
   > We're all bound to go!

3. 'Oh, yes I have got a packet-ship, I have got one or two,
   I've got the *Jinny Walker* and I've got the *Kangaroo*.

4. 'I've got the *Jinny Walker* and today she does set sail,
   With five an' fifty emigrants an' a thousand bags o' meal.'

5. The day was fine when we set sail, but night had barely come,
   An' every lubber never ceased to wish himself at home.

6. That night as we was sailin' through the Channel of St. James,
   A dirty nor'west wind came up an' druv us back again.

7. We snugged her down an' we laid her to, with reefed main tops'l set,
   It was no joke I tell you, 'cos our bunks an' clothes wuz wet.

8. It cleared up fine at break o' day, an' we set sail once more,
   An' every son-o'-a-gun wuz glad when we reached Amerikee's shore.

9. Bad luck to them Irish sailor-boys, bad luck to them I says,
   For they all got drunk, broke into me bunk, an' stole me clothes
   [meal] away.

10. 'Twas at the Castle Gardens, oh, they landed me ashore,
    An' if I marry a Yankee boy, I'll cross the seas no more.

HEAVING AT THE OLD-FASHIONED BRAKE WINDLASS

'An' away, me bully boys, we're all bound to go!' (Windlass Shanty)

Verse 3 was sometimes sung:

> 'Oh, yes,' sez Mr. Tapscott, 'I have got ships of fame,
> I've got one in the Clarence Dock—the *Dreadnaught* is her name.'

Two final verses sometimes added are:

> Now I'm in Philadelphia an' workin' on the Canal,
> To go home in one of them Packet Ships I'm sure I never shall.

> But I'll go home in a National boat that carries both steam an' sail,
> With lashin's o' corned beef every day an' none of yer yeller meal.

Of course in the story the emigrant is a *girl*, but in these final verses it is a man. Many shantymen seemed to get their sexes mixed. For instance Doerflinger's singer sings in verse 2:

> 'Oh, yes, my noble *Irish blade*, I have a ship or two . . .'

and then later he has:

> 'I'll marry some fine Yankee boy, stay all my life on shore.'

L. A. Smith gives a verse:

> 'Now I am in New York and I'm walking through the street,
> With no money in my pockets and scarce a bit to eat.'

Incidentally the words of this Packet Ship song were sometimes sung to the tune of *Can't Ye Dance the Polka?*

Couplets from another Western Ocean forebitter and shanty—*The Banks of Newfoundland*—were sometimes sung to *Heave Away, Me Johnnies*:

> You rambling boys o' Liverpool, ye sailormen beware,
> *Ch.* Heave away, me Johnnies, *etc.*
> An' never sign in Packet Ships where they dungaree jumpers wear,
> *Ch.* An' away, me bully boys, *etc.*

Harlow in his book *The Making of a Sailor* suggests that the ship *Josie Walker* was a hell-ship:

> 'You'll not sail me on a Walker ship, I'll not climb over her rail,
> To hell with you and your packet ship and your thousand bags o' mail.'

(Note that Harlow gives 'mail', not 'meal'.)

But the most popular way of singing this shanty in the latter days of sail was the following:

HEAVE AWAY, ME JOHNNIES (b)

2. Sometimes we're bound for Liverpool, sometimes we're bound for France,
   Ch. Heave away, me Johnnies, heave away—away!
   But now we're bound to New York town to give the girls a chance,
   Ch. An' away, me bully boys, we're all bound to go!

3. Our advance note's in our pocket, boys, it sure will take us far,
   An' now a cruise down Lime Street, boys, an' to the American Bar.

4. In two days' time we'll be outward bound an' down the Mersey we'll clip,
   The gals'll all be waiting, boys, when we get back next trip.

5. The Peter's flyin' at the fore, the Pilot's waiting the tide,
   An' soon we'll be bound out again, bound for the other side.

6. An' when we're homeward bound again, our pockets lined once more,
   We'll spend it all with the gals, me boys, an' go to sea for more.

7. So gaily let yer voices ring, me bullies heave 'n' bust,
   'Tain't no use a caterwaulin'—growl yer may, but go yer must.

   This version appears to be one sung from a Yankee seaman's point of view. The opening stanzas are very like those of *The Gals o' Dublin Town*.
   A final theme is that of the 'milkmaid'. This theme is to be found in many shanties, all stemming from the shore folk-song. Here is a milkmaid version closely akin to that given by Cecil Sharp.

HEAVE AWAY, ME JOHNNIES (c)
(*Same tune as Version (a)*)

1. As I walked out one mornin' fair, all in the month of May,
     Ch. Heave away, *etc.*
   I overhauled a pretty maid and unto her did say,
     Ch. An' away, me bully boys, *etc.*

2. 'Oh, where are ye goin' to, my pretty maid?' I unto her did say.
   'I'm going a milking, sir,' she said, all in the month of May.

3. 'Shall I go with you, my pretty maid?' I unto her did say.
   'Oh, yes, if you please, kind sir,' she said, all in the month of May.

4. 'Oh, what is your father, my pretty maid?' I unto her did say.
   'My father's a farmer, kind sir,' she said, all in the month of May.

5. 'Oh, what is your fortune, my pretty maid?' I unto her did say.
   'My face is my fortune, sir,' she said, all in the month of May.

The rest is mainly unprintable.

Since this shanty has the word 'heave' in its refrains we will now start a series of work-songs which have the word 'heave' in their titles. The first two are from the West Indies and this is the first time they have been in print. Strangely enough, in spite of them both using the word 'heave' in their refrains, they are halyard shanties. The first I learnt from a coloured seaman of St. Vincent, B.W.I., and, like most Negro shanties—as opposed to white men's shanties which usually had a tale to tell—after the first few stanzas it called for improvisation.

HEAVE AWAY, BOYS, HEAVE AWAY (a)

Heave a-way, heave a-way, for the White Man's dollars, Heave a-way boys, heave a-way! Heave a-way, heave a-way for the White Man's dollars, heave a-way boys, heave a-way!

2. Heave away, heave away, for the merchant's money,
     Ch. Heave away, boys, *heave* away!
   Heave away, heave away for the merchant's money,
     Ch. Heave away, boys, *heave* away!

3. Heave away, heave away for the buckra's silver,
   Heave away, heave away for the buckra's silver.

4. Don't let this money bring contention,
   Don't let this money bring contention.

5. Heave away, heave away an' let's get goin',
   Heave away, heave away an' let's get goin'.

And the second one for which we have the same title is:

HEAVE AWAY, BOYS, HEAVE AWAY (b)

2. An' when we are happy we tolls de ol' bell,
     Ch. Heave away, boys, *heave* away!
   An' when we is sad yiz can all go to hell,
     Ch. Heave away, boys, *heave* away!

3. I love a fat widow down Rotherhithe way,
   An' when she next sees me, to me she will say.

4. 'Oh, Johnny I've waited for you to return,
   So I can spend freely all the money you earn.'

5. Oh, roll the ol' chariot, long may she roll,
   Why don't the mate shake 'er, oh, God damn his soul.

6. Oh, heave away, bullies, for ol' Mobile Bay,
   The gals there will help yer to spend yer pay-day [half-pay].

7. When I was a young man an' well in me prime,
   I'd love all them yaller gals two at a time.

8. But now I'm an old man an' don't feel so young,
   I'd sooner have lashin's an' lashin's o' rum!

9. Oh, I've got a sister nine foot tall,
   She sleeps in the kitchen with her feet in the hall.

I learnt this from a coloured shantyman known as 'Harry Lauder' of St. Lucia, B.W.I., in 1932. I am inclined to think that the use of the word 'heave' in these hauling songs indicates that at some time or another both of the foregoing shanties were used by the Negroes of Mobile Bay and elsewhere at the jackscrews when stowing cotton aboard the old wooden ships.

Our next 'heave' shanty is *Heave Away Cheerily O!* Only two collections give it. Davis & Tozer give it as capstan, Harlow as both pumps and windlass. Davis & Tozer state that the words and music of their version are 'entirely original'. If by this the editors mean that they composed it then seamen, obviously, must have taken it from their book in 1887 (first edition) and made use of it at sea— a magnificent gesture! For Harlow mentions it having been sung many times aboard his ship. He declares that there were many unprintable verses. I learnt my version from a Geordie shipmate in the twenties.

HEAVE AWAY CHEERILY O!
Alternative title, *As Off to the South'ard We Go*

2. They're shoutin' goodbye, an' the gals they do cry,
   Ch. Heave away cheeri-lye o-ho!
   So sing up, me darlin's, an' wipe yer tears dry,
   Ch. As off to the south'ard we go-o,
   As off to the south'ard we go!

Full Chorus. Sing, me lads, cheeri-lye,
Heave, me lads, cheeri-lye,
Heave away cheeri-lye o-ho!
For the gold that we prize an' for sunnier skies,
Away to the south'ard we go!

3. They're cryin', 'Come back, my dear John an' dear Jack,
There's water in front an' no door at the back.'

4. But we're Johnnies bold who can work for our gold,
An' stand a good dousin' wi'out catchin' cold.

5. The gals to the south'ard are bully an' fine,
When we gits to Melbourne we'll have a good time.

6. A John he is true to his Sal an' his Sue,
So long as he's able to keep 'em in view.

7. We'll heave her up, bullies, an' run her away,
We'll soon be a-headin' out on a long lay.

This is much the same as that of Davis & Tozer. Harlow gives
verses 1 and 2 in similar vein, then:

3. They're crying, 'Come back, my dear sailor in blue,
For no one can fill the place vacant by you.'

4. They love us for money, whoever he be,
But when it's all gone we are shanghaied to sea.

5. Then sing, 'Goodbye, Sally, your wonders I'll tell,
But when with another, I'll wish you in hell.'

(From *The Making of a Sailor*, with permission)

'Geordie', my friend, always sang the word 'cheerily' as 'cheeri-lye' in accordance with typical sailor usage when singing any word ending with '-ly'.

The word 'cheerily' means 'quickly' and was often used at capstan and halyards when exhorting the men to harder efforts . . . 'Heave away cheerily, me hearties!' . . . 'Cheerily, lads, hand over hand!' It was used in both the Navy and Merchant Marine and Shakespeare uses it in Act I, Scene I, of his play *The Tempest*, where the bosun calls out: 'Heigh, my hearts, cheerly, cheerly, my hearts; yare, yare! Take in the topsail . . .'

'Cheerily' had an opposite number, 'handsomely'. This meant heave or haul slow and steady but appears to have been used more in the Navy than in the Merchant Service.

At this point we will leave our 'heave' series for a page or so and give the shanty which uses the word 'cheerily' more than any other—

Cheerily Man—although here it was never pronounced 'cheeri-lye'; sometimes it would be 'cheer'y' or 'cheer'ly'.

Cheerily Man—a halyard shanty—is only just faintly removed from singin'-out and is probably the most primitive, and one of the oldest of all these heaving and hauling songs of the sea.

It was obscene to a degree and most versions have had to be camouflaged, although C. F. Smith points out that the very fact that it was sung in passenger-carrying ships of the John Company and later in Green and Wigram's passenger ships proves without doubt that it had clean words, since indecent shantying was tabu aboard passenger sailing vessels.

Miss Colcord gives it as a 'British shanty' and mentions the fact that an early writer in *Harper's Magazine* wrote that it was frowned upon in Yankee ships, and quotes him as having written: 'No American crew would ever ape customs prevailing under the flag of an effete monarchy by singing *Cheerily Man*.' Miss Colcord then says that time must have conquered this prejudice, as this shanty was fairly familiar, though not common, in Yankee ships in the latter days of sail. Well, well . . . I wonder what Dana would have thought about this? For he, in the eighteen-thirties, aboard the brig *Pilgrim*, often joined in the singing of *Cheerily Man*. As a matter of fact never once does he mention the hoisting of a topsail or of a t'gallants'l, or the catting of an anchor, without referring to the fact that *Cheerily Man* was the shanty with which they did the job.[1]

CHEERILY MAN (MEN)

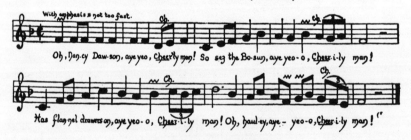

Oh, Dan-cy Daw-son, aye yeo, Cheer'ly man! So ses the Bo-sun, aye yeo-o, Cheer-i-ly man! Has flan-nel drawers on, aye yeo-o, Cheer-i-ly man! Oh, haul-ey, aye-yeo-o, Cheer-i-ly man!"

2. Oh, Sally Rackett, aye yeo!
   *Ch. Cheer*ily man!
   In her pea-jacket, aye yeo!
   *Ch. Cheer*ily man!
   Shipped in a packet, aye yeo!
   *Ch. Cheer*ily man!
   Oh, hauley aye yeo!
   *Ch. Cheer*ily man!

[1] *Two Years Before the Mast.*

3. Oh, Flora Fernanah
   Slipped on a banana,
   Can't play the pianner.

4. Oh, Susie Skinner
   Sez she's a beginner,
   Prefers it to dinner.

5. Oh, Missus Duckett,
   She's kicked the bucket,
   Oh, nip an' tuck it.

6. Oh, Polly Riddle
   Has a hole in the middle
   Of her new fiddle.

7. Oh, Betty Baker,
   Kissed by a Quaker,
   Oh, rock 'n' shake 'er.

8. Oh, Jenny Walker,
   Kissed by a hawker,
   He wuz a corker.

9. Oh, Jennifer Bell,
   She drinks as well,
   An' never will tell.

10. Oh, Katie Karson
    Slept with a parson,
    She's got a bar-son.

11. Oh, Polly Hawkins
    In her white stockings
    Has done some rockin's.

12. Oh, haughty cocks,
    Oh, split the blocks,
    Oh, stretch her luff.

13. Oh, rouse 'n' shake 'er,
    Oh, shake 'n' wake 'er,
    Oh, go we'll make 'er.

14. Avast there, avast!
    Make the fall fast,
    Make it well fast.

When used for catting the anchor the following stanzas would also
be used:

235

CHEERILY MAN (MEN)

Haul all together,
Haul for good weather,
She's light as a feather.

To the cathead,
We'll raise [shift] the dead,
She's heavy as lead.

We'll haul again,
With might an' main,
Pay out more chain.

Chain stopper bring,
Pass through the ring,
Oh, haul an' sing.

She's up to the sheave,
At the cathead we'll leave,
Soon the tackle unreeve.

Pull one an' all,
On the ol' catfall,
An' then belay all!

Strangely enough the piratical flavoured 'yeo' of such shouts as 'Yeo heave ho!' and 'Yeo ho 'n' a bottle of rum!' did not find its way into shanties to the extent it did in sea-songs of the Dibdin type. Apart from those in *Cheerily Man*, *Good Morning, Ladies All*, and our next shanty, neither the 'yo' nor 'yeo' syllables, favoured by the seamen of Drake's day, found much support from the seamen of the nineteenth century. I wonder why?

Sharp gives an interesting version with only three solos and three refrains.

CHEERILY MAN (Sharp)

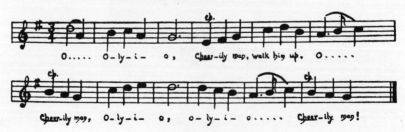

O..... O–ly–i– o, Cheer-ily man, walk big up. O.....

Cheer-ily man, O–ly–i– o, o–ly–i– o..... Cheer-ily man!

Frank Shay in his *Deep Sea Shanties* and in his *American Sea Songs and Shanties*[1] gives:

1. O haul pulley, Yoe!
   Ch. Cheerily men.
   O long and strong, yo ho!
   Ch. Cheerily men.
   Yo-ho and with a will,
   Ch. Cheerily men,
   Cheerily, cheerily, cheerily O!

2. A long haul for Widow Skinner,
   Kiss her well before dinner,
   At her, boys, and win her.

3. A strong pull for Mrs. Bell,
   Who likes a lark right well,
   And what's more will never tell.

4. Oh, haul and split the blocks,
   O haul and stretch her luff,
   Young lovies, sweat her up.

As well as being a deep-water shanty, *Cheerily Man*, under the title of *Sally Rackett*, was a common cargo-working song among the timber stowers of Quebec and elsewhere.

A variant of this shanty is one which was very popular among Negro or 'chequerboard' crews. This was called *Haul 'Er Away*, *Haul Him Away*, or *Sally Rackett*, and is of West Indian origin, hailing either from Barbadoes or Jamaica. I learnt it from Harding. The stanzas are those of *Cheerily Man*. It was a splendid hauling song.

HAUL 'ER AWAY! (a)
Alternative titles, *Haul Him Away!*, *Sally Rackett*

Lit-tle Dan-cy Daiw-son, Haul 'er a-way! She's got flap-pel drawers on, Haul 'er a-way! So say

our ol' Bo-sun, Haul 'er a-way! Wid a haul-ey high-O! Haul 'er a-way!

[1] Published by W. W. Norton & Co., N.Y.

2. Little Sally Rackett,
   Ch. Haul 'er away!
   She shipped in a packet,
   Ch. Haul 'er away!
   An' she never did regret it,
   Ch. Haul 'er away!
   Wid a hauley high-O!
   Ch. Haul 'er away!

3. Little Betty Baker
   Ran off wid a Quaker,
   Guess her Mum could shake 'er,
   Wid a hauley high-O!

4. Little Susie Skinner
   Sez she's a beginner,
   But prefers it to 'er dinner.

5. Little Flo Fanana
   Slipped on a banana,
   Now she can't play the pianner.

6. Little Rosie Riddle
   Broke her brand new fiddle,
   Got a hole right in the middle.

7. Little Polly Walker
   Ran off with a hawker,
   Oh, he was a corker.

8. Little Kitty Karson
   Ran off with a parson,
   Now she's got a little parson.

9. Little Dolly Duckett
   Washes in a bucket,
   She's a tart but doesn't look it.

10. Up me fightin' cocks, boys,
    Up an' split 'er blocks now,
    An' we'll stretch 'er luff, boys.

The tune of the foregoing has something in common with that of the Jamaican song *Missy Ramgoat*, and also with *Hill an' Gully Rider*, another Jamaican song featured in the film *Moby Dick*, and later spliced to the West Indian work-song *Banana Boat* and turned into a 'pop' song.

A closely related song which bears the same title is the following. I learnt this also in the West Indies. Olmstead in his book *Incidents of a Whaling Voyage* (1841) gives stanzas about 'Nancy Fanana' and my 'Flora Fernaner', so it appears to be fairly old. It was essentially a hauling song—and a good one too—although Olmstead's chorus runs: 'Heave her away, and heave her away!'

HAUL 'ER AWAY! (b)

Young Salty Rackett, she shipped in a packet, Haul 'er a-way, oh, haul 'er a-way! Hoo-raw, hoo-raw for young Salty Ra-ack-ett, Haul 'er a-way, oh, haul 'er a-way!

2. Miss Nancy Dawson, she's got flannel drawers on,
   Ch. Haul 'er away, oh, *haul* 'er away!
   Hooraw, hooraw for ol' Nancy Dawson,
   Ch. Haul 'er away, oh, *haul* 'er away!

3. Little Miss Muffet, she sat on a tuffet.

4. Nancy Fernaner, she married a barber.

5. Susy Skinner, she sure is a winner.

6. Young Kitty Carson ran off with a parson.

7. Ol' Missus Duckett, she lived in a bucket.

8. Betsy Baker, she married a Quaker [Shaker].

9. Polly Riddle, she broke her new fiddle.

10. Little Miss Walker's a hell o' a talker.

11. We all love the gals, oh, rouse an' shake 'er,
    Hooraw, hooraw for the gals o' Jamaicker!

Now to return to our 'heave' series: our next shanty is one given by Davis & Tozer, and L. A. Smith, and I should think by its form and music that it must rank as one of the earliest of the capstan shanties. This is *Yeo Heave Ho!* and I wonder whether this song is the one referred to in Chapter 36 of Dana's *Two Years Before the Mast*:

All hands manned the windlass; and the long-drawn *Yo heave, ho!* which we had last heard dying away among the desolate hills of San Diego, soon brought the anchor to the bows.

On the other hand he may have been referring to the sing-out which uses the same words—always popular when breaking the anchor out of the ground.

YEO HEAVE HO!

2. Yeo heave ho, cheerily we go,
   Heave men with a will,
   Tramp and tramp it still,
   The anchor grips the ground—the anchor grips the ground.
   Ch. Yeo ho, heave ho, yeo ho, heave ho!

3. Yeo heave ho, raise her from below,
   Heave men with a will,
   Tramp and tramp it still,
   The anchor's off the ground—and we are outward bound,
   Ch. Yeo ho, *etc.*

4. Yeo heave ho, round the capstan go,
   Heave men with a will,
   Tramp and tramp it still,
   The anchor now is weighed—the anchor now is weighed.
   Ch. Yo ho, *etc.*

The last shanty of this series is one sometimes called *Mainsail Haul* but more commonly *Paddy, Lay Back!* It was both a forebitter and a capstan song and a very popular one too, especially in Liverpool ships. My versions I learnt from my father and from a Liverpool-Irish sailing-ship man, John Connolly, who often sang the last line of the chorus in this fashion:

For we're bound for Val-laparaiser 'round the Horn!

It is a fairly old song dating back to the time of the Mobile cotton hoosiers and has two normal forms: one with an eight-line verse—this was the forebitter form; and the second with a four-line verse—the usual shanty pattern. Doerflinger gives a two-line verse pattern as the shanty—a rather unusual form, and further on in his book he gives the forebitter with both four- and eight-line verses. He gives the title of the shanty as *Paddy, Get Back* and both his versions of the forebitter as *Mainsail Haul.* Shay, Sampson, and Bone all suggest that it was a fairly modern sea-song and give no indication that any form was sung as a shanty, but all my sailing-ship acquaintances always referred to it as a shanty, and it was certainly sung in the Liverpool–New York Packets as such—at least the four-line verse form. Writing of capstan shanties L. A. Smith says: '*Valparaiso, Round the Horn,* and *Santa Anna* are all much in the same style as *Rio Grande.*' There is of course a mistake here—either a printer's error or hasty preparation for the press—for the first two titles are one and the same song, *Valparaiso Round the Horn,* an alternative title for *Paddy, Lay Back.*

Here is my capstan version with the repetitions which were so popular.

PADDY, LAY BACK
Alternative titles, *Mainsail Haul, The Liverpool Song, Valparaiso Round the Horn*

Alternative final line of chorus:

2. That day there wuz a great demand for sailors (for sailors),
   For the Colonies and for 'Frisco and for France (an' for France),
   So I shipped aboard a Limey barque the *Hotspur* (the *Hotspur*),
   An' got paralytic drunk on my advance ('vance, 'vance),
       Ch. Paddy, lay back (Paddy, lay back)!
          Take in yer slack (take in yer slack)!
   Take a turn around the capstan—heave a pawl—heave a pawl!
   'Bout ship, stations, boys, be handy (be handy)!
          Raise tacks, sheets, an' mains'l haul! [For we're bound for
          Valaparaiser 'round the Horn!]

3. Now I joined her on a cold December mornin',
   A-frappin' o' me flippers to keep me warm.
   With the south cone a-hoisted as a warnin',
   To stand by the comin' o' a storm.
       Ch. Paddy, lay back, *etc.*

4. Now some of our fellers had bin drinkin',
   An' I meself wuz heavy on the booze;
   An' I wuz on me ol' sea-chest a-thinkin'
   I'd turn into me bunk an' have a snooze.

5. I woke up in the mornin' sick an' sore,
   An' knew I wuz outward bound again;
   When I heard a voice a-bawlin' at the door,
   'Lay aft, men, an' answer to yer names!'

6. 'Twas on the quarterdeck where first I saw 'em,
   Such an ugly bunch I'd niver seen afore;
   For there wuz a bum an' stiff from every quarter,
   An' it made me poor ol' heart feel sick an' sore.

7. There wuz Spaniards an' Dutchmen an' Rooshians,
   An' Johnny Crapoos jist acrosst from France;
   An' most o' 'em couldn't speak a word o' English,
   But answered to the name of 'Month's Advance'.

8. I wisht I wuz in the 'Jolly Sailor',
   Along with Irish Kate a-drinkin' beer;
   An' then I thought what jolly chaps were sailors,
   An' with me flipper I wiped away a tear.

9. I knew that in me box I had a bottle,
   By the boardin'-master 'twas put there;
   An' I wanted something for to wet me throttle,
   Somethin' for to drive away dull care.

242

10. So down upon me knees I went like thunder,
    Put me hand into the bottom o' the box,
    An' what wuz me great surprise an' wonder,
    Found only a bottle o' medicine for the pox.

11. I felt that I should skip an' join another,
    'Twas plain that I had joined a lousy bitch;
    But the chances wuz that I might join a worser,
    An' we might git through the voyage without a hitch.

12. I axed the mate a-which a-watch wuz mine-O,
    Sez he, 'I'll soon pick out a-which is which';
    An' he blowed me down an' kicked me hard a-stern-O,
    Callin' me a lousy, dirty son-o'-a-bitch.

13. Now we singled up an' got the tugs alongside,
    They towed us through the locks an' out to sea;
    With half the crew a-pukin' o'er the ship's side,
    An' the bloody fun that started sickened me.

14. Although me poor ol' head wuz all a-jumpin',
    We had to loose her rags the followin' morn;
    I dreamt the boardin'-master I wuz thumpin',
    When I found out he'd sent me around the Horn.

15. I swore I would become a beachie-comber,
    An' niver go to sea no ruddy more;
    For niver did I want to be a roamer,
    I'd shanghai the boardin'-master an' stay ashore.

16. But when we got to bully ol' Vallaparaiser,
    In the Bay we dropped our mudhook far from shore;
    The Ol' Man he refused ter let us raise 'er,
    An' he stopped the boardin'-masters comin' aboard.

17. I quickly made me mind up that I'd jump 'er,
    I'd leave the beggar an' git a job ashore;
    I swum across the Bay an' went an' left 'er,
    An' in the English Bar I found a whore.

18. But Jimmy the Wop he knew a thing or two, sir,
    An' soon he'd shipped me outward bound again;
    On a Limey to the Chinchas for guanner, boys,
    An' soon wuz I a-roarin' this refrain.

19. So there wuz I once more again at sea, boys,
    The same ol' ruddy business over again;
    Oh, stamp the caps'n round an' make some noise, boys,
    An' sing again this dear ol' sweet refrain.

Verses from 11 onwards are fairly modern and nothing to do with the Packet Ship seamen, but with the chorus of 'For we're bound for Vallaparaiser round the Horn' are what were sung by Liverpool seamen engaged in the West Coast Guano Trade.

The version I give was often brought to a close by singing verse 14 as follows:

> The mate he lost his head—he didn't savvy 'cos
> The Johns wuz talkin' lingoes all galore;
> So the Old Man thought the only thing to do was
> To pay the ugly bastards off an' ship some more.

The eight-line verse form of the forebitter ran as follows, and often these verses were sung as two four-liners with the same chorus, using the tune of the verse as far as the asterisk only. In this latter fashion it would be sung at the capstan.

MAINSAIL HAUL
or
PADDY, LAY BACK

Another shanty with a similar opening line to *Paddy, Lay Back* is the Swedish pumping song *Albertina*. I have two versions of this, one from *Sång under Segel* and one from Professor J. Glyn Davies who gave me the English translation.

ALBERTINA or SKONNERT ALBERTINA
(Capstan and pumps)

(Tune: German; shanty of Norwegian origin; taken down by
J. Glyn Davies, October 1926, Uppsala)

A schooner was built on the Baltic, Alber-ti-na that was the schooner's name, Pump 'er dry! Albert-i-na, says the sto-ry, Albert-i-na's all for glo-ry, Albert-i-na that was the schooner's name, Pump 'er dry!

Note. A repeat of the lines, '*Albertina*, says the story, *Albertina*'s all for glory, *Albertina*, that was the schooner's name' was used as a full chorus after each verse.

2. And the schooner is painted already,
   She is painted in red and violet—
   Ch. Pump her dry!
   She is painted, says the story, she is painted all for glory,
   She is painted in red and violet.
   Ch. Pump her dry!
   Full Chorus. Albertina, says the story, Albertina's all for glory,
   Albertina that was the schooner's name.

3. And the schooner is rigged out already,
   She is rigged out with tackles and with ropes,
   Ch. Pump her dry!
   She is rigged out, says the story, she is rigged out all for glory,
   She is rigged out with tackles and with ropes.
   Ch. Pump her dry!
   Full Chorus. Albertina, says the story, *etc.*

4. And the schooner is charted already,
   She is charted from Hamburg, homeward bound,
   She is chartered, says the story, she is chartered all for glory,
   She is chartered from Hamburg, homeward bound.

5. And the schooner is loaded already,
   She is loaded with beer and with wine,
   She is loaded, says the story, she is loaded all for glory,
   She is loaded with beer and with wine.

6. And the schooner is sailing already,
   She is sailing away from sight of land,
   She is sailing, says the story, she is sailing all for glory,
   She is sailing away from sight of land.

7. And the schooner is stranded already,
   She is stranded between the surf and reef,
   She is stranded, says the story, she is stranded all for glory,
   She is stranded between the surf and reef.

8. And her headstone is written already,
   It is written in Latin and in gold,
   It is written, says the story, it is written all for glory,
   It is written in Latin and in gold.

9. On the beach there is a maiden weeping,
   She is weeping for her lover on the beach,
   She is weeping, says the story, she is weeping all for glory,
   She is weeping for her lover on the beach.[1]

Returning to our previous shanty *Paddy, Lay Back* I think the name 'Paddy' is a good link with which to start us off on a 'Paddy' series. And our first shanty is *Paddy Doyle*.

This was a very common song or rather 'chant' in the days of sail and was dedicated to one job only—that of getting the mass of sodden, bellying canvas rolled up on to the yard, or 'tossing the bunt' as it was called. It was a job common in the older class of ships that carried single topsails or else had double topsails with 'bunt-stow' t'gans'ls and royals. It was also used on courses when they had clewlines leading in to the quarters of the yard and not to the yard-arms, as was the later practice. Some ships combined both yard-arm and bunt stow. When singing this chant the haul usually came on the word BOOTS! Normally there was no need for more than two or three verses at the most.

---

[1] Translation by Professor J. Glyn Davies, 1929.

There seems to have been three patterns:

(a) A wild 'way-ay-ay' followed by 'We'll pay Paddy Doyle', *etc.*, or variants, the whole being sung by all hands, the haul coming on either the final grunted-out YA!, on BOOTS!, or on both. (*Bullen, Colcord, Doerflinger, Sampson, Sharp, Terry, and Whall.*)

(b) The solos are varied with the same chorus throughout, the pull coming on BOOTS! (*Davis & Tozer, C. F. Smith.*)

(c) Pull on *three* words. (*Shell.*)

Harlow gives a version where both solo and chorus change.

> *Solo.* We'll roll up the sail as we swing a-yah!
> *Ch.* Oh, Paddy can't dive for his boots.
>
> *Solo.* We'll haul away with a will a-yah!
> *Ch.* And hang Paddy Doyle for his boots.

Captain Slocum gives: 'We'll pay Darby Doyl for his boots!'

As to the method of singing this chant, opinions are divided. Some favour the solo-refrain, as an all hands affair; others declare that all hands came in on the refrain only. Patterson, who was a seaman, says that all hands came in only on the word 'boots'. Normally I believe there was a solo and a thundering all-hands-in chorus . . . but, different ships, different long splices!

Some writers declare that it was only used to put a 'harbour-stow' on the courses, etc., when in port, but I can hardly believe this. To bunt a sail in port was a comparatively easy job, but at sea, off the Horn say, a 'good pull an' a strong 'un' was needed, hence the use of the shanty.

C. F. Smith seems to think that the tune of this shanty bears a resemblance to the closing bars of *The Queen's Jig*, which may have been acquired from the ship's fiddler (in the Blackwallers and other East Indiamen).

PADDY DOYLE'S BOOTS (a)

Timme way ay-ay-ay high *ya*!
We'll all throw muck at the *cook*!

Timme way-ay-ay-ay high *ya*!
We'll all drink whisky an' *gin*!

Other last lines were:

> We'll all *shave* under the *chin*!

247

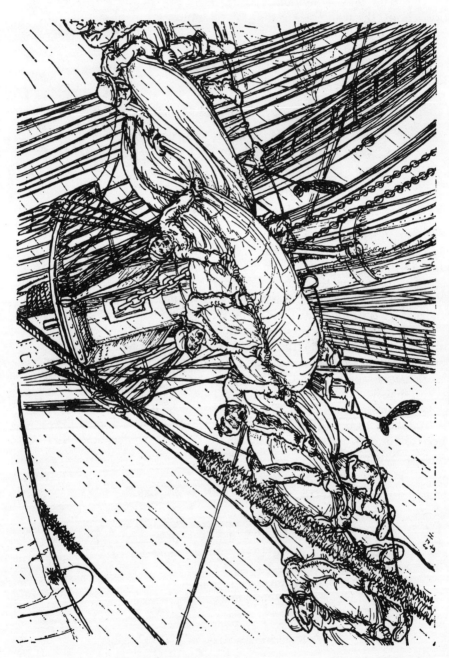

STOWING THE MAINSAIL

'We'll pay Paddy Doyle for his boots!' (Bunt Shanty)

PADDY DOYLE'S BOOTS

Who stole poor Paddy Doyle's *boots*!

We'll bouse her up an' be *done*!

We'll order brandy an' rum!

The dirty ol' man's on the *poop*!

Naturally many of these lines are unprintable in their original state.

PADDY DOYLE'S BOOTS (b)

Yeo aye—an' we'll sing aye,
    Ch. To pay Paddy Doyle for his *boots*!

We'll bunt up the sail with a fling aye!
    Ch. To pay Paddy Doyle for his *boots*!

We'll tauten the bunt an' we'll furl aye,
    Ch. To pay, *etc.*

We'll skin the ol' rabbit an' haul aye,
    Ch. To pay, *etc.*

PADDY DOYLE'S BOOTS (c)

We'll sing, *way*!
An' we'll *heave*!
An' we'll pay Paddy Doyle for his *boots*!

So we'll *heave*!
With a *swing*!
An' we'll pay Paddy Doyle for his *boots*!

As to who Paddy Doyle was we have no historical evidence, but probably he was some Liverpool boarding-master from whom a clever seaman had swiped a pair of seaboots, the boots themselves being now made famous for ever. The hero of our next shanty—Paddy West—however was a real, live personage.

249

He is usually said to have lived in Great Howard Street, Liverpool, where he kept a seaman's boarding-house of singular fame. For here he would make a farmer into an able-bodied seaman in a couple of days! In his backyard he had a ship's wheel rigged up where the candidate would learn to steer, while Paddy's wife would chuck a bucket of cold water over him to 'git yer used to the cold nor' westers'. Practice in furling sail was gained on the window sill of the attic, and the final ceremony was the stepping over a piece of string and the circling of a cow's horn standing on the front parlour table.[1] Then, fitted out in dungarees, with a 'nice clean ropeyarn for a belt', and with 'wan suit av oilskins 'tween ye an' yer mate . . . I'll tell the mate ter put ye in diff'rent watches!' . . . and a dead seaman's discharge papers in his pocket, the newly-made A.B. would be introduced to some hard-case packet, and as he trundled aboard with a sea-bag filled with bricks covered with an old jersey and a torn shirt, Farmer Jack, now Sailor John, had little idea of what awaited him out on the broad Atlantic!

These Paddy Westers were supposed to be a shade better than shanghaied drunks, and the equal, at any rate, of pierhead jumps. They'd had a *little* coaching in the craft of a seaman, even if it was darned little!

Many writers consider this song to be a forebitter only, but most of my Liverpool informants declare it to have been a regular and ever-popular capstan shanty as well. It dates back to the time of the Western Ocean Packets.

PADDY WEST

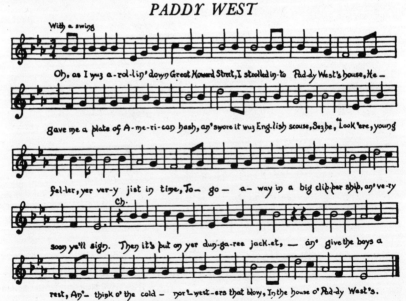

Oh, as I wuz a-rol-lin' down Great Howard Street, I strolled in-to Paddy West's house, He gave me a plate of A-me-ri-can hash, an' swore it wuz Eng-lish scouse, Sez he, "Look 'ere, young fel-ler, yer ver-y jist in time, To go — a-way in a big clip-per ship, an' ve-ry soon ye'll sign. Then it's put on yer dun-ga-ree jack-et, — an' give the boys a rest, An'— think o' the cold — nor'west-ers that blow, In the house o' Pad-dy West's.

[1] 'When the mate axes ye where ye've sailed, tell him ye've crossed the Line, and bin three times around the Horn but don't tell him it wuz a cow horn!'

2. Now he axed me if I had ever been to sea,
   I told him not till that morn;
   'Well, be Jasus,' sez he, 'a sailor ye'll be,
   From the hour that yiz wuz born;
   Just go into the parlour, walk round the ol' cow horn,
   An' tell the mate that ye have bin, oh, three times round the Horn!'
       Ch. Then it's put on yer dungaree jacket,
           An' give the boys a rest [an' we'll find all the rest],
           Oh, think of the cold nor'wester that blows
           In the house of Paddy West's!

3. When I got into ol' Paddy West's house,
   The wind began to blow;
   He sent me up to the lumber-room,
   The fore-royal for to stow;
   When I climbed up to the attic, no fore-royal could I find,
   So I jumped upon the window sill [So I took a tumble to meself] and
       furled the winder-blind.
       Ch. Then it's put, etc.

4. It's Paddy, me bhoy, he pipes all hands on deck,
   Their stations for to man.
   His wife, Sarah Ann, stood in the backyard,
   A bucket in her hand;
   His wife let go the bucket, the water flew on its way;
   'Clew up yer fore t'gallant, me sons, she's takin' in a say!'

5. To every two men that graduates,
   I'll give wan outfit free,
   For two good men on watch at once
   Ye never need to see;
   Oilskins, me bhoys, ye won't want, carpet slippers made o' felt
   I will dish out to the pair o' ye, an' a ropeyarn for a belt.

I rather think that several verses are missing. The line in the chorus which runs: 'An' give the boys a rest' has several variants. 'An' we'll find all the rest' refers to a man's gear which Paddy was supposed to supply. Sometimes it was: 'An' ye'll find all the rest,' indicating that Paddy didn't supply *everything*. 'An' give the gals a rest' suggests that 'tis time you shipped! 'An' then we'll have a rest' or 'Sit down and take a rest' suggests the 'smoke-o' Paddy would allow the candidates between 'wheels' and stowing the attic blind. 'An' then yer in yer best' indicates that Paddy considered his 'fittings' to be good.

Captain Frank Shaw gives the final line of the chorus as: 'In the land of Paddy West.' Others give 'That blows at Paddy West's' or 'Ye had down at Paddy West's' or 'That ye had in Paddy West's house', the previous rhyming line being 'And give them all a rouse'.

Sometimes 'garret' was sung instead of 'attic'. And the last two lines of verse 1 are sometimes given as:

> Sayin', 'Cheer up, me heartie, for ye are just in time,
> Now 'tis put yer name down on the list, an' very soon ye'll sign.'

Our next 'Paddy' shanty is *Poor Paddy Works on the Railway*. This was sung mainly at pumps or capstan and I, like Bullen, wonder why it gained any popularity—but it did! Most authorities seem to think that it started life as a music-hall song, only Terry disagreeing. Alden in *Harper's Magazine* (July 1882) declares that it is a 'sailors' song tamed to do land service . . . on the minstrel stage'. But a land version was also sung by the early railroad workers of Young America around the forties and fifties of last century. It probably became popular in the Western Ocean Packets about the time of the Irish potato famine. C. F. Smith came across a reference to it in the MS. of a magazine called *Young America*, published aboard the *James Baines* in 1865. Captain W. H. Angel, mistakenly I feel sure, calls it a hoisting shanty. The tune varies but little.

Here is the shanty:

POOR PADDY WORKS ON THE RAILWAY

2. In eighteen hundred an' forty-two,
   I did not know what I should do [I had some work that I must do],
   So I shipped away wid an Irish crew,
   To work upon the railway.
      Ch. The railway,
         I'm weary of the railway,
         Oh, Poor Paddy works on the railway!

3. In eighteen hundred an' forty-three,
   I packed me gear an' went to sea [I sailed away across the sea],
   I shipped away to Amerikee,
      Ch. To work, *etc.*

4. In eighteen hundred an' forty-four,
I landed on Columbia's shore,
I had a pick-axe an' nothin' more.

5. In eighteen hundred and forty-five,
When Dan O'Connell he wuz alive,
To break me leg I did contrive. [The wonder is I kept alive.]

6. In eighteen hundred an' forty-six,
Me drinks no longer I could mix,
So I changed me trade to carrying bricks. [The Temperance League
me there did fix.]

7. In eighteen hundred an' forty-seven,
Me children numbered jist eleven,
Of girls I'd four, of boys I'd seven. [So I sold me clothes an' sailed to
Heaven.]

8. In eighteen hundred an' forty-eight,
I made a fortune, not too late,
An' shipped away to the River Plate.

9. In eighteen hundred an' forty-nine,
I for a sight of Home did pine,
So I sailed down south to a warmer clime. [So I hired a Pullman car
so fine. So I sailed down south to fair Caroline.]

After this verse some shantymen carried on with the year 1851,
missing out 1850, improvising as they went:

> In eighteen hundred an' fifty-three,
> I lost me coin an' went to sea,
> For I no longer cared you see,
> To work, *etc.*

Or else they used verses unconnected with dates or the railway:

> Oh, I had a sister, her name was Grace,
> Bad cess unto her ugly face,
> She brought me to a deep disgrace,
> A-workin' on the railway. (*Terry*)

Verse 1 had many variants:

In eighteen hundred and forty-one,
I did what many men have done,
I sent me boy, the younger one, [I sailed away but not for long, With a
stick in me fist about two foot long,]
To work, *etc.*

The bosun of the last British squarerigger—*Garthpool*—would
sing these date stanzas to the tune of *Roll the Cotton Down*. Sometimes
instead of the forties the fifties would be sung about.

Terry vouches for the antiquity of this next shanty and claims that his great-uncle often sang it. He thinks that the Christy Minstrels 'pinched' the tune of *Poor Paddy* from this earlier capstan song. He declares that the first two verses only are printable. I doubt even this! From an old Irish seaman, Spike Sennit, I learnt that this was one of the very few shanties in which the obscenity took a homosexual form. Although such things did (and do) exist at sea, in both services, sailors rarely if ever sang about them.

The last line of each stanza has been altered.

THE SHAVER

When I was a lit-tle hair-less boy, I went to sea in Stor-my's employ, Oh, I shipped away as a ca-bin boy, When I was just a sha-ver, a sha-ver, Oh, I was fed up with the sea, When I.. was just a sha-ver.

2. Oh, they whacked me up, an' they whacked me down,
   The Mate he cracked me on the crown,
   They whacked me round an' round an' round,
   Ch. When I was just a shaver, a shaver,
      Oh, I was fed up [weary] with [of] the sea,
      When I was just a shaver.

3. When I went aloft through the lubber's hole,
   The Mate he cried, 'Lord darn yer soul,
   Ye'll do, me son, what yer bloomin' well told!'
   Ch. When I was just, *etc.*

4. An' when we lollop'd around Cape Horn,
   I wisht to hell I'd niver bin born,
   I felt like a sheep with its wool all shorn.

5. When we left behind the ice an' rain,
   An' once more to the tropics we came,
   The Mate came hazin' me once again.

6. When we made port, well I skipped ship,
   I'd had enough for one bloomin' trip,
   I'd stay ashore an' never more ship.

Paddy working on the railway reminds us of the fact that in the early days of America's development, when railways were being thrust across the new continent, many new work-songs were originated by the Negro and Irish work-gangs who laboured on the Iron Road. Some of these songs eventually arrived at sea and our next shanty was most certainly one of them. Apart from myself, Sharp is the only collector who gives it. I had my version from Harding, who said it was sung at the capstan. Sharp gives only one verse and he believes that the shanty is a variant of the Irish folk-song *Shule Agra*. The 'too-rer-loo' of the chorus indicates an Irish connection, giving it the typical Irish–Negro combination found in many shanties of the forties.

THE OLD MOKE PICKIN' ON THE BANJO
Alternative title, *He-bang, She-bang*

2. Pat, get back, take in yer slack, heave away, me boys,
   Heave away, me bully boys, why don't ye make some noise?
   Ch. We're all from the railroad—too-rer-loo,
   Oh, the ol' moke pickin' on the banjo.
   Full Chorus. Hooraw! What the hell's the row?
   We're all from the railroad—too-rer-loo,
   We're all from the railroad—too-rer-loo,
   Oooh! The ol' moke pickin' on the banjo!

3. Roll her, boys, bowl her, boys, give 'er flamin' gip,
   Drag the anchor off the mud, an' let the barstard rip!
   Ch. We're all from the railroad, *etc.*

4. Rock-a-block, chock-a-block, heave the caps'n round,
   Fish the flamin' anchor up, for we are outward bound.

5. Out chocks, two blocks, heave away or bust,
   Bend yer backs, me bully boys, kick up some flamin' dust.

6. Whisky-O, Johnny-O, the mudhook is in sight,
   'Tis a hell-ov-a-way to the gals that wait, an' the ol' Nantucket Light.

Here is another 'banjo' shanty. It was sung to me by Harding who said it was a very popular hauling song aboard ships in the West Indian and Honduras Logwood Trade. It appears to have no regular story.

GIMME DE BANJO

This is the day we make our pay-day —, Dance, gal, gimme de banjo! Oh, that banjo, that se-ven string banjo, Dance, gal, gimme de banjo!

2. Haul away for Campeachy Bay,
    Ch. Dance, gal, *gimme* de banjo!
 Oh, haul away an' stretch out for yer pay-ay,
    Ch. Dance, gal, *gimme* de banjo!

3. A dollar a day is a buckera's pay,
 Oh, bend yer high shoes an' lavender breeks, boys.

4. There's my Sal, she's the gal for me, boys,
 Oh, I know that she'll be, a-waitin' for me-e.

5. I'll bang on the banjo—to show her my love-o,
 Oh, that banjo—that ping-a, pong-a banjo!

There is a definite Spanish touch to the tune and rhythm, the opening bars are like those of the Spanish-American song *Cielito Lindo*, and its timing is much like *Do Let Me 'Lone, Susan*. Doerflinger gives a version; it was sung to him by William Laurie, one of the crew of the Yankee ship *Kit Carson* (1877). My version has two pulls in the refrains—Doerflinger gives only one. There is, writes Doerflinger, a variant of this shanty in the MS. of Mr. Nathaniel Silsbee with the title *Banjyee*. Here are William Laurie's words which Mr. Doerflinger has kindly allowed me to reprint:

1. Oh, dis is de day we pick on de banjo,
    Ch. Dance, gals, gimme de banjo!

2. O dat banjo, dat tal-la-tal-la wango,
    Ch. Dance, gals, gimme de banjo!

3. O dat banjo, dat seben-string banjo.

4. Ah was only one an' twenty.

5. Ah was sent to school for to be a scholar.

6. Mah collar was stiff an Ah could not swaller.

7. O der's mah book, down on de table.

8. An' you can read it if you're able!

(From *Shantymen and Shantyboys*, The Macmillan Co., New York, 1957)

His tune is much the same as mine.

Another shanty which may have started life on the railroad is *Run, Let the Bulgine Run!* It is definitely Negro and Miss Colcord sees a similarity between it and *Roll the Cotton Down*. It was a halyard song, although Sharp gives it as capstan. Miss Colcord gives it as halyards and has the solos and refrains in their right places, but Terry and Bullen, although they give it as halyards, have refrains more suitable for capstan, for they give a long refrain similar to Sharp's—unwieldy to use at halyards.

'Bulgine' was an American slang term for a railway engine.

RUN, LET THE BULGINE RUN

2. Oh, she's lovely up aloft an' she's lovely down below,
   Ch. Run, let the bulgine *run!*
   Oh, high ya! Oh aye yah!
   Ch. Run, let the bulgine *run!*

3. She's a dandy clipper [flier] an' a sticker too.

4. With a dandy skipper an' a bully crew.

5. Oh, we'll run all night till the mornin'.

6. Oh, we'll rock an' we'll roll her over.

7. Oh, we sailed all day to Mobile Bay.

8. Oh, we sailed all night across the Bight.

9. Oh, drive her, cap'ten drive her.

10. Oh, cap'ten make her ol' nose blood.

Improvisation was the rule, as in most Negro shanties, but there was a theme of sorts which some shantymen adopted, that of running the 'bulgine' to and from all sorts of places:

> Oh, we'll run from Callyo to Dover.
> Oh, we'll run down south to old Cape Horn.
> Oh, we'll run all day to 'Frisco Bay.
> Oh, we'll run her snorty to the Roarin' Forties.
> Oh, we'll run her far to old Mersey Bar.
> Oh, we'll run across the map, to old Saccarapp'.

And so on.

Another shanty bringing in the 'bulgine' is *Clear the Track, Let the Bulgine Run*. This was a capstan song and Terry states it was a favourite in the Yankee Packets. It has almost the same tune as an Irish folk-song *Shule Agra* but the refrains have wording showing Negro influence. It was another typical mixture of Irish and Negro sentiments and is one of the many shanties that passed through the shanty mart of Mobile, in this case I should think the tune came from Ireland to Mobile, where the Negroes took it in hand and then at a later date it returned to sea with a few more alterations. Whall says it was a minstrel ditty.

Here is my version:

CLEAR THE TRACK, LET THE BULGINE RUN
Alternative title, *Eliza Lee*

2. Oooh, the ol' Wild Cat of the Swallowtail Line,
   Ch. Ah-ho! way-ho! are you mos' done?
   She's never a day behind her time,
   Ch. Sooo, clear the track, let the bulgine run!

> *Full Chorus.* To me high rig-a-jig in a jauntin' [low-backed] car,
> Ah-ho! way-ho! are you mos' done?
> Wid Eliza Lee all on my knee,
> Sooo, clear the track, let the bulgine run!

3. Oooh, we're outward bound for New York town,
   Them Bowery gals we'll waltz around.

4. When we've stowed our freight at the West Street Pier,
   We'll be homeward bound to our Liverpool beer.

5. Oooh, them Bowery gals will give us fun,
   Chatham Street dives is home from home.

6. Oooh, the gals are walkin' on the pier,
   Let's all go ashore an' have some beer.

7. Oooh, them gals are walkin' on the strand,
   Oh, heave a pawl, oh, lend a hand [bear a hand].

8. Oooh, wake her, shake her afore we're done,
   Oh, wake that gal wid the blue dress on.

9. When we all gits back to Liverpool town,
   I'll stand ye whiskies all around.

10. Oooh, in Liverpool town them gals hang round,
    An' there me Liza will be found.

11. Oooh, when I gits home across the sea,
    Eliza, will you marry me?

Apart from that of Whall most versions sing of the glory of some
clipper or packet. Davis & Tozer's book has a Blackball version:

> Oh, the smartest clipper you can find,
> Is the fair *Rosalind* of the Blackball Line. . . .

following on with *Eliza Lee* verses:

> Oh, the day was fine, the wind was free,
> And Eliza Lee sat on my knee.
>
> Oh, Eliza Lee all on my knee,
> Was as pretty a sight as ye could see.

Sampson gives the Blue Star Line . . .

> Oh, the smartest clipper you can find,
> Is the *Margaret Evans* of the Blue Star Line.
>
> Oh, Liza Lee, will you be mine?
> I'll dress you up in silk so fine.
>
> I'll stay with you upon the shore,
> And back to sea will go no more.

Terry and Sharp both have the *Margaret Evans* of the Blue Cross Line, and similar verses about *Eliza Lee*.

Another shanty which uses the expression 'high-rig-a-jig' is the capstan song *Roller Bowler* which appears to me to be another of the Negro–Irish type of sailor work-song. I picked up my version out in Trinidad. Sharp's version, the only one in print until now, seems to be a Liverpool shanty although he collected it in Bristol, I think. Anyhow it is definitely a shanty that was sung aboard of the West Indian Sugar and Rum Traders, since it was well known by most of my West Indian shipmates. Sharp gives an introductory chorus.

ROLLER BOWLER
Alternative title, *Good Morning, Ladies All*

2. I axed her for to come wid me,
   Ch. Hooraw, you roller bowler!
   I axed her for to come wid me
   A-down the Bristol Docks,
   Ch. Timme high-rig-a-jig an' a ha-ha!
   Good mornin', ladies all.
   Full Chorus. Hooraw, you roller bowler,
         Timme high-rig-a-jig an' a ha-ha!
         Good mornin', ladies all.

3. She left me and she ran away,
   She left me and she ran away,
   She didn't like me jib.

4. I squared me yards an' sailed away,
   I squared me yards an' sailed away,
   An' to the pub I went.

A Liverpool version sung to me by an ancient mariner from Bootle is the following:

1. Oh, I met her once in Liverpool,
   Ch. Hooraw, *etc.*
   Oh, I met her once in Liverpool,
   This saucy gal of mine,
   Ch. Timme high, *etc.*

2. Oh, the first time that I saw her,
   Oh, the first time that I saw her,
   'Twas down in Parkee Lane.

3. She winked and tipped her flipper,
   She winked and tipped her flipper,
   She thought I wuz a Mate.

4. But when she found that I wuz skint,
   But when she found that I wuz skint,
   She left me standing there.

5. She left me there in Parkee Lane,
   She left me there in Parkee Lane,
   An' I went back on board.

The line 'Good morning, ladies all' brings us to two more shanties which include this fairly obvious Negro phrase, and I feel certain that I am right in saying that any shanty including it can be said to be of Negro origin. Here is a 'genuine Negro song given by a southern slave owner' from *Negro Minstrelsy Ancient and Modern*, Putnam's Monthly, January 1855, page 77 (quoted by N. I. White in his book *American Negro Folk Song*, page 457, Harvard University Press, Cambridge, Mass., 1928):

De ladies in the parlour,
Hey come a-rolling down,
A drinking tea and coffee,
Good morning, ladies all,
De genmen in de kitchen,
Hey come, etc.
A drinking brandy toddy,
Good morning, ladies all.

Our first shanty is a capstan one and Sharp, who also gives it, believes it to have some affinity with *Heave Away, Me Johnnies*. I had my version from Tobago Smith, a West Indian shantyman.

GOOD MORNIN', LADIES ALL (a)

Our ol' man said to me one day, High-ee-yo-ho-ho, high-ee-yo-ho-ho-ho ho! Let's git a-board of our pack-et ship, an' we'll roll 'er 'crosst the Bay-, Ah-ha-! me yel-lar gals, Good-morn-in' la-dies all!

2. Oh, fare-ye-well, I wish ye well,
    Ch. High yo-ho-ho, high-yo-ho-ho-ho-ho!
   We're outward bound on the mornin' tide, this packet wuz bound ter
      hell.
    Ch. Ah-ha, me yaller gals,
       Good mornin', ladies all.

3. We sailed away to the White Man's Grave,
   The Yaller Jack it wiped us out, the divil a man wuz saved.

4. We shipped some monkeys for the crew,
   Our bosun wuz a great big ape, the 'sails' a kinkajou.

Obviously there is more of this shanty, but I have not been able
to get a complete set of words. It may be the shanty which tells the
tale of a crew of monkeys taking charge of the ship—a shanty which
Miss Stephens, the librarian of the Mystic Maritime Museum, has
heard about and wondered whether I had it in my collection. Our
next *Good Mornin', Ladies All* has no connection with the foregoing.
It is a pump song, although Terry gives it as halyards. The words
'heave' and 'haul' coming together in a shanty normally indicate
that it was sung at the pumps, although in many cases these songs
are ones that were used by the hoosiers of Mobile to work the great
jackscrews. Terry gives it with verses from *Outward and Homeward
Bound*. My version I had from West Indian seamen.

GOOD MORNIN', LADIES ALL (b)

We are out-ward bound for Mo-bile Town, With a heave-o, haul—! an' we'll

heave the ol'—wheel round an' round, Good morn-in' la-dies all!

2. An' when we get to Mobile town,
   Ch. With a heave-O, haul!
   Oh, 'tis there we'll drink an' sorrow drown.
   Ch. Good mornin', ladies all!

3. Them gals down south are free an' gay,
   Wid them we'll spend our hard-earned pay.

4. We'll swing around, we'll have good fun,
   An' soon we'll be back on the homeward run.

5. An' when we get to Bristol town,
   For the very last time we'll waltz around.

6. With Poll and Meg an' Sally too,
   We'll drink an' dance wid a hullabaloo.

7. So a long goodbye to all you dears,
   Don't cry for us, don't waste yer tears.

PART FOUR

~~~~~~

*The Haul Family; Rosie
and Roses; Susanna and Polkas;
Girls' Names; Transportation and
Place Names; Men's Names and
Professions; Ships both Famous and
Fictitious*

~~~~~~

*H*AVING reached a shanty with the word 'haul'
in its refrains we will carry on with similar work-
songs—a 'haul' series, and the first of our series is the
once-perennial favourite, *Haul the Bowline.*
It is quite possible that this is the most ancient of the
shanties, seeing that the bowline was a rope of prime importance in
medieval times. When stays'ls were put in ships—about the fifteen
hundreds—this rope degenerated—as more and more fore 'n' aft
sails came into use—into a light line upon which a shanty was un-
necessary. The use of the bowline was to stretch the weather leach
of a squaresail as far out to wind'ard as possible, and it was a most
important factor in the sailing of a ship to wind'ard in the days
before fore 'n' aft sails were invented. The oldest form of bowline
shanty is that given in the *Complaynt of Scotland* referred to in the
Introduction—'Hou, pulpela, Boulena'.

Coming to more modern times 'bowline shanties' were used at
tacks, sheets, or 'sweating-up' and the pull came on the last word of
the chorus. My first version of *Haul the Bowline* I learnt many years
ago from a certain Mr. Dowling of Bootle, who had sailed in the
Colonial Packets.

HAUL THE BOWLINE (a)
Alternative title, *Haul Away the Bowline*

Haul the bowline, for Kit-ty she's me dar - lin', Haul the bowline, th' bowline haul!

Alternatives:

Haul away th'   Haul away th'

2. Haul the bowline—Kitty lives in Liverpool,
 Ch. Haul the bowline—the bowline *haul!*

3. Haul the bowline—Liverpool's a fine town.

4. Haul the bowline—so early in the morning.

5. Haul the bowline—before the day wuz dawnin'.

6. Haul the bowline—the fore 'n' main t'bowline.

7. Haul the bowline—the fore t'gallant bowline.

8. Haul the bowline—the Cape Horn gale's a-howlin'.

9. Haul the bowline—the cook he is a-growlin'.

10. Haul the bowline—we'll either break or bend it.

11. Haul the bowline—we're men enough ter mend it.

12. Haul the bowline—an' bust the chafin'-leather.

13. Haul the bowline—oh, haul away tergether.

14. Haul the bowline—we'll hang for finer weather.

15. Haul the bowline—we'll bowl along tergether.

16. Haul the bowline—the bonnie, bonnie bowline.

17. Haul the bowline—the packet is a-rollin'.

18. Haul the bowline—the long, the long-tailed bowline.

19. Haul the bowline—the Old Man he's a-moanin'.

Many shantymen prefaced the refrain with 'We'll'.

Some authorities seem to see this shanty as a fragment of an Irish air. The final word 'haul' was shouted out staccato, or rather the full value of the note was given and then a final upward grunt or yelp as the men fell back on the rope. Another version of this—a type

HAULING ON THE FORESHEET

'Haul the bowline—the bowline HAUL!' (Sheet Shanty)

used when this shanty was sung as a capstan song, as it sometimes was—is the following, which I learnt from a Welsh deep-water man.

HAUL THE BOWLINE (b)

A certain lady in Aberdovey once told me that they used to man the capstan and haul the sailing lifeboat up the slipway in this little Welsh port to the singing of this form of *Haul the Bowline* some forty years or so ago. Sharp gives this capstan form, as also does Patterson in his *The Sea's Anthology*, but unfortunately he gives no tune. Here is his version:[1]

> The bully ship's a-rolling,
> *Ch.* Haul away the bowline!
> It's raining and it's snowing,
> *Ch.* Haul away the bowline!
> It's raining and it's snowing,
> *Ch.* The bowline haul!
>
> 2. A Blackball liner lies a-lee,
> She'll lead us a chase, I'll bet a spree,
> She'll lead us a chase, I'll bet a spree.

Of course, these forms were also used for hauling; in this case my form would be sung with the first line of the final chorus as a solo—the third solo. The same applies to Sharp's version. Patterson's is already in this form. Patterson gives another unusual form, also without the music:[1]

[1] Both these songs are reprinted from *The Sea's Anthology* by J. E. Patterson, published by William Heinemann, Ltd., London.

HAUL AWAY, BOYS, HAUL AWAY!

1. Haul on the bowline, so early in the morning,
   Ch. Haul away—haul away the bowline.
   Haul away the bowline, so early in the morning,
   Ch. Haul away, haul, the bowline *haul!*

2. O London Docks, they are so fine, in the morning. (*Repeat*)

3. And there lives Kitty on my half-pay, in the morning. (*Repeat*)

4. When I get back, I'll marry her, in the morning. (*Repeat*)

5. And if she's married another man, in the morning. (*Repeat*)

6. I'll black his eyes and I'm off to sea, in the morning. (*Repeat*)

Our next 'haul' shanty is another one that has not been in print before. It is a fine hauling song, which I learnt from my West Indian friend Harding. It was sung with many wild yelps, and was fairly common on the decks of West Indian ships.

HAUL AWAY, BOYS, HAUL AWAY!

Oooh! Haul a-way for the win-dy weather boys, Haul a-way boys, haul a-way! Oo! Haul a-way an'
pull ter-ge-ther boys, Haul a-way boys, haul a-way!

2. Oooh! Haul away an' let's git goin', boys,
   Ch. Haul away, boys, *haul* away!
   Ooooh! Haul away for the merchant's money, boys,
   Ch. Haul away, boys, *haul* away!

3. Haul away like jolly young sailor-boys,
   Haul away an' roll her over, boys.

4. Oh! God made the bees an' the bees made the honey, boys,
   An' God sent the food, but the Divil sent the cooks, boys.

5. Oooh! God made man an' man made money, boys,
   But the Divil sent the woman for to rob us of our money, boys.

6. Oooh! We're rollin' down to Cuba for to load up sugar, boys,
   Rollin' down to Cuba fer to meet our Creole doudous, boys.

7. Oooh! The packet's now rollin' down the river, boys,
   As she rolls down her tops'ls shiver, boys.

8. An' soon we'll be in red-hot Cuba, boys,
   Oh! Haul away an' the wind 'll move her, boys.

9. Soon we'll see our bright-eyed women, boys,
   Ooh! Haul an' shake her as she rolls, boys.

10. Haul away for finer weather, boys,
    Ooooh! Haul away for the better weather, boys.

Our next is another famous tack and sheet shanty—*Haul Away, Joe!* I learnt much of my version from Paddy Griffiths, who told me it was used mainly for hauling aft the foresheet after reefing the fores'l. On account of the numerous couplets known to fit this shanty I am inclined to think that at some time or other it was used as a halyard song, since any sheet shanty employed at the most no more than three or four verses. Captain F. H. Shaw in *Splendour of the Seas* says that it was sometimes used as a bunt shanty (like *Paddy Doyle*) but I doubt this. It was sung in both a major and a minor key. Terry writes that the major version was more common, however, in the latter days of sail. Very often the stanzas used in *Haul the Bowline* were fitted to it. Doerflinger gives one version showing this. My friend T. E. Elwell told me that that 'pull' or 'haul' was often sung instead of 'Joe' at the end of the refrain. It was on this word that the vigorous, concerted 'drag' came. With some crowds the word was not *sung* but grunted out staccato, with others the final note was given its full value followed by an upward groan of the voice as the pull came, i.e. 'Joe-ugh!' Here are the three tunes of this shanty.

HAUL AWAY, JOE (a)

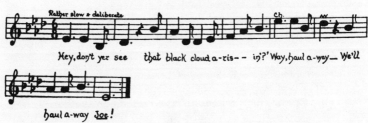

Hey, don't yer see that black cloud a-ris- - -in'?' Way, haul a-way— We'll haul a-way Joe!

HAUL AWAY, JOE (b)

Hey, don't yer see that black cloud a-ris - - in'?' Way, haul a-way, we'll haul a-way Joe!

HAUL AWAY, JOE (c)

Hey, don't yer see that black cloud a-ris......in'? 'Way, haul a-way—, we'll haul a-way

Joe!

And here are the verses which can be fitted to any of these tunes. The tune is repeated in each verse.

HAUL AWAY, JOE

1. Hey don't yer see that black cloud a-risin'?
   Ch. 'Way haul away, we'll haul away *Joe!*
   Hey don't yer see that black cloud a-risin'?
   Ch. 'Way haul away, we'll haul away *Joe!*

2. Naow whin Oi wuz a little boy an' so me mother told me,
   That if Oi didn't kiss the gals me lips would all grow mouldy.

3. An' Oi sailed the seas for many a year not knowin' what Oi wuz missin',
   Then Oi sets me sails afore the gales an' started in a-kissin'.

4. Naow first Oi got a Spanish gal an' she wuz fat an' lazy,
   An' then Oi got a nigger tart—she nearly druv me crazy.

5. Oi found meself a Yankee gal an' sure she wasn't civil,
   So Oi stuck a plaster on her back an' sent her to the Divil.

6. Sheepskin, pitch, an' beeswax, they make a bully plaster;
   The more she tried ter git it off it only stuck the faster.

7. Then Oi got meself an Oirish gal an' her name wuz Flannigan,
   She stole me boots, she stole me clothes, she pinched me plate an' pannikin.

8. Oi courted then a Frenchie gal, she took things free an' aisy,
   But naow Oi've got an English gal an' sure she is a daisy.

9. So list while Oi sing ter yer about me darlin' Nancy,
   She's copper-bottomed, clipper-built, she's jist me style an' fancy.

10. Ye may talk about yer Yankee gals [Liverpool, London, Havre, *etc.*]
    an' round-the-corner-Sallies,
    But they couldn't make the grade, me bhoys, wid the gals from down
    our alley [Girls in Booble Alley, Darlings in the forest].

11. We sailed away for the China Seas, our bhoys so neat an' handy,
    The Ould Man in his cab'n, bhoys, a-drinkin' rum an' brandy.

12. We loaded for the homeward run, all hands so free an' aisy,
    And in his galley sat the doc, a-makin' plum-duff graisy.

13. We squared our yards an' away we rolled, with the fiddles playin'
    handy,
    Wid a roll 'n' go, an' a westward ho, an' a Yankee Doodle Dandy.

14. Oh, King Louis wuz the King o' France, afore the revolution,
    But the people cut his big head orf an' spoiled his constitution.

15. Then they sent the King away ter sea, to larn him how ter swim,
    They sent him wid a Bluenose mate who put a squarehead on him.

16. Oh, once Oi wuz in Oireland a-diggin' turf an' taties,
    But naow Oi'm on a Limejuice ship an' a-haulin' on the braces.

17. Saint Patrick wuz a gintleman, an' he come of daycent paypul,
    He built a church in Dublin town an' on it set a staypul.

18. From Oireland thin he druv the snakes, then drank up all the whisky,
    This made him dance an' sing an' jig, he felt so fine an' frisky.

19. He held High Mass for forty days before he blessed the staypul,
    He held High Mass, 'twas a sorry pass, but he couldn't fool the
    paypul.

20. Yiz call yerself a second mate an' cannot tie a bowline,
    Ye cannot even stand up straight when the packet she's a-rollin'.

Other verses from *Haul the Bowline* often sung were:

> 'Way haul away, we'll haul for finer weather,
> 'Way haul away, we'll haul away tergether.

> 'Way haul away, we'll surely make her render,
> 'Way haul away, we'll either bust or bend 'er.

> 'Way haul away, the Cape Horn gale's a-howlin',
> 'Way haul away, the Ould Man he's a-growlin'.

This shanty, like *Heave Away, Me Johnnies*, was usually sung with
an Irish accent. Verses 6 and 7 are probably from the shore-song
Aunt Jemima's Plaster.

Sharp's version is as follows:

> Haul away, haul away, haul away, my Rosie,
> O you talk about your Aver girls and round the corner Sally.
> Once I had a nigger girl and I loved her for her money.
> O once I had a nice young girl and she was all a posy.
> And now I've got an English girl, I treat her like a lady.
> Now up aloft this yard must go, we'll pull her free and easy.
> Another pull and then belay, we'll make it all so easy.

This last stanza of Sharp's strengthens my belief that this shanty
was once used for 'long drags' at halyards.

Some of Harlow's verses run as follows:

> Oh, once in my life I married a wife and damn her she was lazy,
> And couldn't stay at home of nights—which damn near set me crazy.
>
> She stayed out all night—oh, hell! what a sight,
> And where do you think I found her?
>
> Behind the pump, the story goes, with forty men around her. . . .
>
> (From *The Making of a Sailor*)

These latter verses came to life again in the 1914–18 War and even the children of that period had a street song (for skipping, I believe) which used them. The Liverpool 'kids' had: 'In the jigger kissing a nigger—with all the kids around her.'

C. Robbins, an old sailor who sang *Haul Away, Joe* to a collector in a Marylebone workhouse, did so in the old style of singing where a 'd' was always inserted before an 'l', e.g.:

> Away audle away, we'll audle away, Joe.

'Rolling' was sung as 'rodling', etc. See Whall's Introduction to his *Sea Songs and Shanties* for further remarks on this kind of old-time singing.

Terry gives a verse from another shore-song:

> Geordie Charlton had a pig, and it was double-jointed,
> He took it to the blacksmith's shop to get its trotters pointed.

On account of many versions of *Haul Away, Joe* starting with a verse 'Haul away my Rosy', this sheet shanty is given this title by some writers. Another shanty singing of 'Rosy' is the halyard song *Walkalong, My Rosie*. Bullen gives it—one verse only—and he calls it a capstan shanty, but my West Indian friend Harding declared that he had never heard it at any other job than that of halyards. It is a pure Negro shanty.

WALKALONG, MY ROSIE

Oh, I am here, an' Ro-sie there. A-way you Ro-sie, walk-a-long! Oh, I am here, an'

Ro-sie there, Walk-a-long my Ro-sie!

> 2. Oh, Rosie! she'm the gal fer me,
>   *Ch.* Away you Rosie—*Walk*along!
> She hangs around the big levee,
>   *Ch.* *Walk*along my *Rosie*!

273

3. My Rosie's young, my Rosie's kind,
   A better gal you'll niver find.

4. So haul me up and hang me off,
   The mate he says we've hauled enough.

Of course, improvisation was the thing with this shanty.

Another shanty singing of 'Rose' is *Coal Black Rose*, also given by Bullen. This is another pure Negro ditty.

The shanty is one for halyards and although Bullen gives the first line as chorus my informant (Harding) said that the final line was the only chorus, and the only place where the pull came.

COAL BLACK ROSE

Oh, me Ro-sie, Coal Black Rose, Don't ye hear the banjo ping-a-pong-a-pong?

Oh, me Ro-sie, Coal Black Rose!

2. Oh, me Rosie, Coal Black Rose,
   Strung up like a banjo,
   Allus taut an' long,
   Ch. Oh, me Rosie, *Coal* Black Rose!

3. Oh, me Rosie, Coal Black Rose,
   The yard is now a-movin',
   Hauley-hauley ho!
   Ch. Oh, me Rosie, *etc.*

4. The Mate he comes around, boys,
   Dinging an' a dang.

5. Give her one more pull, boys,
   Rock an' roll 'er high.

It lends itself, like most pure Negro shanties, to easy improvisation.

Another 'Rose' shanty is the halyard song sometimes called *Bunch o' Roses*. This was a real 'Cape Horner', very popular in Liverpool ships, and yet overlooked by most collectors. It was fairly popular too in Yankee ships but it appears to be a British shanty, probably derived from a song about Napoleon and the British soldiers—'Redcoats' or 'Blood-red Roses' as they were called on account of the red jackets they invariably wore. Several variants of the refrain are known:

Come down, ye blood-red Roses, come down!
Hang down, ye bunch o' Roses, hang down!
Go down, ye blood-red Roses, go down!

This halyard shanty has four solos and four refrains like *Cheerily Man*. Adams in his book *On Board the Rocket* refers to a Negro crew mastheading a tops'l to its vigorous tune, and my version comes from my coloured shantyman Harding of Barbadoes, but still I don't think it is of Negro origin. Several shore-songs are built around the words 'bunch o' roses' and 'bonnie bunch o' roses', but in every case they are non-Negro in origin, being true English folk-song. Of course, the shanty may have passed, like many others, through the Gulf Ports' shanty mart. It probably started life about the early part of the nineteenth century.

Doerflinger gives a version with similar tune, some of the verses being from the shanty *Hog-eye Man*. This version, which he had from the MS of Nathaniel Silsbee, of Cohasset, Mass., gives a full chorus as in a capstan song, but he has listed it under halyard shanties. A version of this shanty was used in the film *Moby Dick*, and there is also a recording of it published by the Worker's Music Association (L.P. *The Singing Sailor*).

BUNCH O' ROSES
Alternative title, *Blood-Red Roses*

2. We're bound out to Iquique Bay,
    Ch. Hang [Come, Go] down, ye bunch o' roses [blood-
        red roses], hang down [come down, go down]!
We're bound away at the break o' day,
    Ch. Hang down, *etc.*
Oooh, ye pinks an' posies,
    Ch. Hang down, *etc.*
Oooh, ye pinks an' posies,
    Ch. Hang down, *etc.*

3. We're bound away around Cape Horn,
We wisht ter hell we'd niver bin born.

4. Around Cape Stiff [that Cape] we all must go,
Around Cape Stiff through the ice an' snow.

5. Me boots an' clothes are all in pawn,
An' it's bleedin' draughty around Cape Horn.

6. 'Tis growl ye may but go ye must,
If ye growl too hard yer head they'll bust.

7. The gals are waitin' right ahead,
A long strong pull should shift the dead.

8. Them Spanish gals are pullin' strong,
Hang down, me boys, it won't take long.

9. Oh, rock an' shake 'er is the cry,
The bleedin' topm'st sheave is dry.

10. Just one more pull an' that'll do,
We're the bullies for ter kick 'er through.

Through the kindness of Mrs. G. C. Beach of New York (who possesses Mr. Nathaniel Silsbee's collection of shanties) and of Mr. W. M. Doerflinger I am able to reprint Mr. Silsbee's version of the words of this shanty:

1. Oh, yes, my lads, we'll roll alee,
    Ch. Come down, you bunch of roses, come down,
We'll soon be far away from sea,
    Ch. Come down, you bunch of roses, come down.
    Full Chorus. Oh, you pinks and posies,
        Come down, you bunch of roses, come down,
        Oh, you pinks and posies,
        Come down, you bunch of roses, come down.

2. Oh, what do yer s'pose we had for supper?
Black-eyed beans and bread and butter.

3. Oh, Poll's in the garden picking peas,
She's got fine hair way down to her knees.

4. I went downstairs and peeked through a crack,
   And saw her stealing a kiss from Jack.

5. I grabbed right hold of a piece of plank,
   And ran out quick and gave her a spank.

Sometimes the fourth solo and fourth refrain as given in my version would be omitted.

Harlow in his *The Making of a Sailor* gives another 'bunch of roses' shanty with a different tune. He writes that he heard it sung by the shantyman aboard his ship—*Handsome Charlie*—when sweating-up halyards or 'swigging'.

O MARY, COME DOWN!

Harlow declares this to be 'Negro' and he calls it a 'semi-chantey', meaning, I suppose, that it was little more than a chant.

The name 'Molly' being used in this shanty gives us the opportunity to start a series incorporating girl's names. For our first we will take that very popular shanty, well known to both British and American seamen, *Away, Susanna* or *Can't Ye Dance the Polka?*

This capstan song has many versions of the words, both those of the verses and chorus, and the song probably started life in the Western Ocean Packets about the thirties or forties of the last century, when the polka reached America from Bohemia. The tune is thought to be that of an Irish air *Larry Doolan*, and one version does start with a verse from this ballad:

> My name is Larry Doolan, Oi'm a native of the soil,
> If yer want a day's diversion, bhoys,
> Oi'll drive ye out in stoile.

The words of the chorus give room for speculation. In my more modern first version the first lines of the chorus run:

> Then away Susanna, my fair maid . . .

These words I've heard sung by Charlie Evans, a fine shantyman, one-time member of the crew of the Yankee ship *William T. Lewis*,

277

by Chenoworth ex-*Mount Stewart*, A. Spencer, ex-*Monogahela*, who had learnt it from a German stevedore in 'Frisco, and many other 'modern' sailing-ship men.

The older Packet ship words were:

> Away you Santi, my dear honey . . .

or

> Away you Santi, my dear Annie . . .

Sometimes too one would hear 'Away you Johnnie, my dear honey' or 'my fair man' (Bullen), but in the main 'Santi' was sung. Now no one has ever given a real reason, or meaning, for this word; it just appears to be a meaningless name of some sort. I thought so too, until I came across a version giving 'Away you Santa, my dear Anna' and the explanation became clear—the mysterious 'Santi' or 'Santa' being nothing more than the two first syllables of our friend 'Santi-anna' or 'Santa-anna' or, as it was usually written, 'Santiana'!

My first version of *Away, Susanna* was invariably sung to the 'shanghaied in San Francisco' theme. Charlie Evans, Arthur Spence, Bosun Chenoworth, 'Artie', an A.B. of the New Zealand brigantine *Aratapu*, and many other shipmates of mine all sang these words. However, I believe that these verses are of comparatively recent date and that they came from a poem (the author of which I have never discovered). Probably some versatile shantyman thought them 'just the job' and spliced them to the old Packet Rat shanty. Nevertheless, they were accepted and sung by hundreds of shantymen in the latter days of sail. Every sailing-ship man I ever knew was acquainted with them.

In the German shanty book *Knurrhahn* and in the Swedish shanty book *Sång under Segel* these words are given to a different tune. The Germans used it at the pumps.

SEAFARERS

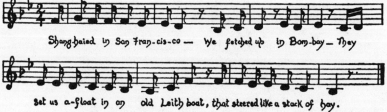

Shang-haied in San Fran-cis-co — We fetched up in Bom-bay — They

set us a-float in an old Leith boat, that steered like a stack of hay.

(From *Sång under Segel*. By permission of Albert Bonniers Forlag, Stockholm.)

278

And here is the 'shanghaiing' version of the shanty:

AWAY, SUSANNA!
Alternative title, *Can't Ye Dance the Polka?* (a)

Shang-haied in San Fran-cis-co, We fetched up in Bom-bay, They set us a-float in an old lease boat, that steered like a bale of hay~ Then a-way Su-san-na! My fair maid, O-ho! ye New York gals can't ye dance the pol-ka?

2. We panted in the tropics,
 Whilst the pitch boiled up on deck,
 We've saved our hides little else besides,
 From an ice-cold North Sea wreck.
  Ch. Then [And] away, Susanna,
   My fair maid!
   Oho! [Sing ho!] ye New York gals,
   Can't ye dance the polka?

3. We drank our rum in Portland,
 We've thrashed through the Behring Straits,
 An' we toed the mark on a Yankee barque,
 With a hard-case Down-east mate.

4. We know the quays of Glasgow,
 An' the boom of the lone Azores,
 We've had our grub from a salt-horse tub,
 Condemned by the Navy stores.

5. We know the track to Auckland,
 An' the light of Kinsale Head,
 An' we crept close-hauled while the leadsman called,
 The depth of the Channel bed.

6. We know the streets of Santos,
 The river at Saigon,
 We've had our glass with a Chinee lass,
 In Ship Street in Hong Kong. [On a house-boat in Canton.]

7. They'll pay us off in London,
 Then it's oh for a spell ashore,
 Then again we'll ship for a southern trip,
 In a week or hardly more.

279

HEAVING AT THE HALYARD WINCH
'O-ho! Ye New York gals . . .' (Capstan Shanty)

8. 'Tis goodbye, Sal an' Lucy,
   'Tis time we were afloat,
   With a straw-stuffed bed, an achin' head,
   A knife an' an oilskin coat.

9. Sing 'Time for us to leave 'er',
   Sing 'Bound for the Rio Grande,'
   An' when the tug turns back, we'll follow her track,
   For a last long look at the land.

10. An' when the purple disappears,
    An' only the blue is seen,
    That'll take our bones to Davy Jones,
    An' our souls to Fiddler's Green.

Here is the normal Packet Rat version—usually sung in a Yankee
drawl:

CAN'T YE DANCE THE POLKA? (b)
Alternative title, *The New York Gals*

2. To Tiffany's [Nelligan's *or* a fancy store] I took her,
   I did not mind expense,
   I bought her two gold earrings [I bought her a slap-up supper],
   An' they cost me fifteen cents [That cost me fifteen cents].
       Ch. Then away you Santee [Susanna],
       My dear Annie [fair maid],
       Ooooh, ye New York gals [them New York gals],
       Can't ye dance the polka? [Can't they dance the polka?]

3. Sez she, 'You Limejuice sailor,
   Now see me home you may.'
   But when we reached her cottage door,
   She this to me did say.

281

4. My flash man he's a Yankee,
   Wid his hair cut short behind,
   He wears a pair o' long sea-boots [red-topped boots, brass-bound
      jacket],
   An' he sails in the Blackball Line [he's Bosun in the Blackball Line].

5. He's homeward bound this evening,
   An' wid me he will stay.
   So git a move on, sailor-boy,
   Git crackin' on yer way.

6. So I kissed her hard an' proper,
   Afore her flash man came,
   An' fare-ye-well, me Bowery gel,
   I know yer little game.

7. I wrapped me glad rags round me,
   An' to the docks did steer.
   I'll never court another maid,
   I'll stick to rum an' beer.

8. I joined a Yankee blood-boat,
   An' sailed away next morn.
   Don't ever fool around wid gals,
   Yer safer·off Cape Horn!

Much of this version is unprintable. Davis & Tozer's version has probably been altered more than most, and the music of the verse of Miss C. F. Smith's version is rather different to the commoner tune.

One day as I went walk-ing, Down by the Cla-rence Dock, It was there I spied an·
I-rish girl, cop-ver-sing with Taps-cott, ... etc.

(C. F. Smith. *A Book of Shanties*, published by Methuen & Co., Ltd., London, 1927.)

It was a fairly common trick to use stanzas from *Heave Away, Me Johnnies*, as in the foregoing version. And again couplets from *The Banks o' Newf'n'land* were also adapted:

      You ramblin' boys o' Liverpool,
      Ye sailormen beware,
      When ye go in a Yankee packet ship,
      No dungaree jumpers wear.
        Ch. And away, *etc.*

Verses from *The Fire Ship* were sometimes used:

> As I walked out one evening,
> Out for a night's career,
> I met a lofty fire-ship
> An' arter her I steered.
>   *Ch.* And away, *etc.*

Other odd verses sometimes heard were:

> My flash man, he's a Packet Rat,
> An' he sails in the Blackball Line,
> An' he'd be a saucy son-o'-a-bitch,
> That'd tackle that man o' mine.

> I went to the Fulton Ferry,
> But I couldn't get across,
> So I jumped on the back of the ferry-boat man,
> And rode him like a hoss. (*C. F. Smith*)

> My fancy man's a loafer,
> He loafs along the shore,
> Git up ye lazy sailorman,
> And lay down on the floor. (*Bullen*)

Our final version is probably the oldest one, going back before the thirties. It is usually called *The New York Gals* and I had my version from an Irish seaman by the name of Spike Sennit, a man who had sailed for years in Yankee windbags. The place-name Shanghai is pronounced in the way old-time seamen used to say it—'Shanghee'.

THE NEW YORK GALS

283

2. Sez I, 'My dear young lady,
   I'm a stranger here in town,
   I left me ship only yesterday,
   From China I am bound.'

       Ch. An' away, you Johnny [Santi]!
         My dear honey [Annie].
         Oh, you New York gals,
         Ye love us for our money.

3. 'Now come wid me, me dearie,
   An' I will stand ye treat,
   I'll buy ye rum an' brandy, dear,
   An' tabnabs for to eat.'

4. 'My friend she has a brother,
   Just now away at sea,
   The last time that she heard from him,
   His ship was in Shanghee.'

5. When we got down to Fourteenth Street,
   We stopped at Number Four,
   Her mother and her sister came
   To meet us at the door.

6. An' when we got inside the house,
   The drinks wuz handed round.
   The liquor wuz so awful strong,
   Me head went round an' round.

7. Before we all sat down to eat,
   We had another drink.
   The liquor wuz so very strong,
   Deep sleep came in a wink.

8. When I awoke next morning,
   I had an achin' head,
   An' there wuz I Jack-all-alone,
   Stark naked on the bed.

9. My gold watch an' me pocket-book
   An' lady friend wuz gone.
   An' there wuz I with nary a stitch,
   All left there on me own.

10. On lookin' all around the room,
    Oh, nothing could I see,
    But a lady's shift an' pantaloons,
    Not worth a damn to me.

11. With a flour barrel for a suit,
    I wisht I'd ne'er bin born.
    A boarding master then I met,
    Who shipped me round the Horn.

12. Now all ye bully sailormen,
    Take warnin' when ashore,
    Or else ye'll meet some charmin' gal,
    Who's nothing but a whore.

13. Yer hard-earned cash will disappear,
    Your rig an' boots as well,
    For Yankee gals are tougher than
    The other side o' Hell!

Sometimes an introductory verse was sung, as in the manner of *Ratcliffe Highway*:

Come, all ye bully sailormen,
Come, listen to me song,
An' I'll tell ye what went wrong wid me,
When I came from Hong Kong.

A writer in *Harper's Magazine* (Alden?) and Miss Colcord give one verse and chorus of this variant:

As I was lumbering down the streets of bully London town,
I spied a Yankee clipper ship to New York she was bound.
  Ch. And hurrah, you Santy,
    My dear honey,
    Hurrah, you Santy,
    I love you for your money.

Doerflinger gives the full version but with the usual 'polka' chorus. His singer uses the introductory verse, and gives the names of famous 'redlight' streets of New York in the days of sail—Chatham Street and Bleeker Street.

He also gives a verse about 'hailing a passing car' in which to go to his new-found friend's home. As Doerflinger points out, this version is from an old forebitter often called *The Shirt and the Apron*.

About the time this shanty was in its heyday the 'redlight' streets of New York thrived on the robbing of seamen, and the method in which a sailor's clothes and money would be stolen was called the 'panel game'. In the wall of the room of assignation a sliding panel was fitted. There would be one chair only in the room, standing near the panel. The sailor naturally would put his clothes on this chair, and some time during the night the panel would slide open and the clothes disappear through the aperture! Around William Street and Chatham Street, both off the Bowery, this game would be played, and also in Greene Street. Low-type concert saloons, brothels, pubs, and shanghaiing dives were in every street along the Bowery and nearly every house had a piano in the front parlour, where cheap liquor was sold, with upstairs bedrooms for hire to the prostitutes. In South Street and Water Street, too, a similar set-up was to be found. Bleeker Street is near Broadway and recently an opera has been written based on the life of its inhabitants in the old days.

Keeping to our theme of 'girls' names', our next shanty is *'Way, Me Susiana!* This is one of Harding's, definitely Negro and a hauling song. Harding also said that it was used for pumping and cargo work. The word 'heave' suggests pumping, although some Negro hauling songs had the word 'heave' in their refrains, indicating most possibly that they had at one time or another been used at the jack-screws aboard cotton-ships. Doerflinger gives a version—his informant giving it for capstan and pumps, and sometimes for hauling. His tune is somewhat similar to mine.

'WAY, ME SUSIANA!

We'll heave him up an a-way we'll go-'Way me Su-si-a-na! We'll heave him up an'a-way we'll go, We're all bound o-ver the moun-ten!

2. We'll heave him up from down below,
   Ch. 'Way, me Sus*iana!*
   That is where the cocks do crow,
   Ch. We're *all* bound over the *moun*ten!

3. An' if we drown while we are young,
   It's better to drown, than to wait to be hung.

4. Oh, growl ye may but go ye must,
   If ye growl too hard yer head they'll bust.

5. Up sox, you cocks, hand her two blocks,
   An' go below to yer ol' ditty box.

6. Oh, rock an' shake 'er, one more drag,
   Oh, bend yer duds an' pack yer bag.

Verse 5 has been camouflaged.

Bullen's *Poor Lucy Anna* may be related. This is a pure Negro shanty and used at capstan or windlass. Bullen writes that this shanty 'is so mournful that one suspects it of being the lament of some just sold slaves sent from one State to another without reference to any human ties they may have possessed'. This shanty was very seldom used except where Negroes formed a considerable portion of the crew. In the Sharp Collection there is a related shanty called *Louisiana*.

POOR LUCY ANNA

(From Frank Bullen's *Songs of Sea Labour*, by permission, Swan & Co., London.)

The remaining verses of this shanty would be improvised.

Our next shanty is a most unusual one—this is its first appearance in print. It is called *Do Let Me Lone, Susan* and I had it from the Barbadian shantyman Harding, who had often sung it at halyards in both British and American ships. It is of Spanish-American origin and similar in timing to a Trinadadian calypso. Much of it is unprintable, since it refers to *all* the parts of the human anatomy! A common trick of Negro shantymen was that of jumping to a higher key every alternate verse.

DO LET ME LONE, SUSAN
Alternative title, *Hooraw, me Looloo Boys (Gels)*

2. Do let me lone, Flora, oh, do let me lone,
    Ch. Hoor*aw*, me looloo boys [gels], do let me lone!
When I put me hand on Jinny's cheek,
Oh, Jinny jump about,
    Ch. Hoor*aw*, me looloo boys [gels], do let me lone!
When I try to play with Jinny's ear,
Oh, Jinny jumps away,
    Ch. Hoor*aw*, me looloo boys [gels]!

3. Do let me lone, Rosy, oh, do let me lone,
    Ch. Hoor*aw*, me looloo boys [gels]!
When I put me arm round Jinny's waist,
Oh, Jinny jumps about,
    Ch. Hoor*aw*, etc.
When I stroke my Jinny on the back,
Oh, Jinny jumps away,
    Ch. Hoor*aw*, etc.

4. Do let me lone, Judy, oh, do let me lone,
    Ch. Hoor*aw*, etc.
When I put me hand in Jinny's lap,
Oh, Jinny jump about,
    Ch. Hoor*aw*, etc.
When I kiss my Jinny on the lips,
Oh, Jinny jump away,
    Ch. Hoor*aw*, etc.

5. Do let me lone Mary, *etc.*

A capstan shanty which may be related to the foregoing is *Do Let Me Go*, given also by Terry and Sharp. The word 'do' was sometimes sung 'doodle' as Terry gives it; Sharp mentions the fact but gives 'do' in his version, and Harding sang both 'do' and 'doodle' indiscriminately. Here are Harding's four verses:

DOODLE LET ME GO
Alternative title, *Do Let me Go, Gels*

Oh, once I met a dou-dou fair, be-longed to Mo-bile Bay— Hoo-raw! me yaller gels,

doo-dle let me go! Doo-dle let me go gels, Doo-dle let me go, Hoo-

raw! me yol-ler gels, Doo-dle let me go—!

288

2. She swung her hips, she tripped her feet, she winked her sassy eye,
   Ch. Hooraw, me yaller [looloo] gels, doodle let me go!
     Doodle let me go, gels,
     Doodle let me go.
     Hooraw, me yaller [looloo] gels,
     Doodle let me go!

3. Ah took her in an' gave her gin, an' danced her on the floor,
   Ch. Hooraw, *etc.*

4. The crew is drunk, the mate is drunk, the Old Man's got a load,
   Ch. Hooraw, *etc.*

Terry gives for the first solo:

    It's of a merchant's daughter, belonged to Callao, *etc.*

The remaining two verses of his version he wrote himself.

In the shanty *Do Let Me Lone* the name *Jinny* keeps cropping up. The heroine(?) of our next shanty was named Jinny—a shanty called *Jamboree* by most collectors, and one very difficult to camouflage. It is one of the shanties that upset the theory that 'unprintable words were kept solely for the solos, the choruses were always above board', or words to this effect, given by many collectors, since the final and noisiest line of this shanty's chorus *is* unprintable! (Worse luck! as the vigour of the line is greatly weakened, and no one seems to have given a good substitute.) Whall says in regard to this line that 'the words "I wonder if my clothes are out of pawn" *were* sung, but with no passengers on board an unprintable version obtained'. Both Terry and Sharp give 'Johnny, get your oatcake done' for this line. Two lines from a Negro song (*American Negro Folk Songs*, by Newman I. White, page 248) have a similarity to the 'oatcake' chorus:

    Sally get your hoe-cake done, my love,
    Oh, Sally get your hoe-cake done.
      (By permission, Harvard University Press, Cambridge,
                Mass.)

I have endeavoured to get nearer to the original than other writers. This shanty was usually sung at capstan or windlass and was a homeward-bound song, in theme reminiscent of *Spanish Ladies*. Sharp writes that the tune is a variant of *Santiana*, but Whall believes, on what grounds I know not, that it is a minstrel ditty. Terry and Sharp and my first version bring the homeward-bounder to Liverpool. Whall brings her to London. Terry gives 'Whoop, Jamboree!'— Sharp gives 'Whip, Jamboree!' Both of these collectors had it from the same shantyman, Mr. Short of Watchet, Somerset. Many of my verses I had from a certain Mr. Jones, a Welsh mate who had served in many sailing ships, his last being Thomas's big four-masted barque *Principality*. The last line of each verse too had an un-printable rhyme.

I have always felt that the tune of this shanty has a near-eastern touch about it.

JAMBOREE

Alternative title, *Jinny, Keep Yer Ringtail Warm, Jinny, Git Yer Oatcake Done*

2. Now, me boys, we're off Holyhead
   An' there's no more casts of the dipsy lead,
   'N' soon we'll be in a lovely fevver bed,
   Ooooh, Jinny keep yer ringtail warm! [Jinny git yer oatcake done, *or* I wonder if me clothes are out of pawn.]
   Ch. Oh, Jamboree, oh Jamboree,
   Ai-i-i! Y'ring tailed black man, sheet it home behind!
   Oh Jamboree, Oh Jamboree,
   Oooh! Jinnie keep yer ringtail warm! [Jinny git yer oatcake, *etc.*]

3. Now the Barship is in sight,
   An' soon we'll be off the ol' Rock Light,
   An' I will clean the flue ternight. [An' I'll be knockin' on yer door ternight.]
   Oooh! Jinnie keep yer ringtail warm, *etc.*

4. Now we're haulin' through the dock [lock],
   All the pretty young gals on the pierhead do flock,
   An' there's my Jinnie in a new pink frock,
   Oooh! Jinny, *etc.*

5. Now we're tied up to the pier,
   Oh, it's 'way down below, an' pack yer musty gear,
   An' I'll soon be a-kissin' o' you, me dear,
   Oooh! Jinnie, *etc.*

6. Now I'm safe upon the shore,
   An' I don't give a damn how the winds do roar,
   For I'll drop me anchor an' I'll go to sea no more,
   Oooh! Jinnie, *etc.*

7. But now I've had two weeks ashore,
   I'll pack me bags [chest] an' I'll go to sea once more,
   An' I'll bid goodbye to me Liverpool whore [the Liverpool shore],
   Ooooh! Jinnie, *etc.*

The London version (much the same as Whall's) runs:

1. The pilot he looks out ahead,
   Oh, a hand in the chains now a-heavin' o' the lead,
   With the Blood an' Guts at our masthead,
   I wonder if me clothes are out o' pawn?
       Ch. Ooooh, Jamboree, *etc.*
            Git away ye black man, don't ye come a-close to me!
            O Jamboree, *etc.*
            I wonder if me clothes are out o' pawn?

2. Now we're past o' the Lizard Light,
   The Start, boys, next will heave in sight,
   We'll soon be abreast of the Isle o' Wight,
   I wonder, *etc.*

3. Now when we git to the Blackwall Docks,
   All the pretty young gals will come down in flocks,
   Some in their petticoats an' some in their frocks,
   I wonder, *etc.*

4. An' on the morrow we will git our pay,
   An' the lads will shout a hip hip hurray,
   An' we'll drop our hooks an' never more go 'way,
   I wonder, *etc.*

Terry gives a Liverpool version with the same first verse as mine, followed by:

2. Now Cape Clear, it is in sight;
   We'll be off Holyhead by tomorrow night,
   And we'll shape our course for the Rock Light,
       Ch. O Jenny get your oatcake done!
           Full Chorus. Whoop Jamboree! Whoop Jamboree!
                        O! ye long-tailed black man poke it up
                          behind,
                        Whoop Jamboree! Whoop Jamboree!
                        O! Jenny get your oatcake done!

3. Now, m' lads, we're round the Rock,
   All hammocks lashed and chests all locked,
   We'll haul her into the Liverpool Dock,
       Ch. O! Jenny, *etc.*

4. Now, m'lads, we're all in dock,
   We'll be off to Dan Lowrie's on the spot,
   And now we'll have a good roundabout,
   Ch. O! Jenny, *etc.*

> (From R. R. Terry's *The Shanty Book*, copyright by
> J. Curwen & Sons, Ltd.)

Sharp says that Dan Lowrie's was a popular playhouse in Paradise Street, Liverpool, near to the Waterloo Dock, much frequented by seamen. Sharp's first verses are slightly different to Terry's. His first verse is Terry's second, and his second verse is as follows:

> Now my boys we're off Holyhead,
> No more salt beef, no more salt bread,
> One man in the chains for to heave the lead,
> Oh—Jenny get your oatcake done!
>   *Ch.* Whip Jamboree! Whip Jamboree!
>   Oh, you long-tailed black man poke it up behind me,
>   Whip Jamboree! Whip Jamboree!
>   Oh, Jenny get your oatcake done.

> (From C. J. Sharp's *English Folk-Chanteys*, 1914)

His next two verses are the same as Terry's, but he gives Waterloo Dock instead of Liverpool Dock. Sharp also gives another Jamboree tune (from Mr. George Conway).

JAMBOREE (C. J. Sharp)

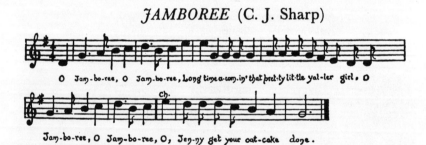

O Jam-bo-ree, O Jam-bo-ree, Long time a-com-in' that pret-ty lit-tle yal-ler girl, O
Jam-bo-ree, O Jam-bo-ree, O, Jen-ny get your oat-cake done.

As can be seen he divides it into solo and chorus, whereas strictly speaking it is only the chorus.

Our next shanty dealing with the 'gels' is the famous old naval song *Spanish Ladies*, although the only other writer apart from myself who calls it a shanty is Captain Frank Shaw, who gives it in his book *Splendour of the Seas*. It was a homeward-bound song sung at the capstan. The way in which the ship is worked up Channel is reminiscent of that in the previous shanty. It has two tunes—the more livelier and faster one being preferred by the later generation of sailing-ship men. I had my versions (*a* and *b*) from my father.

SPANISH LADIES (a)
Alternative title, *Farewell and Adieu to You*

Repeat tune for chorus

> We'll rant an' we'll roar, like true British sailors,
> We'll rant an' we'll rave across the salt seas,
> 'Till we strike soundings in the Channel of Old England,
> From Ushant to Scilly is thirty-four leagues.

2. We hove our ship to, with the wind at sou'west, boys,
   We hove our ship to for to take soundings clear.
   In fifty-five fathoms with a fine sandy bottom,
   We filled our maintops'l, up Channel did steer.
   > *Ch.* We'll rant and we'll roar, *etc.*

3. The first land we made was a point called the Deadman,
   Next Ramshead off Plymouth, Start, Portland, and Wight [off Portsmouth the Wight].
   We sailed then by Beachie, by Fairlee and Dungeyness [and Dover],
   Then bore straight away for the South Foreland Light.
   > *Ch.* We'll, *etc.*

4. Now the signal was made for the Grand Fleet to anchor,
   We clewed up our tops'ls, stuck out tacks and sheets [And all in the Downs that night for to lie].
   We stood by our stoppers, we brailed in our spankers [Stand by your bow-stoppers, let go your shank painters, *or* Let go your shank painters, let go your cat stoppers],
   And anchored ahead of the noblest of fleets [Haul up your clew-garnets, let tacks an' sheets fly].

5. Let every man here drink up [toss off] his full bumper,
   Let every man here drink up his full bowl,
   And let us be jolly and drown melancholy,
   Drink a health to each jovial an' true-hearted soul [Singin' here's a good health to all true-hearted souls *or* Singin' here's a good health to each true-hearted lass].

In addition to the headlands mentioned above, Bullen gives 'the Nab and the Owers'.

293

SPANISH LADIES (b)

Repeat all for chorus—
'Then we'll rant an' we'll roar, *etc.* . . . .'

(Same verses as Version (a))

The distances given from Ushant to Scilly by different collectors are:

34 leagues—Davis & Tozer, and myself;
35 leagues—Sharp, Whall, Sampson, Shell;
45 leagues—Bullen.

Sharp and Whall give 45 fathoms as the depth of the Channel.

A version altered to suit a Bluenose ship approaching its home-port was to be heard among Nova Scotian seamen fifty years ago.

Our next shanty mentioning the girls, one called *The Sailor's Way*, was used as both an outward- and homeward-bound capstan song, and it was also sung at the pumps, so my informant J. Reed told me. I believe it was very popular in the ship in which he served his time—*St. Mirren*. Doerflinger is the only other writer who gives this song, but he gives it as a 'main-hatch song'—what British seamen would call a 'forebitter'. He had it from the mate of a schooner (Frank Vickery of the *Avon Queen*) who sang it to one of the many tunes of *Off to Sea Once More (Go to Sea No More)*, and this version had no chorus. His two verses are:

1. I've sailed among the Yankees, the Spaniards, and Chinees,
   I've lain down with the yellow girls beneath the tall palm trees,
   I've crossed the Line and the Gulf Stream, and around by Table Bay,
   And around Cape Horn and home again—oh, that's the sailor's way!

2. Oh, Bobby'll go to his darling, and Johnny'll go to his dear,
   And Mike will go to his wife and fam'ly, and Andrew for pipes and beer,
   But I'll go to the dance hall to hear the music play,
   For around Cape Horn and home again, oh, that is the sailor's way!

(W. M. Doerflinger, *Shantymen and Shantyboys*, published by The Macmillan Co., New York, 1951)

294

Doerflinger's singer said that there were many more stanzas, and according to him it is a British song. Bill Adams quotes a few lines in one of his books, but none of the foregoing persons give it as a *shanty*. However, that is what my version is, and here it is:

THE SAILOR'S WAY

We've court-ed gay Peru-vi-an gals, French gals an' Chi-nee — Span-ish gals an' Dutch gals too, an' dain-ty Jap-a-nee — To far Aus-tra-lia, Ho-no-lu-lu, where th' Ha-wai-ian maid-ens play — Just a diff-rent gal in ev'ry port, an' that's the Sail-or's Way! — Then it's good-bye ma-vour-neen, We're off to sea a-gain — Sail-or Jack al-ways comes back to the gal he's left be-hind!

2. In calm or storm, in rain or shine,
   The shellback doesn't mind,
   When on the ocean swell, he'll work like hell,
   For the gal he's left behind.
   He beats it north, he runs far south,
   He doesn't get much pay,
   He's always on a losin' game,
       Ch. An' that's the Sailor's way.
           Full Chorus. Then it's goodbye, Mavourneen [*or* Little
                   Sing Loo, My little Rosy, Sweet, little
                   Marie, *etc.*—a different girl's name
                   being used for each chorus],
               We're off to sea again.
               Sailor Jack always comes back
               To the girl he's left behind!

3. Oh, shinin' is the North Star,
   As it hangs on our stabbud bow.
   We're homeward bound for Liverpool town,
   An' our hearts are in it now.
   We've crossed the Line and the Gulf Stream,
   Bin round by Table Bay,
   We've rounded Cape Horn, we're home again,
       Ch. An' that's the sailor's way!
       Ch. Then it's goodbye, *etc.*

4. We'll get paid off in Liverpool,
   An' blow our money free,
   We'll eat an' drink an' have our fun;
   An' forget the ruddy sea,
   Oh, Johnny'll go to his sweet Marie,
   An' Pat with his 'cushla play,
   But I'll get drunk an' turn in me bunk,
      Ch. An' that's the sailor's way!
      Ch. Then it's goodbye, *etc.*

Probably two or three more verses exist but I have failed to find them. To me the whole song is definitely of Irish origin, but the mention of Honolulu in verse 1 makes it a fairly modern shanty, since Honolulu hardly existed in the early nineteenth century, and also its earliest spelling was 'Honoruru'.

Carrying on with our 'girl' theme we next have *Sing, Sally O!* There were two versions of this, one for use at capstan and one for use at halyards. These I had from Harding, who declared they were both used *ashore* in the West Indies for any job where a work-song was needed. Bullen gives the capstan version, Miss Colcord and Sharp give it as a halyard song. Miss Colcord fails to indicate the solos and refrains; Sharp does indicate them, but gives only one line as a solo and the following three lines as chorus—and since he lists it as a halyard song this is obviously wrong. Nevertheless, he puts the hauling marks in their right places! Sharp sees, in the halyard version, a connection with *Haul Away, Joe*, declaring that, although the words are Negro, the tune is in the Dorian mode. Here is the capstan version:

SING, SALLY O! (a)
(Capstan)
Alternative title, *Mudder Dinah*

Good morn-ly' Mud-der Di-nah, I won-der what's the mat-ter? Sing Sal-ly O, an' a fol-lol-day! Hur-

raw, hur-ray me bul-ly boys, for ol' Mud-der Di-i-(-nah), Sing Sal-ly O, an' a fol-lol-day!

2. As she went down to the market,
   She met her high brown sailor boy,
      Ch. Sing, Sally-O! an' a fol-lol-day!
      Hurraw, hurraw, me bully boys,
      For ol' Mudder Dinah,
      Sing, Sally-O! an' a fol-lol-day!

3. An' now he's gone an' left her,
   That man who was her keeper,
   Ch. Sing Sally-O, *etc.*

4. But still she loves all sailors,
   She buys 'em rum an' ter-bac-ker.

And here is the halyard version:

SING, SALLY-O! (*b*)

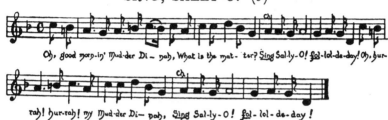

Oh, good morn-in' Mud-der Di - nah, What is the mat- ter? Sing Sal-ly-O! fol-lol-de-day! Oh, hurrah! hur-rah! my Mud-der Di— nah, Sing Sal-ly-O! fol- lol - de- day!

2. The news is goin' round, the packet's homeward bound,
   Ch. Sing, Sally-O, *fol*-lol-de-day!
   O kiss yer gals an' drinks all round, boys,
   Ch. Sing, Sally-O, *fol*-lol-de-day!

3. We'll drink hot rum an' let's all have some fun,
   We'll soon be headin' for the homeward run.

4. Goodbye to Mudder [Mammy] Dinah, there ain't no gal finer,
   Goodbye, goodbye to all the gals.

I feel that both of these shanties are English folk-songs that have
passed through the shanty mart, erstwhile chants of the hoosiers.
They had very few regulation words, to extemporize was the thing.

Another shanty singing of Sally is the halyard song mentioned by
Dana in his *Two Years Before the Mast*—*Round the Corner, Sally*. The
phrase 'round-the-corner-Sallies' is often found in nigger minstrelsy
and means anything from a female species of 'corner boy' to a fully-
fledged prostitute. In one of the many Christy Minstrel books is a
song *Aunt Sally*, the last line of the chorus of which runs: 'Re, ri, ro,
round the corner, Sally.' Terry and Sharp are the only two collectors
who give it and both had it from the same shantyman, Mr. Short of
Somerset. My version is one of Harding's.

ROUND THE CORNER, SALLY

'Round the cor-ner an' a - way we'll go, 'Round th' cor-ner Sal-ly! 'Round th' cor-ner where them
gals do go, 'Round th' cor-ner Sal- ly!

2. Oh, Sally Brown she's the gal for me,
   Ch. Round the corner, *Sally!*
   She's waitin' there by the mango tree,
   Ch. Round the corner, *Sally!*

3. She loves me good, she loves me long,
   She loves me hot, she loves me strong.

4. Was ye ever down in Mobile Bay?
   Where the gals all spend a white man's pay?

5. I wisht I had that gal in tow,
   I'd take her in tow to Callyo.

6. To Callyo we're bound to go,
   Around that corner where there's ice an' snow.

7. So round 'er up an' stretch 'er luff,
   I think by Gawd we've hauled enough!

The 'corner' indicated in this shanty seems to be Cape Horn. Terry's 'Madame' is obviously a 'Round-the-corner-Sally' awaiting round the corner (Cape Horn) in Callyo for sailor victims:

To Madame Gashee's we will go,
   Ch. Round, etc.
For Mademoiselle ye all do know,
   Ch. Round the corner, etc.

O Mademoiselle will take her in tow,
We'll take her in tow to Callao.

O I wish I was at Madame Gashee's,
It's there we'll sit and take our ease.

Then around the corner we will roll,
For Madame is a cheery soul!

(From *The Shanty Book*, by R. R. Terry. Copyright by J. Curwen & Sons, Ltd.)

Although a typical West Indian Negro work-song, it appears from all the earmarks to have been sung mainly aboard ships in the West Coast of South America Guano and Saltpetre Trade, and of course, as we know from Dana, in ships of the earlier Hide Trade of the west coast of North America.

Another typical West Indian or Southern States' work-song taken to sea and turned into a shanty is *Sister Susan* or *Shinbone Al*. Shinbone Alley, by the way, is a location often mentioned in American Negro songs. I learnt it from a coloured shantyman, 'Harry Lauder' of St. Lucia, B.W.I., who gave it as a hauling song. Bullen, the only writer who prints it, also heard it in the West Indies, and the circumstances in which he learnt it are to be found in his book *The*

Log of a Sea Waif, but he gives it as a windlass or capstan shanty. He gives the second (capstan) refrain as:

Gwine ter git a home bimeby,
Gwine ter git a home bimeby—high!
Gwine ter git a home bimeby,

the third line of which is a *solo* in my hauling version.

SISTER SUSAN
Alternative title, *Shinbone Al*

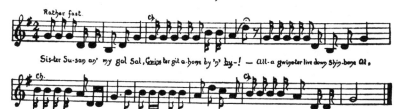

2. Portugee Joe came down our Al,
   Ch. Gwine ter git a-home by'n'*by!*
   Portugee Joe he got my Sal,
   Ch. Gwine ter git a-home by'n'*by!*
   He went an' ran off with my Sally,
   Ch. Gwine ter git a-home by'n'*by!*

3. So I thought I'd take a trip to sea,
   So I shipped aboard o' a big Yankee,
   I went an' shipped out of Nantucket.

4. A whaler's life is no life for me,
   I jumped her an' I left the sea,
   I ran right back to Shinbone Alley.

Our next shanty—a halyard one—is called *Walkalong, Miss Susiana Brown* and is another West Indian or Southern States' work-song. As Miss Colcord, who also gives a version, points out, it was probably used by the hoosiers of Mobile to screw cotton. Miss Colcord gives 'Juliana' instead of 'Susiana'.

WALKALONG, MISS SUSIANA BROWN
Alternative title, *Miss Juliana Brown*

2. She loves her rollo sailor,
    *Ch. Hau*le*y* high! *Hau*le*y* low!
Oh, she loves her rollo sailor,
    *Ch. Walka*long Miss *Susia*na [Juliana] Brown!

3. He's gone north in a whaler,
Oh, he's gone north in a whaler.

4. My doudou she's a lady,
Oh, she's neither dark nor shady.

5. We'll haul an' stretch her luff, boys,
The bastard's gittin' tough, boys.

6. I'll see her boys, tomorrow,
An' I'll make the beggar holler.

Another shanty mentioning 'Julia' is given in the *Journal* of the Folk Song Society (Vol. 5). It was collected by Cecil Sharp and is definitely Negro. It was sung at the capstan.

SOUTHERN LADIES

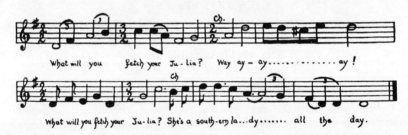

2. One bottle of Florida water,
    Ch. Way-ay-ay-ay!
One bottle of Florida water,
    Ch. She's a southern lady—all the day.

Another shanty with West Indian connections is *Miss Lucy Long*. The Broomielaw is in Glasgow—and Glasgow at one time had strong connections with the Jamaica Sugar and Rum Trade. This shanty was used at the capstan, and quite a rousing song it is. Terry and Sharp give versions, both similar to mine which I picked up in Trinidad in 1931. Miss Lucy Long is a girl often met with in Negro songs, e.g.:

Oh, take yer time, Miss Lucy,
Take yer time, Miss Lucy Long,
Oh, take yer time, Miss Lucy,
Take yer time, Miss Lucy Long.

Both Terry and myself give 'ring, Miss Lucy Long', a word which *was* sung sometimes, but Sharp spells it 'wring'—incorrectly I feel! But it doesn't really matter, because in both cases the word was used only to replace a much cruder one!

MISS LUCY LONG

Was ye ni-ver down on the Broo-mi-low, where the Yan-kee boys are all the go? Tim-me way hay-ey hay,

hay, hay, hay, ah-ha — me John-ny boys, ah-ha! — Why— don't ye try for to ring Miss Lu-cy Long?

2. Oh, as I walked out one mornin' fair, to view the view an' take the air,
   Ch. Timme way-hay-hay-hay-hay-, hay-hay-ah-ha, me Johnny [bully] boys, ah-ha!
   Why don't ye try for to ring Miss Lucy Long?

3. Oh, 'twas there I met Miss Lucy fair, 'twas there we met I do declare,
   Ch. Timme way, *etc.*

4. I raised me hat an' said 'how do?' Sez she, 'I will not walk with you.'

5. 'You dirty sailor, ye stink o' tar, besides I know what sailors are!'

6. 'My friend's a Mate in the Blackball Line, in his uniform and his peak-cap fine.'

7. I left her there upon the quay, that gal she were too smart for me!

It may be noticed that the tune of the first solo is identical with that of *The Sailor Likes His Bottle-O.*

A fine hauling song built around a similar name—Miss Lucy Loo—I also picked up in Trinidad. My informant told me that it has been used by West Indian seamen both ashore on the wharves and at sea at halyards. There is no regular story. The phrase 'rock 'n' roll' in verse 7 was a very common cry among shantymen—a shout of encouragement when hauling or heaving—and of course it emanated, just as the name for 'rock 'n' roll' dancing did, from the American Negro.

MISS LUCY LOO
Alternative title, *Rollin' Down to Trinidad*

2. Bend yer backs, take in the slack, roll me over, Lucy,
    Ch. To me *way*, hay, hay, ho, *hu*!
   Oh, bend yer backs, take in the slack, roll me over, Lucy,
    Ch. We're *roll*in' down to Trinidad to *see* [*meet*] Miss Lucy Loo!

3. The ship's all right, the crew is tight, the Ol' Man's all in clover [never sober],
    Ch. To me way, *etc.*
   Oh, the ship's all right, *etc.*

4. O sing a song, O blow along, turn the blanket over.

5. O haul away an' get yer pay, O Lucy's on the towline.

6. Hoist her high, an' hoist her dry, come rock 'n' roll me over.

7. Now stretch her luff, she's high enough, the end is just in sight, boys.

A rather notorious halyard shanty bearing a Spanish lady's name was *Serafina!* This used to be very popular at t'gallant halyards in ships in the West Coast of South America Saltpetre Trade. I had it from an old Irish sailor called Jack Connolly, and I've had to tone down the original theme quite a lot, a reason probably why it has never been in print before! Many verses are missing.

SERAFINA

2. She's the Queen, me boys, of all the gals that live in the ol' Casino,
   Ch. Serafina! Serafina!
   She used to kiss for monkey nuts but now she works for vino,
   Ch. Serafina! oh, Serafina!

3. At robbin' silly sailors, boys, no gal was ever keener,
   She'll make ye pay right through the nose, that lovely Serafina.

4. She'll guzzle pisco, beer, an' gin, on rum her mum did wean 'er,
   She smokes just like a chimney stack, or a P.S.N.C. steamer.

5. Serafina's got no shoes, I've bin ashore an' seen 'er,
   She's got no time to put 'em on, that hard-worked Serafina.

6. When I wuz young an' in me prime, I first met Serafina,
   In Callyo we saw the sights an' then went up to Lima.

7. But the finest sight I ever saw wuz little Serafina,
   But the very next day as we sailed away I wisht I'd never bin there.

8. For I wuz skint, me clothes wuz gone, an' so wuz Serafina,
   She'd done me brown, she'd sunk me down, that dirty she-hyena!

A verse given to me by another Liverpool seaman runs:

I used to love that little gal, whose name is Serafina,
But she's gone off with a Dago man who plays a concertina.

A very favourite capstan song in Liverpool ships was that known as *The Liverpool Judies* or *The Liverpool Girls*, sometimes called *The Towrope Girls, Roll (Row), Bullies, Roll (Row)*, or *Roll, Julia, Roll.* It is of Irish origin and was usually sung in imitative Irish or Liverpool-Irish fashion. It probably dates from the forties, since it was popular in the Western Ocean Packets. Two themes were common and three tunes were used, with slight variants of these tunes among different sailor-groups, like those of the Tyne, Liverpool, Bristol Channel, London, etc.

THE LIVERPOOL JUDIES (a)

Alternative titles, *Roll, Julia, Roll! Roll, Bullies, Roll! The Towrope Girls*

2. A smart Yankee packet lies out in the Bay, [I shipped on the *Alaska*
     lying out in the Bay,]
   A-waitin' a fair wind to get under way,
   With all of her sailors so sick and so sore,
   They'd drunk all their limejuice [whisky] and can't git no more.
     Ch. Singin' ro-o-o-oll, o-o-o-oll, roll, bullies [Julia], roll!
     Them Liverpool judies have got us in tow!

3. Oh, here comes the mate in a hell of a stew [in his jacket of blue],
   He's lookin' for graft [work] for us sailors to do,
   Oh, it's 'Fore [jib] tops'l halyards!' he loudly does roar,
   An' it's lay along Paddy, ye son-o'-a-whore!
     Ch. Singin', *etc.*

4. One night off Cape Horn I shall never forget,
   'Tis oft-times I sighs when I think o' it yet,
   She was roundin' Cape Horn with her main-skys'l'set [She was divin'
     bows under wid her sailors all wet],
   She wuz roundin' Cape Horn wid us all wringin' wet [She was doin'
     twelve knots wid her mainskys'l set].

5. An' now we are haulin' 'way on to the Line,
   When I thinks o' it now, sure, we had a good time,
   Them sea-boys box-haulin' their yards all around,
   For to beat that flash packet called the *Thatcher MacGowan*.

6. An' now we've arrived in the Bramleymoor Dock,
   An' all them flash judies on the pierhead do flock,
   The barrel's run dry an' our five quid advance,
   An' I guess it's high time for to git up an' dance.

7. Here's a health to the Capen wherever he may be,
   A friend to the sailor on land or on sea [a bucko on land an' a bully at
        sea],
   But as for the chief mate, the dirty ol' brute,
   We hope when he dies straight to hell he'll skyhoot.

I had this version from an erstwhile shipmate Paddy Griffiths; he
said the last two verses were sometimes sung the other way about,
number 6 being last.

Here is the same theme but a different tune, one very common in
Liverpool ships, taught me by an old Irish seaman of the sail,
Paddy Delaney. It is a fascinating air.

THE LIVERPOOL JUDIES (b)

The second set of words are those of the following version, but both
the set about the passage from 'Frisco to Liverpool, and the set
about the passage from Liverpool to New York, are interchangeable
and were sung to all three tunes given here. Here is the third tune
and second theme obtained by me from Spike Sennit. The tune is
very like Bone's (*Capstan Bars*).

THE LIVERPOOL JUDIES (c)

2. For forty-two days we wuz hungry an' sore,
   Oh, the winds wuz agin us, the gales they did roar,
   Off Battery Point we did anchor at last,
   Wid our jibboom hove in an' the canvas all fast.
      Ch. Singin' ho! ro! ho! bullies ho!
         Them Liverpool judies have got us in tow.

3. De boardin' house masters wuz off in a trice,
   A-shoutin' an' promisin' all that wuz nice,
   An' one fat ol' crimp he got cottoned to me,
   Sez he, 'Yer a fool, lad, ter follow the sea.'

4. Sez he, 'There's a job as is waitin' for you,
   Wid lashin's o' liquor an' beggar-all to do.'
   Sez he, 'What d'yer say, lad, will you jump her too?'
   Sez I, "Ye ol' barstard, I'm damned if I do.'

5. But de best o' intentions dey niver gits far,
   Arter forty-two days at the door of a bar,
   I tossed off me liquor an' what d'yer think?
   Why the lousy ol' barstard had drugs in me drink.

6. The next I remembers I woke in de morn,
   On a three-skys'l yarder bound south [out] round Cape Horn,
   Wid an ol' suit of oilskins an' two pair of sox,
   An' a bloomin' big head, an' a sea-chest o' rocks.

7. Now all ye young sailors take a warnin' by me,
   Keep a watch on yer drinks whin de liquor is free,
   An' pay no attintion to runner or whore,
   Or yer head'll be thick an' yer throat'll be sore.

The last line of verses 6 and 7 are pretty rough in the original and have here been camouflaged. Bone gives as a camouflage: 'And a flooring of bricks at the foot of me box', and Shell gives: 'And a flooring of brickbats to ballast me box.' Bone and myself are the only two writers giving this song as a shanty; all other collectors give it as a forebitter. Doerflinger calls it a 'main-hatch song'. The words of verse 2 of the first theme are also to be found in one version of the halyard shanty *A Long Time Ago*, and those of the second couplet of verse 3 are also in *Blow the Man Down*. The second couplet of verse 4 is one used in one of the versions of *Sacramento*, and the second line of verse 7 is found in *Time for Us to Go*. Which 'pinched' from which is difficult to say, but it is possible that all these lines and couplets were purloined from *The Liverpool Judies*. The shanty might quite well have been a whalers' rowing song, explaining perhaps why some versions give 'Row, Julia, row', in the chorus. Whalers must have had many rowing songs, but unfortunately none have survived. I have also heard this shanty sung to a tune almost identical with the shore-song *Villikins and his Dinah*, a tune to which I will refer later (see *The Flash Packet*).

And now we come to a shanty which I'm surprised no other collector has mentioned, one about a very famous Liverpool 'judy' called Maggie May, although as to who she was or where she lived and when, no one seems able to state. But whether an historical character or fictitious, it matters not, seeing that she represents a type of sailor's inamorata ever with us yet. Apparently she acted once too often and was caught and transported to the Colonies. It was sung at the capstan in many Liverpool ships and still survives in a mangled form in Liverpool even today, with verses altered to suit steam and firemen. Its most recent appearance however is over the air as a skiffle item!

It was probably a forebitter as well as a shanty. The tune resembles *Nelly Gray* and some old-timers maintain that it was once sung to this tune. The words I give here are modified somewhat.

MAGGIE MAY

2. I paid off at the Home, after a voyage from Sierre Leone,
   Two pound ten a month had been my pay;
   As I jingled in me tin, I wuz sadly taken in,
   By a lady of the name of Maggie May.
   Ch. Ooh, Maggie, Maggie May,
        They have taken you away,
        To slave upon Van Dieman's cruel shore,
        Oh, you robbed many a whaler an' many a drunken sailor,
        But you'll never cruise round Liverpool [Park Lane, Paradise Street] no more!

3. When I steered into her, I hadn't got a care,
   I wuz cruisin' up an' down ol' Canning Place;
   She wuz dressed in a gown so fine, like a frigate of the line,
   An' I bein' a sailorman gave chase.
   Ch. Oh, Maggie, *etc.*

4. She gave me a saucy nod, an' I like a farmer's clod,
   Let her take me line abreast in tow;
   An' under all plain sail, we ran before the gale,
   An' to the Crow's Nest Tavern we did go.

5. Next mornin' when I woke, I found that I wuz broke,
   I hadn't got a penny to me nyme;
   So I had to pop me suit, me John L's an' me boots,
   Down in the Park Lane pawn shop Number Nine.

6. Oh, you thievin' Maggie May, ye robbed me of me pay,
   When I slept wid you last night ashore,
   Oh, guilty the jury found her, for robbin' a homeward-bounder,
   An' she'll never roll down Park Lane [Peter Street, Paradise Street]
      no more.

7. She wuz chained and sent away, from Liverpool one day,
   The lads they cheered as she sailed down the Bay,
   An' every sailor lad, he only wuz too glad,
   They'd sent the ol' whore out to Botany Bay.

Regarding the streets referred to in this shanty, Peter Street intersects Victoria Street and Whitechapel, but nowadays it has none of the romantic, if sordid, atmosphere of Liverpool's old-time Sailortown. To include all the other streets mentioned in various versions it would appear that Maggie May's habitat stretched from Park Lane and Canning Place (old Liverpool Custom House) along Paradise Street to Whitechapel including Peter Street. Wind Street given in the next version is in Swansea. In the more modern versions and the skiffle number of *Maggie May*, Lime Street, Liverpool, is given as her haunt. A twisted version of the chorus I once heard gives 'Bantry Bay' for Botany Bay.

During 1955–6 at odd intervals a series of letters in connection with this old song were printed in the nautical magazine *Sea Breezes*. One version given by D. H. Williams of South Wales runs as follows:

> Now, you jolly sailor boys,
> Come listen to my tale,
> I'm sure you will have cause to pity me,
> I was a darned young fool,
> In the Port of Liverpool, when I called there,
> On my first trip home from sea.

I was staying at the Home,
In a ship from Sierre Leone,
And two-pound-ten a month was all my pay,
Was all my pay.
As I jingled with my tin,
I was easily taken in by a little girl up there called Maggie May.

In the morn when I awoke,
I found that I was broke,
No shoes or shirt or trousers could I find.
When I asked her where they were
She said, 'My dear sir,
They're down in Lewis' pawnshop No. 9.'

So to Lewis' I did go,
But no clothing could I find,
And the policeman took that wicked girl away,
And the judge he guilty found her
Of robbing a homeward-bounder
And now she's doing time in Botany Bay.

Oh, Maggie, Maggie May,
They've taken her away,
No more she'll roam around our Wind Street way,
For she robbed so many sailors,
And also lots of whalers,
For now she's doing time in Botany Bay.

Here the singer seems to have things mixed—first she is in Liverpool and later in Wind Street, Swansea. Also, according to this version, a Liverpool version of the New York 'panel game' seems to have been played!

Another correspondent in the same issue of *Sea Breezes* (Captain J. R. Hodgson of Devon) writes:

I was serving in the barque *Pharos* in 1908 . . . we had a number of seamen who had served in some of the famous clipper ships in the Australian trade and . . . one of these shipmates . . . used to sing the story of 'Nellie Ray'. . . .

I was paid off at the home,
From a voyage to Sierre Leone
Three pounds monthly was my pay.
When I drew the cash I grinned,
But very soon got skinned
By a lass that lived in Peter Street called Ray.
Oh, my charming Nellie Ray,
They have taken you away,
You have gone to Van Diemen's cruel shore,
For you've skinned so many tailors,
And you've robbed too many sailors,
That we look for you in Peter Street no more.

In *The Trade Winds*, by C. Northcote Parkinson, p. 117, this song is referred to and it also states the source of his information is a diary by Charles Picknell, an able seaman aboard the convict ship *Kains* which sailed from London on July 8, 1830, for Van Diemen's Land. Extracts from this diary were published in the *Blue Peter* in 1930.

In the extract referred to the name is given as 'Nellie Ray' as we used to sing it.

Captain A. Hodgson of Maryport, answering a correspondent, Captain Cole of Yarmouth, in *Sea Breezes* (February 1955), states that he heard *Maggie May* sung aboard the full-rigged ship *Aberfoyle* of Glasgow, but he could only remember the following verse:

> Oh! my dear Maggie May—they have taken you away,
> To die upon Van Diemen's cruel shore,
> For you robbed so many tailors,
> And skinned so many sailors,
> That you'll never shine in Peter Street no more.

This Peter Street is possibly the Glasgow one.

A further correspondent in *Sea Breezes*, R. F. P. Halliday of St. Luke's, Jersey, C.I., writes (February 1956):

I was shipmates with an old Yankee sailor in the barque *Ville de Dieppe* a few years ago before the First World War and he used to sing:

1. If you'll listen for a while, I will tell to you a tale
   Of what happened not very long ago to me,
   How I was made a fool, in the town of Liverpool,
   The first time I arrived home here from sea.
   I was paid off at the Home[1] from a ship from Sierre Leone—
   Five pound ten a month, that was my pay,
   When I got my tin I grinned but I very soon got skinned
   By a girl who lived in Peter Street called May.
   Ch. Oh, my darling Maggie May they have taken you away,
   To toil upon Van Diemen's cruel shore,
   For you robbed a lot of tailors and skinned so many sailors,
   That you'll never walk down Peter Street no more.

2. Oh, I'll never forget that day when I first met Maggie May
   She was standing at the corner at Canning Place,
   In a full-sized crinoline, like a frigate of the line,
   And as she saw I was a sailor she gave chase.
   So I hauled aboard my tacks when I saw her catch aback,
   Her signal hoisted up for me to stay,
   Says she you're homeward bound so you'd better wear around,
   And together in Peter Street we'd rum and tea.
   Ch. Oh, my darling Maggie May, *etc.*

[1] The 'Home' is the Sailors' Home in Liverpool.

3. Next morn when I awoke in bed, with a sore and aching head,
   I looked around about for my clothes but they were gone,
   And with such a knowing stare, she said the Lord knows where,
   You had better ask old Uncle in the pawn.
   When I heard this dreadful news I went raging in the blues,
   When two coppers came and took her right away,
   And old Raffles guilty found her, for she'd skinned a homeward-
        bounder,
   And he sentenced her to Van Diemen's right away.

4. Oh, the rain came down in torrents, as in my pants and boots and
        socks
   I made my way down to the Princes Dock.
   But there I could not linger, so I turned a comic singer,
   And I made my first appearance at the 'Clock'.
   A crowd soon gathered round, and to them my tale I told,
   Some of them seemed to think it served me right,
   But when Liverpool more I go, my pockets shall be low,
   And I won't care if they skin me every night.

Mr. Halliday writes that the tune used was that of *My Darling
Nellie Gray*, and it seems that this tune does suit his set of words
better than the usual one. His fourth verse too is unusual and a very
interesting one I must say!

Bob Roberts, the skipper of a Thames barge, has also sung a version of *Maggie May*: much of it is altered to suit a bargeman's life,
with references to local places where Thames barges sail. Instead of
'Liverpool' he has the 'Port of London Pool', and the hero is paid off
at 'Greenhithe', after a voyage from 'north of Blythe'. And the
Viper Skiffle Group has used the more modern line of 'and she'll
never walk down Lime Street any more'.

The Geordie song—*Keep Yer Feet Still, Geordie Hinnie*—has a
related tune.

Having brought Botany Bay and the penal settlements of the
Colonies into the picture we will take for our next shanty a song
which was originally a shore ballad and later a forebitter, but which
was used at times as a capstan song. This is *Ten Thousand Miles
Away*. It is said to be the ballad on the chorus of which the chorus of
Sacramento was based. The song first appears to have been sung by
street singers in Ireland in the early part of last century, and under
the name of *Botany Bay* it was a favourite song of the old London
music-halls of the fifties and sixties. I have come across many shore
versions of the older pattern, but in later times it was given a set of
nonsense verses and renamed *A Capital Ship*. The version I give here
I had from my mother's father (J. Southwood), and it is the usual
version that was sung at sea at the capstan or as a forebitter.

TEN THOUSAND MILES AWAY

With vigour.

Sing ho! for a brave an' a gallant ship, an' a fair an' favorin' breeze, Wi' a bully crew an' a cap'n too, to carry me over the seas, To carry me over the seas me boys, To me true love far a-way, For I'm takin a trip in a Gov-ern-ment ship, Ten thousand miles a-way! Then blow ye winds an' blow! An' a-rov-in' I will go, I'll stay no more on. England's shores to hear sweet music play, ay, ay, ay, For I'm on the move to me own true love, Ten thou-sand miles a-way!

2. My true love wuz beautiful,
   An' my true love wuz gay,
   But she's taken a trip on a Government ship,
   Bound out to Botany Bay,
   Bound out to Botany Bay, m'boys,
   An' though she's far away,
   I'll never forget me own true love,
   Ten thousand miles away!
       Ch. Then—blow, ye winds, an' blow!
           An' a-rovin' I will go,
           I'll stay no more on England's shore,
           To hear sweet music play [the fiddler play],
           For I'm on the move to me own true love,
           Ten thousand miles away!

3. Oh, it wuz a summer's mornin',
   When last I seed my Meg,
   She'd a Government band around each hand,
   An' another one round her leg,
   Oh, another one round her leg, m' boys,
   As the big ship left the Bay,
   Adieu she sez remember me,
   Ten thousand miles away! [When I'm in Botany Bay].

4. I wisht I wuz a bosun bold,
   Or a sailor widout fear [even a bombadier]—
   I'd man a boat an' away I'd float,
   An' straight for me true love steer.
   An' straight for me true love steer, m' boys,
   Where the whales an' dolphins play,
   Where the whales an' sharks are havin' their larks,
   Ten thousand miles away!

5. Oh, the sun may shine through the London fog,
   Or the river run quite clear,
   Or the ocean brine turn into wine, or I forget me beer,
   Or I forget me beer, m' boys,
   Or the landlord's quarter-day,
   But I'll never forget me own true love,
   Ten thousand miles away!

The Meg in this song obviously didn't follow the same profession as Maggie May, or did she? Anyhow both had to be transported for their 'crimes'.

There is a folk-song in Volume 2 of the *Journal* of the Folk Song Society called *Ten Thousand Miles* with a similar theme as the foregoing but with non-nautical wording. In the same book a version of the *Lowlands of Holland*, entitled *Abroad as I was Walking*, also has a theme about manning a boat in search of the hero's sweetheart.

Still in the realms of convict ships and transportation, we have next the old forebitter often used as a capstan song, *The Banks of Newf'n'land*. Its convict connection is the fact that it was really a parody on an older forebitter, itself originally a shore ballad, called *Van Dieman's Land*, a song often sung in Liverpool and as a forebitter often heard in Liverpool ships. A note attached to the record *Singing Sailor* (mentioned in the Introduction) states that 'Versions can still be heard in Scotland and Ireland, but is in Liverpool and Salford (Lancs.) that the song lives most vigorously'. It tells of the sufferings of poachers transported to Van Diemen's Land. Here it is for comparison with *The Banks of Newfoundland* (from T. W. Jones of Liverpool).

VAN DIEMAN'S LAND

Ye ramb-lin' boys o' Liv-er-pool, I'll have ye to be - - ware, 'Tis when ye go a- hunt-in' wid yer

dog, yer gun, yer snare, Watch out boys for the game-keep-ers, Keep yer dog at your com -

mand, Just think on all the hard - - ships, go-in' to Van Die - - man's land.

2. We had two Irish lads on board, Mickey Murphy an' Paddy Malone,
   And they were both the stoutest friends that ever a man could own,
   But the gamekeeper he'd caught them, and from ol' England's strand,
   They were seven years transported for to plough Van Dieman's Land.

3. We had on board a lady fair, Bridget Reilly [Johnson] wuz her name,
   An' she wuz sent from Liverpool for a-playin' of the game.
   Our captain fell in love wid her and he married her out of hand,
   And she gave us all good usage, boys, goin' to Van Dieman's Land.

4. The moment that we landed there, upon that fatal shore,
   The planters they inspected us, some fifty score or more,
   They marched us off like hosses, an' they sold us out of hand,
   Then yoked us to the plough, me boys, for to plough Van Dieman's
   Land.

5. As I lay in me bunk one night, a-dreamin' all alone,
   I dreamt I wuz in Liverpool, 'way back in Marybone,
   Wid me own true love beside me, an' a jug o' ale in me hand,
   Then awoke so broken-hearted, lyin' on Van Dieman's Land.

Apparently romances blossomed in both convict- and packet-
ships, for in the next song—*The Banks o' Newf'n'land*—we have too
some semblance of a romance. An old friend of mine, 'Scottie' of
Port Adelaide, who never shipped in steam in all his long sea career,
told me that he heard it when young sung at the capstan with all the
twiddles and quavers seamen of the old school would adorn this
type of song with. Nearly all forebitters and many capstan songs were
sung in this fashion by the older seamen.

THE BANKS O' NEWF'N'LAND

Ye ram-blin' boys o' Liv-er-pool, Ye sail-or-men be- ware, when yis go in a Yan-Kee pack-et ship, no dun-ga-ree jump-ers wear, Bu-ut have a mon-key jack-et all up-to your com-mand, For there blows some cold nor'-west-ers on the Banks of New-f'n-land, We'll wash 'er, an' we'll scrub 'er down, wid ho-ly-stone an' sand, An' we'll bid a-dieu to the Vir-gin Rocks, on the Banks of New-f'n-land.

2. We had one Lynch from Ballynahinch, Spud Murphy an' Paddy
   Malone [Moike Moore].
   'Twas in the winter of seventy-three those sea-boys suffered sore,
   They popped their clothes in Liverpool, sold them all out of hand,
   Not thinkin' of the cold nor'winds on the Banks o' Newf'n'land.
      Ch. We'll wash her an' we'll scrub 'er down, wid holystone an'
          sand,
          An' we'll bid adieu to the Virgin Rocks an' the Banks o'
          Newf'n'land.
             [Alternatives for the last line of the chorus—An' we'll let the
              flag at the gangway fly on the Banks, etc., or For 'tis
              while we're here we can't be there, on the Banks, etc.]

3. We had a lady fair aboard, Bridget Reilly wuz 'er name,
   To her I promised marriage an' on me she had a claim.
   She tore up her red flannel petticoats [drawers], me bhoys, to make
      mittens for our hands,
   For she could not see them sea-boys freeze, on the Banks of New-
      f'n'land.

4. I dreamt a dream the other night, an' t'ought I wuz at home,
   I dreamt that me an' my Judee, wuz back in Dublin Town,
   We both wuz in the ale-house wi' a jug o' beer in hand,
   But when I woke I found no jokes on the Banks o' Newf'n'land.

A version given me by Mr. D. McDonald of Glasgow is:

1. Oh, come, all you roving sailors, and sporting blades, beware,
   When you jump on board a packet ship, no dungaree jumpers wear,
   But always have good monkey-jackets at your command
   Think of the cold nor'westers on the Banks of Newf'n'land.

2. Now there was one Lynch from Ballynahinch, Jim Kane and Mick
   O'Moore,
   It was in the year of sixty, the mariners suffered sore,
   With all their clothes in Liverpool, they'd spent money with either
   hand,
   Not thinking of the cold nor'westers on the Banks of Newf'n'land.

3. Oh, there was a girl on board that ship, Kate Conner was her name,
   I promised I would marry her, for on me she had a claim.
   She tore up her flannel petticoat, to make mittens for my hands,
   For I won't see my true love freezing on the Banks of Newf'n'land.

4. Oh, now we're off the Hook, me boys, the land all covered with snow,
   The towboat is ahead and to New York soon we'll go.
   We'll scrub her deck, we'll scrub her down with holystones and sand,
   So we'll bid adieu to the Virgin Rocks on the Banks of Newf'n'land.

5. Oh, I had a dream, a happy dream, I dreamt that I was home,
   Alongside of my own true love and she in Marybone,
   A jug of ale all on my knee, a glass of ale in my hand,
   But when I woke my heart was broke, on the Banks of Newf'n'land.

I should say the foregoing was sung as a forebitter; when it was
used as a capstan shanty the full chorus I give was added.
   Some shantymen started off with 'Ye Western Ocean labourers...'
Doerflinger's version gives 'stockings' for 'mittens', 'Bridget Murphy'
for 'Bridget Reilly', and 'Marylebone' for 'Dublin Town'. Here is
his fine tune and first verse:

This version is from the singing of Richard Maitland of Sailors'
Snug Harbor, and Doerflinger has given his slightly different way of

singing verses 2 and 3 and their choruses. Doerflinger notes the reference that G. P. Jackson makes to the similarity between this tune and that of the white spiritual *Wedlock* (in the latter's book *Spiritual Folk Songs of Early America*).

Now that we have given a shanty having a place-name for its title we may as well carry on with other shanties similarly named.

Our next is a halyard shanty I picked up from my old friend Harding. It is obviously of West Indian or Guiana origin and needed a Negro shantyman to do it justice, having its full complement of yells and hitches. This is the first time it has been in print. It was probably also used ashore for jobs where pulling was needed. Most of these West Indian shanties were first used for jobs such as moving shanties, working cargo, etc., and then were later taken to sea by coloured seamen shipping aboard Yankee, Bluenose (Nova Scotian), and British wind-jammers, on the decks of which they would be adapted for work at halyard and capstan.

ESSEQUIBO RIVER

2. Essequibo Capen is the King o' Capens aaall!
   Ch. Buddy tanna na we are *some*body O!
   Essequibo Capen is the King o' Capens aaall!
   Ch. Buddy tanna na we are *some*body O!
   Somebody O, Johnny, somebody O!
   Ch. Buddy tanna na we are *some*body O!

3. Essequibo Bosun is the King o' Bosuns aaall!
   Ch. Buddy, etc.
   Essequibo Bosun is the King o' Bosuns aaall!
   Ch. Buddy, etc.
   Somebody, *etc.*
   Ch. Buddy, etc.

4. Essequibo sailors is the Chief o' Sailors aaall!

5. Essequibo Sallies is the Queen o' Sallies aaall!

6. Essequibo maidens is the Queen o' Maidens aaall!

Naturally there was much room for improvisation in this type of song. The word 'all' at the end of each solo was pronounced 'arl' and drawn out.

Our next shanty *Sing a Song, Blow-along O!* or as it was sometimes called *Dixie Land* was used at halyards. Patterson gives a version, without the music, with a theme very similar to mine, or rather Smith's of Tobago. This shanty the latter declared was one of the best in his repertoire.

SING A SONG, BLOW-ALONG O!
Alternative title, *Dixie Land*

'Way down in Dix-ie! 'Way down in Dix-ie where de cot-ton grows, Sing a song, blow-a-long, O- o - o!

2. 'Way down in Dixie!
  'Way down in Dixie, oh, I had a gal,
  Ch. Sing a song, blow along *o-o-o*!

3. 'Way down in Dixie!
  Her name it was Fore-tops'l Nell,
  Ch. Sing a song, *etc.*

4. 'Way down in Dixie!
  She was so dark she broke me heart,

5. 'Way down in Dixie!
  She had black eyes an' a lovely nose,

6. Oh, around the world I had to sail.

7. But I'm as tough as a six-inch nail.

8. When I got back, she'd done me down.

9. She'd ran off wid a circus clown.

10. If I could cotch that thievin' [sneakin'] tyke.

11. I'd give him one wid a marline-spike.

12. But I left her there an' sailed away.

Patterson has a 'big, buck nigger' as the chap who 'pinched' the girl whose name was 'Jemima Joe'. This halyard song was one probably used by the hoosiers of Mobile for heaving on the jack-screws when loading cotton.

318

Next we have a version of a once well-known shore-song called *Baltimore*. It was a shanty very popular in German sailing ships, usually sung at the capstan when making sail by leading the halyard to the capstan instead of hauling on the fall. I have taken part in the singing of it myself aboard a German barque, and it was sung as late as 1951 aboard the German four-masted barque *Pamir* on her passage to Rio. It was never heard in British ships, and it helps to strengthen my theory that German and Scandinavian seamen adapted British and American shore-songs and turned them into shanties long after the art of 'inventing' shanties had died out aboard British and American ships. The first couplet of its full chorus reminds one of the shanty *We'll go to Sea No More*. An almost identical version is given in *Knurrhahn*. Of course many of the final verses have had to be censored!

BALTIMORE
Alternative title, *Up She Goes*

2. And he kissed her on the cheek, an' the crew began to roar,
   Ch. Oh, ho! an' up she goes! We're bound for Baltimore!
   And he kissed her on the face, an' the crew began to roar,
   Ch. Oh ho! an' up she goes! We're bound for Baltimore!
   Full Chorus. No more . . . no more . . . no more!
   We'll go to sea no more!
   As soon as we reach port tonight,
   We're headin' for the shore!

3. And he kissed her on the neck, *etc.*

4. And he kissed her on the lips, *etc.*

5. And he kissed her on the arms, *etc.*

6. And he kissed her on the legs, *etc.*

Our next 'geographical' shanty takes us to the once savage Riff Coast of North Africa, lair of the Corsairs, with the romantic name of High Barbaree, the name also of the song. Apart from myself, Sampson alone gives it as a shanty. Whall gives it but only as a forebitter. It had several tunes, the liveliest one being used for the shanty, the solos of which are related to those of the first version I give of *Lowlands Low*. It was sometimes called the *Salcombe Seaman* and was sung solely at the capstan. First I will give the forebitter, the older and minor tune, for comparison. This was the tune my father would sing accompanied by a 'squeeze-box'.

HIGH BARBAREE
(Forebitter)

And here is the shanty form, which I had from my old friend Bill Fuller.

HIGH BARBAREE

2. 'Aloft there, aloft!' our bully [jolly] bosun cried.
  Ch. Blow high! Blow low! An' so sailed we!
  'Look ahead, look astern, look to weather an' a-lee!'
  Ch. All a-cruisin' down the coasts of the High Barbaree!

3. 'There's naught upon the starn, sir, there's naught upon the [our] lee,'
  Ch. Blow high, *etc.*
  But there's a lofty ship to wind'ard an' she's sailin' fast an' free.'
  Ch. All a-cruisin', *etc.*

4. 'O hail her! O hail her!' our gallant cap'n cried,
   'Are you a man-o'-war or a privateer?' cried he.

5. 'Oh, no I'm not a man-o'-war, nor privateer,' cried he,
   'But I'm a salt sea pirate, all a-lookin' for me fee!'

6. For broadside, for broadside a long time we lay [we lay all on the
   main],
   Till at last the *Prince o' Luther* shot the pirate's mast away [in twain].

7. 'O quarter! O quarter!' those pirates they did cry,
   But the quarter that we gave 'em, was to sink 'em in the sea [was we
   sank 'em in the sea].

Another tune—a West Country one—which was a forebitter but
may have been sung at the capstan, is the following:

HIGH BARBAREE

The original old English ballad on which this shanty and forebitter is based is to be found in Patterson's *Anthology*. It is entitled
*The Sailor's Onely Delight: Showing the Brave Fight between the George
Aloe and the Sweepstake and certaine Frenchmen on the Sea.* A version I
once heard—with a slightly different tune, gave for the second
refrain: 'An' the warm winds are blowin' down the High Barbaree.'

The wording of all the versions is very much alike, with some
differences in the names of the ships concerned and so on. Colcord
gives *Princess of Luther* and 'India merchantman or Yankee privateer'
in the question and answer. Some give: 'There's a rock upon the
quarter and a ship upon the lee.' Others sang: 'There's a wreck
away to wind'ard, and a ship all on the lee.' Some give the second
refrain as 'Cruisin' down along the coasts of the High Barbaree'.

Sharp's third and fourth verse come from the old forebitter called
The Princess Royal:

Then back up your topsails and heave your vessel to,
For we have got some letters to be carried home by you.

We'll back up our topsails and heave our ship to,
But only in some harbour and alongside of you.

The first couplet is also related to a verse in 'the Gam' version of *Rio Grande*.

Returning to our 'place name' shanties, both *Maryland* and *Marching Through Georgia*—marches of the American Civil War—were sung by seamen at the capstan, but since seamen did not alter their original words to any extent we will not repeat their well-known tunes and words here.

However, other marches were taken and altered somewhat, one of these being *Sebastopol*. Masefield gives it in his *Sailor's Garland*. It was popular from the Crimean War onwards and was used at the capstan. It was probably adapted for this use by seamen in the early steam troopships which carried a fair amount of square sail At one time, as Captain Robinson has pointed out, it was an unwritten law aboard these early sail-rigged steamers that steam power was not to be used when setting sail, etc., so shanties were still kept alive even in steam. The shanty is a broken-down version of the original march, or rather of its chorus. The original march tune was known as the 'Loth-to-depart, played by drum and fife bands when a regiment goes abroad' (*The Minstrelsy of England*, Duncan).

SEBASTOPOL
Alternative title, *Cheer, Boys, Cheer!*

2. The Russians they've bin put to flight,
   Ch. Sebastopol, *etc.*
   The Russians they've bin put to flight,
   Ch. Sebastopol, *etc.*

   Full Chorus. So sing cheer, boys, cheer,
   Sebastopol is taken!
   And sing cheer, boys, cheer,
   Old England gained the day!

322

OLD SWANSEA TOWN ONCE MORE

3. Our soldiers they are homeward bound,
   Our soldiers they are homeward bound.

4. We'll drink a health to all our men,
   We'll drink a health to all our men.

(*From F. Shaw*)

Our next item is also about a town. This is the very famous Welsh capstan song *Old Swansea Town Once More*. It was very popular in Welsh ships out of the Bristol Channel. Mr. Sullivan of Cardiff wrote and told me that it was always sung homeward bound in the little Welsh barques engaged in the Copper Ore Trade of the seventies and eighties. Scotch and Irish versions too exist, but first I will give the proper sailor version as sung at windlass and capstan.

OLD SWANSEA TOWN ONCE MORE (a)

323

2. Now when we're homeward bound, my dear,
   I'll bring you silks galore,
   I'll bring you jewels an' rings an' things,
   An' ye won't wear the weeds no more, old gal, old gal!
      Ch. You're the one I do adore,
         An' all I'm livin' in hopes to see,
         Is ol' Swansea Town once more, old gal, old gal!
         You're the one I do adore,
         So take me ropes an' make me fast,
         In ol' Swansea Town once more!

3. Now when we're leavin' 'Frisco Town,
   Outside of the Golden Gate,
   I'll write my last letter to you, me dear,
   Then ye won't have so long to wait, old gal, old gal!
      Ch. You're the one, *etc.*

4. An' when we're leavin' the old Fallerones,
   Bound for my ol' Swansea,
   I know ye'll pull, gal, on the string,
   For to haul me in from sea, old gal, old gal!

5. An' then when we've rounded old Cape Horn,
   Climbin' the hill for home,
   Passed the Western Islands into the Bay,
   We'll have no further for to roam, old gal, old gal!

6. An' then when we up Channel do sail,
   I'll pray that you'll be there,
   To wait, me dear, on Swansea pier,
   My lovely presents for to share, old gal, old gal!

7. When Swansea Town we're off once more,
   We'll see the lights so clear,
   I know that's Megan down on the pier,
   In her dimity apron dear, old gal, old gal!

The 'old gal, old gal!' at the end of each verse was usually sung in chorus.

Doerflinger gives a version much the same as this but he classes it as a main-hatch song and gives two slightly different choruses. The more usual form of this shanty, or rather, its forebitter form, is one that has been collected by G. B. Gardiner in Hampshire. I had this from Mr. Mansell Thomas (Head of Welsh Music, B.B.C., Cardiff).

OLD SWANSEA TOWN ONCE MORE (b)

With a swing.

Oh, fare-well to you my Nan-cy, Ten thou-sand times a- dieu, I'm bound to cross the o-cean girl, once

more to part with you, Once more to part from you fine girl, You're the girl that I.. a- dore, But ..

Ch.

still I live in hopes to see old Swan-sea town once more, Old Swan-sea town once more, fine girl, You're the

girl that I a- dore, But still I live in hopes to see, old Swan-sea town once more .

2. Oh, it's now that I am out at sea, an' you are far behind,
Kind letters I will write to you, of the secrets of my mind,
Of the secrets of my mind, fine girl!
You're the girl that I adore,
But still I live in hopes to see, old Swansea Town once more,
   Ch. Old Swansea Town once more, fine girl!
      You're the girl that I adore,
      But still I live in hopes to see,
      Old Swansea Town once more!

3. Oh, now the storm is rising, I can see it coming on,
The night so dark as anything, we cannot see the moon;
We cannot see the moon, fine girls!
Our rigging is all tore,
But still I live in hopes to see, old Swansea Town once more.

4. Oh, it's now the storm is over, and we are safe on shore,
We'll drink strong drinks and brandies too, to the girls that we
      adore,
To the girls that we adore, fine girls!
We'll make the tavern roar,
And when our money is all gone, we'll go to sea for more.

This version has obviously been 'toned down' a lot from original
sailor singing, but it is the version that is current and accepted
throughout the folk-song world. A slightly different version was
given me by Mr. H. G. Owen, Hon. Secretary of the Swansea and
District Shiplovers Society.

OLD SWANSEA TOWN ONCE MORE

Goodbye my lovely Nancy, ten thousand times adieu,
I'm going away for to leave you, once more to part from you . . .

and right throughout the song the plural is used . . .

You are the girls *we* adore.
Now *we* are out on the ocean.
And still *we* live in hope to see, *etc.*

Verse 3 is:

The night is dark and stormy, and our road seems all forlorn,
The good old ship is tossed about, our rigging is all torn.

And the last verse:

And the one that I adore,
We will drink strong wine and brandy too,
And we will make those taverns roar,
And when our money is spent and gone,
We'll go around Cape Horn for more, fine girls.

Other contributors (including an American collector, Mr. Lodewick) have given me *four-line* stanzas instead of eight. The four-line versions would be as a shanty, the eight-line when sung, as a forebitter. Mr. J. Hughes of the M.T. *Hoegh Eagle* has sent me the following:

1. Farewell, my lovely Diana, ten thousand times adieu,
I'm bound across the ocean, far, far away from you.
    Ch. Old Swansea town once more, fine girls you are!
    You're the girls I do adore,
    And still I live in hopes to see,
    Old Swansea town once more.

2. Now I'm on the salty seas, and you are safe behind,
Fond letters I will write to you, of the secrets of my mind.

3. The night was dark and stormy, you could scarcely see the moon,
And the good old ship was tossing about, her rigging was all torn.

4. Now the voyage is all over, and we are safe on shore,
We'll drink strong ale and porter, till we make the taprooms roar.
    Ch. And when the money is all spent, fine girls you are!
    We will go to sea for more,
    And still I live in hopes to see,
    Old Swansea town once more!

Note that here, instead of 'fine girl' or 'fine girls', 'fine girls you are!' is given, a line which in the Irish version was shouted out by all hands staccato.

Now we come to the Irish version. Not only was this sung aboard Irish ships at the capstan but it was also popular among the dockers of Cork and Cobh. Seamus Ennis of the B.B.C. obtained the following version from a colleague of his, Sean Mac Reamoinn (Radio Eireann), who picked it up from the dockers in 1949. The 'Holy Ground' is a poor quarter of Cobh, inhabited mainly by fishermen. This shanty is often referred to as *The Cobh Sea Shanty* and under this title has been broadcast from Radio Eireann. Mr. D. Maloney of Portchester, Hants, told me that his father, a native of County Cork, often sang this shanty in his youth, so it seems to be fairly old. The shouting out of the words 'Fine girls you are!' makes this shanty an unusual one.

THE HOLY GROUND ONCE MORE

2. And now the storm is raging, and we are far from Cobh,
   And the poor old ship she's sinking fast, and her riggings they are tore,
   And the secrets of my mind
       Ch. FINE GIRLS YOU ARE!
   You're the girl that I adore,
       Ch. And now we live in hopes to see,
           The Holy Ground once more,
           FINE GIRLS YOU ARE!

3. And now the storm is over, and we are safe in Cobh,
   And we'll drink one toast to the Holy Ground, and the girl that we adore,
   And we'll drink strong ale and porter,
       Ch. FINE GIRLS YOU ARE!
   And we'll make the tap-room roar,
       Ch. And when our money is all spent,
           We'll go to sea once more,
           FINE GIRLS YOU ARE!

Sometimes after the second verse the chorus went:

> And here's a toast to the Holy Ghost,
> And the Holy Ground once more!

This Irish version has much in common with that of Mr. J. Hughes' *Old Swansea Town*. Which port can claim to be the home of this shanty and forebitter it is difficult to say. Mr. D. Collings, a Naval officer friend of mine, declared he could see a likeness in its melody to that of the old folk-song *Prick'ty Bush* (Prickly Bush).

Our next shanty also refers to a town—Derby—and although it is given in many forms as a shore folk-song, and although Miss Colcord gives it as a forebitter, the version I give here *was* a shanty, according to my friend Bill Fuller, who had had it from older sailing ship men along with the information that it was sung mainly at pumps but sometimes at the capstan as well. The shore version, often referred to as *The Old Tup*, is of great antiquity and may have some connection with Ram and Goat Rituals of the Middle Ages. I have had to camouflage quite a lot as the sailors' version was markedly obscene.

DERBY RAM

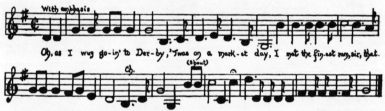

2. This ram an' I got drunk, sir, as drunk as drunk could be,
    An' when we sobered up, sir, we were far away out at sea,
        Ch. That's a lie, sir, that's a lie, sir,
            Oh, yes, me bullies, yer know yer tellin' a lie!

3. This wonnerful ol' ram, sir, wuz playful as a kid,
    It swollered the cap'n's spy-glass along wid the bosun's fid.

4. The night wuz very rough, sir, the wind like ice did feel,
    He borrowed me suit of oilskins an' took me trick at the wheel.

5. He climbed aloft so full of vim to stow the tops'l tight,
    But halfway up he lost his nerve, he had an awful fright.

6. One mornin' on the poop, sir, afore eight bells wuz struck,
   He climbed up to the skys'l yard an' sat down on the truck.

7. This wonnerful ol' ram, sir, he tried a silly trick,
   He tried to jump a five-barred fence an' landed in a rick.

8. This wonnerful ol' ram, sir, it grew two horns of brass,
   One grew out o' his shoulder blade, t'other turned into a mast.

9. An' when this ram wuz killed, sir, the butcher wuz covered in blood,
   Five and twenty butcher boys wuz carried away in the flood.

10. An' when this ram wuz dead, sir, they buried it in St. Joan's,
    It took ten men an' an elephant to carry one of its bones.

11. The crew of the good ship *Toxteth* is handsome, strong an' brave.
    The finest crowd of Jack-sprites that ever sailed over the wave.

In the original 'St. Paul's' was sung. In the last stanza the name of the ship would normally be the one the singer had shipped in.

Variants of the chorus are many. One was:

> Riddle to my rye, riddle to me rye,
> Yes, yes, a riddle, a riddle to me rye!

Miss Colcord gives:

> That's a lie, that's a lie, that's a lie, a lie, a lie!

But the commonest alternative found at sea (given by Bill Adams) was:

> Dinky, Dinky Derbyshire, dinky, dinky day!
> It was the finest ram, sir, that ever was fed on hay!

Our final 'geographical' item is *Alabama*, or as it was sometimes called *John Cherokee*. This is a typical work-song dating back to the days of Negro slavery either in the West Indies or the Southern States. Harding said it was in fairly common use among coloured crowds in the old West Indian Traders. He said it was a hauling song, and it certainly has a good rhythm in the refrains for two short drags, but Captain Robinson, who gives a slightly different version (in *The Bellman*, Minneapolis, 1917), states that it was used at the capstan. It probably was introduced to seamen by way of the cotton hoosiers of Mobile.

ALABAMA
Alternative title, *John Cherokee*

Oh, this is the tale of — John Cher-o-kee, A-la-ba-ma-John Cher'-kee! The In-jun man from Mi-ra-me-shee,

A-la-ba-ma, John Cher'-kee! With a haul-ey high an' a haul-ey low! A-la-ba-ma-John Cher'-kee!

2. They made him a slave down in Alabam,
   Ch. Alabama—John Cher'kee!
   He run away every time he can,
   Ch. Alabama—John Che'kee!
   With a hauley high, an' a hauley low!
   Ch. Alabama—John Cher'kee!

3. They shipped him aboard of a whaling ship,
   Agen an' agen he gave 'em the slip,
   With a hauley high an' a hauley low!

4. But they cotched him agen an' they chained him tight,
   Kept him in the dark widout any light.

5. They gave him nuttin' for to eat or drink,
   All of his bones began to clink.

6. An' now his ghost is often seen,
   Sittin' on the main-truck—all wet an' green.

7. At the break o' dawn he goes below,
   That is where de cocks dey crow.

Captain Robinson's version has a repeat of the third solo and refrain, with 'Way-aye-yah!' instead of my 'With a hauley high an' a hauley low!' His tale is much the same but Alabama in his song apparently dies on shore:

> So they bury him by the old gate post,
> And the day he died, you can see his ghost.

We will now bring in shanties bearing men's names as titles, commencing with a West Indian one called *Dan, Dan*. This is little more than a chant, and according to my informant, Harding, was one of the work-songs used ashore in the Antilles for hauling wooden shanties from one place to another, for working cargo, and so on, which later was taken to sea by coloured seamen and often heard aboard of West Indian squarerigged traders at halyards, the pull coming on the shouted 'ho!'. The Creole patois phrase is, I believe, a rather crude one.

DAN DAN

Our next is the rather notorious *Abel Brown the Sailor*. Miss Colcord is the only other writer who gives it, but she gives it as a forebitter, calling it *Abram Brown,* and the tune she gives is that of the fairly modern gramophone recording *Barnacle Bill the Sailor* (1930s). It was used for 'long drags' at t'gallant halyards and also for hand-over-hand hauling. I have marked my version for 'long drags'. I learnt this shanty on my first voyage to sea and I must say that it is entirely obscene. I have had to camouflage rather a lot but have kept partly to the original theme. 'Abel Brown' is probably the personification of all sailing ship A.B.'s or Able-Bodied Seamen.

ABEL BROWN THE SAILOR

(Verse 3 is sung to the same tune as verse 1; verse 4 to that of verse 2, etc.)

3. Oh, the mat is rough an' me skin ain't tough,
    Ch. Sez *Abel* Brown the Sailor!
   Oh, the mat is rough an' me skin ain't tough,
    Ch. Sez *Abel* Brown the Sailor!

4. You can sleep upon the shelf,
    Ch. Cried *the fair* young maiden!
   You can sleep upon the shelf,
    Ch. Cried *the fair* young maiden!

5. What 'ave yer got upon the shelf?
    Ch. Sez Abel Brown, *etc.*
   What 'ave yer got upon the shelf?
    Ch. Sez Abel Brown, *etc.*

6. I've got some rum upon the shelf,
    Ch. Cried the fair, *etc.*
   I've got some rum upon the shelf,
    Ch. Cried the fair, *etc.*

7. Me throat is long an' me thirst is strong,
    Ch. Sez, *etc.*
   Me throat is long an' me thirst is strong,
    Ch. Sez, *etc.*

8. What if you roll from off the shelf?
    Ch. Cried, *etc.*
   What if you roll from off the shelf?
    Ch. Cried, *etc.*

9. I'll bounce on the floor an' ask for more,
    Ch. Sez, *etc.*
   I'll bounce on the floor an' ask for more,
    Ch. Sez, *etc.*

10. What if the police should come to the house?
    Ch. Cried, *etc.*
   What if the police should come to the house?
    Ch. Cried, *etc.*

11. I'll take 'em on in two's and three's,
    Ch. Sez, *etc.*
   I'll take 'em on in two's an' three's,
    Ch. Sez, *etc.*

12. Then I'll let you stay with me,
    Ch. Cried, *etc.*
    Then I'll let you stay with me,
    Ch. Cried, *etc.*

This shanty would often be sung by two soloists or shantymen in similar manner to *Mobile Bay* and *Billy Boy*, one singer for the questions and one for the answers.

Now we have a shanty based fairly accurately on the life and times of Napoleon Bonaparte. This is called *Boney* which some authorities give as a halyard song and others as a 'short haul' or fore-sheet shanty. Both could be right; in the former the pulls would be as I have marked them in my version, in the latter cases the pull would be on the 'yah!' and '-swor!' The story was always the same, and no dirty versions, to my knowledge, existed. It probably had its origin in one of the many street ballads that emanated from the Napoleonic Wars. Doerflinger gives a couplet from two of these old ballads that have wording very similar to verses found in the shanty. I have stated that it was fairly accurate historically, but according to Miss Colcord a version exists in which Boney crosses the Rocky Mountains(!) and is sent to St. Helena all on account of a woman!

Sharp says that the name 'Boney' was usually pronounced 'Bonny', but, from what I can gather from shipmates and so on, I think this pronunciation was rare.

BONEY

2. Boney beat the Prussians,
    Ch. Way-aye-*yah*! [Away aye yah!, Timme way, hey, hya!]
   The Osstrians and the Rooshians,
    Ch. Johnny Franswor! [François]

3. Boney went to school in France,
   He learnt to make the Russians dance.

4. Oh, Boney marched to Moscow,
   Across the Alps through ice an' snow [Lost his army in the snow].

5. Boney wuz a Frenchyman,
   But Boney had to turn agen.

6. So he retreated back agen,
   Moscow wuz in ruins then.

333

7. Boney went to Elbow,
   There he got his overt'row
   [*or* Boney went to Elba,
      Wisht he'd niver bin there.]

8. He beat the Prussians squarely,
   He whacked the English nearly.

9. We licked him in Trafalgar's Bay,
   Carried his main topm'st away.

10. 'Twas on the Plains of Waterloo,
    He met the boy who put him through [The big-nosed Duke he put
    him through.]

11. Boney marched to Waterloo,
    And there he met his overt'row.

12. He met the Duke of Wellington,
    That day his downfall had begun.

13. Boney went a-cruisin',
    Aboard the Billy Ruffian.

14. Boney went to Saint Helen',
    An' he never came back agen.

15. They sent him into exile,
    He died on Saint Helena's isle.

16. Boney broke his heart an' died,
    In Corsica he wisht he styed.

17. He wuz a rorty general,
    A rorty, snorty general.

In verse 13 the 'Billy Ruffian' is of course the *Bellerophon*. Miss
L. A. Smith (*The Music of the Waters*) gives a verse about the Battle of
Marengo, and gives both refrains as 'Wae! Hae! Ha!' Other shanty-
men sang:

> Drive her cap'n, drive 'er. (*Repeat*)
> Give her the t'gallant sails. (*Terry*)
> It's a weary way to Mobile Bay ['Frisco Bay, *etc.*].

Most shantymen finished with:

> One more pull an' then belay.

In Doerflinger's book there is a version from the collection of James
H. Williams with refrains from *A Long Time Ago*.

When used for a long hoist it was usually sung at royals, heavy
stays'l, or light t'gallants'l, never, as Terry says, at topsails, for which
it would have been too fast.

There has been quite an argument as to why British sailors sang about a famous enemy—a senseless argument to my way of thinking. Sailor John in the main was, and still is, a cosmopolitan type of fellow, and if he spoke of 'furriners' with derision it was entirely without hate. In fact he liked to use 'furrin' words and phrases, as a glance at any old-time nautical dictionary will show.

A relation of *Boney* is *Hilonday* or as it might well be written *Highland Day*. Miss L. A. Smith has a pumping shanty, without the tune, which may be related:

> Highland day and off she goes,
> Off she goes with a flying foretopsail,
> Highland day and off she goes!

(From The Music of the Waters)

Both Terry and Miss L. A. Smith have a version, but mine comes from Harding.

HILONDAY

2. Oooh! Boney beat the Prussians,
   Ch. Ah *hilon*day!
   Rise me up, my yaller, yaller gals,
   Ch. Ah *hilon*day!

Subsequent verses are those of *Boney*.

This shanty was used at t'gallant halyards, and the second solo was always the same throughout. Alden and L. A. Smith give for this second solo: 'Sigh her up my yaller girls!' and Terry gives 'Oh, rise you up my yellar girls', and his final verse is: 'Oh, captain, make her nose blood' (*Twice*).

The next shanty *Billy Boy* is given by Terry as a Northumbrian capstan shanty, and he gives it in the Northumbrian dialect, but I rather fancy it had a wider field than Northumberland. I have met many seamen from London, Liverpool, and South Wales who also knew this shanty. Like Terry states, it had many unprintable stanzas not lending themselves to easy camouflage. There are two main versions, the well-known one and one in a minor key. Of course they have both stemmed from similar shore-songs of which there are many. At times two shantymen would sing, one for the questions and one for the answers. Bill Fuller, who had sailed in *Sunbeam I*, told me that Sir Walter Runciman would often sing it at the windlass aboard that vessel.

BILLY BOY (a)

Where have ye bin all the day, Bil-ly Boy, Bil-ly Boy? Where have ye bin all the day, me

Bil-ly Boy—? I've bin walk-in' on the quay-, With me charm-in' Nan-cy Lee-, An' sweet

Nan-cy tickled me fan-cy, oh, me charm-in' Bil-ly Boy—!

2. Is she fit to be yer wife, Billy Boy, Billy Boy?
    Ch. Is she fit to be yer wife, me Billy Boy?
  Aye, she's fit to be me wife as the fork is to the knife.
    Ch. An' sweet Nancy kittl'd [tickl'd] me fancy, oh, me charmin'
    Billy Boy!

3. Can she cook a bit o' steak, Billy Boy, Billy Boy?
    Ch. Can she cook a bit o' steak, me Billy Boy?
  She can cook a bit o' steak aye an' make a gridle [girdle] cake,
    Ch. And sweet Nancy, *etc.*

4. Can she make an Irish stew, *etc.*
  She can make an Irish stew, aye, an' singin' hinnies too [an' a Cornish
    pasty too], *etc.*

5. Does she sleep close unto thee, *etc.*
  Aye, she sleeps close unto me, like the bark is to the tree, *etc.*

6. Can she make a feather bed, *etc.*
  She can make a feather bed, fit for any sailor's head, *etc.*

7. Can she heave the dipsy lead, *etc.*

8. Can she strop a block, *etc.*

Here is the minor version:

BILLY BOY (*b*)

2. Can she cook, can she bake, Billy Boy, Billy Boy?
   Ch. Can she cook, can she bake, Billy Boy?
   Aye she can cook an' she can bake, she can make a saffron cake,
   Ch. She's the Nancy o' me fancy, and a sailor's pride an' joy!
   [*or* Sweet Nancy tickled me fancy, oh, me charmin' Billy Boy!]

3. Can she darn an' can she sew, Billy Boy, Billy Boy?
   Ch. Can she darn, *etc.*
   Aye she can darn an' she can sew, there is nought she cannot do,
   Ch. She's, *etc.*

4. Can she wash an' can she clean, Billy Boy, *etc.*
   Aye she can wash an' she can clean, an' she plays the tambourine,

And similar verses to the preceding version.
   Shore versions I have come across all have a common final refrain:

(*a*)

Oh, where have you been, Billy Boy, Billy Boy?
Oh, where have you been, charming Billy?
I've been to seek a wife, she's the joy of my life,
She's a young thing and cannot leave her mother.

(*b*)

Can she wash the linen clean, my boy Billy?
Can she wash the linen clean, could yer please tell me?
Aye, she can wash the linen clean, she can play a tambourine,
But she is too young to be taken from her mummy!

(*c*)

Can she cook, oh, can she bake, my Boy Billy?
Can she cook, oh, can she bake, my Boy Billy?
Yes she can cook and she can bake,
She can make a wedding cake,
But she is too young to be taken from her mammy!

(*d*)

Can she cook a cherry cake, Billy Boy, Billy Boy?
Can she cook a cherry cake, my charming Billy?
She can cook a cherry cake, she can cook and she can bake,
Because she was too young for to leave her mammy! (O!)

These 'young things' that cannot leave or be taken from their 'Mammies' seem to tie up *Billy Boy* with the timber droghers' shanty *My Bonnie Highland Lassie.*

And a recent popular radio number *Willie, can you cook?* seems to be another member of this 'Billy Boy' family.

There is a remarkable resemblance between our next two shanties *Billy Riley* and *Tiddy High O! Billy Riley* probably started life as a cotton-hoosiers' song, but at sea it was used at halyards. Several collectors give versions, and according to C. F. Smith it was known in Green's Blackwall ships about the eighteen fifties. The verses are mainly impromptu, subsequent verses sing about Little Jackie Riley, Missie Riley, and Billy Riley's other occupations. Miss Colcord has a different refrain for each stanza, substituting Missus Riley, Missy Riley, etc., for Billy Riley.

BILLY RILEY

2. Old Billy Riley wuz master of a drogher,
   Ch. Yo-*ho!* Billy Riley *oh!*
   Old Billy Riley screw [walk] him up so cheer'ly,
   Ch. Yo-*ho!* Billy Riley *oh!*

3. Old Billy Riley wuz a ladies' man, *etc.*

4. Old Billy Riley—little Missus Riley, *etc.*

C. F. Smith gives the refrain as 'Old Billy Riley O!' and she gives 'master of a drogher sailing to Antigua'. Sharp gives 'wake him up so cheerily' and has one pull in the refrains on the 'oh' after 'Billy Riley'.

Tiddy High O! was also a halyard song. Sharp gives a version slightly different in tune. This is one of Tobago Smith's who told me it was often heard aboard of the old West Indian traders. It is fairly safe to say that it is of West Indian origin and probably came to England aboard the rum and sugar traders of Bristol.

TIDDY HIGH O!

An' now we are bound for ol' Bris-tol town, Tid-dy high O! high hay! Good-bye to them black gals, the

yel-lars an' the browns, Tid-dy high O! high hay, high hay!

2. Oh, old Sally Rackett of Kingston Town,
   Ch. Tiddy high O! high *hay!*
   I spent quite a packet on her new silk gown,
   Ch. Tiddy high O, high *hay!* high hay!

3. We loaded our packet with sugar an' rum,
   Goodbye to Jamaicy, its gals, an' its sun.

4. We're bound to the nor'ard, to the ice an' the snow,
   We're bound to the nor'ard—O Lord let 'er go!

5. An' when we gets back to ol' Bristol Town,
   'Tis there we will drink an' sorrow soon drown.

Our next item was usually sung as a forebitter and probably started life in the Navy, on the China Coast. It was very popular with seamen of both services who had shipped 'out East'. I had my version from Bill Fuller, who declared that it was often used as a shanty when pumping ship. I have sung it myself in such capacity and how we used to roar out the chorus 'Hitchee Kum, Kitchee Kum, Ya! Ya! Ya!' 'Pidgin-English' songs were always very popular with Seamen of the Sail, and in the Swedish shanty book *Sång under Segel* and in the German shanty book *Knurrhahn* two or three are given, but they were only sung as forebitters so far as I know.

THE CHINEE BUMBOATMAN

2. Now Wing Chang Loo he fell in love, with a gal called Ah Chu Fong.
   She 'ad two eyes like pumpkin seeds, an' slippers two inches long,
   But Ah Chu Fong loved a pirate bold with all her heart an' liver,
   He wuz capitan of a double-decked junk, an' he sailed the Yang-Tze
     River-eye-iver-eye!
   Ch. Hitchee-kum, kitchee-kum, ya! ya! ya!
     Sailorman no likee me,
     No savvy the story of Wing Chang Loo,
     Too much of the bober-eye-ee, Kye-eye!

3. When Wing Chang Loo he heard o' this, he swore an' 'orrible oath:
   'If Ah Chu marries that pirate bold, I'll make sausage meat o' 'em
     both.'
   So he hoisted his blood-red battle flag, put into the Yang-Tze River,
   He steered her east an' south an' west, till that pirate he did diskiver-
     eye-iver-eye.
   Ch. Hitchee-kum, *etc.*

4. The drums they beat to quarters an' the cannons did loudly roar,
   The red-'ot dumplin's flew like lead, an' the scuppers they ran with
     gore.
   The pirate paced the quarter deck with never a shake nor a shiver,
   He wuz shot in the stern wi' a hard-boiled egg, that pinitrated his
     liver-eye-iver-eye.

5. The dyin' pirate feebly cried, 'We'll give the foe more shot,
   If I can't marry Ah Chu Fong, then Wing Chang Loo shall not.'
   When a pease-pudden 'ot hit the bumboat's side, it caused a 'orrible
   scene,
   It upset a pot of 'ot bow-wow soup, an' exploded the magazye-eenee-
   aye-eenee!

I think this is the first time that any version of our next contribu-
tion has been in print, that is tune and words. This is *The Bosun's
Alphabet* which, although a forebitter, was also used at the pumps.
I have not had the opportunity of seeing a version which Doerflinger
says is to be found in Thompson's *Body, Boots and Britches* (Philadelphia, 1940) called *The Sailor's Alphabet*. There is a version without
music in *Adventure* and Doerflinger has in the section of his book
Shantymen and Shanty Boys devoted to the songs of lumbermen a
related song called *The Lumberman's Alphabet*, which he states is
probably a hundred years old, being based, in all probability, on
the sailors' song. My tune is entirely different, but the wording of
my chorus bears some resemblance to his. I learnt this from Jack
Birch of Plymouth.

THE BOSUN'S ALPHABET
Alternative title, *The Sailor's Alphabet*

341

2. E is for the Earring when reefing we haul,
   F is for the Fo'c'sle where the bullies do brawl,
   Oh! G is for the Galley where the saltjunk smells strong,
   H is for the Halyards we hoist with a song.
      Ch. Soooo! merrily, so merrily, so merrily sail we,
         There's no mortal on earth like a sailor at sea,
         Blow high or blow low! as the ship rolls along,
         Give a sailor his grog an' there's nothing goes wrong!

3. I is for the Eyebolt—no good for the feet,
   J is for the Jibs, boys, stand by the lee sheet,
   Oh! K is for the Knightheads where the shantyman stands,
   L is for the Leeside hard found by new hands.

4. M is for the Maindeck—as white as new snow,
   N is for the Nigger gals in the land to which we go,
   Oh! O is for the Orlop, 'neath the 'tweendecks it lays,
   P is for the Peter flown on sailin' day.

5. Q is for the Quadrant—to the wheel it lies near,
   R is for the Rudder—it helps us to steer,
   Oh! S is for the Sheerpole over which we must climb,
   T is for the Topmen, 'way aloft every time.

6. U is for Uniform—only worn aft,
   V is for the Vangs running from the main gaff,
   Oh! W is for the Water—we're on pint an' pound,
   X marks the Spot where Ol' Stormy wuz drowned.

7. Y is for Yardarm—needs a good sailorman,
   Z is for Zoe—I'm her fancy-man,
   So this is the end of me bully ol' song,
   Heave away, bullies, oh, heave long an' strong!

An alternative chorus is:

BOSUN'S ALPHABET

So merrily, so merrily, so merrily sail we. There's no-one on
earth like a sailor at sea, Sing high, sing low, as the ship rolls a-
long. Give a sailor his rum an' there's noth-ing goes wrong!

Our next shanty is a pumping one, given only by Davis & Tozer
as a shanty and by other collectors as a forebitter. Apparently it

came to life in the eighteenth century as a shore ballad and several versions and variants are known both in Britain and in the United States. The Davis & Tozer version however could never have been sung as a shanty, since there is no refrain, not even the repeat of the last line—so common in Scandinavian and French shanties—that I and other collectors give. I have heard this sung by many wind-jammer men, and it was most certainly used when pumping ship out, but as far as I can ascertain it was never sung at capstan or elsewhere. The tune is reminiscent of *My Darlin' Clementine.*

THE SAUCY SAILOR BOY
Alternative titles, *The Saucy Jack Tar, Jack Tar*

2. 'No indeed I'll wed no sailor, for they smell too much of tar.
   You are ragged, you are sassy, get you gone, you Jackie Tar,
   Ch. You are ragged, you are sassy, get you gone, you Jackie Tar!'

3. 'I have ships all on the ocean, I have gold in great galore,
   Me clothes they may be all in rags, but coin can buy me more,
   Ch. Me clothes they may be all in rags, but coin can buy me more!'

4. 'If I'm ragged, if I'm sassy, it may be of tar I smell,
   Yet I've silver in my pocket, more than you can ever tell,
   Ch. Yet I've silver in my pocket, more than you can ever tell!'

5. When she heard him, that distressed her, down upon her knees she fell,
   Sayin', 'Ragged, dirty sailor boy, I love more than words can tell,
   Ch. Sayin', ragged, dirty sailor boy, I love more than words can tell!'

6. 'Do you think that I am foolish, do you think that I am mad,
   That I'd wed the likes of you, Miss, when there's others to be had,
   Ch. That I'd wed the likes of you, Miss, when there's others to be had!'

7. 'No indeed I'll cross the ocean, an' my ships shall spread her wings,
You refused me, ragged, dirty, not for you the wedding ring,
   Ch. You refused me, ragged, dirty, not for you the wedding ring!'

We will now include shanties which are woven round the ships themselves and their escapades, both factual and fictitious.

Our first has several titles. As an early Naval ballad it was called *La Pique* or *The Flash Frigate*, as a Sailor John's forebitter it was named *The Dreadnaught*, and as a capstan shanty its title, usually, was *The Liverpool Packet* or *Bound Away!* but quite often the last three titles were used indiscriminately.

Sampson and Patterson give it as a capstan shanty, other collectors as a forebitter.

THE 'DREADNAUGHT' (a)
Alternative title, *The Flash Packet*
(Tune same as *The Flash Frigate*)

1. There's a saucy wild packet, a packet o' fame,
She belongs to New York, an' the *Dreadnaught*'s her name;
She's bound to the west'ard where the wide waters flow,
Bound away to the west'ard in the *Dreadnaught* we'll go!

2. The time of her sailin' is now drawin' nigh,
Farewell, pretty maids, we must bid ye goodbye;
Farewell to ol' England an' all we hold dear,
Bound away in the *Dreadnaught*, to the west'ard we'll steer.

3. An' now we are haulin' out o' Waterloo Dock,
The boys an' the gals on the pierhead do flock;
They'll give us three cheers while their tears freely flow,
Sayin' 'God bless the *Dreadnaught* where 'ere she may go!'

4. Oh! the *Dreadnaught*'s awaitin' in the Mersey so free [in the River Mersey]
For the old *Independence* to tow her to sea [Awaitin' the tugboat to tow her to sea];
For to round the Rock Light [Black Rock] where the Mersey does flow;
Bound away in the *Dreadnaught*, to the west'ard we'll go!

5. Now the *Dreadnaught*'s a-howlin' down the wild Irish Sea,
Her passengers are merry, an' their hearts full o' glee;
Her sailors like tigers they walk to an' fro [like lions walk the decks to an' fro],
She's a saucy flash packet, O Lord let her go!

344

6. Now the *Dreadnaught*'s a-sailin' the Atlantic so wide,
   Where the high roarin' seas roll along her black side;
   With her topsails set taut for the Red Cross to show [With her sails
      tautly set for the Red Cross to show],
   Bound away to the west'ard—O Lord let her go!

7. Now the *Dreadnaught*'s becalmed on the Banks o' Newf'n'land,
   Where the water's so green an' the bottom's all sand;
   Where the fish o' the ocean do swim to an' fro,
   Bound away in the *Dreadnaught* to the west'ard we'll go!

8. Now the *Dreadnaught*'s a-lyin' off the Long Island shore,
   Awaitin' the pilot as we've waited oft before;
   'Fill away yer maintops'l, board yer main-tack also!'
   Bound away to the west'ard in the *Dreadnaught* we'll go!

9. Now the *Dreadnaught*'s arrived in New York once more,
   So go ashore, shipmates, to the land we adore;
   With wives an' wi' sweethearts so merry we'll be,
   An' drink to the *Dreadnaught* where'er she may be.

10. Then a health to the *Dreadnaught* and all her brave crew,
    To bold Cap'n Samuels an' his officers too;
    Ye may talk o' yer fliers Swallow-tail an' Blackball,
    But the *Dreadnaught*'s the flier [bloodboat] that can beat 'em all!
    [Talk about yer flash packets Swallow-tail an' Blackball,
    Now the *Dreadnaught*'s the flier that outsails 'em all!]

11. Now me story is ended and my tale she is told,
    Forgive me old shipmates if ye think that I'm bold;
    For this song was composed while the watch was below,
    Bound away to the west'ard in the *Dreadnaught* we'll go!

In 'Old Songs Men Have Sung' (*Adventure*), verse 9 runs:

> Now the *Dreadnaught*'s arrived in New York once more,
> We'll go up to Old Brannigan's, whom we all do adore;
> We'll call for strong liquor and be merry and free,
> An' we'll drink to the *Dreadnaught* where'er she may be.

As a forebitter the last line of each verse would often be sung in chorus, but when used as a shanty at the capstan this chorus would be added:

> Bound away! Bound away! Where the wide [wild] waters flow,
> Bound away to the west'ard in the *Dreadnaught* we'll go!

All versions I have heard or seen in print give the same geographical sequence, but Whall becalms her on the Banks (like the above) while others 'howl' her over the Banks; Whall 'howls' her through the Irish Sea. Frothingham's version (*Adventure*) has her 'a-bowling' down the Irish Sea and 'a-humming' down the Long Island shore, whereas others have her 'sailin'' down that shore. Doerflinger's singer names the 'bank'—the George's.

This forebitter was often sung, with the inconsequence typical of seamen, to the tune of another forebitter called *The Dom Pedero*, the first stanza of which ran:

> There is a flash packet, a packet o' fame,
> She hails from New York an' *Dom Pedero*'s her name,
> She's jammed up an' rammed up on deck an' below,
> We're bound for Shanghai in the *Dom Pedero*,
> *Ch.* Singin' down, down, down, derry down!

Here is the tune of *The Dom Pedero* joined to the words of *The Dreadnaught*.

THE DREADNAUGHT (*b*)

The *Dreadnaught* was a flash American clipper packet launched in 1853 and she was famous for her many smart passages across the Western Ocean (Atlantic). She belonged to the Red Cross Line and had a red cross on her fore tops'l. In verses 3 and 9 of my version (first tune) the lands of the singers' sweethearts and wives appear to get a bit mixed. Sometimes too the home port of the ship gets a bit mixed—no one seems to worry about the difference between *A* Liverpool Packet (one hailing from Liverpool and hence English) and *The* Liverpool Packet (one which trades to Liverpool—a Yankee).

THE LIVERPOOL PACKET

Now we have the capstan version.

THE LIVERPOOL PACKET (a)

At the Liv-er-pool Docks at the break o' the day, I saw a flash pa-cket bound west-ard a-way, She was bound to the west-ard where the wild wa-ters flow, She's a Liv-er-pool pack-et, Oh, Lord let 'er go! Bound a-way-ay! Bound a-way-ay! Through the ice, sleet an' snow, She's a Liv-er-pool pack-et, oh, Lord let 'er go!

2. Oh, the time of her sailin' is now drawin' nigh,
   Stand by all ye lubbers we'll wish ye goodbye;
   A pair o' clean heels to ye now we will show,
     Ch. She's a Liverpool packet—O Lord let her go! [O Lord let us go!
     or Good God let us go!]

   Full Chorus. Bound away! Bound away!
       Through the ice, sleet, an' snow,
       She's a Liverpool packet,
       Oh, Lord let 'er go! [Good God let 'er go!]

3. An' now we are leavin' the sweet Salthouse Docks,
   All the boys an' the gals on the pierhead do flock;
   All the boys an' the gals are all shoutin' hurro!
     Ch. She's a Liverpool packet—Oh, Lord let 'er go!
     Full Chorus. Bound away! Bound away! *etc.*

4. An' now we are waitin' in the Mersey so free,
   Awaitin' the tugboat to tow us to sea;
   An' we'll round the Rock Light where the salt tides do flow, [But
       when she's off soundings you shortly will know,]
     Ch. She's a Liverpool packet—Oh, Lord let 'er go!

5. Sheet home yer big tops'ls, haul aft yer jib sheets,
   Sheet home fore 'n' aft, boys, ye'll git no darn sleep;
   Come aft now, God damn yers, come aft one an' all,
     Ch. For over yer heads flies the bonnie Blackball!

347

6. An' now we are howlin' down the wild Irish Sea,
   Our passengers are merry, an' their hearts full of glee;
   Our sailors like tigers they walk to an' fro,
   Ch. She's a Liverpool packet—Oh, Lord let her go!

7. An' now we are sailin' the Atlantic so wide,
   An' the hands are now ordered to scrub the ship's side;
   Now then, holystones boyos, the bosun do bawl,
   Ch. For Kickin' Jack Williams commands this Blackball!

8. An' now we are off the Banks o' Newf'n'land,
   Where the bottom's all fishes an' fine yeller sand;
   An' the fishes they sing as they swim to 'n' fro,
   Ch. She's a Liverpool packet—Oh, Lord let 'er go!

9. An' now we're arrivin' in old New York town,
   We're bound for the Bowery, an' let sorrow drown;
   With our gals an' our beer, boys, oh, let the song flow,
   Ch. She's a Liverpool packet—Oh, Lord let 'er go!

The final line of each stanza used as chorus was, I feel certain, sung the same throughout originally, those of verses 5 and 7 being later interpolations. These two verses seem to have been purloined from *Blow the Man Down*. The packet here is not a Red Cross one as in the forebitter but a Blackball liner.

Sometimes the first verse ran:

There is a crack [flash] packet—crack [flash] packet of fame,
She sails [hails] from New York—ye all know her name [the so-and-so's her name].

Patterson as usual gives an intermediate chorus in the verse, but owing to the absence of melody he puts the collector at a disadvantage; we cannot decide whether such versions were sung or not:

And when we go sailing up the Long Island Sound,
   Ch. Bound away! Bound away!
With flags a-flying and shore-boats around;
   Ch. Bound away! Bound away!
Then the band's striking up, 'Yankee Doodle' will flow,
All welcome to the *Dreadnaught*,
O God, let us go!
   Ch. Bound away! Bound away!
      Through gale, hail, and snow,
      She's a Liverpool packet,
      O God let us go!

(J. E. Patterson, *The Sea's Anthology*, published by
                              W. Heinemann Ltd., London, 1913)

Our next shanty was very popular at capstan and pumps, in particular in ships in the South American Saltpetre Trade. My version comes from McArty, who served many years in this trade. Doerflinger gives a version and his singer, on what grounds I do not know, reckons the *Campanayro* (*Campañero*) was a vessel engaged in the Brazil Coffee Trade. It was well known to Liverpool seamen and lasted until the end of sail. I never heard any bawdy version. McArty, whose last ship was the *Falls of Garry*, told me that it was a fine song for getting out the anchors after having laid in some West Coast port for two or more months, and that there were many more verses, but these were all he could remember.

THE HANDY BANDY BARQUE

Alternative title, *The 'Campanayro' ('Campañero')*

2. I wuz not very long ashore in a place called Baltimore,
   When I shipped away to Rio de Janeiro,
   This packet oh I jined, I wuz sorry that I'd signed
   Ch. In that handy bandy barque the *Campanayro!*

THE HANDY BANDY BARQUE

Full Chorus. 'Tween the skipper, bosun, an' the pump,
They nearly druv me off me chump
In the handy bandy barque the *Campanayro,*
An' if ever I go to sea, no more West Coast Packets
for me,
Like that handy bandy barque the *Campanayro!*

3. Oh, she had a shanghaied crew from Hell an' Timbucktoo,
An' the bullies in six lingoes they did swear-O!
Her skipper wuz a dandy-O, far too fond o' brandy-O,
Ch. In that handy bandy barque the *Campanayro!*
Full Chorus. 'Tween the skipper, *etc.*

4. In the roundin' of Cape Stiff, we had a little tiff,
With the snifters of Tierra del Fuaygo,
It blew like hell all day, carried our tops'ls all away,
Ch. In that handy bandy barque the *Campanayro!*

5. In Cally-o we lay, just inside the Bay,
When the wind it blew up so bloomin' rare-O,
It blew like Barney's Bull, an' it nearly wrecked our hull,
Ch. In that handy bandy, *etc.*

6. A dose of Yeller Jack put the bullies on their back,
An' it even made the Old Man share his grog-O,
A Jonah's bitch wuz she, not meant for you or me,
Ch. Oh, that handy bandy, *etc.*

7. I skinned out in the port, by the jaunties I wuz caught,
But their hoosegow wuz a pleasant place to stay-O,
It wuz a home from home, better far than havin' to roam,
Ch. In that handy bandy, *etc.*

8. Ye may sail the whole world round, but never I'll be bound,
Will ye find a worser barque than this'n 'ere-O,
If ye'll take my advice, ye'll never jine her twice,
Ch. Oh, that handy bandy, *etc.*

An alternative way of singing bars 4 and 5 of the Introduction and
8 and 9 of verse 1 is the following:

Doerflinger's singer, Captain Patrick Tayleur, has three verses all
more or less in a mixed-up condition, as though the singer's memory
had failed him.

Another little-known capstan song, referring to a ship (probably fictitious) was *Aboard the 'Kangaroo'*. It appeared in the 'Port of Bristol Guide and Sailing List' (August 1949), and later in *Sea Breezes* (September 1949), both versions being those of Mr. Stanley Slade (who has since died), a Bristol seaman, then in his seventies, who stated that he had heard it sung as a boy in ships out of Bristol. Later he recorded his version with the idea of its being used in a film about Bristol; but for some reason or other this scheme did not mature. A copy of the recording was kindly sent me by Mr. Jack Knapman, who made it. My friend Mr. Elwell of the Isle of Man also knew this shanty and he informed me that it was often sung in Liverpool, in the 'free'n'easies' of the last century, along with two other ditties— *The Cruise of the 'Calabar'* and *Across the Western Ocean*. Mr. Slade stated that there were many verses, some unfit for publication. One verse went:

> He shipped as cook and cabin boy,
> On the Cardiff old Canal.

ABOARD THE 'KANGAROO'

2. I thought I'd like seafarin' life, so I bid my love adieu,
   And sailed away as bosun's mate, aboard of the *Kangaroo*.
     Ch. Oh, I never thought she would be false,
         Or ever prove untrue,
         As we sailed away from Bristol quay,
         On board of the *Kangaroo*.

3. You would not say it was her wealth that stole me heart away,
   She was starcher at a launderer's for eighteen-pence a day.

4. My love she was no foolish girl, her age it was two-score,
   My love she was no spinster, she'd been married twice before.

5. Paid off I sought her dwelling 'way on Bristol Down,
   Where an ancient dame upon a line was hangin' out her gown.

6. 'Where is my love?' 'She's married, sir, about six months ago,
   To a smart young man who's commander of a barge that trades in coal.'

7. Farewell to dreams of married life, to soapsuds and the blue,
   Farewell to all the Bristol gals, they're fickle-minded too.

8. I'll seek some distant foreign clime, no longer will I stay,
   An' on some Chinese Hottentot I'll throw this life away!

Mr. Elwell wrote in *Sea Breezes* (October 1949) that he re-membered a 'verse in the Bristol Chanty stating that the laundress used "Glenfield" starch', and Mr. Slade, writing in the same magazine, states that: 'A sailor in my young day always bought his young wife a washing tub so that she could earn some money while he was away at sea.'

I remember my own grandmother on my father's side—a sailor's wife—talking about 'the takkin' in o' washin'' which sailors' wives would do in the port of Plymouth whence she hailed.

In the recorded version which I have, Mr. Slade sings two of the above verses to one chorus, probably so as not to tire the listener! He also sings 'Be'minster Down' instead of 'Bristol Down'. As to the name of the ship Mr. Slade writes: 'There was a schooner named *Kangaroo*, 84 registered tons, built at Douglas in 1867, and owned by Mrs. Eleanor Qualtrough of Douglas, I.O.M. There were also two others, one owned in Halifax, N.S., and one in St. John's, New-foundland.' There was a sailing steamer also named *Kangaroo*.

Although this shanty bore the title *Bristol Sea Shanty* (in *Sea Breezes*) it appears that it was not the property of sailors sailing from Bristol alone, since my friend Seamus Ennis, the well-known folk-song collector (B.B.C.), found the following version in Ireland. As will be seen it gives Milford Bay (South Wales) as the port concerned, but the tune is definitely Irish. Seamus had it from Mrs. Elizabeth Cronin of Macroon, County Cork.

ON BOARD OF THE 'KANGAROO'

At first I was a waiter man that lived at home at ease - But now I am a ma-rin-er that ploughs the ang-ry seas - I al-ways liked sea-far-ing life and bid my love a-dieu - I shipped as stew'd and cook, my boys, on board of the 'Kan-ga-roo". Oh, I nev-er thought she would prove false or ei-ther prove un-true - Till we sailed a-way through Mil-ford Bay, On board o' the "Kan-ga-roo"!

2. 'Oh, think of me, oh, think of me,' she mournfully did say,
'When you are in a foreign land and I am far away.
Take this lucky threepenny bit, 'twill make you bear in mind
Of a loving, trusting faithful heart you have left in tears behind.'
    Ch. Oh, I never thought she would prove false,
        Or either prove untrue,
        Till we sailed away through Milford Bay,
        On board o' the *Kangaroo.*

3. 'Cheer up, cheer up, my own true love, don't weep so bitterly,'
She sobbed, she sighed, she choked, she cried, and could not say
        goodbye.
'Oh, I won't be gone so very long, just but a month or two,
And when I will return again, of course I'll marry you.'
    Ch. Oh, I never, *etc.*

4. Our vessel she was homeward bound from many a foreign shore,
And many a foreign present unto my love I bore.
I brought tortoises from Teneriffe and ties from Timbuctoo,
A china rat, a Bengal cat, and a Bombay cockatoo.

5. Paid off I sought her dwelling in a suburb of the town,
Where an ancient dame upon a line was hanging out her gown.
'Where is my love?' 'She's married, sir, about six months ago,
To a smart young man that drives the van for Chapping, Son and Co.'

6. Here's a health to dreams of married life, to soap, to suds, and blue,
Hearts, true lovers, patent starch and washing soda too.
I will go unto some distant shore, no longer can I stay,
And on some China Hottentot I'll throw myself away.

7. My true love she's not a foolish girl, her age it is two score,
My love she's not a spinster, she was married twice before.
I cannot say it was her wealth that stole me heart away,
She's a starcher and a laundress for eighteen-pence a day.

Another rather humorous shanty often sung at the pumps according to Paddy Delaney, another fine old seaman of the days of sail, was *The Ebenezer.* The air is probably an Irish fiddle tune. Doerflinger gives a version in his chapter on 'Forecastle Songs of the West Indies Trade', which has not my repeat of chorus, but otherwise in tune and wording is much the same. It is a typical product of the Irish Packet seamen. One or two parts have had to be altered to meet the demands of the censor. It has many Liverpool 'trimmings'!

THE EBENEZER

I shipped on board of the "E-ben-e-zer", Ev'-ry day 'twas scrub an' grease 'er, Send us a-loft to scrape 'er down, Ay

Ch.

if we growled they'd blow us down, Oh, git a-long boys, git a-long do, Han-dy me boys, so han - dy!

Git a - long boys, git a - long do, Han-dy me boys, so han - dy!

2. The Old Man wuz a drunken geezer,
   Couldn't sail the *Ebenezer*,
   Learnt his trade on a Chinese junk,
   He spent mos' time, sir, in his bunk.
       Ch. Oh, git along, boys, git along do,
       Handy, me boys, so handy!
       Git along, boys, git along do,
       Handy, me boys, so handy!

3. The Chief Mate's name wuz Dickie Green, sir,
   The dirtiest beggar ye've ever seen, sir,
   Walkin' his poop wid a bucko roll,
   May the sharks have his body an' the devil have his soul!
       Ch. Oh, git along, *etc.*

4. A Boston buck wuz second greaser,
   He used to ship in Limejuice ships, sir,
   The Limey packets got too hot,
   He jumped 'em an' he cursed the lot.

5. The Bosun came from Tennessee, sir,
   He always wore a Blackball cheeser,
   He had a gal in every port,
   At least that's what his missus thought.

6. The *Ebenezer* wuz so old, sir,
   She knew Columbus as a boy, sir.
   'Twas pump her, bullies, night an' day,
   To help her git to Liverpool Bay.

7. Wet hash it wuz our only grub, sir,
   For breakf'st, dinner, an' for supper,
   Our bread wuz tough as any brass,
   An' the meat wuz as salt as Lot's wife's ass.

8. We sailed away before a breezer,
   Bound away for Vallaparaiser,
   Off the Horn she lost her sticks,
   The molly-hawks picked up the bits.

PART FIVE

Pot-pourri of British, American,
French, German, and other Foreign
Shanties; Sweatin'-up and Hand-over-hand
Shanties, and Sing-outs; Go to Sea No More

E will now deal with a pot-pourri of shanties that
we have been unable to deal with in our previous
sequences.

Our first is *Handy, Me Boys* or as it was sometimes
sung *Handy, Me Girls*. This was a halyard song,
although some authorities give it as hand-over-hand. Lines from
this song were often purloined and sung to other hauling songs.
In fact, it seems that it was the shantyman's 'fall-back' when he ran
out of verses telling the regulation story—a few stanzas from this
would help him to 'string out' and complete the hoist. The shantyman normally started the song with an introduction. Some forms of
the tune of the refrains tend to sound like the bugle call 'Officers'
wives get pudding and pies'.

HANDY, ME BOYS (HANDY, ME GIRLS) (a)

Introduction. (Rather slow)

So ha-an-dy me boys, so han-dy, Why can't ye be - so han-dy-O! Ha-an-dy me boys, so
han-dy! Oh, up a-loft this yard must go, Ha-an-dy, me boys, so han-dy! Ooh! up a-lo-oft from
down be-low, Ha-an-dy me boys, so han-dy!

357

HAND-OVER-HAND AT THE FLYING JIB HALYARDS

'Hand, over hand, lads, we must reach . . .' (Hand-over-hand shanty)

HANDY, ME BOYS (HANDY, ME GIRLS)

2. Growl ye may, but go ye must,
     Ch. Handy, me boys, so *handy!*
   It matters not whether yer last or fust [Growl too much an' yer head
        they'll bust],
     Ch. Handy, me boys, so *handy!*

3. Oh, a bully ship an' a bully crew,
   Oh, we're the gang for to kick 'er through [put her through],

4. Yer advance has gone, yer at sea agen,
   Bound round the Horn through the hail an' rain.

5. Two months' advance we've blown away,
   So make yer port an' take yer pay.

6. Oh, up aloft wid tautened leach,
   Hand-over-hand gang ye must reach.

7. Rouse an' shake 'er is the cry,
   The bloody topm'st sheave is dry.

8. Oh, stretch it aft an' start a song,
   A damn fine song an' it won't take long.

9. Oh, up aloft from down below,
   To the sheave-hole she must go.

10. Haul away an' show yer clew,
    Oh, we're the bullies for ter drive 'er through.

11. Round Cape Horn we're bound ter go,
    Round Cape Stiff through the ice an' snow.

12. We're bound down south around Cape Horn,
    Ye'll git there sure as yiz wuz born. [Ye'll wish ter Hell ye'd niver bin
        born, *or* Yer boots an' clothes are all in pawn.]

13. I wish Jack Sprite'd keep his luff,
    The blighter thinks we've hauled enough.

14. Sing an' haul, an' haul an' sing,
    Up aloft this yard we'll swing [bring]. [Give one good jerk, the yard
        will spring.]

15. Up aloft that yard must go,
    For we are outward bound ye know. [For Mister Mate he told me so.]

16. To set the sail haul out each sheet,
    Haul upon the fall lads, two blocks meet.

17. A handy ship an' a handy crew,
    A handy Mate an' Old Man too.

359

18. A handy Bosun an' handy sails,
    A handy Chips ter drive the nails. [A handy rig, an' handy sails.]

19. A handy Cook an' Steward too,
    Who spoil the grub they give the crew.

20. We'll hoist 'er high afore we go,
    We'll hoist 'er high an' leave 'er so.

21. Oh, shake 'er up an' away we'll go,
    Be handy there wid a handy-O!

22. Be handy wid yer washin' [dhobi] gals,
    Oh, handy Round-the-corner Sals!

23. My fancyman's a dandy-O,
    He loves the gals who are handy-O. [But far too fond o' brandy-O.]

24. I thought I heard the Old Man say,
    Another pull an' then belay. [One more pull, lads, then belay.]

Davis & Tozer give a different tune:

SO HANDY, MY BOYS

Oh, up a-loft the yard must go, So han-dy, my boys, so han-dy, Oh, up a-loft, from down be-low, So han-dy, my boys, so han-dy

Shell too gives a widely different tune:

HAND O'ER HAND

A han-dy ship and a han-dy crew, Han-dy, my boys, so han-dy! A han-dy ship and a han-dy crew, Han-dy, my boys, a-way-O!

(From *The Shell Book of Shanties*, by permission of E. H. Freeman Ltd., Brighton.)

And finally here is another tune I picked up in Australia:

HANDY, ME BOYS (b)

A han-dy ship an' a han-dy crew, Han-dy me boys, so han-dy! A han-dy ship an' a han-dy crew,

Han-dy, me boys, so han-dy!

Sharp's shantyman (Short, I think) has, as usual, an interesting verse:

> Whenever you go to Playhouse Square,
> Gipsy Pole she do live there.

Our next item is a shanty I picked up in St. Lucia, B.W.I. I learnt it from a coloured shantyman, 'Harry Lauder', who told me that it was a very popular hauling song in his younger days in the West Indian Traders. But I have a feeling that it probably originated aboard Jimmy Nourse's 'coolie ships', where the crews, in the main, were Lascaris from India. If this is so then it is the only example we have of the type of shanty sung aboard of these ships—shanties in which pidgin English and shipboard Hindustani were freely mixed. In this example the words 'Eki dumah!' are probably a corruption of the Hindustani expression '*Ek dom*', i.e. one man. This shanty was used at halyards, the pull coming on the word 'Eki'.

EKI DUMAH! (KAY, KAY, KAY)

Kay, Kay, Kay, Kay! E-ki du-mah! Kay, Kay, Kay, Kay! E-ki du-mah! Som-er-set a-Kil-la cool-ie

man, E-ki du-mah! Som-er-set a-kil-la Bo-sun's mate, E-ki du-mah! Som-er-set a-Kil-la wire-fall, E-ki du-mah!

Som-er-set a-Kil-la cool-ie-man, E-ki du-mah! Kay, Kay, Kay, Kay! E-ki dumah! Kay, Kay, Kay, Kay! E-ki du-mah!

2. Kay, kay, kay, kay!
   Ch. *Eki* dumah!
   Kay, kay, kay, kay!
   Ch. *Eki* dumah!
   Sailorman no likee Bosun's Mate,
   Ch. *Eki* dumah!
   Bosun's Mate no likee Head Serang,
   Ch. *Eki* dumah!
   Head Serang no like Number One,
   Ch. *Eki* dumah!
   Number One no likee coolie man,
   Ch. *Eki* dumah!
   Kay, kay, kay, kay!
   Ch. *Eki* dumah!
   Kay, kay, kay, kay!
   Ch. *Eki* dumah!

Now we have a shanty which, as its name implies, was sung just prior to the ship arriving at the 'payin'-off' port. This was *One More Day*. It was sung at both windlass and pumps and was more of a favourite with Yankee crews than British. The collectors, as usual, differ as to its job aboard ship. Terry and Sharp give it as capstan, Bullen and Whall as halyards, Davis & Tozer at pumps, and Miss Colcord as windlass or capstan.

(*ONLY*) *ONE MORE DAY*
Alternative title, *Charlie, One More Day*

On-ly one more day me John-nies, One more day! Ooh, come rock 'n' roll me o - ver, On-ly one more day!

2. Don't ye hear the Old Man growlin'?
   Ch. One more day!
   Don't ye hear the Mate a-howlin'?
   Ch. Only one more day!

3. Don't ye hear the caps'n pawlin'?
   Don't ye hear the pilot bawlin'?

4. Only one more day a-howlin',
   Can't ye hear the gals a-callin'?

5. Only one more day a-rollin',
   Can't ye hear them gulls a-cawin'?

6. Only one more day a-furlin',
   Only one more day a-cursin'.

7. Oh, heave an' sight the anchor, Johnny,
For we're close aboard the port, Johnny.

8. Only one more day for Johnny,
An' yer pay-day's nearly due, Johnny.

9. Then put out yer long-tail blue, m'Johnny,
Make yer port an' take yer pay, Johnny.

10. Only one more day a-pumpin',
Only one more day a-bracin'.

11. Oh, we're homeward bound today, me Johnny,
We'll leave 'er without sorrer, Johnny.

12. Pack yer bags terday, me Johnny,
Oh, an' leave her where she is [lies], Johnny.

13. Only one more day a-workin',
Oooh, come rock 'n' roll me over.

Very often the second solo line was the same in each verse, merely a repeat of 'Oooh, come rock 'n' roll me over!' and many seamen sang for the final refrain, 'Charlie, one more day!'

It was quite common too to carry on with a grand chorus after the above two solos and two refrains. This chorus would be nothing more than a repeat of the solos and refrains:

> Only one more day, me Johnnies,
> One more day,
> Oooh, come rock 'n' roll me over,
> Only one more day!

Miss Colcord gives in her *Songs of American Sailormen* a rather different tune with a full chorus.

ONE MORE DAY

Oh, have you heard the news, my Johnny? One more day! We're home-ward bound to-morrow,

One more day! On-ly one more day, my Johnny, One more day! Oh, rock and row me

O-ver.., One more day!

(By permission of W. W. Norton & Co., N.Y.)

It is fairly certain that this shanty was one used by the cotton hoosiers of Mobile, later taken to sea by white seamen, but some of its features point to it being originally a riverman's song. The rivermen were the 'ditch-hogs' already mentioned in reference to the *Hog-eye Man*, men who worked on the inland waterways, the great rivers and canals, of America. These men had many songs of their own, some of which undoubtedly reached deep water. The *Hog-eye Man* of course was one, *Shenandoah* may have been another—the Missouri, Mississippi, and Ohio being the chief rivers where these rivermen were to be seen at work. *Roll the Woodpile Down* was another shanty connected with the rivers, probably the Mississippi, on the banks of which woodpiles would be dotted awaiting the fuelling of the early paddle-steamers, which burnt only wood.

As will be noticed both 'Rock 'n' *roll* me over' and 'Rock 'n' *row* me over' were sung in this shanty—the 'row' pointing to its river origin and being probably the older refrain.

A Bluenose shipmate of mine, Ezra Cobb, used to sing a version with different words and tune which places the shanty fairly definitely as a river-song. Here it is:

ROCK 'N' ROW ME OVER

2. Oh, row me to my lover,
    Tell him I won't delay,
    Soon we will be in clover,
    One more day.
        Ch. Only one more day for Johnny,
            One more day,
            Oh, rock 'n' row me over,
            One more day!

3. Oh, Johnny he's a rover,
    He says he'll sail away,
    He wants to leave the river,
    One more day.

4. But stay, my John, and tarry
   For just another day;
   'Tis you I want to marry,
   One more day.

Captain Robinson in *The Bellman* gives a version with a tune very similar, with 'row' instead of 'roll', and although his verses tell the same sort of story they are much more sentimental than Cobb's. 'The tempest loud is storming'—one of his lines—would never have been concocted by a sailor, and I doubt if even rivermen would have reached such a poetic flight of fancy.

The phrase 'rock 'n' roll!'—so popular with modern youth!—goes back quite a bit with seamen, being a very common shout at both capstan and halyards to encourage the effort. It is, I think, of Southern State origin.

Sharp's verses are reminiscent of *South Australia* and *Lower the Boat Down*.

There is one thing that grieves me,
   Ch. For one more day,
There is my wife and baby,
   Ch. For one more day.

I'm bound away to leave you,
Don't let this parting grieve you.

The following shanty is given by Miss C. F. Smith only. She says: 'This rather pretty little anchor song, which I think does not appear in any other collection, dates back to the early fifties, when it was a favourite in ships outward bound from the London River. . . . The first verse only is traditional. . . .' Miss Smith adds two more verses, having taken 'the liberty of acting shantyman for once'. She seems to think that originally it may have been an emigrant song.

I'M BOUND AWAY

For the sake of you, my lassie, I'm bound a-way, my lassie, For the sake of you, my lassie, I'm bound a-way!

(From C. F. Smith, *A Book of Shanties*, Methuen & Co., Ltd., 1927—By permission.)

Our next item, *Home, Dearie, Home*, is obviously a shore-song taken over by seamen for use at the capstan. Several variants of the tune exist, although the versions of all those sung as forebitters have similar words. Apart from myself, Davis & Tozer, and Miss L. A. Smith are the only collectors who give it as a shanty, although in each case their version is the forebitter one which probably was often used at the capstan. Both the North Country and the West Country have versions; it was an equal favourite among seamen of the Tyne and of the Bristol Channel. W. E. Henley apparently rewrote the old folk-song version about 1878. The original Northumbrian tune was in a minor key, giving Amble as the home port concerned. First I will give the West Country forebitter which may have been sung as a shanty at the anchor capstan.

HOME, DEARIE, HOME
Alternative title, *The Oak and the Ash*

2. In Plymouth town a-walkin' a lady I did meet,
   With her babe on her arm as she walked down the street,
   And I thought how I'd left with the cradle standing ready,
   An' the pretty little babe that had never seen its daddy.
   Ch. Then its [Singin'] home, dearie, home, oh 'tis home I wanter be,
   An' 'tis home, dearie, home, far across the rollin' sea.
   For the oak an' the ash an' the lovely ellum tree
   Are all a-growin' green in my own counteree [the West Counteree].

3. Oh, an' if it 'tis a girl, she shall then live with me,
   And if it be a boy he shall ship away to sea,
   With his tarpaulin hat an' his pea-jacket blue,
   He shall walk the quarterdeck like his daddy used to do.
   Ch. Then it's home, *etc.*

And here is the North Country form, which Davis & Tozer give as an anchor shanty, calling it *Hame, Dearie, Hame.*

366

HOME, DEARIE, HOME

2. The clouds are high an' steady, the wind is comin' free;
   We'll hoist our main t'gans'ls an' speed across the sea;
   We'll head across the seas, m'boys, your love shall be my guide,
   An' soon we'll be safe moored at last an' by my dear one's side.
   Ch. Then 'tis home, dearie, home, aye, 'tis home I want to be,
       Our tops'ls are hoisted an' we must out to sea.
       For the oak an' the ash an' the bonnie birchen tree
       Are all a-growin' green in the North Countree [North-a-
       countree].

3. Ye told me in my dreams last night that a little one had come;
   Your face was shinin' clear an' bright, you bade me hurry home.
   Ye said, 'My dear, the days are long, when ye are far from me.'
   So now I'm sailin' for my home, my wife an' babe to see.

4. An' if it be a lass she shall dress in silken sheen,
   But if it be a boy he shall serve our gracious Queen;
   He shall walk the quarterdeck like a sailor bold an' true,
   An' fight for home an' countree like his daddy used to do.

As both the foregoing were rather sentimental, as shanties run,
Sailor John produced another—a true shanty—which in its entirety
was obscene to a degree. I had this from a former sailing-ship
carpenter called Anderson who had often shipped in Vickers' big
four-posters of Liverpool, where he told me it was one of the most
popular of homeward-bound shanties for use at the capstan.

HOME, HOME, HOME

2. She took her fine young sailor-boy an' asked him in to tea,
An' for a while the pair did dine an' sing quite merrily,
An' then he brought his rum-flask out and offered her a dram,
And from that moment onwards, oh, her troubles they began.
    Ch. Singin' home, home, home I wanna be,
        Singin' home, home, in the only counteree,
        For the pine an' the ash an' the bonnie ellum tree,
        Are all a-growin' green in sweet Nort' Amerikee!

3. She had no lovin' husband for to save her from his spell,
She had no kind young sister, did our sorry little Nell,
An' very soon she'd furled her sail an' struck her colours down;
An' then he left that fair young maid, that gal from London town.
    Ch. Singin', *etc.*

4. The very next day he sailed away, but before he went aboard,
He gave her a silver dollar for to pay her for his board,
An' as he waved a last farewell, our little Nell she knew
She'd never see that lad again, her darlin' o' the crew.

5. He said to her before he sailed, 'Now when our babe do come,
You will make a sailor o' him, if he do be a son;
With his tarpaulin hat an' his coat o' navy blue,
Oh, let him climb the riggin' like his daddy used to do.'

6. Now all you young maidens, oh, a warnin' take from me,
   Never let a sailor give you drinks too fast an' free.
   For I trusted one and he deceivèd me,
   An' now he's gone an' left me with a daughter on my knee.

Alternative ways of singing the stanzas are:

1. There once was a servant girl in Sackville Street did dwell,
   Well in with the Missus an' the Master as well,
   Early one mornin', oh, a sailor came from sea,
   And that was the beginning of all her sweet miseree.
2. (*First couplet*) He asked for a candle for to light him up to bed,
   He asked for a handkerchief to wrap around his head. . . .

(A similar couplet to this is to be found in verse 9 of *The Wexford Girl* in *Ballads and Sea Songs From Nova Scotia*.)

3. . . . that girl from Dublin town.

4. (*First couplet*) Early next mornin' the sailor he awoke,
   Put his hand in his pocket an' he pulled out a note. . . .

5. (*First couplet*) Now if it be a daughter, oh, bounce her on yer knee,
   And if it be a son pack the laddie off to sea. . . .'

In the chorus besides birchen tree and ellum tree some singers would give ivy tree.

This was one of the several homeward-bound songs which upset the theory offered by collectors that the homeward-bound shanty was never polluted with dirty themes. *Jamboree* is another.

A 'pop' song of fairly recent years—*Lulu had a Baby*—has used stanzas from this shanty, with a chorus taken from an old forebitter—a proper rude one—which ran:

Muck-shoot, cap-box, ditty-box,
She was one of the flash gals,
Dressed in the rig of the day!

Another shanty I picked up from old 'Harry Lauder' was *Pay Me the Money Down*.

This I think is a typical example of a West Indian shore work-song being taken to sea and adapted by sailors for use as a hauling song. Miss L. A. Smith who gives the words and music of one verse in her *Music of the Waters* (1888) writes that it was used at the pumps, but my West Indian friend said that it was used on shipboard as a halyard song. I have been unable to track down the origin of the modern 'pop' number *Pay Me My Money Down*, a number sung in the calypso manner by skiffle groups, but I feel sure that there is a relationship between this and the shanty, at any rate some of the verses seem to be related.

Miss L. A. Smith writes that the tune of the shanty is a variant of that of *Paddle Your Own Canoe*.

PAY ME THE MONEY DOWN

Your mon-ey young man is ye ob-ject to me, Pay me the mon-ey down! Oh, mon-ey down, oh,

mon-ey down, Pay me the mon-ey down!

2. I went for a cruise, boys, around the town,
   Ch. Pay me the money *down*!
   I there met a gal called Sally Brown,
   Ch. Pay me the money *down*!

3. I put me arm around her waist,
   Sez she, 'Young man, yer in great haste.

4. 'My price for love is half a crown,
   An' money down, 'tis real money down.'

5. Oh, the Yankee dollar some gits for their pay,
   Will buy us rum, boys, for many a day.

6. A dollar a day is a white man's pay,
   Stowin' cotton all the day.

7. Oh, if I had silver dollars galore,
   I'd pack me bags and stay on shore.

8. I wisht I had ten thousand pound,
   I'd sail this ol' world, around an' around.

9. I wisht I wuz Ol' Stormy's son,
   I'd build a ship o' a thousan' ton.

10. We'd stay at the ports where we wuz in,
    Drinkin' beer an' whisky an' gin.

11. When the ship it ties up an' the voyage is through,
    I wants me pay, sir, every sou.

English and American terms for money were, and still are, used indiscriminately in the West Indies.

Here are some extra stanzas given by Harding.

> The bumboatman he said to me,
> 'Bottles o' rum I don't give free.'

> My fancy gal she said to me,
> 'I don't give me favours free.'

370

The Madam said to me one day,
'You've had yer fun so don't delay.'

The tailorman he said to me,
'Ye'll pay me 'fore ye leave for sea.'

The judge he said, 'Look 'ere you mug,
Ye'll pay yer fine or ye'll go to jug!'

SLACK AWAY YER REEFY TAYCKLE

Ev'ry good ship has an an-chor, Ev'ry an-chor has a shank, An-y boy'll chase a mai-den if she's mop-y by the ... Slack a-way yer reef-y tay-ckle, reef-y tay-ckle, reef-y tay-ckle, Slack a-way yer reef-y tay-ckle, me sheets they are jammed!

2. Every good ship has a lifeboat, every lifeboat carries oars,
   Every boy forgets the maidens left on foreign ——
   Ch. Slack away yer reefy tayckle, reefy tayckle, reefy tayckle,
   Slack away yer reefy tayckle, me sheets they are jammed!

3. Every good ship has a sidelight, every sidelight has a screen,
   Every boy forgets the maiden left on the village ——
   Ch. Slack away, *etc.*

4. Every good ship has a mains'l, every mains'l has a clew,
   Every maiden loves a sailor rigged in navy ——

5. Every good ship that goes alongside, makes fast to the quay,
   Every girl likes a sailor who spends fast and ——

Slack Away Yer Reefy Tayckle was both a capstan and pumps song
as well as an old forebitter. Doerflinger gives a fragment in his
'Main Hatch Songs' section of *Shantymen and Shantyboys*, but his
version, probably of Naval origin, and recorded by Tayluer, has a
different tune from mine, a tune reminiscent of *Believe Me If All
Those Endearing Young Charms.* I had this shanty from 'Big Mac',
an A.B. called MacDonald, who, in the First World War, when
ships of all kinds were in great demand, had sailed from New
Zealand, round the Horn, to Europe, in a resuscitated squarerigger
—she had been a coal-hulk after a lifetime of deep-sea sailing—

called the *Dartford*, if I remember rightly. Jack Birch of Plymouth also gave me some stanzas, although he sang the refrain:

Heave away yer tops'l halyards, tops'l halyards, tops'l halyards,
Heave away yer tops'l halyards—the good ship lies low!

The omission of the last word of each stanza is correct, but I have had to use a different word at the end of each first line, and camouflage each second line a little.

Jack Birch would often sing a pseudo-Dutch or German version :

Mein fader vos ein Dutchman, ein Dutchman, ein Dutchman,
My fader vos ein Dutchman, Ach! Gott for dommey!
Ch. Heave away yer tops'l halyards, tops'l halyards, *etc.*

Another pseudo-Dutch shanty was *Yaw, Yaw, Yaw*, usually sung at the pumps. It was obscene throughout and both Doerflinger and my friend the late Professor J. Glyn Davies give camouflaged versions.

YAW, YAW, YAW! (JA, JA, JA!)

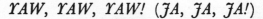

2. Und der polis-man, fireman, steeple-man,
   Ch. Mit mein yaw, yaw, yaw!
   Und der polis-man, fire-man, steeple-man,
   Ch. Mit mein yaw, yaw, yaw!
   Dey all climb upon de steeples,
   Und dey laugh do all the peoples,
   Ch. Mit mein yaw, yaw, yaw!

3. Oh, ven I vos ein sailor,
   Ch. Mit, *etc.*
   Oh, ven I vos ein sailor,
   Ch. Mit, *etc.*
   Vell ve trink up all de visky,
   An' it make us all feel frisky,
   Ch. Mit, *etc.*

4. Ve did all de bublic-houses,
   Ve did all, *etc.*
   Und ve hitched up all der trousers,
   Und ve catch 'em all de louses.

5. Ve chase all der bretty frauleins,
   Ve chase, *etc.*
   Und ve catch 'em und ve tease 'em,
   Und ve hook 'em und ve kees 'em.

Our next is one I picked up in the West Indies—*Won't Ye Go My Way?* This was a common hauling song among coloured seamen and was even a favourite with white sailors. Terry and Sharp both give a version much the same as mine. The pull came on the word 'go' in both refrains.

WON'T YE GO MY WAY?

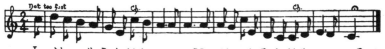

I met her on the Bow-ry. Won't yiz go my way? I met her on the Bow-ry. Won't yiz go my way?

2. She backed her main-tops'l smartly,
   Ch. Won't yiz *go* my way?
   Yo-ho, me Jack-me-hearty,
   Ch. Won't yiz *go* my way?

3. She spent me money freely,
   She grabbed the lot or nearly.

4. An' now that I am married,
   I'm glad I didn't tarry.

5. Oh, round her up so hearty,
   Yo-ho, oh, Jack-me-hearty.

6. Oh, Julia, Anne, Maria. (*Repeat*)

The pumping song we now give is in print for the first time. Owing to its ribald theme much 'blue-pencilling' has been done. It was popular in British ships only. It may have given rise to the popular war-song *Roll Me Over in the Clover!*

373

PUT YER SHOULDER NEXT TO MINE AND PUMP AWAY!

Oh, once I had a girl, had a girl, Had a girl! Oh, once I had a girl, had a

girl, Had a girl! Oh, once I had a girl, she put me in a whirl, Put yer shoul der next to

mine, an' pump a-way—, pump a-way, Put yer shoul-der next to mine, an' pump a-way!

2. She had me on a string, on a string,
    Ch. On a string!
She had me on a string, on a string,
    Ch. On a string!
She had me on a string, I bought her everything,
    Ch. Put yer shoulder next to mine an' pump away, pump away,
    Put yer shoulder next to mine an' pump away!

3. When I came home from sea, home from sea,
    Ch. Home from sea!
When I came home from sea, *etc.*
When I came home from sea I brought her gifts so free,
    Ch. Put yer shoulder, *etc.*

4. I brought her presents one, presents one, *etc.*
I brought her presents one, she said I shouldn't have done, *etc.*

5. I brought her presents two, *etc.*
    . . . and her heart she let me woo.

6. I brought her presents three . . .
    . . . and she caught me by the lee.

7. I brought her presents four . . .
    . . . and she met me on the shore.

8. I brought her presents five . . .
    . . . she was very much alive.

9. I brought her presents six . . .
    . . . and that one did the trick.

10. I brought her presents seven . . .
    . . . she said she was in heaven.

11. I brought her presents eight . . .
    . . . and I took her for my mate.

12. I brought her presents nine . . .
    . . . the baby's doing fine.

13. I brought her presents ten . . .
    . . . now we start all over again.

A halyard shanty which is related to *A Long Time Ago* is the one called *A Hundred Years Ago* or *'Tis Time for Us to Go*. I believe this to be the shanty mentioned by Dana (*Two Years Before the Mast*) which he calls *Time for Us to Go*, although it is possible that he may have been referring to a version of *Leave Her, Johnny, Leave Her*, often called *Time for Us to Go*.

Chorus variants

      First—Oho, yes, oho!
           Oh, yes, oh!
           Oh, aye, oh!

    Second—A hundred years ago.
           'Tis time for us to go.
           Oh, time for us to go.

This shanty has two main tunes, both equal favourites at halyards. The first I had from an English sailor, the second I learnt in the States. It was sung mainly at t'gallant halyards.

A HUNDRED YEARS AGO (a)
Alternative title, *'Tis time for us to go!*

Oh, a hun-dred years is a ve-ry long time. Oh, aye oh! A hun-dred years is a ve-ry long time, A hun-dred years a-go!

2. Oh, a hundred years on the Eastern Shore,
    Ch. Oh, aye oh!
  A hundred years on the Eastern Shore,
    Ch. A hundred years ago! ['Tis *time* for us to *go!*]

3. Ol' Bully John from Baltimore,
    Ch. Oh, aye, etc.
  I knew him well on the Eastern Shore [that son-o'-a-whore],
    Ch. A hundred, etc.

4. Ol' Bully John was the boy for me,
  A bully on land, an' a bucko at sea.

5. Ol' Bully John I knew him well,
  But now he's dead an' he's gone to hell.

375

6. He's as dead as a nail in the lamproom door,
   He's dead as a nail, that son-o'-a-whore. [He won't come hazin'
   us no more.]

7. A hundred years have passed an' gone,
   'Tis a hundred years since I made this song.

8. They used to think that pigs could fly,
   Can you believe this bloody lie?

9. They thought the stars were set alight
   By a bunch o' angels every night.

10. They thought the world was flat or square,
    That old Columbus never got there.

11. They thought the moon was made o' cheese;
    You can believe it if yer please.

12. They thought that mermaids were no yarn,
    But we know better 'cos we can learn [larn].

13. They hung a man for making steam,
    They pitched his body in a stream.

14. Oh, a very long time an' a very long time,
    'Tis a hell o' a time since I made this rhyme [line].

15. Oh, don't yiz hear the Old Man say,
    Just one more pull, lads, then belay!

Here is the second tune to which the same words were sung.

A HUNDRED YEARS AGO (b)

A hun-dred years op the East-ern Shore, the yes, ho! a hun-dred years op the East-ern Shore, a hun-dred years a-go!

This tune is given by Terry and others. The Blackball version as well as other versions of *A Long Time Ago* were also fitted to this halyard shanty.

The shanty I have named *Saltpetre Shanty* was a great favourite with crews of ships in the Saltpetre and Guano Trades of the West Coast of South America; it is one of four shanties rarely heard in other trades, the other three being *Rollocky Randy Dandy O!*, *Serafina*, and *The Girls of Chili*. They were all well known to Liverpool sea-men, but have rarely found their way into print owing to the difficulty of camouflaging them: they were all obscene to a degree, even the refrains and choruses being extremely bawdy. Captain Robinson in *The Bellman* is the only person who has 'had a go' at titivating them up. As he points out: 'many of these bawdy refrains were nothing more than Sailor John's obscene renderings of snatches of "Dago" phrases picked up in the Chilian ports.'

I had this one from Spike Sennit, an old sailing-ship A.B. It was used at the capstan.

SALTPETRE SHANTY

To ol' Cal-ly-o we are bound a-way-ay, Oh, rooll! To ol' Cal-ly-o we are bound a-way-ay, Oh,

rooll! We're bound a-way from Liv-er-pool Bay, oh, then pu-tas o'Chi-li will grab all our pay, Oh,

rooll! Rock yer bars! Heave 'er high-O, rock 'er, oh, rooll!

2. Old Pedro the crimp, boys, we know him of old,
   Ch. Oh, rooooll!
   Old Pedro the crimp, boys, we know him of old,
   Ch. Oh, rooooll!
   He's primin' his vino an' dopin' his beer,
   To the Chinchas he'll ship us if we don't steer clear,
   Ch. Oh, rooooll! Rock her bars!
   Heave 'er high-O, rock 'er, oh rooll!

3. Them putas o' Chili, they're hard to beat,
   Ch. Oh, rooll!
   Them putas o' Chili, they're hard to beat,
   Ch. Oh, rooll!
   They'll greet us an' love us an' treat us to wine,
   But them bastards is robbin' us most of the time,
   Ch. Oh, rooll! Rock yer bars,
   Heave her, *etc.*

Miss Colcord has reprinted Robinson's version which both call *Slav Ho!* One verse only is given, camouflaged even more than mine, with imitative Spanish words in the refrains.

And now we come to a great favourite for pumping the ship out. This is *Fire Down Below*. It has two main verbal forms as well as three distinct tunes. The first version I give, which in the main was the form sung by Bosun Chenoworth, is the last shanty to have been

sung aboard a British squarerigger since it was sung at the pumps
aboard the four-masted barque *Garthpool* sometime towards the end
of October 1929, a week or so before being wrecked on Ponta Reef,
East Sandhead, Bōa Vista, Cape Verde Islands. I had the honour
of being the shantyman at the time.

FIRE DOWN BELOW (a)

She wuz just a vil-lage mai-den with red an' ro-sy cheeks, To mee way, hay, hee, high, ho! Oh, she
went to church an' Sun-day school an' sang this an' they sweet, Oh, there's fi-yer down be-low!

2. The passon wuz a misery, so scraggy an' so thin,
   Ch. To mee way, hay, hee, high, ho!
   Sez he, 'Look 'ere, you shellbacks, if yer lead a life of sin,'
   Ch. Oh, there's fiyer down below!

3. He took his text from Malachi an' he pulled a weary fayice,
   Oh, I took french leave an' I sailed away, but now I've fell from
   grace.

4. This passon had a daughter who wuz sweet as sugar candy,
   I said to her, 'Us sailors would make lovers neat an' handy.'

5. She sez to me, 'You sailors is a bunch o' bloomin' liars,
   An' all of yiz is bound ter Hell, ter feed the bloomin' [flamin'] fiyers.'

6. She wuz a very naughty gal was this passon's only daughter,
   She went down to a creek for to wash her locks in water.

7. The fiyer down below, me lads, is very hot an' jolly,
   But the fiyer there's not 'arf so 'ot as my sweet clipper Polly.

8. There's fiyer in the cabin, boys, an' in the galley too,
   But there's no fiyer in the fo'c'sle an' it's cold is the crew.

9. There's fiyer all around us, boys—it's playin' hide an' seek,
   It's tryin' to find a bunk, m' lads, where it can git some sleep.

10. There's fiyer in the galley an' it's runnin' down below,
    There's fiyer in the bosun's pipe—it's time for us to go!

11. If the rotten boats won't hold us when it's time for us to go,
    We'll complain to Havelock Wilson when we gits him down below.

12. There's fiyer up above me, boys, there's fiyer down below,
    There's fiyer in the main-top, boys, it's rouse all hands below.

378

After mentioning any part of a ship where the fire could be, the final verse was usually as follows:

Oh, fiyer up! Oh, fiyer up! Oh, fiyer down below,
The bonnie lassies are awaitin' for us in Dundee, y'know.

Trevor Jones, a Welsh shipmate of mine, sang a different tune to the former minor tune. Any or all of the preceding stanzas would be sung to it.

FIRE DOWN BELOW (b)

Another version of the above forms is given by C. Sharp in the *Journal* of the Folk Song Society. It was taken down from the singing of Mr. H. Perry.

FIRE DOWN BELOW (c)

These forms were popular with men I have sailed with, but there was another not so musical pattern. This form has become popular with radio shanty-singers.

379

FIRE DOWN BELOW (d)

2. Fire in the fore-top, fire in the main,
   Fire in the 'wilderness' and fire in the chain.
     Ch. Fire! Fire!
         Fire down below,
         [It's] Fetch a bucket o' water, girls [boys],
         [There's] Fire down below!

3. Fire in the fore-peak, fire down below,
   Fire in the fore-chains, the bosun didn't know.
     Ch. Fire, *etc.*

4. Fire in the lifeboat, fire in the gig,
   Fire in the pig-stye roasting the pig.

5. Fire in the lower-hold, fire down below,
   Fire in the main-well, the Old Man didn't know.

6. Fire up aloft, me boys, fire all aglow,
   Fire in the galley, the 'Doc' he didn't know.

7. Fire on the royal yard, fire on the main,
   Fetch a bucket o' water, gals, an' put it out again.

8. Fire in the orlop, fire in the hold,
   Fire in the strong-room, melting the gold.

9. Fire in the cabin an' in the galley too,
   No fore in the fo'c'sle an' it's cold all through.

10. Fire at the caps'n, fire at the mast.
    Fire on the main-deck, a-burnin' fast.

11. Fire in the store-room, burnin' the food,
    Fire at the knightheads, burnin' the wood.

12. Fire up above, me boys, fire down below,
    Douse it with the water, boys, an' let us roll 'n' go!

Some shantymen would leave out the word 'boys' or 'girls' in the chorus.

Terry gives one of two alternatives for the second solo line in every stanza:

(1) It's fetch a bucket of water, girls, there's fire down below.

(2) It's fetch a bucket of water, girls, and put it out **again**.

rhyming either 'below' or 'again' with the last word of the first solo line of the verse, e.g.:

> Fire in the fore-top, fire in the chain,
> Fetch a bucket o' water, girls, and put it out again.

or

> Fire in the fore-peak, the bosun didn't know,
> Fetch a bucket o' water, girls, there's fire down below.

A variant of this form is one sung to Cecil Sharp by George Conway (aged seventy-one) at the London Sailors' Home in 1914.

FIRE DOWN BELOW (e)

Fire up the mid-dle door, fire down be-low, O fire in the main-top, fire down be-low,

Fire! fire! fire! O here's an aw-ful go! Let's hope that we shall nev-er see,

Fire down be-low!

(From the *Journal* of the Folk Song Society.)

Before leaving this shanty I must point out the fact that as wooden ships were superseded by iron ones and pumping became much rarer, *Fire Down Below* was taken over for use at the capstan.

Another halyard shanty of Negro origin which I came across in the West Indies is *Bully in the Alley*. Sharp gives a version sung to him by Mr. John Short of Watchet in which all the refrains are the same—'Way, ay, bully in the alley', but I feel that this version has all the signs of being in a worn condition, as though Mr. Short's memory, in this case, didn't serve him well.

'Shinbone Al' is a place often referred to in Negro songs.

BULLY IN THE ALLEY

So 'elp me bob, I'm bul-ly in the al-ley, Way-ay-ay ay-ay-ay, bul-ly in the al-ley! So

'elp me bob I'm bul-ly in the al-ley, Bul-ly down in Shin-bone Al !

2. Sally am de gal down in our alley,
   Ch. Way-ay-ay-ay-ay-ay, *bully* in the alley!
   Sally am de gal that I spliced nearly,
   *Ch. Bul*ly down in Shinbone *Al*!

3. I'll leave my Sal an' I'll go a-sailin',
   I'll leave my Sal an' go a-whalin'.

My informant 'Harry Lauder' told me that from here on improvisation was the thing. This shanty may have been one used originally by cotton screwers.

An old song known to most Irish and Liverpool-Irish seamen was *Bound to Australia,* sung to the air *I'm a man ye don't meet every day*—a variant of *Believe me if all those endearing young charms.* It was not a true forebitter perhaps, although it *was* sung in the dog-watches in the old sailing ships; but I never heard that it was used as a capstan shanty until I read in Doerflinger's *Shantymen and Shantyboys* that according to Captain P. Tayleur it was often sung by seamen in the Australian Emigrant Trade as they 'hove in their mooring lines' and 'brought the anchor to the hawse-pipe'. Captain Tayleur calls his song *The First of the Emigrants* and in the main it is the same as mine, which I had from old Paddy Griffiths. Gold was found in Australia in 1851 and from that time onwards for the rest of the century sailing ships packed to the scuppers with emigrants and gold-seekers headed for the 'Colonies'. No doubt it lent itself to being a fine capstan song.

BOUND TO AUSTRALIA

I'm leav-ing Old Eng-land the land that I love, And I'm bound far a-cross the sea, Oh, I'm

bound for Aus-tra-lia the land of the free, Where there'll be a welcome for me, So fill up yer glas-ses an'

drink what ye please for whatever's the dam-age I'll pay, So be ai-sy an' free whilst yer drink-in' wid me, Sure I'm a

man yiz don't meet ev'ry day!

2. When I board me ship for the south'ard to go,
      She'll be lookin' so trim an' so fine,
      And I'll land me aboard, wid me bags an' me stores,
      From the dockside they'll cast off each line.
         Ch. So fill up yer glasses an' drink what ye please,
            For whatever's the damage I'll pay,
            So be aisy an' free, whilst yer drinkin' wid me,
            Sure I'm a man yiz don't meet every day!

3. To Land's End we'll tow, wid our boys all so tight,
      Wave a hearty goodbye to the shore,
      An' we'll drink the last drop to our country's green land,
      An' the next day we'll curse [nurse] our heads sore.
         Ch. So fill up yer glasses, *etc.*

4. We'll then drop the tug, and sheet tops'ls home taut,
      An' the hands will crowd sail upon sail,
      Wid a sou'wester strong, boys, we'll just tack along,
      By the morn many jibs will turn pale.

5. We'll beat past the Ushant and then down the Bay,
      Where the west wind it blows fine an' strong,
      We'll soon git the Trades an' we should make good time,
      To the south'ard then we'll roll along.

6. Round the Cape we will roll, take our flyin' kites in,
      For the Forties will sure roar their best,
      An' then run our Eastin' wid yards all set square,
      Wid the wind roaring out of the west.

7. We'll then pass Cape Looin[1] all shipshape an' trim,
   Then head up for Adelaide Port,
   Off Semaphore Roads we will there drop our hook,
   An' ashore, boys, we'll head for some sport.

8. When I've worked in Australia for twenty long years,
   One day will I head homeward bound,
   Wid a nice little fortune tucked under me wing,
   By a steamship I'll travel I'm bound!

9. So 'tis goodbye to Sally an' goodbye to Sue,
   When I'm leavin' Australia so free,
   Where the gals are so kind, but the one left behind
   Is the one that will one day splice me!

Heave, My Boys, Away! I learnt from 'Big Skan', a Swedish shipmate. How popular it was in British ships I've no idea, but apparently Scandinavians sang it at the capstan. A version is given in the Norwegian shanty book *Opsang*, and there is a very similar version in Bradford and Fagge's collection. In these two printed versions it is called *The Capstan Bar* or *Capstan Bars*.

HEAVE, MY BOYS, AWAY

Walk 'er round for we're rollin' homeward, Heave me boys to-geth-er! The bul-ly ol' ship is a-lyin' wind-ward,

Heave me boys, a-way! We're taut an' trim an' the wind is blow-in', Snug up a-loft an' the ship she's go-in',

Heave 'er an' we'll break 'er, for the old ship's a-rol-lin' home!

2. Sing an' heave an' heave an' sing,
     Ch. Heave, me boys, together!
   Heave an' make the capstan spring,
     Ch. Heave, me boys, away!
   'Tis blow ye winds for London Town-O!
   Where the gals are dressed so fine-O!
     Ch. Heave 'er an' we'll break 'er [Bust 'er, strand 'er],
       For the old ship's a-rollin' home!

3. Sails trimmed taut an' the ship she's goin',
   Ch. Heave, *etc.*
   Move her round for the winds a-blowin',
   Ch. Heave, *etc.*
   So goodbye, gals, we're bound to leave you,
   Goodbye, Sally, and goodbye, Lulu,
   Ch. Heave 'er, an' we'll break 'er,
   For the old ship's a-rollin' home!

The British shanty called *The Little Ball of Yarn* by some may be considered a countryman's ditty, and perhaps it was, but it was often heard at the pumps in the old days, and I'm sure that, in actual fact, 'balls o' yarn' were more likely to be associated with sailormen than countrymen! A shipmate of mine, Jack Reid, who had served his time in the ship *St. Mirren* gave me the following version. It was rather bawdy—but its chorus went down well with the 'crowd'.

THE LITTLE BALL O' YARN

One sun-ny morn in May, As I was on my way, To vis-it my grand-father's farm, I spied a pret-ty maid, a-rest-in' in the shade, She was wind-ing up her lit-tle ball o' yarn, Oh, the black-bird an' the thrush, sing out from ev'-ry bush Keep yer hand up-on yer lit-tle ball o' yarn, Oh, the black-bird an' the thrush, sing out from ev'ry bush, Keep yer hand up-on yer lit-tle ball o' yarn!

2. A pretty gal was May, as she lay there in the hay,
   The scene it was so quiet and so calm,
   I dropped down where she lay, an' unto her did say,
   'Let me wind up yer little ball o' yarn.'
   Ch. Oh, the blackbird an' the thrust sing out from every bush,
   Keep yer hand upon yer little ball o' yarn!
   An' the blackbird an' the thrush sing out from every bush,
   Keep yer hand upon yer little ball o' yarn!

3. 'No, kind sir,' said she, 'you're a stranger unto me;
To other gals you may possess some charm.
You'd better go away, an' come back some other day,
To wind up my little ball o' yarn.'
    Ch. Oh, the blackbird, *etc.*

4. I kissed that pretty maid, just underneath the shade,
Intending to do her no harm,
'Cos the blackbird an' the thrush sang out from every bush,
To remind her of her little ball o' yarn.

5. Twelve months have passed away, since that sunny morn in May,
When I spied that maid—a baby on her arm.
She would not look at me, the reason plain to see—
'Cos I helped to wind her little ball o' yarn.

There are a few more verses. Mr. D. Maloney says that my final verse was the pre-penultimate one and gives it thus:

Ten weary months had passed, ere I saw that maid at last,
And I met her with a baby on her arm.
But she didn't know 'twas me, till I told her I was he
Who had wound up her little ball of yarn.

He says that the penultimate verse contained a moral or warning, and the final verse referred to the blackbird and thrush.

Apropos winding balls o' yarn in the old squareriggers, this was a regular job; winding up tarry lengths of yarn into rope, usually done in dirty weather under the fo'c'sle-head, when pipes and the telling of tales would be in order—hence the expression—'Spin a yarn, sailor!'

In Terry's collection there is a rather unusual item which he sets down as a shanty. Terry himself was of the opinion it was a shore-song until Mr. James Runciman informed him he had heard it sung as a shanty. He says that it is 'redolent of the Venetian gondola' and that the words are of a sentimental type 'beloved of sailors'. I'm afraid I disagree with his rather persistent idea that sailors liked sentiment—they did in shore-songs maybe, but rarely if ever in their shanties, as the shanties themselves prove. He gives this song as a capstan shanty with the title of *My Johnny*.

A favourite forebitter occasionally used as a capstan or pumps shanty—Miss L. A. Smith gives it as capstan—is *Homeward Bound* or as sometimes called *Outward and Homeward Bound*. Different towns and docks are given in the many versions to be found on both sides of the Atlantic, and the names of the inn and its landlord also vary. It was presumably a naval song originally and may be of great age. The words of this song are to be found in many shanties—*Goodbye, Fare-ye-well* being most prominent. The version I give here I learnt in the main from my mother who had it from her sailor father, John Southwood.

OUTWARD AND HOMEWARD BOUND
Alternative title, Homeward Bound

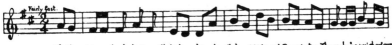

To the Liv-er-pool docks we'll bid a-dieu, to Sal an' Kate an' Bes-sie too. The an-chor's a-weigh an' our

Sails are un-furled, An' we're bound to plough the wat-ty world, Oh, say we're out-ward bound, Hur-rah we're out-ward bound!

2. Oh, the wind blows hard from the east nor'east,
   The ship will sail ten knots at least,
   The purser will our wants supply,
   An' while we've rum [grog] we'll never say die.
     Ch. Hurrah, we're outward bound,
        Hurrah, we're outward bound! [Oh, say we're outward bound,
        Hurrah, we're outward bound!]

3. An' if we touch at Malabar or any other port as far,
   The purser then will tip the chink,
   An' just like fishes we will drink,
     Ch. Hurrah, *etc.*

4. An' when our three years they are out,
   'Tis jolly near time we went about,
   An' when we're home an' once more free,
   Oh, won't we have a jolly spree,
     Ch. Hurrah, we're homeward bound,
        Hurrah, we're homeward bound! [Oh, say we're homeward
        bound, Hurrah, we're homeward bound!]

5. At last our cap'n comes on board,
   The sails are bent we're manned an' stored,
   The Peter's hoisted at the fore,
   Goodbye to the girls we'll ne'er see more,
     Ch. Hurrah, we're homeward bound, *etc.*

6. One day the man on the look-out,
   Proclaims a sail with a joyful shout,
   'Can ye make her out?' 'I think I can,
   She's a Pilot headin' out from the land.'
     Ch. Hurrah, *etc.*

7. An' when we gits to the Liverpool Docks,
   The pretty gals come down in flocks,
   One to the other ye can hear them say,
   Here comes Johnny wid his three years' pay.
       Ch. Hurrah, *etc.*

8. An' then we'll haul to the Bull an' the Bell,
   Where good liquor they do sell.
   In comes the Landlord with a smile,
   Sayin', 'Drink up, lads, while 'tis worth yer while.'

9. But when the money's all spent an' gone,
   None to be borrowed, none to be lent,
   In comes the Landlord with a frown,
   Sayin', 'Git up, Jack, let John sit down!'

10. Then poor ol' Jack must understand,
    There's ships in port all wanting hands.
    He goes on board as he did before,
    An' he bids adieu to his native shore.

Of course sailors from different ports sang of their own home town—'To the Bristol docks we'll bid adieu', or 'To Sunderland town . . .' The Yankees would use 'Pensacola' or 'Boston town'. Some Britishers would sing of leaving the 'Salthouse Docks' or 'Wapping Stairs'. Also the final port would vary according to the soloist. I've heard: 'An' when we gits to the Blackwall Docks' and 'the London Docks.' 'The home port docks,' 'Katherine Docks', 'Milbay Docks', and 'Millwall Docks' were also used. As to the landlord of the pub (usually the Dog and Bell), he was sometimes called by the name of Archie or Archer, but as Whall points out, 'Americans sang of Mother Langley, and the Londoner of "Old Grouse".'

Old Paddy Griffiths with whom I once sailed had another variant of this song, but his, as he pointed out, was a proper capstan shanty —a homeward-bound song. It was connected with Liverpool and sung aboard ships in the Saltpetre Trade to Chili and aboard Guano Traders to Peru. The only other writer who gives it, and he only gives one verse, is Captain Robinson (in *The Bellman*).

HOMEWARD BOUND

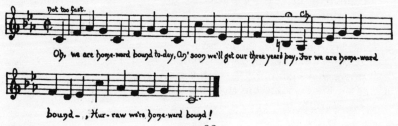

Oh, we are home-ward bound to-day, An' soon we'll get our three years' pay, For we are home-ward
bound—, Hur-raw we're home-ward bound!

2. We're homeward bound for Liverpool town,
Where all them gals they will come down.
Ch. For we are homeward bound,
Hurraw, we're homeward bound!

3. An' when we gits to the Liverpool docks,
Them pretty gals will come in flocks.
Ch. For we, *etc.*

4. Goodbye to the gals of ol' Callyo,
Them Liverpool judies have got us in tow.

5. Them Spanish gals we've left behind,
Were fine an' free an' very kind.

6. We'd sing an' dance an' have good fun,
When we wuz on the outward run.

7. But when the boys had had their fun,
An' all our money it wuz done [gone].

8. The Madam in her best silk gown,
Said 'Get up, Jack, let John sit down.'

9. 'Twas time for us to roll 'n' go,
An' give some other John a show.

10. So now our pay-day soon will come,
Up [Down] Paradise Street we'll have good fun.

This capstan song in all probability stemmed from the old fore-bitter, a process often repeated in the days of sail.

The ceremony known as 'paying off the dead horse' became a rather half-hearted affair in the latter days of sail, whereas in days gone by it was a spectacular effort, particularly in the emigrant ships, and one of the best descriptions of it is given in *Reminiscences of Travel in Australia, America and Egypt*, by R. Tangye (London, 1884).

Of course it has been described many times and all I need to say here is that it mainly consisted—at the end of the first month at sea—of dragging a canvas horse stuffed with shavings and a few holy-stones along the deck, followed by tricing the effigy up to the main yard-arm, and firing a blue flare at the same time as a seaman on the yard cut the gantline to allow the 'hoise' to 'drop into the drink'. It was to celebrate the start of the crew earning their pay, since their first month's wages had been drawn in advance when they had signed on, and normally found their way into the pockets of the boarding-masters. The 'horse' was hoisted up to the yard-arm to the shanty called *The Dead Horse*. This shanty was originally consecrated for use at this ceremony only, but in later days, when the ceremony fell into disuse, it was utilized as a halyard song.

Some authorities seem to think that it was developed from the nigger minstrel ditty *Clear the kitchen, young folks, Ol' Virginny never tire*, but I fail to see any connection. Others believe it to have had some connection with a shore folk-song the first verse of which begins: 'Once I was reared in a stable so warm . . .' and finishes with 'Poor old horse, poor old horse'.

Sometimes the shanty is about 'Poor Old Joe':

> Old Joe is dead an' gone to Hell,
> Poor Old Joe!

Variants of the first and second refrains are as follows:

> Oh we say so, an' we hope so!

> An' they say so an' they hope so!

> And they say so, an' I hope so!

> For they says so, an' they knows so!

> Oh, Poor old horse!

> Oh, Poor old man!

> Oh, Poor old Joe!

My version is from both the Bosun of the *Garthpool* and Reed, an Australian sailmaker.

THE DEAD HORSE
Alternative titles, *Poor Old Horse, Poor Old Man, Poor Old Joe*

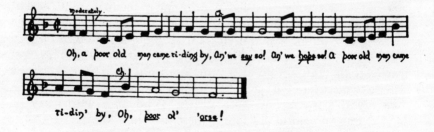

2. Sez I [They say], 'Ol' Man, yer 'orse will die,'
   Ch. An' we *say* so, an' we *hope* so!
   Sez I, 'Ol' Man yer 'orse will die,'
   Ch. Oh, *poor* ol' 'orse [man, Joe]!

THE CEREMONY OF THE DEAD HORSE

'An' we say so, an' we hope so!' (Halyard Shanty)

3. An' if he dies we'll tan his hide,
   Ch. An' we say, *etc.*
   An' if he don't we'll ride him agin,
   Ch. Oh, poor, *etc.*

4. For one long month I rode him hard,
   For one long month we rode him hard.

5. One month a hell-bent life we've led,
   But ye've laid in a nice warm [fevver] bed.

6. But now yer month is up, ol' Turk,
   Git up, yer swine, an' look for work.

7. Git up, yer swine, an' look for graft,
   While we lays on an' yanks ye aft.

8. After hard work an' sore abuse,
   We'll salt ye down for sailor use.

9. An' if ye think this ain't not true,
   In the horse-cask look, an' ye'll find his shoe.

10. He's as dead as a nail in the lamproom door,
    He won't come a-hazin' [worryin'] us no more.

11. We'll use the hair of his tail to sew our sails,
    We'll use the hair of his tail to sew our sails.

12. We'll yank him aft to the cabin door,
    An' hopes we never sees ye more. [An' now goodbye, ye son-
    o'-a-whore.]

13. We'll hoist him up to the main yard-arm,
    We'll hoist him up to the main yard-arm.

14. An' drop him down to the depths o' the sea,
    An' drop him down to the bottom of the sea.

15. We'll sink him down with a long, long roll,
    Where the sharks'll have his body, an' the devil have his soul.

16. Oh, 'tis growl ye may but go ye must,
    It matters not whether yer last or fust. [If ye growl too hard
    yer head they'll bust.]

17. I thought I heard the Old Man say,
    Just one more pull, lads, then belay!

Doerflinger's singer—Richard Maitland of Sailors' Snug Harbor—
has a verse which obviously is one of the additions to the song when
it became a proper halyard shanty in later days:

> Round Cape Horn through frost and snow,
> Round Cape Horn I had to go.

Many of the lines and couplets in this shanty were taken from a 'chant' commonly known as the 'Sailor's Grace', as it was recited or sung when the first barrel of 'salt horse' (salt beef or pork) was opened on the outward passage. A leading hand would solemnly chant or sing the following staves whilst all hands would come in on the dirge-like 'Salt horse, salt horse, what brought ye here?'

I give two tunes—one little more than a Gregorian chant. It was not a shanty.

THE SAILOR'S GRACE (a)

Salt horse, salt horse, We'd have ye know, That to the gal-ley ye must go, The cook with-out a
sign o' grief, Will boil ye down, an' call ye beef, An' we poor sail-ors stan-din' near, must eat ye though ye
look so queer, Salt horse, salt horse, What brought ye here?

2. Salt horse, salt horse, both near an' far,
   Yer food for every hard-worked tar.
   In strongest brine ye have been sunk,
   Until yer hard an' coarse as junk.
   To eat such poor an' wretched fare,
   Would whiten any nigger's hair,
       Ch. Salt horse, salt horse, what brought ye here?

3. Salt horse, salt horse, what brought ye here?
   After carryin' sand [stones] for many a year,
   From Bantry Bay to Ballywhack,
   Where ye fell down an' broke yer back,
   An' after years of such abuse,
   They salt ye down for sailors' use,
       Ch. Salt horse, salt horse, what brought ye here?

THE SAILOR'S GRACE (b)

(Rather fast)

Salt horse, salt horse, we'd have ye know, That to the galley you must go, The cook without a
sign o' grief, will boil ye down an' call ye beef, An' we poor sailors standin' near must eat ye tho' ye
Ch. (Slower)
look so queer, Salt horse — salt horse, what brought ye here?

In American ships the geographical places in the third verse were: 'Portland Bay to Saccarapp'.

Other couplets are:

> They tan yer hide an' burn yer bones,
> An' pack ye off to Davy Jones.
>
> They'll salt ye down for sailors' use,
> They'll pick yer bones an' suck yer juice.
>
> An' if ye don't believe this true,
> In the harness-cask ye'll find his shoe.

A version sent me by Mr. W. A. Bryce of Sutton Coldfield runs:

> Old horse! Old horse! What brought you here?
> From Saccarap' to Portland Pier.
> I carted stone for many a year,
> I laboured long and well a-lack,
> Till I fell down and broke my back.
> They picked me up with sore abuse,
> And salted me down for sailors' use.
> The sailors they do me despise;
> They pick me up and damn my eyes,
> They eat my flesh and gnaw my bones,
> And throw the rest to Davy Jones.

* * *

'Sweatin' up' and 'swiggin' down' were endless tasks in the ships that carried sails, and short staves of many and varied types must have been used in bygone days. But, owing to the lack of interest in the collecting of such brevities, we have very few to offer at so late a date. Whall gives one or two and an odd one is found here and there in sailing-ship yarns, but generally speaking hundreds of these little work-chants must have passed into oblivion. They were little more than enlargements on the ordinary 'singin'-out' which one still hears and usually consisted of one or two verses. Two given by Whall in his *Sea Songs and Shanties* are as follows:

ROYAL ARTILLERY MAN

My bleed-in' fan-cy-man, he's a R'yl Ar-til'ry-man, He wears spurs!

The 'drag' in all these kinds of work-song came on the final word of the chorus. Both this one and the next were probably used aboard troopers.

ST. HELENA SOLDIER

You stole my boots, You Saint Helena sol-dier... You stole my boots, ah-ha!

2. You stole my boots so early in the morning,
   Ch. You stole my boots ah-*ha*!

'St. Helena sojer', 'Port Mahon baboon', and similar phrases were used by shellbacks to designate seamen poor at 'sailorizing'.

An old Irish shipmate of mine—I believe he died at sea while serving as lamptrimmer aboard a steamer in the New Zealand trade —once sang to me a little ditty which he said was very popular for 'sweatin' up'. He called it *Hauley, Hauley-ho!* Later I came across a one-verse version of this in C. F. Smith's book of shanties. Her informant told her it was popular in Green's Blackwall ships, and she writes that the tune is part of the opera *Der Freischütz* (Huntsman's chorus), which makes this shanty a good illustration of the theory that 'all was fish for the shantyman's net'. She calls it *England, Old Ireland* and her refrain—'Rumptsty, Bumpsty haul!'—certainly smacks of great antiquity. Here is Paddy's version.

HAULEY, HAULEY-HO!

Eng-land, ould Oi-er-land, Eng-a-land, ould Oi-er-land, Eng-land, ould Oi-er-land, Hauley, hauley ho!

2. Paddy M'Ginty—Paddy, Jock, and little Jackie too,
   Oh Paddy M'Ginty—Hauley, hauley-*ho*!

SWEATIN'-UP AT THE UPPER BRACES
'Oh, fiddle-string 'im!' (Sing-out)

3. Shamrock an' Rose, boys, Shamrock, Rose, and pricky Thistle too,
Shamrock an' Rose, boys—Hauley, hauley-*ho*!

Another brief sweatin'-up chant in fairly common use is to be found in both Harlow and Sharp.

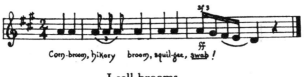

I sell brooms,
Squeegees,
And *Swabs*!

I myself have used

O-ho-o . . . *Jul*ia!
Oh rise him, O . . . *Jul*ia!
Lay back, O . . . *Jul*ia!

Whall also gives:

but doesn't indicate the pull which I fancy would come on 'Running'.

Sailors also used odd phrases in other languages; here are two examples from Whall (*Sea Songs and Shanties*).

It may be of interest to note that at the Outward Bound Sea School, Aberdovey, we still keep alive a short drag-song—used when hauling boats up the slipway—which has its origin in the wild chants of the Indian Tamils. This one can shift mountains!

Hul-la-ba-lay-lay, Ar-lis! Hal-ran dai-ran, Ar-lis! Hi-ra ben-da-ri, Ar-lis!

Rock 'n' shake 'er, Ar-lis! etc.

Of the wild hand-over-hand sing-outs very few have ever been put down on paper. Harlow, in his *The Making of a Sailor*, gives us:

A-way-a-a-ah-hay-a-a-hay, etc.

and

A-way... hey! Oh, haul him high-O! Way...

hey! Oh, haul him high-O! Way... hey! Oh, haul him-high-

O! High-O! Raise him and haul him high-O!

Professor J. Glyn Davies once told me that among Welsh crews a bawdy version of the following was often sung out hand-over-hand.

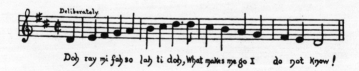

Doh ray mi fah so lah ti doh, What makes me go I do not know!

Captain D. W. Bone gives:

> Ho, yo, ho, roust 'r up!
> Ho yo, yeh, ho, yeh!

And he also has the very popular hand-over-hand chant which runs:

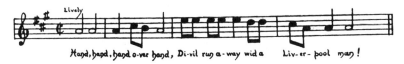

Hand, hand, hand o-ver hand, Di-vil run a-way wid a   Liv-er-pool man!

Bone gives 'West Country man' (*Capstan Bars*).

And a very well known one—given by Doerflinger from the singing of Captain J. Barker of *Tusitala*—is:

Hel-lie, hel-lie shum-ra, shum-ra, shum-ra, Hel-lie, hel-lie, shum-ra, hay, hay, hay,

Hel-lie, hel-lie shum-ra, shum-ra, shum-ra, Hel-lie, hel-lie, shum-ra, hay, hay, hay.

(From *Shantymen and Shantyboys*, with permission.)

I myself have sung out some wild efforts too, learnt from older seamen:

(1) O-o-o, o-o-o, her-ree-up-ah! etc.

(2) Hey, ha, ho, ah — hey, ha, ho, ah!   etc.

(3) Way hey, up she ris-es! Oh, ah, up she ris-es!   etc.

(4) Oh, hil-ly hol-ly, hol-ley hil-ly! Hil-ly hol-ly, hol-ly hil-ly, etc.

(5) Way, hey, hee, ho ya! Way, hey, hee, ho, ya!   etc.

(6) Lee-ay, lee-ay, ho-ro, ho-yah! etc.

But it is extremely difficult, in fact impossible, to translate by means of cold standard music notes on paper the wild and fearsome effect of these cries. No landsman could ever hope to imitate them!

CLEWING UP THE MAINS'L
'*Hee-lay-oh-yu!*' (Sing-out)

Other sing-outs for sweatin'-up were:

> Oh, *fiddle*-string 'im!
> Oh, *Johnny*!
> Ah-ha, *stretch* me!
> Oho, *bunt*-a-bo!
> High-*bully*!
> Two *block* 'im!
> Oho, *Jew*!
> Oh, *come* 'n' see me!
> Long 'n' *strong*!
> Heavy *arses*!
> High 'n' dry for a wet *sail*!

At the capstan such encouraging shouts as follow would be heard when the anchor was being lifted:

> Heave 'n' pawl!
> Heave-o-heave!
> Heave, ye parish-rigged barstards!
> Roundy come roundy for Liverpool town!
> Roundy come roundy—squarey come squarey!
> Heave 'n' bust 'er!
> Heave round hearty!
> Heave 'n' break her, bullies!

Other odds and ends used for holystoning the decks and so on are to be found in other books. C. F. Smith has one for this latter task.

HOLYSTONING

Leave her John-ny and a-way we'll go, Leave her John-ny.

The following chant is from C. F. Smith's collection. It was used to help keep time in the days when on the West Coast of South America seamen would swing heavy wooden mallets or 'commanders' with which they stowed the bags of saltpetre into the holds of their vessels.

> There goes *one*,
> Hurrah my boys, strike *one*,
> For one now is *gone*,
> And there's many more to *come*,
> For to make up the *sum*,
> For one hundred so *long* . . . (*ad lib*).

*   *   *

For our final shanty I have chosen a song which was probably more of a forebitter than a real shanty, but nevertheless most of my old shipmates seem to think that it *was* used as a shanty at both capstan and pumps.

The reason I have kept it for our winding-up song is its title—*We'll Go To Sea No More!*—the ever-present thought in the mind of the old shellback, who swore regularly at the end of every voyage that he would carry an oar over his shoulder and tramp inland until he met someone who would ask him what the object was he was carrying, and there he would drop his 'pick' and go to sea no more! Alas, this rarely happened and once Sailor John had spent his money, he was soon to be found outward bound around Cape Stiff again; here he could give voice once more to the old saying 'Who'd sell a farm 'n' go to sea?'

My first version of this ditty I learnt from my shipmate, A. Spencer, who had sung it aboard the American four-masted barque *Monongahela.* He only remembered the first verse and chorus.

WE'LL GO TO SEA NO MORE

No more I'll haul on a lee fore brace, By the roy-al hal-yards stand, Nor a-loft I'll fly when I hear the cry, With a tar-pot in me hand, No more I'll fork a-Flem-ish horse, nor ride a stay-s'l down . . . , But I'll stay on shore for-ev-er-more, An' be mayor of me lit tle home town, No more, no more, we'll go to sea no-more. No more, no more, we'll go to sea no more!

Our next version is very often called *Shanghai Brown.* This was the commonest version of all, known to every seaman. It is given as a forebitter by Doerflinger, and is also to be found in the American magazine *Adventure* (30 January 1923), but in both cases they give the song as *Off To Sea No More.*

GO TO SEA NO MORE
Alternative title, *Shanghai Brown*

When first I went to Fris-co, I went up-on the spree, Me hard-earned cash I spent it fast, Got

drunk as drunk could be- Be-fore me mon-ey was all gone, or spent wi'some ol'whore, I was

ful-ly in-clined, made up me mind, To go to sea- no more, No more- no

more- no more, no more, no more! There goes Jack Rack, poor sail-or boy, who's

go-in' to sea no more!

2. That night I slept wid Mary Ann, too drunk to turn in bed,
   Me clothes wuz new, me money wuz too, next morn wid them she'd
   fled.
   A-feelin' sick I left the house an' went down by the shore,
   Oh, an' then as I went, me head all bent, the crimps they all did
   roar.
      Ch. No more, no more,
         No more, no more, no more!
         There goes Jack Rack, poor sailor boy,
         Who's goin' to sea no more!

3. The first chap I ran foul of wuz Mister Shanghai Brown.
   I axed him neat, for to stand treat he looked me up an' down.
   Sez he, 'Last time yiz wuz paid off, wi' me yiz chalked no score,
   But I'll give ye a chance, an' I'll take yer advance, for to go to sea
   once more!'
      Ch. No more, *etc.*

4. Oh, he shipped me aboard of a whalin'-ship, bound for the Arctic
   Seas,
   Where the cold winds blow an' the frost an' the snow makes even hot
   rum freeze.
   I had no clothes, I had no gear, me cash spent on a whore,
   Oh, 'twas then that I swore when once on shore I'd go to sea no
   more.

5. Some days we caught our sparm whales, boys, some days we did
   catch none.
   Wid a twenty-foot oar stuck in yer paw we pulled the whole day long,
   And when the night it came along an' ye nod upon yer oar.
   Oh, a man must be blind fer ter make up his mind fer ter go ter sea
   once more.

6. Come, all ye bully sailormen, an' listen to me song.
   O, I hope ye just will listen till I tell yiz what went wrong,
   Take my advice don't drink strong rum, nor go sleepin' wid a whore,
   But just git spliced, that's my advice, and go ter sea no more!

Another tune very popular with Liverpool seamen was the
following, but this was a forebitter since it had no all-hands-in
chorus.

GO TO SEA ONCE MORE

2. That night I slept wid Angeline, too drunk to roll in bed.
   Me clothes wuz new and me money wuz too, next morn wid them
   she'd fled.
   An' as I rolled the streets about, the tarts they all did roar,
   Oh, there goes Jack Ratcliffe, poor sailor boy, who must go to sea
   once more.

3. Now as I wuz rollin' down the street I met ol' Rapper Brown.
   I axed him then to take me in, but he looked at me wid a frown.
   Sez he, 'Last time yiz was paid off wid me yiz chalked no score,
   But I'll take yer advance an' I'll give yiz a chance an' I'll send yiz to
   sea once more.'

4. He shipped me aboard of a whalin'-ship bound for them Arctic
   Seas,
   Where the cold winds blow, an' there's ice an' there's snow an'
   Jamaicy rum do freeze.
   I can't stay here, for I have no gear, an' I spent all me money ashore,
   An' 'twas then that I said that I wished I wuz dead so I'd go to sea
   no more.

5. Sometimes we catched our sperm whales, boys, some days we did
   catch none,
   Wid a twenty-foot stuck in yer paw we rowed the whole day long,
   An' then the night it came along an' ye dozed upon yer oar,
   Oh, yer back's so weak ye never could seek a berth at sea once more.

6. Come, all ye bold seafaring men, and listen to me song;
   When yiz come off of them damn long trips I'll tell yiz what goes
   wrong.
   Take my advice, don't drink strong drinks, nor go sleepin' wid a
   whore,
   But get married, lads, an' have all night in, an' go to sea no more!

The tune of the foregoing is reminiscent of *Greensleeves*.

Rapper Brown was a Liverpool 'Shanghai Brown', and whaling
did operate to some extent from Liverpool many years ago. The
street Jack rolls down is sometimes 'Battery Street'. A variant of this
forebitter is given in Mackenzie's *Ballads and Sea Songs from Nova
Scotia* under the title *Dixie Brown*. The version given in *Adventure*
(Frothingham) is just different enough to justify its inclusion here.
As it has a chorus this may have been used as a shanty.

OFF TO SEA ONCE MORE

1. I met with a gay young 'Frisco gal, and my heart was not my own,
   But when I kissed her goodbye at last, my money and watch was
   gone.
   As I was walking down the street and people was gazing at me,
   Said they, 'There's a brave young sailor lad who's off once more to
   sea.'
   Ch. Once more, once more, he's off to sea once more,
       Oh, there's a brave young sailor lad who's off to sea once more.

2. A boarding-master picked me up; his name was Shanghai Brown,
   And I'll tell you the truth, he wasn't so ill, for he gave me half a
   crown.
   'Look here, my brave young sailor lad, there's no more work ashore,
   But here's your chance; take ten pounds advance, and go to sea once
   more.'
   Ch. Once more, *etc.*

3. So I shipped me aboard of a whaler that was bound for the Arctic
  Sea,
  Where ice and snow and the cold winds blow, froze my toes all off'n
  me.
  And the worst of it was I had no clothes to keep me dry and warm,
  And then I swore, if I ever get ashore, to go to sea no more.
    Ch. No more, no more, he's off to sea no more,
      Oh, there's a brave young sailor lad; he goes to sea no more.

4. Look here, my brave young sailor boys, take this as a warning from
  me,
  Steer wide of the gay young 'Frisco gals and do not go to sea;
  Drink no more whisky, smoke no more cigars, and run with the gals
  no more,
  But get married, my boy, and stop ashore, and go to sea no more.
    Ch. Once more, once more, they all go to sea once more,
      Oh, there's a brave young sailor lad, who goes to sea once more.
        (By permission of Popular Publications Inc., New York)

In her *Songs of American Sailormen* Miss J. Colcord gives the
following ditty, which appears to have been based on the two
versions of *Go To Sea No More* which I have already given. She
states that it was 'composed' by a shantyman called Sam Peck. This
may be true, but even so the fact of the matter is that within a very
short period of time it became popular as a capstan shanty aboard
the ships of many nations.

THE RIVER LEA

It was one fine day in the month of May, And I was out-ward bound, I had-n't any tin to buy some gin, So I walked the streets all round, My shoes were out at the el-bows, And I was sore in need, So I shipped as a jol-ly sail-or, On board of the "Riv-er Lea", No more I'll go to sea, beat down the Bay of Fun-dy, For-ev-er more I'll stay on shore, I'll go to sea no more!

2. No more I'll take my first look-out,
No more I'll take my wheel;
No more at the cry up aloft I'll fly,
While, 'Aye, aye, sir,' I squeal;
No more I'll reef those tops'ls,
For it is no more my trade,
No more I'll brail that spanker in,
On board of the River Lea.
    Ch. No more I'll go to sea,
        Beat down the Bay of Fundy,
        Forever more I'll stay on shore,
        I'll go to sea no more.

3. No more I'll pull on a lee fore brace,
Nor by royal halyards stand;
No more I'll ride those swifters down,
With a tarpot in my hand;
No more I'll cross those royal yards,
Nor furl that flying jib,
No more I'll shift gaff-tops'l tacks,
On board of the River Lea.

4. I've crossed the Western Ocean,
I've sailed the raging main,
But I've made it a rule, that I won't be a fool,
And go to sea again,
I'll stay at home in comfort,
And good advice I'll give:
Don't ever ship as a sailor,
On board of the River Lea.
    (By permission of W. W. Norton & Co., New York)

This version I now give was sent to me by a Belgian master mariner—Captain Popieul of Antwerp. He told me it was popular when he was serving his time 'in the Norwegian sailing ship *Ingrid* of Larvik (ex-*Anglesey* of Liverpool) in the year of 1906'.

THE ANGLESEY

It was one fine day in the month o' May, an' I was out-ward bound, I had-n't an-y tin to pay for gin, so I walked the streets all round, My coat was out at the el-bows, an' I was sore in need, So I shipped as a lit-tle sail-or boy, on board of the "Angle-sey," Then no more I'll go to sea, a-cross the West-ern O-cean, a-haul-in' an' a-pul-lin' I nev-er will a-gain, Then no more I'll go to sea, a-cross the West-ern O-cean, For e-ver-more I'll stay on shore, an' go to sea no more!

2. No more for me the first look-out,
   No more the wheel I'll take;
   No more gaff-tops'l tacks I'll shift, nor a-haul till me back does
       break;
   No more I'll shout 'All's well, sir!' nor pump away for life,
   But I'll go ashore an' get a wife,
   From on board of the *Anglesey*.
       Ch. Then no more I'll go to sea,
       Across the Western Ocean,
       A-haulin' an' a-pullin' I never will again;
       Then no more I'll go to sea,
       Across the Western Ocean,
       For evermore I'll stay on shore,
       An' go to sea no more!

3. No more will I reef, no more will I furl,
   Square in the crojik yard;
   No more the brightwork I will scrape with sand and canvas hard;
   No more up aloft will I fly, with a grease-pot in me hand,
   But I'll go ashore for evermore,
   From on board of the *Anglesey*.

408

4. No more I'll stand by the royal halyards,
   Nor eat their crackerhash;
   No soul an' body lashin's tie, nor in saltwater wash;
   No tarring down of backstays, no haul on the lee-fore-brace.
   But I'll pack me bag an' go ashore,
   From on board of the *Anglesey*.

*   *   *

And with this we clew up our record of working songs of seamen
of the world. The ships aboard which they were sung and the men
who sang them have gone, never to return. The songs themselves are
passing into the realm of ordinary folk-song, and the wild yelps and
savage howls with which Sailor John of the days that are gone
roared out these 'wild hooraw choruses' are now lost in the more
sedate radio renderings of them. But we hope that our effort to give
these shanties in as truthful a manner as possible will help those who
are interested to savour, for perhaps the last time, the genuine saltiness, rhythm, and vigour of the inimitable true song of the sea . . .

THE SHANTY

GLOSSARY

ADVANCE NOTE. A month's advance of wages has always been the custom at sea; in the days of sail two or even three months' were common. The idea was to enable the potential voyager to fit himself out with oilskins, mattress, etc., but normally the piece of paper—the NOTE—found its way into the hands of the boarding-house masters, publicans, ship-tailors, or money-lenders. The sailor received the Note when he signed on his ship—if it was worth two pounds ten (the usual monthly wage), the seaman would be lucky if he received two pound's worth of booze, female charm, or 'gear' out of it!

AMERICAN BAR. A well-known pub on Lime Street, Liverpool, famed both sides of the Atlantic. It still exists, but has become more popular with Yankee naval seamen since the Second World War. Photos of the crews of Yankee men-o'-war adorn its walls.

BACK THE MAIN TOPSAIL. When a sailing ship wished to 'heave to' or stop without using her anchor, the sails on the mainmast were trimmed so that the wind would be on their wrong side, working in opposition to the sails on the other two masts, thus causing the vessel's way to be checked. The manoeuvre was called 'backing the main-yard' or 'backing the main tops'l'.

BARBARY COAST, THE. A notorious water-front district of San Francisco, in the days of sail consisting mainly of boarding-houses, tailor shops, bar-rooms, and brothels, and the home of such famous crimps as Shanghai Brown, Larry Marr, etc. Probably so named on account of its 'riff-raff', comparable to the Riffs and pirates (corsairs) of the original North African Barbary Coast.

BIGHT, THE. A stretch of water, very often stormy, washing the shores of South and West Australia.

BLACKBALL CHEESER. A type of peak-cap with no stiffening in the crown worn by seamen of famous Blackball Line of Western Ocean (Atlantic) Packet Ships.

BLOODBOAT. Sailor name for hard-case sailing ship (usually Yank or Nova Scotian) from which crews would desert and fresh ones be supplied by the medium of shanghaiing.

BLOOD 'N' GUTS. Deep-water term for the Red Ensign of the Merchant Service.

BOW-CHASER. A small cannon fitted in the bows of merchant ships, particularly those engaged in the China Trade—East Indiamen and the like—useful when meeting up with Chinese pirates.

BOW STOPPERS. (1) Chain or hemp lashings with which to fasten the ring of an anchor to the cathead. (2) A brake of sorts controlling the anchor chain, open when the anchor is about to be dropped, closed when the ship is lying at anchor or when sailing.

BUMBOAT. Type of small rowboats found in most tropical ports surrounding deep-water ships at anchor, their owners vociferously shouting their wares—fruit, booze, curios, etc., for which in the old days seamen would exchange a shirt or bar of soap—'Black dog, white monkey!' would be the cry. Nowadays they demand money, Yankee dollars in particular!

BURGEE. A small flag, sometimes triangular (pennant) sometimes with two tails (swallowtail), having a special meaning.

CAPE STIFF. Usual sailor name for Cape Horn.

CATFALL. A three-fold tackle sometimes rigged from the head of the fore topmast or sometimes shackled to the head of a cat-davit. In older ships the upper block was the cathead itself, the latter having three sheaves in its outboard end. Sometimes the lower block was fitted with a hook, or else a wire pendant with a hook attached was shackled to the lower block. Used in catting the anchor, i.e. hoisting the anchor to the cathead.

CATHEAD. A heavy baulk of oak or teak projecting from either bow—often with three sheaves in its outboard end—to which the anchor was 'catted'. After the ring of the anchor was made fast to the cathead the lower part of the anchor was 'fished' also with the hook of the cat-tackle and hoisted inboard. Hence the expression 'cat an' fish the anchor'. Many of the older patterned catheads had the face of a cat carved in their outboard ends.

CHAFIN' LEATHER. A strip of leather sewn over the bolt-rope of the foot of a squaresail to prevent the sail chafing against the wire standing rigging.

CHALK NO SCORE. It was the usual thing in ports such as Liverpool, 'Frisco, New York, etc., for a paid-off seaman to 'chalk up a score' with a boarding-house master, i.e. spend all his hard-earned wages with the boarding-house master in booze, lodgings, and female company, in return being found a berth in an out-ward-bound ship by the same boarding-house master when his money had been 'blown'.

CHOWLAH. A girl, in particular a street-walker; possibly a word of Hindustani origin.

COUNTER. The overhanging part of a ship's stern; the buttocks.

CRACKERHASH. Hard dog biscuits or 'Liverpool Pantiles' crushed and mixed with water into a paste and jam or some other sweetener added, the result baked in the galley oven—a sailing-ship 'bonne bouche'!

DAN O'CONNELL. An Irish politician who lived from 1775 to 1847, a leader in the struggle for Catholic emancipation, often called the Liberator.

DIGGER RAMREES. Diego Ramirez, island near Cape Horn in the South Atlantic.

DONKEY. 'Donkey's breakfast', the name of the straw palliasse on which a seaman slept, this along with his plate and pannikin he would buy at some ship's chandler prior to joining his ship.

DOUDOU. A West Indian Creole word meaning 'sweetheart'.

DOWN EASTER. By Britishers, ships and men hailing from the Eastern American ports—Boston, Salem, New Bedford, etc.—were so called, but the term really meant those from Maine only.

DUNGAREE JUMPERS. The 'denim' jumpers popular with seamen in any trade except that of the North Atlantic.

FAITHFUL LOVER. Tobacco carried in a ship's 'slop chest' for sale to the crew was usually 'plug' tobacco, for both smoking and chewing. Faithful Lover, Fair Maid, Cornucopia were some of the brands carried in British ships.

FLAT ABACK. Said when a ship was caught by the wind on the wrong side of her sails putting great strain on her masts.

HALYARDS RACKED. Lashing the parts of the tackle of a halyard together by means of a light line in figure-of-eight fashion to prevent someone letting go the halyards at night when a ship was being driven by some hard-case racing master.

HANDY BILLY. A watch tackle, sometimes called 'Convenient William', used for many purposes aboard ship but mainly for clapping on the fall or hauling part of another tackle to get extra purchase. Particularly useful in under-manned ships.

HIGH SHOES. Paddy Griffiths told me that in his young days it was customary for Merchant Johns to 'bend' shore-going shoes which possessed rather higher heels than those worn by landsmen.

HOLY JOE. Sailor name for a parson.

HOME, THE. The Sailors' Home in Canning Place, Liverpool.

HOOSEGOW. Prison, from the Spanish word 'juzgb', hence 'jug' or 'jughouse'.

IRISH PENNANTS. Bits of spunyarn flying from stays, or frayed ends of rope dangling from aloft, sign of a 'slack' ship.

JAMES BAINES. Blackball liner, later in the Australian Trade; once sailed 420 miles, noon to noon, running the Easting down in a sixty-three day passage from Liverpool to Melbourne.

JUDY. Liverpool-Irish slang expression for a girl or sweetheart.

KNEES. Pieces of oak, grown to an L-shape, used in the construction of a wooden ship.

KNIGHTHEADS. In the older wooden ships great baulks of timber to which the inner end of the bowsprit was secured. In later ships,

413

with spike jibbooms, such erections were smaller or even non-existent.

LASH UP 'N' STOW! A naval expression for the unrigging of hammocks after night use.

LARRY MARR. One of the most infamous crimps of the Barbary Coast, San Francisco, who is reputed to have shanghaied all types of beings, from dead men and bank clerks to clergymen aboard hellships of all nations.

LAZAREET. A name originating in the countries which border the Mediterranean meaning a leper quarter; used aboard of sailing ships for a room set aside as a sick-bay, or store-room when no one was sick.

LOBSCOUSE. A Liverpool dish from which Liverpool seamen took their name of 'Scousers.

MARCO POLO. A famous clipper of the Australian Gold Rush days; her most famous captain was Bully Forbes who lies buried in Smithdown Road Cemetery, Liverpool. His famous words 'Hell or Melbourne in sixty days' are said to be cut in the headstone above his grave.

MATLOW. From the French; a word originally meaning a naval seaman.

MIRAMASHEE. Miramichi, a river in New Brunswick, well known to timber-droghers.

MOLLEY DEL RAY. Molina del Rey (Monterey), the place where the battle was fought between the American General Taylor and the Mexican General Santa Aña. The latter 'lost the day'.

MONKEY JACKET. A short heavy cloth coat worn by seamen in cold climes.

MOTHER CAREY'S CHICKENS. Sailor name for Stormy Petrels, seabirds found flying close to the crests of the great seas of the high latitudes.

NANTUCKET. An island and port off the coast of Massachusetts, from whence hailed prime ships and seamen of the South Sea or Yankee Sperm Whaler days.

PAWLS. Short bars of metal at the foot of a capstan or close to the barrel of a windlass which engage a serrated base so as to prevent the capstan or windlass 'walking back'. Records are in existence of capstans stripping their pawls—in a big ground swell for instance—running backwards and killing or maiming many of the crew. The clanking of the pawls as the anchor cable was hove in was the only musical accompaniment a shanty ever had!

PISCO. A fiery liquor common along the Chile Coast.

RED-TOPPED BOOTS. Seamen at one time wore long leather sea-boots the insides of which were tanned red, the top part of the boot being turned down to show this red leather.

RIDE A SPANKER DOWN, RIDE A STAYS'L DOWN. The brailed-in type of spanker and stays'ls bent to the upper stays which had little slant, often jammed when being lowered, so boys were detailed off to 'ride down' such sails—a dangerous feat in which the 'victim' had to hang on to the canvas and rope and by the sheer weight of his body drive the sail downwards.

RUNNING BOWLINE. An ordinary bowline with a noose formed by putting a bight of the rope through the bowline. Used to lasso the end of a swinging spar or objects difficult to reach normally.

RUNNING GEAR. The numerous ropes and wires that 'move' as opposed to the standing rigging which 'stays put'.

SACCARAPPA. Old name for the port of Westbrook in Maine, U.S.A.

SAKE. Japanese national drink made from rice.

SALT HORSE. Salted beef usually, also pork, sometimes called 'salt junk', stowed in a harness-cask (the 'horse' in its 'harness') was the staff of life in the days of sail. Dried in the sun it was possible for it to become as hard as teak and without smell, and many a seaman in days gone by has carved a model ship, etc., from it.

SAMSHU. Chinese bean-wine, very fiery and potent.

SCOTCHMEN. Battens lashed to wire stays to prevent the canvas of the lower sails from being chafed by the wire when the ship is close-hauled.

SCUPPERS. Gutterways either side the deck near the bulwarks pierced with holes to carry off surplus water when seas pour aboard, or when washing down decks.

SHANK PAINTERS. Lashing of hemp or chain securing the shank of the anchor inboard. In the older and in all small ships when about to drop the anchor the shank painter was cleared away and then the anchor hung by the bow stopper at the cathead, the stopper being released to drop the anchor. In later ships the anchor was rolled over the side from the fo'c'sle-head by means of 'tumblers'.

SHEBANG. Irish name for a shack wherein illicit whisky (potheen) was distilled; any sort of low 'dive'.

SHEERPOLES. Rounded-off spars of timber fastened to the shrouds just above bottle-screws where the rigging is 'turned-up'. In ships with dead-eyes and lanyards they were much bigger affairs than in 'modern' ships, often being pierced for to hold belayin'-pins.

SHIFT GAFF TOPS'L TACKS. A job more common in fore 'n' afters than in squareriggers; to haul the tack of a gaff-tops'l over the peak halyards of the gaff-sail, first down to loo'ard and then to wind'ard of the gaff beneath it.

SHORT-CUT HAIR. This phrase goes back to the days when Yankee seamen, not wishing to ape the British matlow who wore a long pigtail known as a 'queue', cut their hair short.

'SIX DAYS SHALT THOU LABOUR . . . and do all that thou art able,
On the seventh day thou shalt holystone the deck an' clean-scrape the rusty cable.'
This ruling was known among seamen as the 'Philadelphia Catechism'.

SLIPPED HIS CABLE. A seaman's expression for 'to die'.

SOUL 'N' BODY LASHINGS. Lashings worn to help keep wind and water out. A full set consisted of one's belt and knife worn outside a suit of oilskins, with a 'gee-string' of spunyarn or ropeyarn fastened to the belt between the legs to prevent the crutch of one's oilskin trousers tearing when climbing around aloft; lashings of the same material just below the knees—like a navvy's 'boweyangs'—to keep water from filling one's sea-boots and allowing oilskin trousers to 'give'; lashings around both wrists to help prevent water running up one's arms when pulling with the arms aloft on buntlines and clewlines; and a 'pigtail' of yarn stretching from the back of one's sou'wester to the belt to help keep the sou'wester from flying over the head when aloft on the yard. The sou'wester usually had its thin 'ties' which would chafe under a man's chin replaced by a broad band of serge or some such material and a large button. Once such a rig was 'bent' it was rarely taken off in the high latitudes —seamen would 'turn-in all standing' until these seas were left behind.

STAY. 'To stay' equals 'to tack', that is bring the bows of the vessel through the wind.

STOW A BUNT. To haul the bulky middle part of a squaresail up on to the yard and lash it in position with lengths of rope called gaskets.

STRETCH 'ER LUFF. To haul either a squaresail or fore 'n' after taut.

STUNS'L BOOM. A light spar projecting from the lower yards from which a squaresail (stuns'l) was hung; in some ships the booms were over the yards in others beneath them.

SWIFTERS. A wire stretched from capstan-bar to capstan-bar helping to keep them secure in their 'pigeon-holes'. A custom more common in the Navy than in the Merchant Service.

TABNABS. Sailor name for a type of rock-cake common years ago.

TAFFRAIL. The rail round the ships poop, to which a piece of canvas called a weather-cloth was fastened, enabling the officer of the watch to have some sort of a 'lee'.

TARPAULIN HAT. The common seamen's hat in Nelson's day worn by both naval and merchant seamen. Shaped like a straw-hat and covered with tarred canvas it was an early form of sou'wester. 'Tarpaulins' was a name used for both oilskins and naval seamen.

THREE SKYS'L YARDER. A ship with three skysails one above each

royal was considered by seamen to be the acme of sail per-
fection. Men who shipped in such a vessel looked with scorn on
ships carrying only royals, and 'brassbounders', i.e. apprentices,
from such queens, considered it their prerogative to walk out
the prettiest girls in ports like Newcastle, N.S.W., Sydney
Town, Melbourne, etc.

TOSS A BUNT. The act of rolling the bunt of a squaresail up on to the
yard. Prime seamen would be at the bunt when furling and at
the yard-arm when reefing, hence the derisive phrase 'a yard-
arm furler an' bunt-reefer'.

TWO BLOCKS. Said when the two blocks of a tackle are hauled close
together.

VALLIPO. A sailor word for Valparaiso. A sailor generic term for this
part of the world was the 'Flaming Coast'.

VINO. Spanish word for any kind of wine, in common use among
seamen.

WEAR. 'To wear' means to pass the stern of the ship through the
wind as opposed to 'tacking' in which the bows pass through
the wind.

WESTERS, PADDY WESTERS. Pseudo seamen also called 'Hoodlums'.
The name comes from the type of 'seamen' shipped by Paddy
West, a Liverpool crimp aboard sailing ships in the latter part
of the nineteenth century.

WHALING TERMS. '*The hundred and ninetieth lay.*' This means the
190th part of the clear net proceeds of a whaling voyage. Seamen shipping aboard whalers received no pay, but signed on
according to certain 'lays'. A good harpooner would get as
much as 'a 90th lay', but 'greenhorns' would be lucky if they
secured a '500th lay', commonly called 'a long lay'.

Tuckoona. Whalers' name for Talcahuano on the West Coast
of South America.

Tonbas. Tumbez at the mouth of the Guayaquil River in
Ecuador.

WHITE-STOCKING DAY. A term, still common in Liverpool. In the
nineteenth century white cotton stockings were the hall-mark
of ladies of quality, but when a sailor's wife or mother went to
draw her 'allotment' of money (sailor's half-pay) she would
unfailingly put on a pair of these stockings, considering herself a
'lady' if only for a day—hence the term.

YARDARM TO YARDARM. Sailing ships sailing abreast or in company.

BIBLIOGRAPHY

Books and articles on Shanties, sea-songs, sailing-ship voyages (with passages referring to the singing of shanties, etc.), minstrel songs, Negro folk- and work-songs, and so on.

ADAMS, CAPTAIN R. C., *On Board the Rocket* (D. Lothrop & Co., Boston, 1879). Contains description of shanty singing and shanties.

ALDEN, W. L., 'Sailors' Shanties and Sea Songs', *Chambers's Journal*, London, 11 December 1869, pp. 794–6.

—— 'Sailors' Songs', *Harper's New Monthly Magazine*, New York, July 1882, pp. 281–6.

—— *More Maritime Melodies* (Commercial Publishing Co., San Francisco, 1894).

ANDERSON, CAPTAIN ALEX, *Windjammer Yarns* (H. F. & G. W. Witherly, London, 1923). Contains songs.

ARNOUX, GUY, *Chansons du marin français au temps de la marine en bois* (Devambez, Paris, 1918). Many of the songs in this book are from an earlier work by G. de la Landelle called *Gaillard d'avant*, published by E. Dentu.

ASHTON, JOHN, *Real Sailor Songs* (Leadenhall Press, London, 1891).

BALTZER, R., *Knurrhahn*, German and English Sailor Songs and Shanties sung aboard German Sailing Ships, 2 vols. (Verlag A.C. Ehlers, Kiel, 1936). A shortened reprint of *Knurrhahn* was published by the Musikverlag Hans Sikorski, Hamburg, in 1952.

BARRA, E. I., *A Tale of Two Oceans* (San Francisco, 1893). Contains a description of a 'shanter'.

BECKETT, MRS. CLIFFORD, *Shanties and Forebitters* (J. Curwen & Sons, Ltd., London, 1914 (Curwen Edition 6293)).

BERNARD, D. H., 'Sea Songs and Chanties', *The Nautical Magazine* (LXXV, 1906).

BONE, CAPTAIN DAVID W., *Capstan Bars* (The Porpoise Press, Edinburgh, MCMXXXI, 1931).

BOUGHTON, CAPTAIN GEORGE P., *Seafaring* (Faber & Gwyer Ltd., London, 1926). Contains shanties with tunes.

BRADFORD, J. and A. FAGGE, *Old Sea Chanties* (Metzler & Co., Ltd., London, 1904).

BRIGGS, L. V., *Around Cape Horn to Honolulu on the Bark 'Amy Turner'* (Charles E. Lauriat Co., Boston, 1926). Contains shanties.

BROADWOOD, LUCY E., 'Early Chanty Singing and Ship Music', *Journal of the Folk Song Society*, London, pp. 55–8, vol. 8.

BROCHMANN, H., Article in the magazine *Signal* on shanties (Christiania, Oslo, 1908).

—— Article in the magazine *Jul Tilsjøs* on Shanties (Christiania (Oslo), 1908(?)).

—— *Opsang fra Seilskibstiden* (Norske Förlags Kompani Ltd., Christiania, 1916). Includes several shanties from the above articles.

BROWN, R. CURTIS, 'Sailors' Shanties', *Nautical Magazine* (XCVII, 1917, pp. 294–9).

BULLEN, FRANK T., and W. F. ARNOLD, *Songs of Sea Labour* (Swan & Co., Ltd., London, 1914).

BURLIN, NATALIE CURTIS, *Negro Folk Songs* (G. Schirmir Inc., New York, 1918).

CARPENTER, DOC., J. M., 'Chanteys in the Age of Sail', *New York Times*, 30 October 1938).

CAREY, C., Shanties in the *Esperance Morris Book* (II) (Curwen Edition, 1912).

CHOVIN, —, *Chansons de marins* (Paris).

CLARK, CAPTAIN A. H., *The Clipper Ship Era* (Putnam's, London, 1910). Contains words of shanties.

CLARK, G. E., *Seven Years of a Sailor's Life* (Adams & Co., Boston, 1867). One of the first writers to use the word 'Chantyman'.

CLEMENTS, REX, *A Gipsy of the Horn* (Heath Cranton Ltd., London, 1924). Contains words of shanties.

—— *Manavilins* (Heath Cranton Ltd., London, 1928).

COLCORD, JOANNA C., *Roll and Go* (Heath Cranton Ltd., London, 1924).

—— *Songs of American Sailormen*, an enlarged edition of *Roll and Go* (W. W. Norton & Co., New York, 1938, and Putnam, London, 1938).

DANA, R. H., JNR., *Two Years Before the Mast* (Harper & Brothers, New York, 1840, and also published many times since).

DAVIES, J. GLYN, *Cerddi Huw Puw* and *Cerddi Portinllaen* (R. H. Rees, The Educational Publishing Co., Ltd., and the Oxford University Press). Welsh versions of British shanties.

DAVIS, J., and FERRIS TOZER, *Sailor Songs or 'Chanties'* (Boosey & Co., Ltd., London, 1887).

DAY, THOMAS FLEMING, *Songs of Sea and Sail* (Rudder Publishing Co., Ltd., 1898).

DERBY, THOMAS, 'Sailors' Chanties or Working Songs of the Sea', *Manchester Quarterly* (XXXIV, 1915, pp. 285–302).

DOERFLINGER, WILLIAM MAIN, *Shantymen and Shantyboys* (The Macmillan Company, New York, 1951).

DOWNES, OLIN, and ELIE SEIGMEISTER, *A Treasury of American Song* (A. A. Knopf, New York, 1943). Contains shanties.

FARNSWORTH, C. H., and CECIL J. SHARP, *Folk Songs, Chanteys and Singing Games* (H. W. Gray Co., New York, 1916).

FAVARA, ALBERTO, *Canti della Terra e del Mare di Sicilia* (G. Ricordi & Co., Milan, 1948).

FINGER, CHARLES J., *Sailor Chanties and Cowboy Songs* (Haldeman-Julius Co., Gerard, Kansas, 1923).

FROTHINGHAM, R., *Songs of the Sea and Sailors' Chanteys* (Houghton Mifflin Co., Cambridge, Mass., 1924). Shanties reprinted from KING (see below).

—— 'Old Songs that Men have Sung', a dept. in *Adventure* Magazine (U.S.A., 20 June 1922–30 June 1923). This dept. was later edited by R. W. Gordon (10 July 1923–15 September 1927).

GAMLE KARLEBY, *Segelförenings Visbok* (Stockholm, 1914).

GRAINGER, P. A., *Grainger Collection*, Hektograph copies of English folk-songs, shanties, etc. (Library of Congress, U.S.A.; see also *Journal of the Folk Song Society*, London).

HALLIWELL, J. O., Ed., *The Early Naval Ballads of England* (The Percy Society, Library of Trinity College, Cambridge, 1841).

HARLOW, F. P., *The Making of a Sailor* (Marine Research Society, Salem, Mass., 1928). Contains shanties with tunes.

—— *Chanteying Aboard American Ships* (American Neptune, Salem, Mass., April 1948, pp. 81–9).

HAY, M. D., Ed., *Landsman Hay, Memoirs of Robert Hay, 1789–1847* (Rupert Hart-Davis, London, 1953).

HAYET, CAPTAIN A., *Chansons de bord* (Editions Eos, Paris, 1927).

—— *Dictons et tirades des anciens de la voile* (Paris, 1934). In this book Captain Hayet gives the reason for his not having published certain French shanties in his previous book.

HURSTON, ZORA NEALE, *Caribbean Melodies* (U.S.A.).

HUTCHISON, P. A., 'Sailors' Chanties', *The Journal of the American Folk Lore Society* (XIX, January–March 1906, pp. 16–28).

JACOBSON and TERRY, 'Sailors' Shanties' (from *The Shanty Book*), (London).

JOURNAL OF THE FOLK SONG SOCIETY, 1899–1931. Published by the Folk Song Society, London. Many shanties with their tunes, words, and variants collected by Miss Gilchrist, H. E. Piggott, Percy Grainger, Hon. Edward Fielding, C. J. Sharp, W. J. Alden, Margaret Harley, Thomas Miners, J. E. Thomas, etc.

KING, S. H., *King's Book of Chanties* (Oliver Ditson Co., Boston, 1918).

KRAMER, A. M., *Salty Sea Songs and Chanteys* (London, ?).

LA LANDELLE, G. DE, *Gaillard d'avant, chansons maritimes* (E. Dentu Paris).

LE BIHOR, JEAN-MARIE, *Chansons de la voile, 'Sans Voiles'* (Dunkirk, 1935). This is a pseudonym for Captain A. Hayet.

LESLIE, R. C., *A Sea Painter's Log* (Chapman & Hall Ltd., London, 1886). Reference to shantying and examples of shanties.

LOMAX, JOHN A. and ALAN LOMAX, *Our Singing Country* (The Macmillan Co., New York, 1941).

LUCE, ADMIRAL S. B., *Naval Songs* (W. A. Pond & Co., New York, 1883). Forebitters and shanties, many from ADAMS (see above).

MACKENZIE, R. W., *Ballads and Sea Songs from Nova Scotia* (Harvard University Press, Cambridge, Mass., 1928). Contains many shanties.

MARSTON and D. ALLEN, *Shanties* (London, ?).

MASEFIELD JOHN, *Sea Songs* (Temple Bar, London, January 1906, pp. 56–80).

—— *A Sailor's Garland* (London, 1924). Words of shanties only.

MELONEY, W. B., 'The Chanty Man Sings', *Everybody's* (1915).

MINSTREL (NIGGER) COLLECTIONS:

> *Nigger Melodies* (Cornish Lamport & Co., New York, 1850. Originally published as *Ethiopian Songs*, circa 1840).
>
> *The Story of the Jubilee Singers*, by J. B. T. Marsh. Appendix contains 130 Jubilee Songs of striking similarity to shanties.
>
> Christy and White's *Ethiopian Melodies*, by T. B. Peterson (Philadelphia, 1855).
>
> Christy's *Plantation Melodies* (Fisher & Brother, New York, 1851, 1853 and 1854.)
>
> *The Ethiopian Glee Book* by Gumbo Chaff (E. Howe, Boston, 1849).

MORTIMER-EVANS, P., 'At Sea in the Eighteen-eighties—Shanties and their Singers', *The Nautical Magazine* (CXXIV, 1930, pp. 129–31).

MURRAY, JAMES, 'Sailors' Songs with California Significance', *California Folklore Quarterly* (April 1946, pp. 143–52).

NORDHOFF, CHARLES, *Nine Years a Sailor* (Moore, Wilstach, Keys & Co., Cincinnati, 1857). In three books: *Man-of-war Life, The Merchant Vessel, Whaling and Fishing. The Merchant Vessel* (with examples of the Chants of the Mobile Bay Hoosiers) was published separately by Dodd, Mead & Co. (New York, 1884).

OLMSTEAD, F. A., *Incidents of a Whaling Voyage* (D. Appleton & Co., New York, 1841). Two shanties with tunes.

PALLMAN, GERHARD, *Seemannslieder* (Hamburg, 1938).

PATTERSON, J. E., *The Sea's Anthology* (G. H. Doran, New York, 1913). Shanties without tunes.

PERCY, BISHOP, *Reliques of Ancient English Poetry* (5th ed., 3 vols., 1812, vol. 2, pp. 431–5 for *The Baffl'd Knight*).

PERRY, *Fair Winds and Foul* (London). Three or four shanties.

ROBINSON, CAPTAIN JOHN, 'Songs of the Chantey Man', *The Bellman* (Minneapolis, Minn., 14 July–4 August 1917).

ROUSE, *Chanties in Greek and Latin*.

ROWLEY, ALEX, *Songs of the Seven Seas*. Pocket shanty book; songs mainly from *The Seven Seas Shanty Book*.

SAAR, R. W., and GILBERT FORSYTH, *Twelve Sailors' Songs or Chanteys* (Paxton, London, 1927).

SAMPSON, JOHN, *The Seven Seas Shanty Book* (Boosey & Co. Ltd., London, 1927).

SANDBURG, CARL, *The American Songbag* (Harcourt, Brace & Co., New York, 1927). Contains several shanties.

SAUNDERS, WILLIAM, 'Sailors' Songs and Songs of the Sea', *Musical Opinion and Music Trade Review* (London, August 1929, pp. 1102–4).

—— 'Folk-songs of the Sea', *Musical Opinion and Music Trade Review* (London, July 1927, pp. 984–5).

SAWYER, E. O., JNR., Ed., *Our Sea Saga; The Wood Wind Ships* (Reeves Publishing Co., San Francisco, 1929). Contains an article 'Sailor Songs in the Days of the Shantyman', reprinted from *Harper's Magazine*, July 1882 (Alden).

SHARP, CECIL J., *English Folk-Chanteys* (Simpkin Marshall, Ltd., Schott & Co., Ltd., London, 1914).

—— *Capstan Chanteys* (Novello & Co., Ltd., London, 1919). Reprint of *English Folk-Chanteys* except *Blow the Winds Wester*.

—— *Pulling Chanteys* (Novello & Co., Ltd., London, 1919). Reprinted from *English Folk-Chanteys*.

—— Collection of Folk Songs (MS), Clare College Library, Cambridge University.

SHAW, CAPTAIN FRANK, *The Splendour of the Seas* (Edward Stanford Ltd., London, 1953). Contains a chapter, 'Ship Savers', all about shanties and shantying.

SHAY, FRANK, *Iron Men and Wooden Ships* (Doubleday, Page & Co., New York, 1924).

—— *Deep Sea Shanties* (London, ?). No music.

—— *American Sea Songs and Chanteys* (W. W. Norton & Co. Inc., New York, 1948).

SHELL BOOK OF SHANTIES, THE (The Shell Petroleum Co. Ltd., London, 1952). Many tunes from BONE (see above).

SMITH, C. FOX, *A Book of Shanties* (Methuen & Co., Ltd., London, 1927).

SMITH, LAURA A., *The Music of the Waters* (Kegan Paul, Trench & Co., London, 1888).

'STEERAGE PASSENGER'—*The Quid, or Tales of my Messmates* (W. Strange, London, 1832). A copy may be found in the Reading Room, Library of the Greenwich National Maritime Museum.

STERNVALL, CAPTAIN S., *Sång under Segel* (Albert Bonniers Förlag, Stockholm, 1935).

STEWART, AUBREY, Trans., *The Book of the Wanderings of Brother Felix Fabri* (Library of the Palestine Pilgrims Society, Vol. VII, 1893).

SUSCINIS, JEAN, *Chansons de la mer en de la voile* (Private Press, Paris).

TEGTMEIER, K., *Alte Seemannslieder und Shanties* (Dr. Ernst Hauswedell & Co., Hamburg, no date).

TERRY, R. R., 'Sailors' Shanties', *The Music Student* (London, November 1917, pp. 95-8).

—— *A Forgotten Psalter* (Oxford University Press, London, 1919).

—— *The Shanty Book*, two parts (J. Curwen & Sons, Ltd., London, 1931 (Curwen Edition)).

—— *Salt Sea Ballads* (J. Curwen & Sons, London, 1931). Forebitters only.

TOYE, GEOFFREY, *Sea Chanties* (London, 1924).

TREVINE, OWEN, *Deep Sea Chanties* (J. B. Cramer & Co. Ltd., London, 1921).

WALTERS, ALAN, *Songs of the Sea* (Temple Bar, London, August 1900, pp. 485-95).

WEBB, ALFRED, 'Sailors' Chanties', *The Irish Monthly* (Dublin, January 1903, pp. 37-42).

WHALL, CAPTAIN W. B., 'The Sea Shanty', *The Yachting Monthly* (October 1906).

—— 'Sea Melody', *The Nautical Magazine* (LXXVI, 1906).

—— 'Real Sea Songs', *The Nautical Magazine* (LXXXI, LXXXII, 1909).

—— 'Real Sea Shanties', *The Nautical Magazine* (LXXXIII, 1910).

—— *Sea Songs and Shanties* (First Edition called *Ships, Sea Songs and Shanties*, 1910) (Brown, Son and Ferguson, Ltd., Glasgow, 1927).

WHITE, N. I., *American Negro Folk Songs* (Harvard University Press, Cambridge, Mass., 1928).

WHITEHEAD, A. W., and S. T. HARRIS, *Six Sea Shanties* (Boosey & Co., Ltd., London, 1925).

WILLIAMS, J. H., 'The Sailors' "Chanties" ', *The Independent* (New York, 8 July 1909, pp. 76-83).

WOOD, THOMAS, *The Oxford Song Book* (Vol. II, Oxford University Press, London, 1927). Contains shanties.

INDEX OF TITLES